Ex Líbrís

Randy Manning

© APCo

Disaster on the Mississippi

Gene Eric Salecker

Disaster on the Mississippi

The *Sultana* Explosion, April 27, 1865

NAVAL INSTITUTE PRESS   ANNAPOLIS, MARYLAND

Library of Congress Cataloging-in-Publication Data
Salecker, Gene Eric, 1957–
   Disaster on the Mississippi : the Sultana Explosion, April 27, 1865 / Gene Eric Salecker.
      p.   cm.
   Includes bibliographical references (p.   ) and index.
   ISBN 1-55750-739-2 (alk. paper)
   1. Sultana (Steamboat)   2. United States—History—Civil War, 1861–1865—Prisoners and prisons.   3. Steamboat disasters—Mississippi River—History—19th century.   I. Title.
E595.S84S25   1996
973.7'71—dc20   95-49585

Printed in the United States of America
on acid-free paper ♾

03   02   01   00   99   98   97   96   9   8   7   6   5   4   3   2

First printing

To my brother Gary—
I knew him such a short time,
and
to Gramma Googy—
I thought she always would be there

Contents

Foreword

For four long and bloody years war had raged across America. Finally, on April 9, 1865, the guns fell silent. The South was defeated. It ended when the tattered Army of Northern Virginia surrendered at Appomattox. America had paid a horrible price during the Civil War. Her soil lay stained by the blood of more than 600,000 of her sons.

The nation, which had been so divided during the war, now faced the task of healing the deep wounds of war and making herself whole again. Peace meant that the soldiers could throw down their arms and return to their homes and families. They had touched the elephant and survived. For a group of these veterans, the dying was not over.

On April 24, 1865, a long column of blue-clad soldiers snaked its way toward the *Sultana* docked at the riverfront at Vicksburg, Mississippi. Built to carry only 376 passengers, when the *Sultana* steamed northward that evening, she had what her first clerk described as the largest number of passengers ever carried by a steamboat up the Mississippi River. In all, there were more than 2,500 on board. Among the steamer's passengers were approximately 2,300 Union soldiers, veterans who had survived the carnage of war and the horrors of the Cahaba and Andersonville prison camps. As the *Sultana* plowed up the flooded river, the soldiers celebrated their freedom. They were finally out of harm's way and on their way home.

At two o'clock on the morning of April 27, 1865, the celebration was brought to a tragic conclusion. When the *Sultana* was seven miles north of Memphis, three of her massive boilers exploded with a volcanic fury. When the sun rose that morning, more than 1,700 people were dead or dying.

Gene Salecker has dedicated years to the researching and writing of this remarkable book. It will be a lasting tribute to those who suffered and died in the darkness of that horrible morning: the men that history forgot.

JERRY O. POTTER
Memphis, Tennessee

Preface

On the Mississippi River, seven miles north of Memphis, Tennessee, the boilers of the sidewheel steamboat Sultana suddenly exploded at 2 A.M. on April 27, 1865. The *Sultana* was carrying more than 2,000 Union prisoners of war recently released from the notorious prison pens of the South. The sick and emaciated soldiers suddenly found themselves caught between the raging flames of the boat and the icy floodwaters of the Mississippi. Their chances of survival were slim.

The burning and sinking of the *Sultana,* the worst maritime disaster in the history of the United States, claimed more than 1,700 lives. In addition to a factual account of the disaster, this book tells the personal stories of the victims, both soldiers and civilians, who faced the horrors of that April morning.

Integral to the soldiers' stories is their background as prisoners. Their time in prison, their movement to a neutral exchange camp, and their experiences in the camp and on the *Sultana,* as well as the disaster itself, were forever etched in the memories of the survivors. When they thought of one, they remembered the others; when they wrote of one, they wrote of the others. Because of this interrelationship, which too often has been overlooked by historians, I was able to gather extensive information about all aspects of the disaster. For this same reason, I decided to include the soldiers' prison and parole camp experiences in this book.

The generally accepted opinion of historians, which I feel obligated to dispell, is that the prisoners were crowded onto the *Sultana* pell-mell, with no semblance of order. This was not the case. An examination of survivor accounts reveals that the prisoners were sent to the *Sultana* in organized groups and that certain regiments and companies laid claim to specific areas of the vessel.

Another myth is that the explosion of the *Sultana*'s boilers went straight up. A careful analysis of the facts, as presented by many of the survivors, shows that the explosion went up and backward at a 45-degree angle. Basically, the explosion cut the *Sultana* in two above the waterline. In order to present an accurate picture of what the prisoners, passengers, and crew faced in front of and behind the explosion, I cover the actions of those trapped on the forward section first and methodically move upward from deck to deck before describing the actions of those trapped on the stern.

Unfortunately, the rescue of the last survivor from the cold waters of the Mississippi did not put an end to the misfortunes of the victims. Many faced agonizing months in hospitals, and, with the loss of the *Sultana,* all of the survivors were stranded in Memphis. For many, the rest of the trip on another steamboat, after their experiences on the *Sultana,* was almost as frightening as the disaster itself.

Immediately after the disaster, many survivors wrote letters to their families and friends at home, but others waited years before telling their stories. The hundreds of accounts collected here, many of them published for the first time in book form, shed light on what it was like on board the *Sultana* that morning. They also describe the hardships encountered by many of the victims and their families for the rest of their lives. Not only did they struggle with physical and mental injuries, but they also had to cope with a government that was unable or unwilling to recognize the scope of the *Sultana* disaster.

Acknowledgments

My most helpful mentor during my efforts to tell the story of the *Sultana* has been Jerry O. Potter, author of *The* Sultana *Tragedy* (Gretna, La.: Pelican Publishing Co., 1992). Jerry loaned me every scrap of paper that he had on the *Sultana* and her ill-fated passengers and also encouraged me to record my thoughts and research, which ultimately resulted in this book.

Gratefully, I acknowledge the helpful enthusiasm of Pam Newhouse, publisher of *The* Sultana *Remembered: Newsletter of the Association of* Sultana *Descendants and Friends.*

I am obliged to Norman Shaw and a group of descendants of the *Sultana* soldiers who meet annually in Knoxville, Tennessee. They contributed valuable information and anecdotes, as did descendants whom I met through the Ohio Civil War Collectors Show.

Military historian Richard A. Sauers contacted me about eyewitness accounts of the *Sultana*'s sinking that appeared in the *National Tribune,* Washington, D.C., and librarian Beth Schurgin-Cutler of Northeastern Illinois University, Chicago, helped me to obtain this information.

Donald Cooper of Hayes Boiler & Mechanical, Inc., Chicago, offered a modern point of view of the disaster; David Helfand of Northeastern Illinois University helped me to "market" my manuscript; and Tom Pappas had invaluable suggestions, including much-needed humor.

I am grateful to the survivors whose diaries, letters, memoirs, and reminiscences provided the groundwork of this work.

Scores of individuals tracked down items relating to the *Sultana* and helped me to compile accurately the lists of the *Sultana*'s crew members, the passengers, members of the guard unit, and the paroled prisoners on board when the boat sank. It is impossible to list everyone by name, but I am especially indebted to Mike Allard, Stewart Bennett, Timothy R. Brookes, Kim Harrison, Gary Holmes, Sue Kerekgyarto, Bonnie Knox, Roger Long, Bernie Paprocki, and Ray Zieliniewicz.

I am particularly thankful for the understanding and cooperation of my family and friends who knew when to leave me alone and when to perk me up.

A special thanks must be extended to Anne Collier, Arlene S. Uslander, and Terry Belanger for helping me to turn my research and writing into this finished product.

Disaster on the Mississippi

1 The *Sultana*

The workmen at John Litherbury's Boat Yard in Cincinnati, Ohio, carefully inched the finished hulls and superstructures of their two newest creations into the icy waters of the Ohio River on January 3, 1863. The first hull was destined to become the *Luminary*. Captain Preston Lodwick, owner of the second hull, would name his ship the *Sultana*.[1]

The hull of the *Sultana* measured 260 feet in length, 39 feet wide at the base, 42 feet wide at the beam, and 7 feet deep.[2] The shipwrights had built the hull to pencil-thin proportions in order to obtain a fast, stable boat. Among experienced rivermen, opinion ran that a long, thin boat could carry the same amount of cargo as a short boat while using less power and therefore was a more efficient and economical investment.[3]

When lowered broadside into the Ohio River, the superstructure of the *Sultana* was a mere shell, with only the huge twin paddlewheels, one on each side of the boat, and the machinery to turn them in place. Built by Moore and Richardson, the pair of waterwheels measured 34 feet in diameter and carried 11-foot-long bucket planks. The wheels would be powered by steam generated in four side-by-side, high-pressure tubular boilers.[4]

In 1848, the first tubular boiler had been fitted on a Mississippi steamboat with the expectation that it would make twice the steam while using only half the fuel consumed by an ordinary flue boiler. The conventional flue boiler consisted, primarily, of an outer shell and two internal flues running the length of the boiler and placed well below the waterline. The heat from the furnaces below the boilers was drawn through the flues by the upward draft from the twin chimneys, or smokestacks, which allowed more of the hot metal to come into contact with the water inside the boiler, thereby producing more steam for the engines.

The tubular boiler, on the other hand, had any number of flues, generally much smaller in diameter than conventional flues. These boilers were usually shorter in length and weighed much less than conventional boilers, yet the number of flues exposed a greater amount of metal to the hot water within the boilers. One of the main drawbacks of tubular boilers, however, was the difficulty in cleaning them, and they needed to be cleaned often on the muddy Mississippi.[5]

The brand-new boilers of the *Sultana* were made of iron, $^{17}/_{48}$ inch thick; they each measured 18 feet in length and 46 inches in diameter. Inside each boiler, twenty-four return flues, five inches in diameter, ran from end to end. Two high-pressure engines, needed to turn the two huge paddlewheels, each had standard horizontal cylinders 25 inches in diameter with an 8-foot stroke.[6]

During January, the hull of the *Sultana* remained at anchor alongside the bank of the Ohio River. A seemingly endless array of artisans swarmed on board to complete the interior and exterior of the superstructure and give the steamboat its overall wedding-cake appearance. Carpenters, joiners, and decorators from half a dozen Cincinnati businesses worked long hours in fashioning the luxurious main cabin and building the hurricane deck, texas deck (officers' quarters), and pilothouse.

Built for the New Orleans trade, the *Luminary* and the *Sultana* were almost identical in appearance. Their design was unique among steamboats of that era. On most steamboats, the long main cabin of the second, or misnamed boiler deck (the boilers were actually below, on the main deck), came forward and enclosed the tall smokestacks poking up through the decks. The main cabin on the *Sultana,* as well as the *Luminary,* however, ended about ten or twelve feet short of the chimneys. This left the twin stacks outside of the cabin, which resulted in a larger deck space so that a greater amount of cargo could be carried.

In the cold January air, carpenters from the Marine Railway Company worked on the capacious main cabin located on the second deck of the *Sultana.* It was flanked on either side by a total of thirty-one staterooms, each with two berths. The typical stateroom of 1863 measured about 6 feet square. In addition to the berths, placed one above the other, it contained a chair or two, perhaps a small table and mirror, and a life preserver for each of the two occupants. A wash basin, water pitcher, and chamber pot were usually provided. Toilet accommodations on the *Sultana,* as on most steamboats, were located fore and aft of the left paddlewheel housing.

The main showpiece in most western river steamboats was the grand saloon, and the *Sultana* was no exception. Joiners and artisans from the Marine Railway Company worked their magic to create beautiful arches, fretwork, pendants, and scrolls along the sides and across the ceiling of the main hall. The Williams Company's painters followed close behind. Decorators from Shillito and Prather then laid a luxurious carpet on the floor of the ladies' cabin, a fifty-foot section at the rear of the hall that was set aside for female passengers, and placed fine pieces of furniture throughout the long, cavernous saloon. The Hunnewell Company provided the *Sultana* with china, glass, and tableware. From above, chandeliers installed by McHenry and Carson illuminated the whole luxurious affair.[7]

An unknown English engineer could have been describing the *Sultana* when he wrote in 1861: "The magnificence of the saloons of the Mississippi river boats is far famed and they form a strange contrast to the rest of the ship. They are, as before stated, unbroken by columns, by tie rods, or by the engines, and there is very little colour used in their decoration, except in the carpets and furniture, for they give a preference to white paneling, covered with florid carving. From each beam, fretwork and open lattice work hangs [*sic*] down, and the constant repetition of this carving, illuminated by coloured light thrown from the painted glass skylights on each side, in a saloon over 200 feet long, produces one of the most beautiful effects of light and shade I have ever witnessed."[8]

On top of the main cabin, carpenters laid the wide, spacious hurricane deck, covered with a mixture of tar and felt to protect against sparks from the smokestacks and sawdust or sand to prevent wear. The hurricane deck was raised a little in the center to form the beautiful skylight roof described by the English engineer. The short, narrow texas deck, housing the sparse rooms of the *Sultana*'s crew, was above the hurricane deck. At the center of the boat, high atop the texas cabin, workmen built the all-important pilothouse.[9]

The pilothouse, the kingdom of the Mississippi riverboat pilot, was pretty much standardized throughout the 1860s. Perched at the highest part of the steamboat, it afforded the pilot an unobstructed view of the river. High windows enclosed the sides and back of the pilothouse, but the front had no glass and was left open to the elements. This ensured that the view of the pilot never would be obstructed by dirty, streaked windows or frosted glass.[10]

As January turned to February, large block letters, nearly six feet high, began to appear on the sides of the two wheel housings that enclosed the huge paddlewheels. The tops of the letters were flush with the border of the boiler deck. The seven letters—SULTANA—each had the hint of a shadow expertly painted to the right and at the bottom behind each letter.

By February 3, 1863, the workmen completed their tasks and the *Sultana* dropped down to the Cincinnati levee to take on her first load of cargo and passengers. Although she weighed 578.22 tons and had the legal capacity to carry 660.38 tons of freight on her main deck, she still trimmed out at a shallow depth and was able to maneuver at a minimum depth of thirty-four inches of water.

As she stood at the foot of the Cincinnati levee, the *Sultana* was "one of the largest and best business steamers ever constructed," according to the *Cincinnati Daily Commercial* (February 4, 1863, 4), the zenith in luxury and safety. With accommodations to carry 76 cabin passengers on her luxurious second deck and another 300 deck passengers on her open main deck, she had a legal passenger capacity of 376. A crew estimated at 80 to 85, including officers, stewards, cooks, firemen, washerwomen, and deckhands, were ready and waiting to make the *Sultana* the epitome of elegance and success.

In terms of safety, she carried the most modern equipment. The safety gauges used alloyed metal with safety guards that fused open in a safe position when the internal boiler pressure reached 150 pounds per square inch, only 5 pounds above the allowed working rate. Captain Lodwick had installed three fire-fighting pumps, although two of them had to be worked by hand. A metallic lifeboat was stored upside down on the aft part of the hurricane deck, and a wooden yawl (small rowboat) was hung at the stern. In addition, the *Sultana* carried 300 feet of fire hose, thirty buckets, and five fire-fighting axes. Seventy-six life belts were provided for stateroom passengers. Floating gangplanks, containing 300 additional feet of space, were apportioned to deck passengers.[11]

Captain Lodwick's steamboat was the fifth boat to carry the name *Sultana*. Meaning the wife, mother, sister, or daughter of a sultan,[12] the name was first used on a boat that ran the lucrative cotton trade between Vicksburg, Mississippi, and New Orleans, Louisiana, during the late 1830s and early 1840s.

Built in 1843, the second *Sultana* worked the Saint Louis (Missouri)–New Orleans trade. She was the largest boat on the Mississippi River at that time and established a number of speed records between 1843 and 1846. In 1846, she collided with another steamboat, which resulted in the loss of a number of lives. The third *Sultana,* built in 1848, quickly set a new speed record in the run from New Orleans to Louisville, Kentucky, by making the trip in five days and twelve hours. In 1851, she caught fire at the Saint Louis wharf and burned to the water's edge. A number of people died in the fire.

Built in 1851, the fourth *Sultana* worked the lower Mississippi cotton trade. Caught in a gale wind in 1853, she lost her twin smokestacks. Four years later, she burned to the water at Hickman, Kentucky. As the fifth *Sultana* was nearing completion, Captain Lodwick was hoping that his boat would have better luck than the other *Sultana*s before her.[13]

Captain Lodwick, noted for producing superior boats, had little trouble finding a well-respected crew. The crew of the *Sultana,* as did other steamboat crews, fell into three distinct groups: officers, cabin crew, and deck crew. Captain Lodwick was the overall master, and it was his job to make the steamboat attractive to both passengers and cargo shippers. Although he was host to all on board, he was first a businessman, whose primary interest was running the boat at a profit.[14]

Second in command was the chief mate. When the boat was under

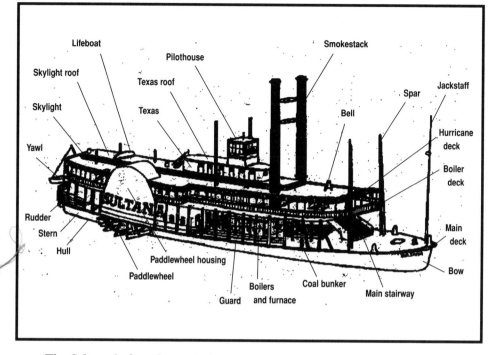

The *Sultana*, before the explosion.

way, his duty was to take charge while the captain slept or was busy. When the boat docked at a landing, the chief mate was responsible for getting the most out of the deck crew and supervising the placement of freight in the hold, on the deck, or out on the guards. He had to make sure that the load was distributed evenly to keep the vessel from careening and that the draft was as light as possible. How much time was wasted at a landing, either loading or unloading freight or taking on coal, depended on the skill of the mate.

Probably the most important men on board were the two pilots, who alternated four-hour shifts in the pilothouse. They had complete authority to decide the movement of the boat—their words were law. The captain could suggest a maneuver or a landing, but pilots had the final say about where the boat went and where she stopped. The pilots had to know every inch of the river in bright daylight, in the dark, in heavy rain, and in thick fog. They had to read every ripple on the water and know every sandbar and chute. Pilots were legally required to be licensed and demonstrate their knowledge of the river.

The only other crew members on a steamboat required to have a license were the two engineers, whose job was to tend to the mechanical workings of the boat. It was their duty to keep the engines and machinery running twenty-four hours a day. They had to perform all kinds of engine and boiler maintenance during transit and make minor adjustments and repairs. In terms of safety, an engineer could overrule the captain or pilot, but he was usually at their beck and call. He had to have sharp ears, ready to pick up the ring of landing or maneuvering bells amid the clump and chug of the engines and pitmans and detect the slightest vibration in an engine or wobble in a valve. Engineers were generally unseen by the public. The job was hot, greasy, and thankless, but proficient engineers were essential to the safe and efficient operation of a steamboat.

Ranking next to the captain in prestige and salary was the clerk of the boat. Except for the captain, most of the other officers spent little or no time interacting with the main cabin passengers. The clerk's office was usually at the front of the long social hall, and the clerk acted as the steamboat's overall business manager. He was in charge of assigning staterooms, soliciting and checking cargo, purchasing fuel and supplies, and handling the payroll of the crew.

The cabin crew of the *Sultana,* little more than a hotel staff on water, consisted of stewards, cooks, waiters, cabin boys, and chambermaids. Although the cabin crew received lower wages than the deck crew, a certain status came with working in the main cabin. At night, the cabin crew were allowed to sleep on the floor of the main cabin and were first to get any leftover food.

The deck crew, about one half of the *Sultana*'s total complement, was made up, for the most part, of unskilled laborers hired solely for the strength of their backs. The deck crew consisted of the firemen and the roustabouts, or deckhands. The firemen, usually covered from head to foot with thick black coal dust, worked four-hour shifts of shoveling coal into the hot furnaces beneath the mammoth boilers. When a steamboat ran out of coal or cordwood, the firemen had to lug buckets or push small wheelbarrows full of fuel up a narrow plank to the empty bin in front of the hungry furnaces. The firemen did hard, hot, dirty work, for which they received little pay.

The deckhands, under the direct supervision of the mate, were the lowest-paid employees on steamboats, but they did some of the hardest work. They slept wherever they could, the most enviable spot being between the fuel piles and the warm furnaces. The deckhands carried freight of every shape and size up the gangplanks in all kinds of weather and at all types of landings. The cursing mate had to be a certain kind of man, able to weave together a veritable tapestry of colorful phrases to get the most out of tough, lowly-paid deckhands.[15]

With such a large, magnificent boat and a fine crew, the agents for the *Sultana* had little trouble acquiring passengers or freight for her

maiden voyage. The *Cincinnati Daily Commercial* reported: "Passengers
. . . may anticipate an agreeable trip on the *Sultana*."[16]

The *Sultana* was slated to proceed upriver from Cincinnati on the icy
Ohio to Pittsburgh, Pennsylvania. On February 11, 1863, she began her
first trip with six hundred tons of freight and a "fair" amount of passengers. The *Daily Missouri Republican* pointed out that she "glided off grace-
fully from the levee, indicating something more than ordinary speed."[17]

Reaching Wheeling, West Virginia, on February 14, Captain Lodwick
found that the smokestacks of his new boat would not fit under the
bridge spanning the Ohio River. Doing the next best thing, he off-
loaded his freight and passengers at the Wheeling wharf, took on a
cargo of coffee and sugar from the East and a few passengers, and
headed back to Cincinnati. On February 17, the *Sultana* was once again
docked at her home port. For the remainder of February and on into
the first two weeks of March, Lodwick continued to book passengers and
freight for regular runs to Wheeling.[18]

On March 12, while the steamboat was in Wheeling, a federal government agent approached Lodwick and told him that, when the *Sultana*
reached Cincinnati, she would be requisitioned by the government for
the shipment of troops and cargo. The captain had no say in the
matter.[19]

With the country involved in a bloody Civil War, captains and owners
of steamboats constantly feared the requisition of their boats, which
were often loaded far beyond their legal carrying capacity. Should a master complain, he would be told by military authorities that it was a necessity. Masters of steamboats soon found that it was useless to protest any
requisition or overcrowding; the military always had its way.[20]

On March 17, the *Sultana*, bearing a full cargo, left Cincinnati for the
Cumberland River and Nashville, Tennessee, in the service of the U.S.
government. Apparently, she had no trouble going over the falls at
Louisville, nor did she have any difficulty when she came back upriver.
On April 2, she once again departed from Cincinnati for Wheeling.[21]

The *Sultana* plied the regular Cincinnati-Wheeling trade during the
rest of April. On May 5, she departed Cincinnati for the last time and
headed down the Ohio River for the "Mighty Mississippi." She successfully went over the Louisville falls on May 8 and was reported to be
"another model of Cincinnati boat building, [that] reflects credit on the
builders and furnishers." Leaving Louisville that same day with "a good
freight and a host of people," the *Sultana* was finally on her way to join
the Saint Louis–New Orleans trade for which she had been built.[22]

The next day, May 9, Captain Lodwick was in Memphis, Tennessee,
in an attempt to prove the *Sultana*'s true worth. At 5:30 P.M., the *Sultana*,
City of Alton, and *Belle Memphis* lined up opposite the city for "one of the

most exciting events . . . which has occurred at the landing during the war"—an old-fashioned steamboat race. With lights aglow, the three steamers jockeyed for position and then surged forward, each trying to be the first to reach Cairo, Illinois. Twenty-eight hours later, the *Belle Memphis,* under Captain J. Cass Mason, a carefree, almost reckless individual who held a number of speed records with the *Belle Memphis* and always pushed for new records, steamed into Cairo far ahead of the other participants.[23] Mason must have liked what he saw in the *Sultana,* even though she lost her first race. Before long, he and the *Sultana* would meet again.

By May 1863, almost the entire Mississippi River was in the hands of the U.S. Army and Navy, the lone exceptions being the small but steadfast Confederate garrison at Port Hudson, Louisiana, and the strong river town of Vicksburg.[24] While Gen. Ulysses S. Grant concentrated on reducing and capturing these two Confederate holdouts, the *Sultana* was again tapped by the government to carry supplies and troops to the forces engaged in the reduction of Vicksburg.[25]

The requisition of the *Sultana,* however, almost cost Captain Lodwick his prized steamer. On May 18, the *Sultana* and four other steamboats were fired on by a Confederate artillery battery near Columbia, Arkansas. Surviving that encounter, the *Sultana* remained in military service throughout May, June, and July. Even after the fall of Vicksburg on July 4, 1863, the government retained the *Sultana,* quite possibly because of her design, which included the extra-wide deck space in front of the main cabin on the second (boiler) deck.[26]

On July 18, almost ten weeks after reaching the Mississippi River, the *Sultana* finally nosed into a berth at the Saint Louis waterfront with a government cargo of 186 horses and 63 mules. From that time on, Saint Louis would be her home port. Although she was still under the auspices of the federal government, her express agents immediately began advertising for a run downriver.[27]

The *Sultana* left Saint Louis for Vicksburg on July 21. Eight days later, she steamed up the Yazoo River, just north of Vicksburg, and took on board a load of Union troops, including the 61st Illinois Infantry. Turning around, she headed back down the Yazoo to its mouth and, turning up the Mississippi, again steamed north. On July 31, she put in at Helena, Arkansas, and disembarked the Union soldiers.[28]

That same day, the *Sultana* left Helena with three top-ranking Union generals. About forty-five miles downriver from Memphis, she was fired on by a small group of Confederates, who badly damaged her upper works before she escaped. Although the fall of Vicksburg and the surrender of Port Hudson placed the entire Mississippi River in Union hands, passage along the river was still hazardous. On August 3, as the *Sultana* steamed upriver toward Saint Louis with 672 bales of precious cotton, she was fired on again but managed to avoid serious damage.[29]

For the remainder of the year, the *Sultana* ran an irregular service between Saint Louis and Vicksburg, with occasional operations for the government.[30] By the new year of 1864, Captain Lodwick had his elegant packet set up in the trade for which she was designed, and the *Sultana* ran down to New Orleans on January 25. When she made a run from New Orleans to Louisville on March 6, however, the steamer was under the command of J. Cass Mason, who, as captain of the *Belle Memphis,* had beaten the *Sultana* in her one and only race in May 1863.[31]

Captain Lodwick had relinquished command of his vessel for these two trips because, at the age of sixty-four, the confirmed bachelor had fallen in love. He was engaged to be married to Sarah C. Halsey before the end of the year and had decided to sell the *Sultana.*[32]

On March 7, 1864, after owning the *Sultana* for little more than a year and registering a profit nearly twice the cost of her construction, Lodwick sold his steamboat to a trio of Saint Louis citizens for the sum of $90,000. Captain William A. Thornburg purchased a one-fourth share; Logan D. Dameron of Nauson, Dameron and Company and Captain Mason each bought a three-eighths interest.[33]

Mason was well known and respected along the waterways of the Mississippi and Ohio rivers. Born in Lynchburg, Virginia, in 1830, Mason had moved to Missouri as an infant. Prior to his investment in the *Sultana,* he had been a part owner and officer of a number of steamboats. In 1860, he had married Mary Rowena Dozier, the daughter of Saint Louis businessman and steamboat magnate James Dozier, and, after a short time, became master of one of Dozier's prized boats, the *Rowena.*[34]

In February 1863, the *Rowena* was stopped by a Union gunboat when she was carrying illegal medicine and trousers for the Confederacy. Mason was not arrested, but the *Rowena* was seized as contraband. A month later, while still in federal hands, she struck a snag near Cape Giradeau, Missouri, and sank.[35] Dozier was unable to forgive his son-in-law, and all business contact between the two came to an abrupt end.[36]

Mason continued his career on the river and eventually became captain of the *Belle Memphis.* Steaming up and down the river, he set a number of speed records. Although he showed a somewhat reckless side, merchants and businessmen were happy about the quick shipment of cargo and generally had a high opinion of him. Mason appeared carefree and a bit wild, but the newspapers reported that he had "one of the clearest heads on the river," and was "very decided, firm and conscientious." When he bought into the *Sultana* in March 1864, the general opinion among other rivermen was that the boat would have a profitable career under his guiding hand.[37]

In late April 1864, the *Sultana* made her first trip under her new owners. With Captain William Thompson as master, she made three successful trips to New Orleans and back. On July 5, Captain Mason took over command of the boat and made a quick run to Vicksburg. Mason remained in command throughout the rest of the year and made regular trips between Saint Louis and New Orleans. During the slow winter months of the new year, the *Sultana* remained relatively quiet. She made only two trips in February, the last with a light load of cargo, including three hundred ducks and four geese.[38]

During the end of February and the beginning of March, the annual spring rains and thaws in the north were causing the usual rise of the Mississippi River. By early March, the Cairo newspapers were reporting that the river had risen "to such stage as to cover a considerable extent of country".[39] Because of the heavy snows during the winter of 1864, the towns along the river were bracing for one of the worst floods in recent history.

The *Sultana* was then in New Orleans, and her carefree captain again developed an itch to engage another boat in a race. On March 5, after informing Captain Ben Tabor of the *Olive Branch* that the *Sultana* would pass his boat on the way back to Saint Louis, Mason waited just above New Orleans while the *Olive Branch* backed away from the flooded levee. Getting up a good headway, the *Olive Branch* shot past the *Sultana* and pulled into a quick lead. She beat Mason to Donaldsonville, Louisiana, about sixty miles upriver. When the *Olive Branch* was unexpectedly detained, however, the *Sultana* slipped ahead and quickly gained a five-minute lead. The race was on.

Not to be outrun by Mason, Captain Tabor poured on the steam and caught up with the *Sultana* at Baton Rouge, Louisiana. The two boats landed simultaneously, but Tabor was again detained. Mason took advantage of his rival's bad luck and continued his run to Saint Louis. Although delayed twenty-five minutes at Baton Rouge, Tabor passed the *Sultana* at Fort Adams, about eight miles over the Mississippi state line, and landed at Natchez, Mississippi, thirty-seven minutes ahead of Mason.

Despite the excitement and drama of the race, it came to an abrupt end at Natchez when the federal government commandeered the *Olive Branch* for a quick return trip to New Orleans.[40] Before leaving Natchez, Mason examined his boilers and found that he would have to lay over a short time for repairs.[41] After almost two years on the muddy Mississippi, the silty brown water and high-pressure racing were beginning to wreak havoc with the finicky tubular boilers.

Leaving Saint Louis at the end of March, Mason and the *Sultana* took more than a week to reach the port of New Orleans because of a delay at Vicksburg for more work on the troublesome boilers.[42]

Undoubtedly feeling secure with the repair work, Mason left New Orleans on April 3 and pushed his aging boilers to the limit. Despite fighting against the rising flood waters, he reached Cairo in record time. "The *Sultana* made the trip from New Orleans in 4 days and 7 hours, the best trip of the season," a Cairo newspaper reported. For his efforts, Mason and the *Sultana* were awarded a set of elk antlers to be placed high on the staging between the two black chimneys, a sign to all passengers and freightmen that the *Sultana* was a fast boat.[43] With his prize antlers in place, Mason readied his packet for her next trip downriver.

Although Mason continued to run regular trips between New Orleans and Saint Louis that spring, a Saint Louis newspaper reported that "business on the landing is dull—unusually dull for the season" and that "steamers are daily lying up to wait for better times." Competition was cutting into Mason's pocketbook. The *Tri-Weekly Missouri Republican* predicted: "Some of [the steamers] will have to suspend soon, or run with disordered safes and display the red ink on the wrong side of the balance sheets."[44]

As Mason ran into more financial trouble, he was forced to sell part of his investment in the *Sultana*. In early 1865, he sold one-eighth of his total share to Sam DeBow of DeBow and Co., New Orleans, and later sold another one-eighth portion to his first clerk, William Jordan Gambrel of Glasgow, Missouri.[45]

Apparently Gambrel, with two young children and his wife expecting their third child, had trouble gathering up enough money to pay Mason. Two months after the transaction, Mason was still waiting for his money.[46] Forced to look elsewhere for capital, he sold half of his remaining one-eighth interest in the *Sultana* to William Shands of Saint Louis.[47] As a result of these transactions, Mason had regressed from a three-eighths majority owner in the *Sultana* to a one-sixteenth minority shareholder. He now owned less interest in the vessel than his first clerk.

Perhaps trying to ensure an income for the *Sultana*, Mason and the other owners entered into a loose association of twenty-two independently owned steamboats and formed the Merchants and People's Steamboat Line, which, in turn, contracted with the U.S. government to transport freight and troops.[48] The *Sultana*, with her wide boiler deck space, was now guaranteed the shipment of Union soldiers and freight.

Mason must have looked on the contract as a lucrative deal. The government was paying $5 per enlisted man and $10 per officer for shipment. With the fall of the Confederate capital of Richmond, Virginia, on April 2 and the surrender of Robert E. Lee's army in Virginia on April 9,[49] Mason, like everyone else, must have realized that the Civil

War was just about over. Soon, thousands of Union troops would be returning to their homes.

On Tuesday, April 11, 1865, the crew of the *Sultana* prepared for a 4:00 P.M. departure from the Saint Louis wharf for a run to New Orleans.[50] Mason had assembled a capable crew for this trip: chief mate, longtime friend William Rowberry; pilots George Kayton and Henry Ingraham; chief engineer, Nathan Wintringer; and assistant engineer, Samuel ("Sam") Clemens (no connection with Mark Twain).

As first clerk, part-owner Gambrel handled office affairs; William Stratton acted as second, or "mud" clerk. Seeing to the needs of the first-class passengers were First Steward Henry Cross and Second Steward George Slater. Independent barkeeps Thomas McGinty and James O'Hara were available to quench the thirst of parched travelers.[51]

Before Mason could leave, however, he was informed by the local Board of Inspectors of Boilers and Machinery that the *Sultana* would have to undergo a periodic safety inspection, which was set for Wednesday, April 12. The *Sultana* would be delayed one day in leaving Saint Louis, and each day spent at the waterfront meant lost revenue. On April 10, Mason had watched Captain Tabor and the *Olive Branch,* now a member of the competing Atlantic and Mississippi Steamship Company, leave Saint Louis. The *Pauline Carroll,* also of the Atlantic and Mississippi line, was scheduled to leave at the same time as the *Sultana.*[52] As Mason stood idly by, he must have felt quite frustrated.

Inspectors John Maguire and John Schaffer arrived at the *Sultana,* as scheduled, and examined the two-year-old steamboat from top to bottom. Both men were probably surprised by what they found tucked away in one of the wheelhouses, a 7½-foot-long alligator! The crew had captured the creature some time before. They had built a crate for it and kept it as sort of a mascot.[53]

Probably more interesting to the two inspectors were the *Sultana*'s aging boilers. They subjected the boilers, which normally operated at a pressure of 145 pounds, to a hydrostatic pressure of 210 pounds without incident. Satisfied that the *Sultana* was safe to operate on her normal Saint Louis–New Orleans run, Maguire and Schaffer issued a safety certificate to Mason and promptly left.[54]

After a delay of more than twenty-four hours, Mason was finally ready to leave Saint Louis. He was still hoping to get away before the *Pauline Carroll,* which, for some unknown reason, had delayed her departure until the morning of the 14th.[55]

At 10:00 A.M., Thursday, April 13, the *Sultana* backed into the strong current of the Mississippi and turned her bow downstream toward New Orleans. Her first scheduled stop was less than one day away at Cairo.[56]

Delivered from Bondage

After almost four long years of civil warfare, more than 600,000 Americans had lost their lives and hundreds of thousands more had been wounded and scarred in battle. In addition, more than 400,000 men from both the Union and the Confederacy had been captured and forced to spend time in captivity.

At the beginning of the American Civil War, both sides, believing that it would be over in a short time, had relied on a cartel of exchange to deal with prisoners. Captives were granted a parole and released on their word of honor not to take up arms again until officially exchanged. By agreement, all exchanges were to be made on a rank-for-rank, man-for-man basis.[1]

Although the cartel started out well enough, it soon broke down as commissioners on both sides failed to agree on various procedures.[2] Forced to hold onto large groups of prisoners, both the Union and Confederacy began to look for adequate facilities to house their captives, and a number of prisons and prison camps began to spring up.

Castle Morgan, a Southern facility, was established in the spring of 1863. An unfinished cotton shed located in Cahaba, Alabama, on the Alabama River about ten miles downstream from Selma, it was originally designed for a few hundred men. Before long, thousands of prisoners were confined in an area measuring 200 by 300 feet.[3] A freshwater stream, the only source of drinking water for the prison, soon became polluted as people in the town used the stream for washing and sewage disposal. Because the stream flowed from Cahaba to the prison, all of the filth was brought into the stockade and the water for the prisoners was tainted.[4]

With the overcrowding at Cahaba and elsewhere, the Confederacy decided to open a new prison near Andersonville, Georgia, twelve miles north of Americus. On February 17, 1864, the first contingent of prisoners arrived at Camp Sumter (Andersonville Prison). Under orders of April 24, all prisoners at Cahaba would be transferred to Andersonville and Castle Morgan would be shut down. By May 3, no prisoners remained at Cahaba except those too sick to travel.[5]

Although the Confederacy had intended to close the stockade at Cahaba, it soon found that to be impossible. Shortly after being emptied, the prison was again crowded with Union prisoners awaiting transfer to Andersonville. For the next two months, the Cahaba prison functioned as a receiving station for prisoners on the way to Georgia. When Andersonville began to overflow, the stockade at Cahaba once more became a permanent stopping place, an unwelcome home for nearly 3,000 Union soldiers.[6]

The prospect of an unknown length of time in prison was a harrowing experience. On entering the stockade, seventeen-year-old Pvt. Charles M. Eldridge (Company G, 3d Tennessee Cavalry) could only sit down and cry after seeing the other prisoners walking around in their deteriorating clothes.[7]

Soldiers coming into the prison stockade and unfinished cotton shed were amazed at the filthy conditions of the place. Pvt. Jesse Marshall Huffaker (Company D, 3d Tennessee Cavalry) awoke the morning after entering Cahaba to find his new jacket covered with body lice, "shining like wheat grains along the seams."[8]

The soldiers also had the problem of guarding what meager possessions they had lest the other inmates steal them. Pvt. William H. Williams (Company F, 18th Michigan Infantry) remembered, "We were robbed of everything we had that was good for anything."[9] Pvt. Harmon A. Christine (Company H, 102d Ohio Infantry) wrote, "You could not lay a pan down and turn around but someone had it."[10]

The usual ration for the men at Cahaba was about a pint of ground cornmeal each day, sometimes supplemented with a bit of beef. Pvt. Truman M. Smith (Company B, 8th Michigan Cavalry) found the meal to be "ground cob and all" and that to be "moldy."[11] As for the beef, Christine noticed that it was so bad he could smell it "before it reached the inside of the prison fence."[12]

The health of the prisoners soon began to deteriorate. Despite the overcrowding and the close quarters, the inhabitants of Castle Morgan were fortunate never to have an outbreak of any killing epidemic, although a few contracted typhoid fever or measles. The major illnesses apparently were diarrhea, dysentery, and pneumonia.[13] Almost every prisoner held at Cahaba, however, suffered from malnutrition.

When Pvt. John L. Myers (Company A, 18th Michigan Infantry) was captured, he weighed 165 pounds. At his release, he was down to a mere 95 pounds. Pvt. Commodore Smith (Company F, 18th Michigan Infantry), who lost 80 pounds, was reduced to a 94-pound skeleton in less than six months.[14] Because of the lack of fresh fruits and vegetables, many of the prisoners suffered from scurvy. Pvt. Alonzo A. Van Vlack (Company F, 18th Michigan Infantry) found his "legs were one raw sore from my knees down to my feet."[15]

On March 1, following a long period of rain, the Alabama River began to rise and flood the entire prison compound. This forced the soldiers either to remain in the water or to find whatever "roosts" they could. Cpl. Spencer Harrison Williams (Company E, 3d Tennessee Cavalry) remembered that the river "overflowed the whole town, and was also half-leg deep all over the prison . . . it was bad tho amayzing to see the yanks (no 2200) [*sic*] climbing from bunk to bunk and building our fires on skillet leds [lead skillets] to do our cooking."[16]

With the whole prison area underwater, the Confederates put about 1,100 prisoners on a steamboat and carried them up the Alabama to a temporary holding area at Selma.[17] Those who remained in the stockade (about 1,700 men) had to deal with the flood as best they could.

Because of the flooding and also as a result of the negotiations taking place at Vicksburg for an exchange of the prisoners at Cahaba, the men were informed on March 6 to get ready to leave. Pvt. John Lowery Walker (Company B, 50th Ohio Infantry) heard a Confederate shout, " 'Come on, Yanks,' which invitation we all accepted without being urged."[18] As the steamboats arrived at the Cahaba landing, lot after lot of prisoners were carted away to the great delight of all. By March 20 or 21, the majority of the prisoners were gone, but some did not leave Castle Morgan until as late as April 12, some five weeks after the release of the first man.[19]

The prison pen at Camp Sumter (Andersonville) was vastly different from that at Cahaba. It was originally intended to hold about 8,000 to 10,000 men. A month after its opening, the prison population was about 7,500 and, in April, jumped to 10,000. As the result of battles in both Virginia and northern Georgia, the number of prisoners at Andersonville rose to more than 22,000 men in June and then 29,000 in July. The number of prisoners during August was almost 33,000, the maximum number ever held at Andersonville.[20]

The overcrowding, a hot and wet Georgia summer, and progressively poor rations quickly led to a breakdown in the health of the prisoners. "There were one hundred to one hundred fifty boys dying every day," Sgt. Joseph Stevens (Company E, 1st Michigan Sharpshooters) witnessed. "A large wagon, drawn by four mules, was used in drawing out the dead. They were laid in as we pile cord wood and taken to the burying ground, generally putting fifty in a grave, and returning would bring mush in on the same wagon, where worms that came from the dead could be seen crawling all over it; but we were starving, therefore we fought for it like hungry hogs."[21]

The Union soldiers at Andersonville, like those in most of the Confederate prisons, suffered from scurvy, diarrhea, dysentery, and gangrene. In the fall of 1864, Joseph Jones, a Confederate doctor, spent several weeks at the prison. Dr. Jones noted: "From the crowded condition, filthy habits, bad diet, and dejected, depressed condition of the prisoners, their systems became so disordered that the smallest abrasion of the skin from the rubbing of a shoe, or from the effects of the hot sun, or from the prick of a splinter, or from scratching a mosquito bite, in some cases took on rapid and frightful ulceration and gangrene."[22]

On the last day of October 1864, all prisoners were suddenly rounded up and marched out of the gates. While they at first thought that they were being exchanged, they soon found out otherwise. With the fall of Atlanta in early September, the Confederates feared that Union Gen. William T. Sherman would send a cavalry raid south to free the prisoners. To prevent the temptation for such a raid, the Confederates decided to move the prisoners farther into the interior of the South out of Sherman's reach.[23]

After moving throughout the southern part of Georgia for almost two months, the prisoners were eventually loaded into boxcars and taken north. "I thought we were going to be released," Pvt. Isaac Noah Davenport (Company K, 7th Tennessee Cavalry) wrote, "but to our sorrow we were in a few hours time . . . penned in that horrible prison called Andersonville." The northbound train had brought them straight back to prison.[24]

On their return to Andersonville, the thousands of poorly clad, underfed soldiers had to put up with an unusually cold southern winter. Capt. J. Walter Elliott (Company F, 44th U.S. Colored Troop) recalled: "Oh! the long and dreary winter in prison; the suffering from cold, [and] hunger."[25] Pvt. William A. McFarland (Company A, 42d Indiana Infantry) found that "when sleeping we were obliged to huddle together to keep warm."[26]

Finally, near the middle of March, with the Confederacy crumbling around them and other Confederate prisons removing their prisoners to mutual exchange camps, the prisoners at Andersonville, only about 5,000 in number now, were told to get ready to go home. "We heard the glad tidings of great joy, that welcome word—exchange," Davenport wrote. "We were soon ordered to fall in line. I tell you there was no time lost."[27]

Captain Elliott, who had been confined with the officers in a smaller prison area, was shocked when he saw the soldiers from the main prison pen. "At the [train] cars we joined some 500 privates from the stockade, and a more pitiable sight [was] never disclosed. All were begrimed and blackened by exposure, without pretense of protection from summer's sun or winter's rain; all weak and lean from starvation; many, too feeble to take care of themselves."[28]

At the dilapidated railcars, there was a mad scramble to get on board; no man wanted to be left behind. According to Lt. Joseph Taylor Elliott (Company C, 124th Indiana Infantry), however, some of the prisoners were so weak that they "were unable to help themselves, and had to be lifted on as little children."[29]

As the first train pulled away from that "hell on earth," Thomas

Horan (Company H, 65th Indiana Infantry) summed up the feelings of his fellow prisoners when he wrote, "God forbid I should ever be taken into bondage again."[30]

The movement of prisoners resulted from a trip by Lt. Col. Howard A. M. Henderson, commander of Cahaba Prison, to Union-held Vicksburg under a flag of truce in mid-February 1865. Because of the deplorable conditions at Cahaba, Henderson sought relief from the government of the United States.

In a meeting with Col. Archie C. Fisk, the assistant adjutant general of the Union Army at Vicksburg, Henderson suggested that the United States send another boatload of medicine and supplies through the lines to Cahaba, as had been done in December.

"Why not bring the men here under parole," Colonel Fisk said, "and detain them in a camp on neutral ground until exchanged?"[31]

The idea sounded simple enough to Henderson, but he stipulated that the arrangement had to be a two-way street. The agreement had to apply to Confederates held in Union hands, as well as to Union troops in Cahaba.

Diligently, Henderson and Fisk began drafting some form of working arrangement. The welfare of the prisoners was a concern on each side, and the two officers worked out a realistic plan. On February 21, 1865, a formal arrangement was drawn up and agreed to by both parties.

As stipulated in the cartel, 3,000 Union prisoners, (understood to be those held at Cahaba) were to be placed on paroles of honor and brought to a neutral exchange camp set up outside Vicksburg, where they would remain until exchanged. The Federals were also to see that an equal number of Confederates held in the North were brought downriver for the same purpose.

The neutral exchange camp would be set up four miles from Vicksburg and officially designated a "parole camp," but it unofficially became Camp Fisk in honor of Colonel Fisk. To ensure its neutrality, the camp would be guarded by U.S. troops. The Union prisoners at the camp were to be supplied and taken care of at the expense of the U.S. government, but they would remain under Confederate control.[32]

Henderson was back at Cahaba in early March. On March 6, some of the first prisoners were loaded on a steamboat and brought up the Alabama River to Selma. After a few days at Selma, the men climbed aboard a string of "dirty box cars" and headed west toward Meridian, Mississippi.[33]

After confinement at Meridian for a night or two, the soldiers were placed back on the cars and carried to Jackson, Mississippi, the end of the rail line. They were kept in a guarded camp for the evening. Excitement began to grow among the prisoners. "Now we were nearing our lines and learned that our troops were near the [Big] Black River—less than forty miles away," Truman M. Smith noted. So close to Union lines, they finally realized that freedom was a reality. They were going home.

The rail line between Jackson and Vicksburg had been long since destroyed and never rebuilt, so the 800 weak, undernourished prisoners were forced to travel the last 40 miles on foot. Tired and hungry, they plodded westward until the evening of March 16. After more than a week and a half of travel, the prisoners came within sight of the Big Black River, eight miles from Vicksburg.

"What a glorious sight met our eyes when we got there!" Smith remembered, as he stood on the eastern bank of the river. "On the opposite side floated the stars and stripes."[34] For many, it had been more than a year since they had seen the red, white, and blue of the United States.

While the prisoners were moving west from Cahaba, a series of communiques had been traveling back and forth between the Union and Confederate authorities involved in an overall prisoner exchange. An agreement reached on March 10 stipulated that all Union soldiers held captive in Georgia, Alabama, and Mississippi should be forwarded to Mobile, Alabama, for exchange. This agreement, then, would have applied to the men from Cahaba, at that instant already en route to Vicksburg.

When it was determined that a group of prisoners had already been forwarded to Vicksburg and that Mobile was impossible to reach because of the threat of an attack by Union forces, Union agents in charge of the exchange issued instructions that the prisoners still held by the Confederates, principally the 5,000 starving wretches at Andersonville, be sent to Vicksburg.

The small cartel drawn up by Colonels Henderson and Fisk suddenly took on new importance. Vicksburg was now the center for all exchanges in the west. Knowing that the cartel would have to be revamped and reworked, both sides sat down on March 16 to define the finer points. Among these was how to protect the prisoners as they moved from the Big Black River, eight miles from Vicksburg, to the neutral Camp Fisk at Four Mile Bridge, four miles closer to town. A strip of land from river to camp, 1½ miles wide on each side of the railroad connecting the two, would be considered neutral ground, a sort of no-man's land to all but the prisoners and agents of the exchange.[35]

A second large group of prisoners had left Cahaba around March 10 to begin their journey to Vicksburg. Taking the same route as the first group, the column arrived at the Big Black on March 19. Private Eldridge, sick and weak and far to the rear, was slowly hobbling along when he suddenly heard shouts coming from the front of the column.

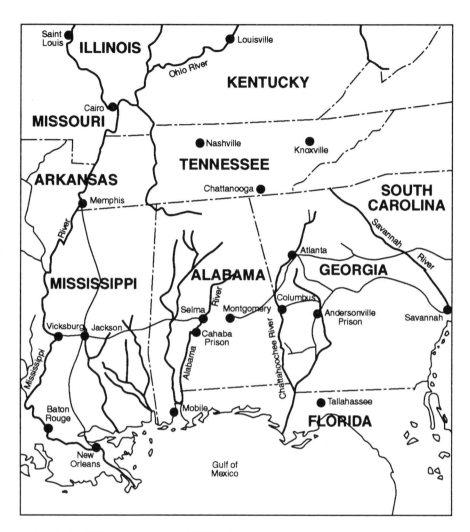

Mississippi River area in the Middle South.

Not knowing what was causing the commotion, he continued forward until he too could see what everybody was cheering about. There, across the Big Black, just barely in sight, was Old Glory. "Then I hollered, too," he wrote, "until I had no more strength in me, and sank down in the road."[36]

The third and last large group of prisoners released from Cahaba trickled away from the prison between March 12 and 18 and, on the way to Jackson, eventually rejoined forces. Arriving at Jackson, they found a supply of Union clothing ready to be issued. Cpl. Erastus Winters (Company K, 50th Ohio Infantry) remembered, however, that there seemed to be more men in need then there were clothes to go around. "All that I remember getting was a pair of socks," he wrote.[37]

The column was hindered by a pouring rain, and the 40-mile walk from Jackson to the Big Black took two days. Even the soldiers dressed in new clothes were soon soaked to the skin. Trudging through the mud, Corporal Winters found that his old worn-out shoes were only an encumbrance, so he tossed them aside and marched along in his new socks. As the rain dampened the morale of the men, Winters was determined to be among the first of the men at the Big Black. He squared his shoulders, took a fresh chew from a twist of tobacco, and forged ahead. Near sundown, the head of the straggling column reached the river. Despite being barely able to lift his feet from the ground as he slid along in his socks, the stiff and sore Winters succeeded in being among the first to reach the Big Black.[38]

While the men from Cahaba were traveling toward Vicksburg, the first of the worn-down skeletons at Andersonville were leaving their horrible prison pen. Beginning on March 18, the prisoners were taken by rail to Columbus, Georgia, and then to Montgomery, Alabama. All along the way, at each little station they passed, the remains of a soldier or two were left behind for burial. "How hard to die on their morning of deliverance," Lieutenant Elliott thought, "with all the bright hopes of meeting father, mother, wife or children."[39]

From Montgomery, the weary prisoners were taken by steamboat to Selma, then by rail to Demopolis, Alabama. Although the rail trip was short, the line was in bad shape; three times, some of the cars derailed, and, twice, some were wrecked as they derailed and flipped over. Many of the prisoners were injured and broke brittle arms and legs in the wrecks.[40]

From Demopolis, the men were transported to Jackson, but the Confederate soldiers escorting them from Andersonville were not as well organized as the escorts from Cahaba. After reaching Jackson, they gave each prisoner a quart of cornmeal and sent him on his way. Lieutenant Elliott remembered that the Confederates "simply turned us loose, and directed us to the road to Vicksburg." A cold rain started early on the morning of March 29. It continued all day and severely impeded the progress of the emaciated, weary prisoners. Despite their best efforts, they traveled only about 17 miles during the first day. Although stiff and sore from being battered about in jolting boxcars and from walking the day before, the men started on their way bright and early on the 30th. What normally took the Cahaba prisoners two days to cover required three days by the men from Andersonville. On the second day, they walked all day but were forced to stop with still 5 miles before them.[41]

On March 31, after a week of constant travel, the men neared the Big Black. There, floating from a tall pole on the opposite side of the river, was the United States flag. Capt. J. Walter Elliott "hailed the glorious flag of our country as it floated in the breeze. Tears flowed at sight of that proud emblem, while Big Black River, Jordan-like, divided the forlorn C.S.A. from our Canaan."[42]

Once across the river, the men had to take one last train ride before they could relax. At Camp Fisk, they were greeted enthusiastically by the men from Cahaba. Corporal Winters, a Cahaba prisoner, looked at the living skeletons: "Poor boys! What a sad plight they were in."[43] Many of the Andersonville prisoners were so emaciated that the Cahaba men had to help them from the cars to the camp.[44]

Throughout the rest of the day and into the next, the men from Camp Sumter exchanged their ragged, lice-ridden clothing for new, clean uniforms. Augmenting the articles of food and clothing given out by the government were items furnished by the U.S. Sanitary Commission. Organized by civilians in 1861 to assist the army in providing care and personal items to sick and wounded soldiers, the commission presented such items as shirts, socks, and underdrawers, as well as an assortment of foods, to the men from Cahaba and Andersonville.[45]

Some of the first rations that the men from both prisons drew from the Camp Fisk commissary were stale and filled with worms. Private Walker found the hardtack "so alive with vermin as to be unfit for a dog to eat."[46] Blaming the quartermaster in Vicksburg who supplied the camp with rations, the men complained to Maj. Gen. Napoleon Jackson Tecumseh Dana, Union Commander of the Department of Mississippi with headquarters in Vicksburg, who quickly had fresh bread furnished daily to the prisoners.[47]

On March 20, even before the arrival of the men from Andersonville, Capt. George Augustus Williams, 1st U.S. Infantry and commissary of musters at Vicksburg, was appointed by General Dana to superintend the exchange of prisoners at Camp Fisk. Williams, a career army officer, was to supervise the arrival of the prisoners, record all of their names, and get them ready for shipment north. He was to consult with Col. N.

G. Watts, the Confederate commissioner of exchange at Vicksburg, and arrange the man-for-man exchange of Union and Confederate prisoners.[48]

After graduating from the U.S. Military Academy in 1852, Williams had spent the prewar years on the Texas frontier and as an instructor at the academy. Shortly after the start of civil hostilities, he had fought with the 1st U.S. Infantry at New Madrid, Missouri; Island No. 10, near New Madrid; and Corinth, Mississippi. While in command of an expedition near Yazoo Pass in March 1863, Williams had suffered a hernia that subsequently relieved him from field service. During the following two years, he had served as provost-marshal in Memphis and, at one time, had faced charges of dismissal because of the filthy conditions found in the prisons under his care. In early 1865, he had been ordered to Vicksburg as General Dana's commissary of musters for the Department of Mississippi.[49]

On his appointment to superintend the exchange, Williams went to Camp Fisk with Brig. Gen. Morgan L. Smith, commander of the Post and District of Vicksburg, and met with Colonel Watts. Instead of finding the smooth-running cartel he had expected, Williams found that a breakdown had occurred and few Confederate prisoners in Union hands were being forwarded to Vicksburg. Because the cartel stipulated that the prisoners were to be exchanged man for man, rank for rank, Colonel Watts refused to release any of the constantly arriving Union prisoners until more Confederate soldiers were sent to Vicksburg.

On March 22, Smith and Williams again met with Watts in an attempt to persuade the Confederate to release the prisoners now in camp. Steadfast in his argument, Watts refused. He told the two men that if the Union-held Confederates were not released, he would have to send the prisoners now at Camp Fisk back to Andersonville and Cahaba. Fearful of what might transpire if the men in camp and en route were sent back to prison, Smith addressed an alarming letter to his superior, General Dana: "It is my opinion, general, that at least one-fourth of them will die and be killed if they are turned back."[50]

To clear up the matter, Dana sent Williams to Mobile, where Union Maj. Gen. Edward Canby was supposed to be holding 3,000 Confederate prisoners. Hoping he could exchange these men for those now in Vicksburg, Williams learned in Mobile that he had been greatly misinformed about the number of men held by Canby. Staring disaster in the face, Dana instructed Williams to proceed to Cairo, Illinois, for direct communication with Washington and further instructions.[51]

As the result of Sherman's sweep through Georgia and the Carolinas and Union Gen. James H. Wilson's destructive cavalry raid through northern Alabama, telegraphic communication throughout the South was almost nil. Messages sent from Washington were taking three or four days, and sometimes more, to reach Vicksburg. If Williams wanted a direct line with Grant or Washington, he had to go to Cairo.[52]

General Dana, feeling that District Commander Smith did not have the requisite authority to transact the exchange of prisoners with parties in Virginia, decided on April 1 to take over the operation of Camp Fisk. With the hope of breaking the deadlock of exchange, Dana immediately appointed Captain Williams to take overall charge of the prisoner exchange.

By this time, Williams was back in Vicksburg, having come up from Mobile on the *Sultana* during her record run from New Orleans to Cairo. Williams was awaiting formal orders to proceed to Illinois when he received his new appointment. It was now up to him to iron out all of the wrinkles that had developed between the Confederate commissioners at Vicksburg and the U.S. War Department in Washington.[53]

Dana's quick actions in trying to straighten out the deadlock might have been prompted by the restless nature of the waiting prisoners and a growing tension at Camp Fisk between the prisoners and their Negro guards, members of the 66th U.S. Colored Troop. On April 4, a near riot resulted over a confrontation between one of the white officers of the Negro guards and an officer of the prisoners. Only with the utmost care were the Union and Confederate authorities at Camp Fisk able to divert a major disaster. That night, in an attempt to diffuse the situation, General Dana replaced the Negro guards with white guards and waited a few days, until tempers had cooled, before returning the Negroes to the camp.[54]

Williams left Vicksburg for Cairo on April 8, and, that same day, Dana sent another telegram to Washington to ask for assistance. More men were coming into Camp Fisk every day, in groups and in squads, and 800 men, some of the last from Andersonville, were expected soon.[55] Although the number of men at Camp Fisk continued to grow, nobody was being sent home. The exchange camp had become a huge bottleneck.

Then, on Palm Sunday, April 9, 1865, Gen. Robert E. Lee surrendered his army to General Grant. Although one major Confederate army still remained in the field, the back of the Confederacy had been broken. The South's premier army had been defeated, and its government was on the run or in hiding.[56] No longer was it feasible for the Confederacy to squabble over the release of Union prisoners at Vicksburg.

The next day, a telegram was sent to the "Confederate Officer Having Charge of Prisoners, Vicksburg." This telegram, which did not reach Vicksburg until April 13 (partly as a result of the damage done to telegraph lines by Wilson's cavalry raid), was the breakthrough for which 5,000 men had been waiting. "All Federal officers and men who are held as prisoners" were to be paroled without the usual man-for-man exchange. "By agreement with General Grant, equivalents are to be given on the James River [Virginia]." By order of his superiors, Colonel Watts was to let his prisoners go.[57]

3 Messenger of Death

The *Sultana* steamed steadily southward from Saint Louis on Thursday, April 13. Passengers and crew watched the Mississippi rising and breaking free of its banks. Water from melting snow in the north was rushing down hundreds of rivers and streams to gorge the mighty river, already swollen from the heavy rains of late February and early March. Along its entire length, the "Old Man" was breaking through war-torn levees and spreading out over the rich farmlands of the North and the battle-scarred cotton fields of the South in one of the worst floods in recent history.

At Cairo, the river had risen 4½ inches in the past twenty-four hours. The *Memphis Argus* reported that the river was "much higher than it has been for years before." Opposite the city, the river completely covered the town of Hopefield, Arkansas. To the north, the waters of the Mississippi devoured the land for several miles on each side of the once placid banks. Large groves of trees, normally high and dry, showed only their top branches above the swirling brown water.[1]

In spite of the heavy flood, the *Sultana* was coming downriver at her usual rate of about nine miles per hour. Captain Mason was hoping to nose her into the Cairo wharf during the early morning hours of Friday, April 14.[2]

Meanwhile, on April 13, General Dana finally received the copy of the Confederate telegram, sent on April 10, that ordered the release of all Union prisoners held at Vicksburg. He passed the telegram to his senior assistant adjutant general, Capt. Frederic Speed, who, in turn, informed the Confederates at Camp Fisk of the good news. Optimistically, Speed asked if they could "deliver us a boatload [of released prisoners] by tomorrow noon."[3]

In spite of this optimism, it was not practical to assume that any of the men would be ready to go north by noon of the 14th. Besides transportation and supply problems that would arise in the movement of such a large, unregimented group, the rolls of the prisoners still had to be made up. When they had arrived in groups of all sizes, their names had been called from rolls held by the Confederates and put into the Federal books. No pattern had been used in recording the names, however; before the men could be sent north, the names had to be broken up by state and recorded on separate rolls. All of this would require more time than Speed had realized.[4]

A highly ambitious young man, Speed had become increasingly involved with the prisoners at Camp Fisk during early April 1865. As the first few contingents of prisoners began to arrive at Vicksburg, Speed had collected the many names and, knowing that relatives and friends were anxiously awaiting word of their interned loved ones, sent the information north for publication in the Saint Louis newspapers. A few days later, he met with Colonel Henderson to arrange for the transfer of all nonmilitary personnel to Benton Barracks, Missouri.[5]

Born in western New York State in 1841, Speed had moved to Portland, Maine, in 1860. As war approached, he had helped to raise the first company of Federal troops from that state, despite being a relative newcomer. He rose to the rank of sergeant major of the 5th Maine Infantry and fought at the first battle of Bull Run. After promotion to the adjutancy of the 13th Maine Infantry, Speed received a commission as captain and assistant adjutant general. In early 1865, he joined the staff of General Dana and the Department of Mississippi.[6] In this capacity, he became increasingly involved in the job of getting the paroled Union prisoners home to their families.

During the first two weeks of April, the men at Camp Fisk rested and recuperated. The majority of them were making the best of their stay at the camp. Many wrote letters home to ask for news from their loved ones, while others told of their exploits in battle and in prison.[7]

Writing to his parents, Pvt. Thomas J. Hinds (Company K, 18th Michigan Infantry) left no doubt as to why the prisoners had been released. "The reasons of the Rebs fetching us here is they could not feed us any more. They are the nearest played out of anything I have seen lately. They are worse than my old shoes and they are good for nothing."[8]

Because the men, technically, were still prisoners of war, they were not drilled, marched, or paraded. Sgt. Richard Jourdan Foley (Company A, 6th Kentucky Cavalry) wrote home that he was "healthy, hearty, fat and saucy" and that he had "nothing to do but eat, drink and sleep."[9] Corporal Winters found that he and the others were slowly beginning "to fill out and look like men once again."[10]

To relieve the boredom, many of the soldiers sought passes to visit Vicksburg. Lieutenant Elliott went into the city day after day to look over the battle lines from the siege of 1863. Inspecting the Confederate earthworks, he marveled at their strength and wondered how Grant and his soldiers could have moved up close enough to succeed in capturing the Bluff City.[11] Hinds was equally impressed with the fortifications. In a letter to his parents, he wrote: "It is the greatest wonder how Grant took this place for it is one fortress."[12]

Corporal Winters also secured a pass to visit Vicksburg. While walking the streets, he suddenly came upon a fifty-cent paper "shin plaster" lying in the gutter and had to admit that "It had been so long since I had any money I came near not recognizing it."[13] On the other hand, Cpl. Spencer Harrison Williams had no trouble recognizing "4 half dollars in silver" that he found while "rambling around hunting for some greens."[14]

Although most of the soldiers at the parole camp were in the same financial straits as Winters and Williams, some managed to get money or considerations from home. Pvt. Lewis W. McCrory (Company A, 100th Ohio Infantry) received so much money that he was able to purchase a good set of civilian clothes, a fine valise to put them in, and a good, ironbound pocketbook. Even after his wild spending spree, McCrory still had more than a hundred dollars to put into his new pocketbook.[15]

Another prisoner, Sgt. Alexander C. Brown (Company I, 2d Ohio Infantry), was not sent money, but he was offered any needed assistance by a southern agent of a Cincinnati express company. Grateful for the offer, Brown had only one request. He asked the agent to purchase a stateroom berth for him when the prisoners were sent north, and the agent readily agreed.[16]

As the prisoners waited for their release, the war was still going on around them. On April 6, word reached the camp that Richmond had been evacuated and was now in Union hands. The prisoners went wild with joy, and one hundred guns were fired in a salute to Grant and his victorious army. Two days later, the men heard of General Sherman's victory in Bentonville, North Carolina. Suddenly, hope ran high that the war soon would be over and the prisoners unconditionally released.[17]

The spirits of most of the men remained high. Many began receiving letters and packages from home, but others watched and waited at every mail call, only to go away empty handed. "You must delay no time in answering this letter," Spencer Harrison Williams wrote, "as I have not heard from home since I was captured."[18] Private Horan, admonishing those at home, wrote: "You know the game is every one for themselves but I think . . . some of you can find time to write me a few lines."[19]

The waiting was becoming unbearable. Then, on April 13, the same day on which the *Sultana* was plowing her way toward Cairo and General Dana received the telegram for release of the prisoners, word hit Camp Fisk that General Lee had surrendered his entire army to General Grant.

"Lee has caved [in] to Grant," 1st Sgt. John Clark Ely (Company C, 115th Ohio Infantry) wrote. "Bully, bully, glorious bully."[20]

The prisoners broke into instantaneous celebration. Again, rumors of their going home began to run wild. A celebration of unequalled magnitude was scheduled for the next day, April 14. "There is to be a Salute of 200 guns fired with speaking [and] military parades," Hinds noted.[21] They would be exchanged in a matter of days. It almost seemed too good to be true.

At one o'clock in the morning of Good Friday, April 14, the *Sultana* slipped into a berth at the Cairo wharf. At first light, the Cairo *War Eagle* was trumpeting that the "regular and unsurpassed passenger packet" *Sultana* would depart for New Orleans by ten o'clock the next morning.[22]

Downriver, in Vicksburg, General Dana sent a telegram to Washington, D.C., in which he stated that there were "about 4,700" prisoners at Camp Fisk and of that number, about 1,100 were grievously sick. "The rest of the prisoners are in excellent health, the Cahaba prisoners particularly," Dana added. "Nearly all the sick are from Andersonville." Dana informed Washington that even now, as he wrote, the Confederates were getting ready to release the men and that they would "be sent North as rapidly as possible."[23]

Meanwhile, a tragic event was about to unfold 1,000 miles away at Ford's Theatre in Washington, D.C. Shortly after 10 P.M., while watching the stage comedy *Our American Cousin*, President Abraham Lincoln was shot and mortally wounded by John Wilkes Booth. As Booth fled like a phantom into the night, Lincoln's large frame was carried across the street to the home of William Peterson, where the president died at 7:22 A.M. on April 15, 1865.[24]

Immediately, the telegraphic wire services began sending across the nation the horrible news that President Lincoln had been assassinated. Before noon of April 15, the Cairo *Democrat* hit the streets with a morning "extra." Bordered in black, the newspaper heralded: "Terrible News President Lincoln Assassinated." The account of Lincoln's death quickly spread throughout the city, and church bells began to peal in sorrowful mourning. When word reached the riverfront, the bells of the docked steamers added to the sullen din. The nation was in mourning. A few hours later, when the *Sultana* backed into the muddy Mississippi waters, she was the first boat to leave Cairo with word of the assassination. Draped in black mourning, she carried extra copies of the Cairo newspaper proclaiming the sad news.[25]

Traveling downriver, the *Sultana* stopped at all points (cities, towns, private landings, and military forts) to report the news of the assassination. Because telegraphic communications throughout the South were still devastated, the *Sultana* was a self-appointed messenger of death.[26]

On the morning of Easter Sunday, April 16, the *Sultana* passed through the flooded lands just north of Memphis. The pilot carefully avoided the partially submerged trees of islands No. 42 through No. 45, known locally as Paddy's Hen and Chickens because one island was large and the rest small. It was still early morning when the *Sultana,* her flag at half-staff, glided up to the Memphis wharfboat. In an instant, the news was on the street. The Cairo "extras" were carried to the military and civilian leaders in the city, and flags were silently lowered to half-mast.[27]

After a short layover in Memphis, Captain Mason was on his way downriver. Aware of the impact of the message he was carrying, he stayed ahead of the other steamboats from Cairo. As a businessman, Mason knew that the *Sultana*'s reputation, and his own, would be greatly enhanced by spreading the word of this national calamity to all points along the river. Such a seemingly humanitarian deed could only help his dwindling pocketbook.

As the nation began to mourn, the people of Vicksburg, still unaware of the assassination, continued with business as usual. Captain Speed sent out another special order on the 16th that would allow all of the sick prisoners in Vicksburg hospitals to go home. At the end of the order, he added: "Quartermaster's Department will furnish transportation."[28] The men were being gradually released, and the energetic Speed was doing all that he could to send them home as quickly and efficiently as possible, but he did not intend to pick the boats to transport the men. That was the job of the quartermaster. Speed had enough to do without the extra burden of choosing the vessels to carry the men home.

That same day, fully aware that Colonel Watts had been ordered to release the Union prisoners on parole without the man-for-man exchange, Speed approached General Dana and volunteered to take over the job of commissioner of exchange while Captain Williams was still in Cairo. Speed knew full well that it would take Williams another five or six days to return to Vicksburg. Because he had been working with the rolls and the prisoners from the start and already had a good working relationship with both Watts and Henderson, Speed felt that the temporary commissioner's job would not be too difficult. Glad to have a volunteer, Dana quickly accepted Speed's offer and gave verbal orders for him to step in for Williams.[29]

Carrying his new temporary title, Speed went quickly to work. On Monday, April 17, he cut another special order that sent all of the Illinois prisoners rushing to their tents for their meager belongings. Taken into the Bluff City by the shuttle train that ran between Vicksburg and

Camp Fisk, the men went on board a steamboat furnished by the Quartermaster's Department and were soon on their way home.[30]

While Speed kept himself busy with the prisoners, the *Sultana* continued her journey southward. Throughout the rest of Easter Sunday and on into Monday, she moved at a steady pace along the crooked bends of the lower river and solemnly spread the news of Lincoln's death. Late Monday evening, she closed in on Vicksburg and found that the corkscrew bend in front of the city was totally awash with the spring flood. The river had spread out for miles over the lower Arkansas bank, and the town of De Soto, Louisiana, situated at the northeast edge of the bend, was completely underwater.[31]

Just as the sun was beginning to set, the *Sultana* nosed up to the wharfboat and Captain Mason sent runners into the city with the news of the assassination. The steamboat was still tying up when Col. Reuben B. Hatch, chief quartermaster of the Department of Mississippi, stepped on board the *Sultana* and sought out Mason.[32]

Joining the army in early 1861, Hatch had quickly secured the rank of first lieutenant and regimental quartermaster of the 8th Illinois Infantry. A few months later, after promotion to captain, he had moved to Cairo as an assistant quartermaster in the Federal service.[33] Undoubtedly, his rise in rank and position came with the help and support of his influential brother, Ozias M. Hatch, the secretary of state for Illinois and a close personal friend and adviser to President Lincoln.

Shortly after arriving in Cairo, Hatch's true nature began to show. As an assistant quartermaster, he had access to large sums of government money. He and two other men entered into a number of contracts with Chicago lumber dealers to purchase lumber at a low price, but they charged the government a higher amount. When the government paid the invoices, Hatch and his friends settled with the dealers at the low price and skimmed the excess into their own pockets.

The scheme might have gone on for an indefinite period, but the lumber dealers, feeling fleeced, went to the *Chicago Tribune* and reported the scandal. General Grant, then in Cairo, began a personal investigation of the allegations. Although Hatch tried his best to cover his tracks—even throwing his ledger books into the Ohio River, only to have them wash back on shore—he was eventually arrested "as an accomplice" and ordered before a court-martial.

Before Grant filed official charges against his assistant quartermaster, further investigations revealed other underhanded dealings between Hatch and the Quartermaster Department. During the five months that Hatch had been in Cairo, such transactions had included his selling army clothing and other supplies for personal gain, chartering steamboats to carry troops and supplies at a specified rate while charging the government a higher rate, and running the quartermaster harness and saddle shop for his personal welfare.

Faced with the near certainty of being found guilty by a court-martial, Hatch turned to his influential brother, who gathered together a group of important people, including the governor of Illinois, and bombarded President Lincoln to intercede in the "frivolous" charges against Reuben Hatch. In answer, Lincoln sent a letter to the judge advocate general stating that he personally knew "R. B. Hatch, and never before heard any thing against his character." He asked the judge advocate to personally look into the matter.

Although Hatch was in the army and this was strictly a military affair, Lincoln suggested that a civilian commission be appointed to investigate the allegations brought against Hatch. After looking into 1,696 claims, the commission found Hatch innocent of all charges. With his name cleared, Hatch was back on active duty by February 1863. He was promoted to chief quartermaster for the eastern district of Arkansas.

That August, Hatch tried to get another promotion and once again called on his brother and his brother's friends. In spite of their help, the promotion was not forthcoming, and a pouting Hatch tendered his resignation. No sooner had his resignation been approved, Hatch decided, for some unknown reason, that he wanted to stay in the army. Again, those in authority were bombarded by letters of recommendation from politically influential men in Illinois and from the desk of President Lincoln. Finally, in March 1864, Hatch was back in uniform. Following his promotion to lieutenant colonel, he was handed the job of chief quartermaster of the 13th Army Corps.

Later in the spring, the 13th Army Corps was abolished after the Union's failure in the Red River campaign. While he awaited assignment elsewhere, Hatch again sought promotion. As before, his brother and brother's friends, in addition to General Grant, who had forgiven Hatch (reason unknown) for his earlier trouble in Cairo, inundated the War Department with letters of recommendation. In spite of their efforts, however, he was not promoted. A disgruntled Hatch tendered his resignation a second time.

While he awaited news about his resignation, Hatch was suddenly ordered before an examining board looking into the qualifications of a number of quartermaster employees. In February 1865, the board reported, "Of the 60 officers who have appeared before this board, not more than 1 or 2 can compare with [Colonel] Hatch in degree of deficiency." It noted that he was "totally unfit to discharge the duties of assistant quartermaster," and, in substance, asked that he be suspended from further duty.

But, before the board's finding could be implemented, Hatch was back in uniform at a new post, his second resignation apparently forgotten. In late February 1865, he was ordered to Vicksburg to act as chief quartermaster, and it was in this capacity that he met the steamer *Sultana* and Captain Mason.[34]

Perhaps Hatch and Mason knew each other during Hatch's stay in Cairo in 1862, and Mason even might have known of Hatch's shady dealings with the government. At the same time, Hatch might have been aware of Mason's financial troubles.

Whether or not each knew of the other's past, however, Mason thought that Hatch, as chief quartermaster at Vicksburg, was the man to see in procuring a shipment of paroled prisoners for his return trip upriver, and Hatch in no way tried to dissuade him.[35]

Mason believed that Hatch had charge of shipping the prisoners out of Vicksburg, and he wanted to get as large a load as possible. He reminded Hatch that the *Sultana* carried a government contract to ship troops and should get preferential treatment in such matters. Hatch acted as if he were in charge and, during his short visit to the *Sultana*, told Mason that he would see what he could do.[36] Although Hatch actually had little control over the prisoners, the combination of his shady character and Mason's financial status left the steamboat captain ripe for another of the quartermaster's fraudulent schemes.

Shortly after Hatch left the *Sultana*, Gen. Morgan Smith arrived to see Mason. Prior to the war, Smith, like Mason, had been a resident of Saint Louis and the captain of a number of steamboats. Possibly, his only reason for visiting the *Sultana* was to greet an old friend, but Mason quickly put Smith on the spot. He wanted a boatload of prisoners when he came back upriver, and he wanted assurances from Smith that he would get them. Although the exchange of prisoners had been officially taken out of Smith's hands by General Dana, Smith promised Mason that he would have his load.[37]

When Smith left the *Sultana*, he offered Miles Sells, the *Sultana*'s steamboat agent in Vicksburg, a ride into town. As the two men rode away, Smith turned to Sells and said, "I will give Captain Mason a load as he comes up and if Hatch or Captain Speed don't turn the men out to him, you let me know it."[38]

That evening, as the *Sultana* backed away from the Vicksburg wharfboat and turned downriver toward New Orleans, Captain Mason felt assured that he would get all the paroled prisoners he wanted.

Meanwhile, the news of Lincoln's murder was spreading through the streets of Vicksburg. All paroled Confederate soldiers and all recognized Confederate sympathizers were rounded up and taken to the city courthouse under heavy guard. Surrounded by the Confederacy, the Federals feared for their lives.

Just outside of Vicksburg, at an impromptu party hosted by Confederate Col. H.A.M. Henderson for most of the officers involved in the functions of Camp Fisk, both Union and Confederate, the terrible news hit like a thunderbolt.

"My God! They have murdered our President!" one of the Federal officers exclaimed when he first heard the news.[39]

Although angry words were exchanged and tempers momentarily flared, cooler heads soon prevailed when it was reasoned that the Confederates at Camp Fisk had taken no part in the assassination. It was quickly decided to rush Colonel Henderson and the other Confederates to their side of the Big Black River before the angered Union soldiers in town knew that they were close by and before the prisoners at Camp Fisk heard the news. Henderson and his staff were soon seated in the tender of a speeding locomotive going full-throttle toward the Confederate lines, eight miles away. As the train sped past Camp Fisk at about two o'clock on the morning of April 18, it was obvious to the Confederates that the prisoners had already learned of Lincoln's murder.[40]

Word of the assassination had spread rapidly throughout the camp. As expected, the prisoners went wild and caused a near riot. A Kentucky lieutenant led a contingent of prisoners toward the headquarters tent to demand the arrest of the Confederate commissioners and their aides. Other men, bent on revenge, cried out for somebody to bring a rope, but not a Confederate was to be found. The few Confederate staff members who had remained in camp that evening were already on the other side of the Big Black River. Highly aggravated, the prisoners sang "Hang Jeff Davis from a Sour Apple Tree" for a while before finally settling down for the night.[41]

In Vicksburg that morning, the first rays of sunlight revealed black crepe hanging from numerous storefronts and Federal buildings and flags flying at half-mast. Eight miles away, on the Confederate side of the Big Black River, Colonel Henderson raised his Confederate flag, intertwined with the white flag of truce, at half-mast. On the Federal side of the river, the 66th U.S. Colored Troop did the same with the United States flag.[42]

A sullen gloom had settled over the men at Camp Fisk. Understandably, the talk that morning was of the assassination. "Sad, sad [news] of this morning," Sergeant Ely wrote in his diary, "our president honest old Abe was shot."[43] Some of the Union soldiers thought that Lincoln's murder had been a Confederate plot. Others feared that Confederate guerrillas were preparing to attack the exchange camp and that the one or two Negro companies assigned to guard the grounds would not be strong enough to resist an attack. Knowing that the Confederates were on the run and the war was all but officially over, the prisoners clamored for immediate release from a defunct government.[44]

Despite the overwhelming gloom of the day, Captain Speed kept at his work and cut another order, this one to release the troops from Wisconsin, Minnesota, and Iowa. Again, in order to avoid crossing over any lines between departments, Speed added to the bottom of the order: "The Quartermaster's Department will furnish the necessary transportation."[45] He did not want to take on any unnecessary responsibility. The men at Camp Fisk were more than enough for him.

As the *Sultana* steamed southward, Captain Mason continued to spread the news of Lincoln's assassination to the Deep South. On April 19, the *Sultana* slid into a berth at the foot of Gravier Street along the crowded New Orleans waterfront, and runners carried the news of Lincoln's death to the New Orleans newspapers. By seven o'clock that morning, the Crescent City had heard the news.[46]

The *Sultana*'s role in spreading the news had been completed. The boat stayed in New Orleans overnight, and then it was business as usual. Mason had a promised load of released prisoners waiting for him in Vicksburg. Nothing was going to keep him from picking up those men and the government money that came with them.

4

Greed and Deception

On April 19, Captain Speed drew up Special Order No. 35 for the purpose of sending all men, then at Camp Fisk, who were from Missouri and Louisiana to Benton Barracks near Saint Louis. Again, the Quartermaster Department was called on to furnish transportation. Captain Speed was gradually emptying the parole camp of its residents. Almost every day, men were being sent home, either in small lots or in large groups. General Dana had instructed Speed to send the men home in lots of about one thousand or as near to that number as conditions permitted.[1]

On arrival at Camp Fisk, each soldier's name, company, and regiment had been recorded on state rolls maintained by the Federal exchange officers and compared with the names in the many ledgers and books turned over to them by the Confederates. When names were found in these documents, they were checked off as they were entered in the state rolls. If a prisoner's name could not be found, the books had to be checked and double-checked and the information added to the correct books and rolls in order to get an exact count for exchange.[2]

Although all of Captain Speed's special orders had carried the sentence, "The Quartermaster's Department will furnish the necessary transportation," Capt. William F. Kerns, assistant quartermaster and master of transportation for the Post of Vicksburg, had had little to do with the shipments up to that time.[3]

Unknown to Kerns, the transportation for the small prisoner shipments had been furnished by his superior, Colonel Hatch.[4] Looked on as a minor gold mine by the business-starved steamboat captains, the shipment of prisoners at the government rate could lead to a nice piece of pocket change for them . To obtain the men, some captains and their agents were not above offering a monetary inducement to any officer willing to be a party to their hustling and scheming. It was no coincidence that such an offer was made in the office of Colonel Hatch.

On April 19, a runner from one of the steamboats rushed into Hatch's office and asked if any of the prisoners were ready for shipment.

"If it takes money to get them," the runner added, "we have as much as anybody."

"It does not take any money in *this* office!" Hatch's chief clerk, George B. Denton, shot back, not wanting to be a part of the shady dealings of the steamboat agents.[5] The same, however, could not be said of Colonel Hatch.

On April 20, while the *Sultana* was tied up at New Orleans, a number of passengers, including young Seth W. Hardin, Jr., with his new bride of only a few weeks, and well-to-do J. D. Fontaine from Dallas City, Illinois, booked passage on the *Sultana*.[6]

William Long from Leavenworth, Kansas, was booked in stateroom No. 10, and Sallie B. Woolfolk from Kentucky took a room off the Ladies' Cabin. Samuel B. Spikes and his wife Elethia from Assumption Parish, Louisiana, were traveling with their three daughters, three sons, and a young niece to establish a new home in the North. Along with his family, Samuel Spikes had brought his entire fortune, $17,000 in gold, which he deposited in the *Sultana*'s safe in the clerk's office.[7]

Hobbling across the *Sultana*'s gangplank on a stiff and useless right leg, ex-soldier Daniel McLeod, who had been wounded at the Battle of Shiloh, was on his way home to Illinois. Another paying passenger, Lt. Col. Charles E. Compton (53d U.S. Colored Troop) was going only as far as Memphis. Fifty-two-year-old Enoch Bent, returning from burying his soldier son Elijah in a New Orleans cemetery, was going home to Kenosha, Wisconsin. Young Elijah, like so many Union soldiers in the South, had succumbed to disease rather than to Confederate bullets.[8]

As passengers continued to board the *Sultana*, more than two hundred hogsheads of sugar, each weighing close to 1,200 pounds, were being manhandled into the hold for shipment to Memphis, where they were destined for the U.S. Quartermaster Department. Along with the sugar, ninety-seven boxes of wine and sixty grunting hogs were en route to Memphis.[9]

An additional item entrusted to the *Sultana* and placed in the clerk's safe beside the gold coins of the Spikes family was $15,000 in cash being sent to Saint Louis by the firm of Nauson, Ober and Company of New Orleans.[10]

While the *Sultana* was in port, Chief Engineer Wintringer drained his troublesome boilers and supervised their scraping and cleaning. Although scheduled to leave at 5 P.M. on the 20th, Captain Mason ran into unspecified trouble and was forced to delay his trip north for twenty-four hours.[11]

In the late afternoon of Friday, April 21, the *Sultana* inched away from the New Orleans waterfront and turned her nose into the onrushing floodwaters coming down from the north. As her twin paddlewheels churned up the dirty brown waters and pushed her toward her destiny, she carried about 40 passengers and a crew of 80, a total number well below her legal carrying capacity of 376.[12] Along with her passengers and a hold filled with cargo, the *Sultana* had the promise of a load of paroled prisoners waiting for her at Vicksburg.

Fighting against the swollen river, the steamboat moved steadily north at her usual rate of nine miles per hour, despite the force of the floodwaters against her bow. The passengers were having a pleasant trip. Wintringer and his second engineer, Sam Clemens, were keeping a close eye on the *Sultana*'s boilers.[13] With the boat running at normal speed against the strong current, the finicky boilers were showing no signs of stress. The earlier repairs and constant cleaning appeared to have done the trick.

In Vicksburg, plans for movement of the paroled prisoners were rapidly moving along. On April 21 in Camp Fisk, a call went out for two men handy with a pen to assist in making up the rolls. Wanting to hasten their release and do their part in the exchange, Pvt. James W. Wells (Company B, 102nd Ohio Infantry) and Sgt. Maj. Hascal M. Cole (Regimental Staff, 18th Michigan Infantry) stepped forward and offered their services. After receiving the necessary writing materials, they immediately went to work.[14] Once special orders were cut, it took about five days to get the men ready and on their way. The eight hundred soldiers from Illinois and Iowa, released on April 17 and 18, were not ready to leave until the morning of the 22nd.[15]

Although Captain Speed was sending the paroled prisoners along as fast as they could be processed, the job was long and hard. Also, small groups of prisoners were still coming into camp and throwing off the rolls even more.[16]

On April 22, as the first large group of prisoners, which included men from Illinois, Iowa, Wisconsin, and Minnesota, began moving into Vicksburg for transportation north, Captain Speed issued another order. All prisoners from the New England states and those from Maryland, Kansas, Alabama, and Mississippi were to be sent to Benton Barracks, Missouri, as soon as possible. As before, Speed ordered the Quartermaster Department to "furnish transportation."[17]

The *Arthur,* a non–contract steamboat, and the *Henry Ames* of the Merchants and People's Steamboat Line, which held a government contract, traveled north to Vicksburg for the intended purpose of transporting the first large group of prisoners. Waiting at the levee to meet them was Lt. William Tillinghast, acting assistant quartermaster for Camp Fisk, who was under the direct command of the unscrupulous Colonel Hatch. James P. McGuire, agent for the *Arthur,* took Tillinghast aside and asked whom he should see to obtain a load of prisoners for the *Arthur.* Knowing that McGuire was inexperienced in the business of troop shipments, Tillinghast told McGuire that he was shipping the men. McGuire knew that the lieutenant had been heavily involved with quartermaster duties at Camp Fisk, and this reply seemed entirely plausible. Figuring he had the right man, McGuire explained that he was employed by the non–contract line (Atlantic and Mississippi Steamship Company) and had been offered ten cents per head by the line if he could get some men for the *Arthur.* If Tillinghast would help, McGuire said, he would see to it that Tillinghast "would lose nothing by it." Although not spelled out in so many words, both men knew that they would end up with a little extra unreported spending money if Tillinghast could acquire a number of prisoners for the *Arthur.*

Apparently driven by the same greed that consumed Colonel Hatch, Tillinghast went to the office of Captain Kerns, who was in charge of river transportation, and asked what line would transport the men of the Illinois, Iowa, Wisconsin, and Minnesota units. Honoring the government contract, Kerns answered that the men would all go on the Merchants and People's Steamboat Line. This was not what Tillinghast wanted to hear, but he had no real control over the shipment of the men, in spite of what he had told McGuire. He returned to the river and stood idly by as the contract boat *Henry Ames* arrived before the *Arthur* and tied up to the Vicksburg wharfboat.

While the *Henry Ames* was tying up, William C. Jones, overall agent for the non–contract boats, approached Lieutenant Tillinghast and questioned him about the prisoner shipments. Tillinghast, perhaps knowing that Jones was an experienced businessman, told the agent the truth— that he knew nothing about the shipments and had no control over the paroled prisoners. He told Jones, however, that he understood that the men were all to go north on contract boats. Apparently satisfied for the time being, Jones left.[18]

Dressed in new clothes issued to them at Camp Fisk, the prisoners from the northwestern states began crowding on board the *Henry Ames,* captained by T. L. Crawford. The men were in high spirits and in much better health than when they had arrived at the Big Black River from the Confederate prisons.[19]

Although the rolls for only about 800 men were complete when the *Ames* arrived at Vicksburg, Captain Speed and his officers had been able to add another 500 names to the rolls before nightfall. By the time the boat was ready to leave late that evening, 1,315 men had been crowded onto her decks.[20]

Even though the special orders for the shipping of the men from the northwestern states had insisted that "Quartermaster's Department will furnish transportation," Captain Kerns, master of river transportation, again had been ignored in the selection of the *Ames.* He was in his office all day but was not informed of the boat selection or of the number of men going north until a runner applied to him for a transportation pass.[21] The selection had been made by Colonel Hatch without notifying Kerns.[22]

The *Ames* finally backed away from the Vicksburg wharfboat late that day. General Dana stood at the foot of the levee and watched her start the long journey to Saint Louis. Having immersed himself in getting the exchange system rolling again and taking great pains to expedite the shipment of the men, Dana wanted to see them safely under way.[23] Although he had issued orders for the men to be transported in lots of 1,000, he had made no comment on learning that more than 1,300 men were on board the *Ames.* He was as happy as the men that they were finally on their way home.

After the departure of the *Henry Ames,* Captain Speed sent two orderlies to ask Colonel Hatch when the next steamboat would arrive. Speed had been able to put down another 700 names and wanted to send the men off as soon as possible. Hatch answered that he did not know when the next boat would be in, but, as soon as he could find out, he would let Speed know.[24]

Later that evening, agent Jones met with Lieutenant Tillinghast. Knowing there were still many men at Camp Fisk, Jones told Tillinghast that he would be compensated if he could secure some of the prisoners for the Atlantic and Mississippi Steamship Company.[25] This offer must have been enticing to the lieutenant.

Captain Tabor's *Olive Branch* nosed up to the Vicksburg wharfboat late that same night. The *Olive Branch,* also a member of the non–contract Atlantic and Mississippi Steamship Company, was met by agent

Jones. Rushing on board, Jones advised Tabor that it probably would be in his best interest to remain at Vicksburg overnight because he was quite certain that Tabor could get some of the paroled prisoners. Tabor wanted assurances before wasting time in port, however, and immediately went to see Colonel Hatch, the man whom he believed had control over the shipping of the prisoners.[26]

Hatch had learned from Captain Kerns that the *Olive Branch* was at Vicksburg, and he made arrangements with Captain Tabor to detain the boat and put a number of prisoners on board.[27] Although Hatch had promised Speed that he would inform him as soon as a steamer arrived, he kept the news of the *Olive Branch* to himself and did not even tell Kerns that he was detaining the boat.[28] Hatch was setting in motion a plan to ensure that the troops would be put on board Captain Tabor's packet.

The *Sultana* had been moving along swiftly and smoothly on her northbound trip until a few hours after midnight on April 23 when, suddenly, the boat slowed considerably. Colonel Compton sought out a crewman and inquired about the change in speed.

"There is a defect in one of the boilers," the crewman said. The boiler could be used only under very low pressure.[29]

While keeping a sharp eye on the boilers, Chief Engineer Wintringer had discovered a small leak in the middle larboard (left-hand) boiler. Looking closer, he found that the third sheet from the forward end bulged out on the straight seam, with a resulting crack in the metal between two or three rivets. Fearing the worst, Wintringer had reduced the pressure in the boilers and notified Captain Mason of a further delay in reaching Vicksburg.[30]

Early that same morning, Captain Speed went down to the waterfront and was amazed to find the *Olive Branch* in port. Although he had given specific instructions that all steamboats were to be reported to him as soon as they arrived, the *Olive Branch* had been at the wharfboat overnight without his knowledge. Irritated, Speed hurried off to see the chief quartermaster, Colonel Hatch.[31]

Speed angrily complained to Hatch and wanted to know why he had not been told about the *Olive Branch*. Sticking to his plan, Hatch told Speed that he knew nothing of the arrival of the *Olive Branch* and, in fact, had just found out about the boat. To help cover his tracks and ensure the shipment of troops on the non–contract *Olive Branch,* Hatch added that he thought Captain Kerns must have taken a bribe from the contract line in the hope that the *Olive Branch* would go unnoticed until a boat from the contract line showed up.[32] Playing right into Hatch's hands, Speed vowed to put every last man ready to leave on the *Olive Branch,* despite the efforts of Kerns, and stormed out of the office. The infuriated adjutant had taken the bait—hook, line, and sinker!

All day, the prisoners from the New England states, as well as those from Kansas, Alabama, and Mississippi, were shuttled from Camp Fisk to Vicksburg and placed on the *Olive Branch.* By the time Ben Tabor's packet was ready to leave, 619 paroled prisoners were on board, not an overly large number but enough to make Tabor's wait in port worth-while.[33]

As the *Olive Branch* started upriver toward Saint Louis, a still angry Captain Speed rushed off to General Dana at department headquarters to lodge a complaint against Kerns. Speed asked Dana to arrest Kerns because he was certain that Kerns was being bribed by the Merchants and People's Steamboat Line to put the prisoners on only its boats.[34]

When Kerns arrived at Dana's headquarters, Speed immediately asked him why the *Olive Branch* had been detained overnight and why she had not been reported as ordered. Stupefied, Kerns stated that he knew nothing of the detention of the *Olive Branch* and had reported her arrival to Colonel Hatch as instructed. Trying to put an end to the incident, Dana instructed Kerns to submit a written explanation of the event, while Speed left to see Hatch concerning further particulars about the prisoner shipments.

In the meeting between Hatch and Speed, the two officers agreed that if the men could be made ready, they should be sent north on the first available steamer. The next group, perhaps the last, would be sent to Camp Chase, just west of Columbus, Ohio. As the two spoke, Hatch managed to steer the conversation around to the *Sultana,* although he did not tell Speed that he had met with Captain Mason a few days prior and promised him a load of prisoners. Instead, Hatch said that because the *Sultana* belonged to the Merchants and People's Steamboat Line, which held a government contract, she should get a nice load of men.

Perhaps Speed had misgivings as a result of the rumored bribe attempt made to Captain Kerns by that line. He told Hatch that he would have only 500 men, at most, ready to go by the next day. He was hoping to have all the rolls finished by Thursday, April 27, and get the men off as soon as possible after that. Although Speed agreed that the contract boats should get the prisoners, he did not think enough men would be ready for the *Sultana* to make a wait worthwhile.[35]

While Speed was meeting with Hatch, Captain Williams, who originally had been in charge of the paroled prisoners, arrived back in Vicksburg from Cairo and reported to General Dana. He learned that the exchange was going nicely and that Captain Speed had stepped forward to perform the duties of commissioner of exchange. Williams still considered the job his and left Dana's office to meet with Speed. He was intent on obtaining the exchange records to familiarize himself with what had taken place during his absence. Speed told Williams that there were only about 1,300 or 1,400 men still at Camp Fisk. Feeling that he was more familiar with what had already transpired, Speed suggested that he continue with the work at the parole camp until the whole business was finished. Williams consented but said that he wanted to accompany Speed to Camp Fisk to help call the rolls.[36]

It was nearly 6 P.M. that evening when the *Sultana* limped into Vicksburg. Immediately, Wintringer went into town to find an experienced boilermaker, a difficult task at that hour on a Sunday. Around 8:45 P.M., he called at the residence of boiler mechanic R. G. Taylor and told him that the *Sultana*'s boilers had given out. At Wintringer's insistence, Taylor accompanied the chief engineer to the *Sultana*.[37]

After inspecting the leak, Taylor asked, "Why did you not have this repaired at New Orleans?"

Wintringer told the mechanic that the boiler had shown no signs of leaking or bulging at New Orleans. He asked Taylor if he could repair the boiler enough to get them back to Saint Louis. Apparently, Wintringer was as concerned about time as Captain Mason. If they were delayed too long at Vicksburg, some other boat would surely get the promised load of prisoners.

As he left the *Sultana*, Taylor said, "If I do anything at all, I will make a job of it or have nothing to do with it."

Wintringer caught up with Taylor and asked him to come back. The engineer was willing to let the mechanic do the best he could in order to get the *Sultana* away from Vicksburg as soon as possible. Convinced that he had won the battle, Taylor turned around and went back on the *Sultana*.[38]

As soon as the *Sultana* reached Vicksburg, Captain Kerns had sent a message to Colonel Hatch, and he made sure that Denton, Hatch's chief clerk, knew about the message.[39] Kerns was not going to be accused of letting a steamer go unreported to his superiors a second time. What headquarters did with the vessel after it was reported was their concern. As before, he had followed orders and reported the arrival of a steamboat to headquarters, but, this time, he made certain that others knew of his actions.

Another person much concerned about the results of Kerns's report of the *Sultana*'s arrival was Captain Mason. He met with Miles Sells, Vicksburg agent for the Merchants and People's Steamboat Line, and learned that two large loads of prisoners had already gone north to Saint Louis. Immediately, Mason set out with Sells to find Colonel Hatch.[40]

The captain had come too far to let the promised load of prisoners slip through his fingers now. He was going to make sure that Hatch delivered on his promise.

5

The Loading

Agent Sells and Captain Mason found Colonel Hatch in his office. Mason got right to the point. He was there to get the promised prisoners for his boat, and he wanted all he could carry.

Hatch was anxious to see Mason get the men and, perhaps at the same time, to line his own pockets. He told Mason that he had just talked to Captain Speed and learned that Speed had the rolls made up for no more than 500 men. Speed probably would not have the rolls completed before Thursday, April 27, but Hatch said he thought that the prisoners could be readied for shipment by Tuesday.[1]

"It will hardly pay me to wait until the next day for that number of men," Mason angrily told Hatch. "If the men are ready I am entitled to them!" Because the *Sultana* was a member of the Merchants and People's Steamboat Line and a contract boat, Mason felt that she was entitled to government freight.[2]

"If Captain Speed can get the men ready, I am anxious to ship them," Hatch said. He blamed the delay on Speed. "Go to Speed and see what you can do," Hatch instructed Mason.[3]

Spurred on by this remark, Mason and Sells went to Speed's quarters, where Sells introduced the two men. "We have just been to see Colonel Hatch," Mason told Speed, "and have come to see you to see how many men you can give the *Sultana*."

Mason then said that he wanted to get a full load of prisoners, as many as he could carry. Knowing about the delay in the rolls, Mason was quick to add, he was willing to wait until the next day for the load. He did not mention that the *Sultana* would be delayed at least until the next morning because of the boiler repair.

"I want to ship the men very badly," Speed told Mason, but the rolls were not yet finished. If Mason wanted, however, Speed would give him all the men that were ready—about 300, perhaps 500 or perhaps even 700.

Not satisfied with Speed's indefinite answer, Mason tried to pin the captain down.

"I am *entitled* to those men," Mason argued. He reminded the captain that the *Sultana* had a government contract and asked for a definite number from Speed. Not about to be maneuvered into a corner, Speed reiterated that he only had between 300 and 500 names on the rolls, but might have 700 by Tuesday morning.

"I want to ship the men, but I can't get the trains," Speed said.

Jumping on the opening he wanted, Mason told Speed that Hatch would supply the trains if preparations were made for the prisoners to depart.

"The prisoners are in a pretty bad condition out there," Speed admitted. "The weather has been very bad, and they are anxious to go forward."[4]

If Mason waited, Speed said, the *Sultana* could have all the men that could be gotten ready. Still disappointed at Speed's vagueness, Mason left without deciding whether or not he would wait.[5]

When he was outside, however, Mason decided to try to find out who could help him get a larger number of paroled prisoners. His ace in the hole was the district commander, General Smith, who had promised him a full load when the two had met on the *Sultana*'s downriver trip, but Mason did not want to disturb the general unless it was absolutely necessary. He still had a few cards to play.[6]

Intent on lodging a formal complaint against those in charge of the exchange, Mason left Sells and went to department headquarters. There, he ran into Captain Williams. Mason had met Williams on the *Sultana*'s last trip upriver and knew that he had been in charge of the prisoner camp outside Vicksburg. Perhaps, Mason thought, this was the man he should see. He informed Williams that he was there to file a complaint against the exchange office because the contract boats could not get a load of prisoners and the opposition lines were transporting all of the men. Williams, perhaps taken by surprise, told Mason that he was "especially anxious" to send the men north because they had been repeatedly promised that they would be sent home. Having just arrived from Cairo and not fully understanding the grounds for Mason's complaint, Williams sent for Speed.[7]

When Speed arrived at headquarters, Williams, with Mason at his elbow, informed him of Mason's complaint and asked if it would be possible to get the men off on the *Sultana*.[8]

Speed said that he did not think any of the prisoners would be ready to leave the following day because the rolls for only 300 to 400 had been completed. Again, he explained that he thought it would be almost impossible to get even those men into Vickburg before the *Sultana* was ready to leave. As he had told Mason, however, the *Sultana* could have the 300 or 400 men.[9]

Despite Mason's threat of a complaint, Williams must have concluded that the shipment of prisoners was being run without malice. He was ending the meeting when he suddenly had an idea. Perhaps the names of the prisoners could be checked off on the books supplied by the Confederate commissioners and the rolls completed afterward from the books. In that way, the men could be placed on board the *Sultana* and sent on their way while the rolls were still being completed.

Seeing nothing wrong with this arrangement and believing that Williams was still acting as overall commissioner of exchange, Speed agreed to check off the names in the Confederate books, ship the men into Vicksburg, count them as they were placed on the *Sultana,* and draw up the rolls later.

Speed informed General Dana of Williams's plan. Dana was satisfied with the arrangement and asked Speed how many men were left to be shipped. Although Speed said that he did not know exactly, he thought there would be only about 1,300, certainly no more than 1,400.[10]

With only one more obstacle standing before them, Speed and Williams called on Colonel Hatch and told him about the new plan. The two asked Hatch if he could arrange the necessary river and rail transportation, and the latter readily agreed. Speed still doubted whether all the prisoners could be shipped the next day, but, as long as the other two officers were willing to help, he would try to get the job done. Promising to aid him in any way possible, Williams agreed to meet Speed at the railroad depot in the morning and ride to Camp Fisk with him. As the three parted company, it was understood that all of the remaining men at Camp Fisk were to be shipped on the *Sultana.*[11]

At no point during any of the meetings were the repairs to the *Sultana*'s boilers mentioned.

Almost everyone connected with the prisoners was advised of the new plan for compiling the rolls and the choice of the *Sultana* to transport the remaining prisoners at Camp Fisk, but a few officers were ignored. One of these was Captain Kerns, who was normally in charge of selecting river transportation.

Early the next morning, April 24, Speed was getting dressed when he received a surprise visit from Colonel Hatch. Although Speed was under the impression that everything concerning the prisoners had been worked out the night before, Hatch indicated, according to Speed's roommate, Capt. William H. H. Emmons, that he was there "in reference to the shipment of prisoners which was to take place on that day." Hatch asked Speed whether all the prisoners at Camp Fisk would go on the *Sultana* in one large load. Repeating his words from the night before, Speed said that he and Williams had decided to send everyone on one boat and that the *Sultana* was indeed the selected craft.[12]

Hatch's intentions in seeing Speed had not been to make sure that all the prisoners got on the *Sultana* but to do the opposite—to see if he could get some of the men diverted to the *Pauline Carroll.* Although it would appear that Hatch was receiving compensation from Captain Mason to put men on the *Sultana,* he might have had an even better deal from the *Carroll.* He had failed in his first attempt to get prisoners for the non–contract boat, but he was not about to give up so easily.

When Hatch left, Speed hurried to department headquarters and ordered Special Order No. 140 to be sent to Camp Fisk immediately. Dated April 24, the order specified: "All the prisoners of war, officers and enlisted men, remaining at the Parole Camp at Four Mile Bridge . . . from the states of [West] Virginia, Tennessee, Kentucky, Ohio, Indiana and Michigan, have been paroled. . . ." The order further stipulated that "Major W. H. Fidler, 6th Kentucky Cavalry, will take charge of the men . . . and will organize them into companies . . . and will proceed with them to Camp Chase, Ohio." This was the standard form, ending with the words, "The Quartermaster's Department will furnish transportation." The general practice in the adjutant's office was to send copies of special orders to General Smith, Colonel Hatch, and Captain Kerns. On this occasion, however, Speed personally made certain that Kerns received a copy of Special Order No. 140.[13]

Finished with his work at headquarters, Speed was about to leave for the parole camp when Captain Williams arrived in the office. Speed informed Williams that special arrangements had been made to have a train meet them at the foot of Cherry Street, close to headquarters.[14]

Around 8:30 A.M., the two officers, accompanied by an orderly, Pvt. Jameson Cox, started down Cherry Street. Speed told Williams that he was inclined to see all of the remaining prisoners placed on boats of the contract line, Merchants and People's. In addition, Speed mentioned a recent conversation with Colonel Hatch, during which Hatch had suggested that there was a possibility of bribes being offered by agents of the non–contract boats to obtain loads of prisoners. Speed said that detention of the *Olive Branch* tended to confirm his suspicions.

Williams stated that General Dana had many enemies intent on besmearing his reputation and good name. He cautioned Speed that they had to be very careful not to give Dana's enemies any occasion to injure him. Mentioning that he had already heard stories of bribery, Williams said that they would be better off delivering the prisoners to a contract boat and letting the quartermaster in charge send them by that boat or take the responsibility for doing otherwise.[15]

When the officers and their orderly finally reached the foot of Cherry Street, they had to wait only a few minutes before the train for Camp Fisk arrived. When they saw that the train consisted of one passenger car and a number of flatcars, Speed went immediately to the conductor.

Concerned for the comfort of the prisoners, who had already gone through so much, Speed told the conductor, G.S. Oakes, that Colonel Hatch had promised the use of only the best cars on the road. He threatened to go to a higher authority if the promise were not kept. Although the conductor knew nothing of Hatch's words, he told Speed and Williams that there were two passenger cars near the engine house that he could let them use.

Somewhat appeased, Speed and the others boarded the train and rode the quarter mile to the engine house. While the train took on wood and water, Speed went to see Edward D. Butler, superintendent of military railroads. When told of the arrangements made with Hatch, Butler hesitantly agreed to release the two idle passenger cars. After the cars were coupled to the train, Butler and Speed climbed aboard and settled back for the four-mile trip to Camp Fisk and the waiting prisoners.[16]

The officers in charge of Camp Fisk had been advised by Lt. Edwin L. Davenport, who had been dispatched to the camp by order of Captain Williams the night before, to have the men ready to leave as early as possible on the 24th.[17] Early that morning, Special Order No. 140 had been telegraphed to the camp—the order that more than 2,000 prisoners had been impatiently awaiting.

"Glad shouts of joy rent the air when the news came to us to pull up camp," remembered Pvt. George S. Schmutz (Company I, 102d Ohio Infantry). "We were soldiers, prisoners of war, who had been shut up in prison pens, some for 6 months, some for 12, some for 18 months. One might think how glad all were to get home."[18]

Immediately, Major Fidler (Regimental Staff, 6th Kentucky Cavalry) began organizing the prisoners into companies and assembling them by state on the open parade ground in front of the train platform. Fidler tried to place a prisoner officer in charge of each company, but there were few officers in camp and some companies were commanded by sergeants.[19]

While the officers counted the men and separated them into companies and squads, the men stood in the morning sun and anxiously awaited the train that would take them into Vicksburg. When it did not immediately arrive, they sat on the ground. Only a heartbeat away from starting the trip home, they were careful not to lose their places in line.[20]

The repair of the *Sultana*'s middle larboard boiler had continued all night. Boiler mechanic Taylor, under Wintringer's supervision, had cut out a patch of metal, measuring 11 by 26 inches, from the ruptured area. When Taylor attempted to force back the bulge that had caused the leak, Wintringer stopped him. He said that such a job would take too long and a new metal sheet would have to be riveted over the bulge. Although he resented this interference, Taylor continued his work as the engineer had instructed. Taylor noticed the condition of the boilers; they looked as though they had been used with little water in them, a dangerous thing to do.[21]

Meanwhile, agent Jones of the rival steamboat line was conferring with Lieutenant Tillinghast. Jones bluntly asked the lieutenant how many prisoners would leave on the *Sultana*.

"I don't know," Tillinghast answered truthfully.

"Will all go on her?" Jones persisted.

Again Tillinghast said he did not know but thought they would not.

Pressing his case, Jones told the lieutenant that he would have a boat up from New Orleans in the afternoon and that she would beat the *Sultana* to Saint Louis.

Previously, Jones had told Tillinghast that he would be compensated for procuring a load of prisoners for the non–contract Atlantic and Mississippi Steamship Line but had failed to give a price. Now he offered Tillinghast fifteen cents for every man he could get, a pretty sum when multiplied by the number of men at Camp Fisk. Eager for the money, Tillinghast accepted the proposal and agreed to try to get a load of men on a non–contract boat.[22]

Early on the morning of April 24, Captain Kerns was busy in his office when the *Sultana*'s captain entered.

"Why are you still in port?" Kerns asked Mason.

Nonchalantly, Mason told Kerns that he was waiting for a load of prisoners. This was Kerns's first notice that the *Sultana* had been selected as a transport. Mason also informed Kerns that the *Sultana* was having one of her boilers repaired. When the boiler work was finished, he would be ready to leave. This was also the first mention to any of the officers in charge at Vicksburg that the *Sultana* was undergoing repairs.

During the conversation, Kerns learned that the *Sultana* had been selected to take all of the remaining men at Camp Fisk. Although Speed, who had repeatedly visited Camp Fisk, was under the assumption that there were only about 1,400 men at the camp, Kerns, who had seldom, if ever, been there, thought that the number was much larger, too many men for the *Sultana* to carry comfortably.[23]

A little after 9:00 A.M., Kerns received Special Order No. 140. The order was a duplicate of the original, with an additional message written in red ink across the bottom: "Copy furnished Captain of Steamer *Sultana*." Kerns knew that it was highly unusual for an order to contain the name of a specific boat. Thinking that special arrangements must have been made under the authority of General Dana, Kerns did not question the order.[24] Again, he realized that he had been bypassed in the selection of transportation for the paroled prisoners.

It was nearly 10:00 A.M. Capt. William S. Friesner (Regimental Staff, 58th Ohio Infantry) was making out his long overdue ordnance returns for the first quarter of the year when an orderly rode up with an order from headquarters. Although irritated at the interruption, he accepted it and read that by order of General Smith, Friesner and twenty-one of his men had been selected as guards for the load of prisoners to be transported on the *Sultana*. Not believing his misfortune, Friesner directed his adjutant to assemble the guard detail, then mounted his horse for the long ride to post headquarters. With all the work he had to do, he was determined to find out why he and his men, among all the commands at Vicksburg, had been selected to go on board the *Sultana*. He must try to have the order rescinded; otherwise, he would have to sit quietly and receive his instructions.[25]

At about the same time, the train carrying Captains Speed and Williams reached the parole camp. The prisoners rose to their feet and eagerly moved closer to the platform. Both captains were glad to see that the Camp Fisk officers were hard at work on the rolls. Speed and several other officers began placing the men on the train. The first to be called were from Ohio, the only state for which rolls were nearly complete. When each name was called, that man stepped forward to the platform. Wells and Cole checked the names off the rolls, and Orderly Cox, under the supervision of Captain Williams, directed the men to the cars, so as to fill them in turn.[26]

For two hours, the officers at the parole camp continued to call names. One by one, the men boarded the train until more than 650 Ohio soldiers had crowded onto the three passenger cars and the flatcars. Fearing that the train was becoming much too crowded, Superintendent Butler complained to Captain Speed that the train had all the men it could carry. Brushing Butler aside, Speed continued to have the names called.[27] An additional 150 to 200 men from Indiana boarded the train until, finally, every available space was filled.[28]

When the train was ready to leave, Speed informed Williams that he would go into town with the men and attend to the shipping. Instead, Williams, who was not feeling well, said that he would go in and "see the men aboard all right." Williams added that he would go down to the levee and count the men as they went on board the wharfboat. Speed could remain at Camp Fisk and continue to call the rolls and get the men ready for the train's return.[29]

Around noon, the train pulled away from Camp Fisk. Captain Speed and his officers and volunteers were hard at work over the little table that had been set up in front of the train platform.[30]

The large steamer *Lady Gay*, a member of the Merchants and People's Steamboat line, nosed in beside the *Sultana* at the Vicksburg wharfboat at around 11 A.M. Captain Kerns immediately reported her to Colonel Hatch. Because he still believed that the *Sultana* could not handle all of the men from Camp Fisk, Kerns asked Hatch to contact Captain Speed about detaining the *Lady Gay*, a contract boat, to take the overflow. For more than an hour, Kerns waited for a reply. Finally, in the early afternoon, he received word that Speed had telegraphed from Camp Fisk: "No they can all go on one boat." Seeing no reason to detain the *Lady Gay* any longer, Kerns told her captain, John A. Williamson, that she was free to go. Perhaps because Williamson noticed Kerns's concern about whether the *Sultana* could take all of the soldiers, he told Kerns not to worry. The *Pauline Carroll*, another large boat, was not far behind and would be up sometime in the afternoon.[31]

When Captain Friesner arrived at General Smith's headquarters, he was met by an aide.

"Captain," the man said, "you will get to Ohio this time."

As much as he wanted to go home, Friesner knew that his responsibility was with his regiment.

"I cannot go," Friesner said, explaining that he had long-overdue ordnance forms to fill out and turn in.

"You need not report until seven this evening," the smiling orderly said, "and I will be at the boat with your instructions."

Facing defeat, Friesner accepted his assignment as guard to the load of prisoners being sent north on the *Sultana*. He quietly rode back to his regiment and hoped that he could complete his work before seven o'clock.[32]

The first trainload of soldiers arrived at the Vicksburg depot around 1:00 P.M. The men were ordered to fall into column and march through the streets of Vicksburg to the wharfboat. Standing at the forward gangway of the wharfboat, Captain Williams counted the men as they began crowding onto it. Each was carrying a little bundle of extra clothing and food, their only possessions except for the clothes on their backs. As the first men passed over the gangway, Williams told them to remain on the wharfboat. Someone from the Quartermaster Department would have to direct them to go on board the selected steamer.[33]

Among the first soldiers to board the *Sultana* was Sgt. Arthur A. Jones (Company C, 115th Ohio Infantry). "It was not necessary to be invited to go on board," Jones recalled, perhaps suggesting that nobody needed to give an official order to board the *Sultana*. Feeling ill, Jones was helped on board by two friends. As they started toward the main stairway, they noticed the repairs being made on the *Sultana*'s boilers. Too ill to care, Jones and his comrades continued on, intent on finding a place near the front of the open hurricane deck.[34]

Pvt. William Boor (Company D, 64th Ohio Infantry) also heard the pounding from the boiler area. After marching up to the hurricane deck, he was told that this was to be his resting place for the next few days, but Boor decided otherwise. Leaving his gear with friends, he went down to the main deck and looked at the boilers. Deciding that they were "not very favorable," Boor returned to his comrades and told them that they had better find another spot to bed down. He said that "if the boat should blow up . . . we [will] go higher than a kite." Heeding his sound judgment, Boor's friends followed him down to the cabin deck and took up a spot near the head of the main stairway.[35]

As Sgt. Alexander C. Brown stepped onto the deck of the steamboat, he was called aside by the agent of the Cincinnati express company who had offered to help him and was introduced to the *Sultana*'s first clerk, William Gambrel. As Brown had requested, Gambrel informed him that first-class cabin passage for him had been paid by the agent. Happy to have a room to himself, Brown followed the clerk up the main stairs to see about his stateroom.[36]

Among those going on board the *Sultana* was Pvt. Adam Schneider (Company C, 183d Ohio Infantry), who, unknown to his friends, had a colorful past. In 1849, while living in his native Duchy of Hesse (now Germany), he had been arrested and accused of attempting to assassinate the Prince of Prussia, who later was to become Kaiser Wilhelm I of Germany. Schneider was thrown into prison, but he was eventually freed for lack of evidence. In 1853, he emigrated to the United States with his family.[37]

As the last man from the train cleared the wharfboat and was safely on board the *Sultana,* the chief medical director of Vicksburg, Dr. George S. Kemble, arrived with 23 patients who were confined to cots. Based on his understanding with Captain Speed that all parolees remaining in Vicksburg should be sent north as soon as possible, Dr. Kemble had instructed the 277 ambulatory Union patients in the Vicksburg hospitals to walk down to the levee and board the *Sultana.* He had left copies of the rolls containing the names of all of his patients with the adjutant general's office.

Dr. Kemble gave instructions for the sick men on the cots to be placed on the forward end of the cabin deck just outside the main cabin and above the boilers, so that their heat would give the men some comfort

flues (the most frequent problem with tubular boilers) appeared to be in good condition, Taylor felt that the safety of the boilers had been further compromised by their constant use with little water in them, a very dangerous practice on any type of boiler. For some unknown reason, Taylor said nothing to the engineer about his feelings.[48]

The non–contract *Pauline Carroll*, which was approximately 25 percent larger than the *Sultana*, nosed into Vicksburg at about 3:00 P.M. that same afternoon. Her captain, H. L. White, was hoping to receive a load of paroled prisoners.[49]

Captain Kerns immediately reported the *Carroll's* arrival to Colonel Hatch. Still believing that there were more men at Camp Fisk than could possibly go on the *Sultana*, Kerns asked both Hatch and General Smith to issue orders to detain the *Carroll*. Although both men were noncommittal, Smith told Kerns that he could detain the boat if he wished; whatever decision Kerns made would meet with Smith's approval.[50]

Returning to the waterfront, Kerns went straight to the *Carroll* and met with Captain White. Expressing his fears about the loading of the *Sultana*, Kerns asked White if he would wait at Vicksburg, without a direct order, until all of the men had arrived from Camp Fisk. Already behind schedule, Captain White argued that he would stay only if he could be guaranteed a load of soldiers. Although Kerns could not give a guarantee, he felt certain that the *Carroll* would get some men. He did not want to order White to remain at Vicksburg but said that he would if the *Carroll* tried to leave. White agreed to wait and waived the need for a direct order.[51]

It was close to 4:00 P.M., and Captain Speed was still working hard to get the men ready for the next train when he received Dana's telegram reporting that the *Sultana* would be ready to leave in two hours and inquiring whether all of the men could be brought into Vicksburg by that time. Knowing full well that they could not, Speed wired back in the negative.[52] If Mason wanted all of the prisoners, he would have to wait.

Shortly afterward, Lieutenant Davenport brought another telegram to Speed; this was the one from Williams telling Davenport to "hurry up the men." Speed was provoked when he read the telegram. He was doing his best to get the men into Vicksburg as quickly as possible, and Williams wanted the men even faster. Irritated over the tone of the telegram and unaware of the rumored bribe he had supposedly taken to delay the men, Speed told Davenport, "Tell Captain Williams when Captain Speed gets ready." These words would subsequently fuel the suspicions of others.[53]

The train arrived at Camp Fisk for the third load of men after 4:00 P.M. This was the train that had taken the first load into Vicksburg; conductor G. S. Oakes had turned the train around and headed back to Camp Fisk for another load.[54]

The men already on the platform, more than likely the remaining Michigan soldiers, quickly began to climb aboard the train, as the names of the men from Tennessee, Kentucky, and West Virginia were called out. Every paroled prisoner at Camp Fisk, except the men deemed unfit to travel, were to go on this last train.[55]

Captain Speed was busy with boarding the men when he received yet another telegram, this one from Colonel Hatch. It asked if there were more men than could be accommodated on the *Sultana* and informed him that the *Pauline Carroll* was available. A bit irritated by the sudden influx of telegrams, Speed answered Hatch: "No the *Sultana* can take them all."[56]

Approximately an hour after the train had arrived at the platform, more than 800 men had crowded on board. Captain Speed and the other officers and men who had helped at Camp Fisk climbed into one of the passenger cars and settled back for the short trip to Vicksburg.[57] After long weeks, the men were finally on their way home—a happier bunch could not be found.

6 The Overcrowding

After meeting with General Dana, Dr. Kemble returned to the *Sultana* around 5:00 P.M. Dana had given Kemble permission to use his own discretion about removing the seriously ill men from the boat and not allowing the ambulatory patients to board when they arrived. Kemble was in the process of having the men on the cots removed when he was accosted by Captain Williams.

Williams objected to the removal of the sick men; he said that if they were removed, there would be a discrepancy in the rolls. Kemble replied that they were not on Williams's rolls and showed him the rolls containing the names of the sick men. Williams then gave his consent to remove the men on the cots.

Returning uptown, Kemble met the other convalescents and turned them back toward the hospital, where they would wait for the hospital boat.[1]

Immediately after hearing from Captain Mason and First Clerk Gambrel that they believed approximately 600 more men were expected on board the *Sultana,* Captain Kerns went straight to department headquarters and saw Colonel Hatch and General Smith. Convinced that the *Sultana* would be grossly overcrowded, he asked Smith to come down to the riverfront to help divide the men. Although Smith had already told Kerns that the prisoner exchange was out of his hands, he agreed to come, as did Hatch.

Satisfied that he had finally made an impression on two people who had the authority to set policy, Kerns returned to the levee. It was almost 6:00 P.M.[2]

From today's perspective, Hatch's sudden change of heart seems puzzling. Although he was the sole officer responsible for the selection of not only the *Sultana* but also the *Henry Ames* and *Olive Branch,* he had led everyone to believe, from the very start, that he had nothing to do with the prisoner exchanges. Perhaps he was worried that not all of the paroled prisoners would fit on the *Sultana* and wanted to make sure that the overflow went on the *Pauline Carroll,* from which he could also expect compensation. Another motive for visiting the levee might have been to get a look at the *Sultana* so that he could better estimate how much money Mason would owe him.

By the time the last trainload of men reached the depot, it was nearly dark. Major Fidler was there to meet them and help them out of the cars. Lieutenant Davenport asked Speed to accompany the column to the *Sultana.* Although Speed had indicated that he was through with the exchange, he agreed to go.[3]

The men formed into columns of four, with Speed, Davenport, and Fidler at the head, and started the march to the river. Pvt. Isaac Davenport noticed that the men were "a set of glad-hearted boys," happy to be finally going home.[4]

Captain Kerns was waiting at the wharfboat. He was determined to make one final attempt to place this last group of men on board the *Pauline Carroll.*[5]

It was dark as the head of the column neared the waterfront. Private Wells and Sergeant Major Cole, who had spent three days working on the rolls, were at the front of the column. They were about to board the *Sultana* when they heard someone calling their names. Retracing their steps, they found Speed waiting for them on the wharfboat. He told them that he needed a copy of their lists, but he did not want to order either of them to stay behind. If they elected to complete the work, however, he would see to it that they were on the next boat going upriver after they had finished. He added that they might have a more comfortable trip on a boat less crowded than the *Sultana*. Wells and Cole agreed to stay behind.[6]

In spite of the confusion and controversy, Speed had successfully brought his charges out of Camp Fisk and down to the river. Feeling that his job was finished, he was on his way to the *Sultana* when Kerns stopped him. The prisoners continued to file past, as they were being counted, and the two officers stepped to one side.

"Would it not be best to put these men on the *Pauline Carroll*?" Kerns asked.

"'I don't know," Speed answered truthfully.[7]

Speed went on to say that the rolls had been made up to send the men on one boat, and he thought it was too late now to try and divide them. Undaunted, Kerns said he understood that there were two majors being shipped with the men, and asked if the men could be divided, with one major taking charge of each section. Speed firmly repeated that the rolls had been made out for the men to go on *one* boat and they could not be divided. Taking a new tack, Kerns lied: "Colonel Hatch and General Smith want it done."[8]

Perhaps not believing the quartermaster or perhaps wishing to refer the matter to Captain Williams, Speed turned from Kerns.

"Let us see about this," Speed said skeptically.[9]

Going over to Williams, Speed halted the counting of the men and said, "Captain Kerns says that General Smith, Colonel Hatch, and yourself want the men divided and part go on the *Pauline Carroll*. How about it?"[10]

Not knowing whom to trust, Williams was still determined to place all of the men on the *Sultana*.

"No, I have been on board," he snapped. "There is plenty of room. They can all go comfortably."[11]

Taken aback by Williams's response, Speed told the men to continue forward and left Williams to his counting. Speed repeated to Kerns that the men could not be divided and that none could go on the *Carroll*.[12]

Speed started toward the *Sultana* when he was stopped again, this time by Lieutenant Tillinghast. Like Kerns, Tillinghast was also still hoping to put some of the men on the *Carroll*, but for the entirely different motive of lining his own pockets. Tillinghast told Speed that there were more men than should go on one boat and the *Carroll* was standing by to take the overflow. Perhaps still angered over his rebuke from Williams, Speed told Tillinghast that there was sufficient room on the *Sul-*

tana, even though he had yet to set eyes on her already crowded decks.[13] He turned away and continued toward the *Sultana.*

When Speed left, Kerns then went over to Williams. He knew that, if anybody had the power to divide the last group of men, it would be the commissioner of exchange.

While Williams continued to count the prisoners, Kerns asked him if some of the men should be placed on the *Carroll.* Unfortunately for Kerns, his genuine concern for the safety and comfort of the men was misconstrued by Williams. After General Dana informed him of Speed's formal complaint against someone in the Quartermaster Department, Williams had learned that the suspect was Kerns. Now, with Kerns showing an interest in putting half the men on the non–contract *Carroll,* Williams felt that his suspicions were confirmed.

"No," Williams told Kerns, "they can all go very well on the *Sultana.* The *Pauline Carroll* has offered twenty cents per man to get these men, and for that reason, she cannot have a man."

Angrily, Williams added, "And you will hear more about it by and by."

A startled Kerns said no more. Taking leave, he went over to the *Carroll,* where he ran into agent Jones.[14]

Once again, thinking that it was impossible to get all the prisoners onto the *Sultana,* Jones told Kerns that he would like to get some of the men for the *Carroll.* He added that it was a shame for so many men to be crowded onto one boat. Although Kerns agreed with the agent, he said that it was beyond his control and he could do nothing about it.[15] He left Jones and boarded the *Carroll* in search of Captain White.

Three officers in Vicksburg had the authority to divide the men on the *Sultana* if she appeared overcrowded. Each did almost nothing. Although General Dana had expressed a desire to see the men off, his interest apparently waned as the day wore on. When night settled on Vicksburg, Dana elected not to visit the waterfront and to leave the loading to those already involved.[16]

General Smith, whom Kerns had repeatedly beseeched to lend a hand in dividing the men, had finally given in to the captain's requests and promised to go down to the levee. On his way, he met "some man connected with the Quartermaster's Department at the parole camp" who informed him that there were only about 300 men left to put on the *Sultana.* Thinking that the number was small and all of the men would be comfortable on the steamer, Smith turned around and went back to his office.[17]

The last officer with authority was Colonel Hatch, who had also told Kerns that he would go to the river and see how crowded the *Sultana* really was. Like Smith, Hatch actually started forward but went only a short distance before turning around. Although he had been involved in the prisoner exchange since its beginning, Hatch suddenly washed his hands of the entire affair.[18]

When the last group of prisoners had boarded the wharfboat and then the *Sultana,* Major Fidler instructed Capt. James M. McCown (Company K, 6th Kentucky Cavalry), his acting aide-de-camp, to place the Kentucky men around the area of the boilers and engines, while he took the rest of the troops, the Tennessee, West Virginia, and remaining Michigan men, to the hurricane deck.

As he boarded the boat, McCown ran into Captain Mason.

"Captain," McCown said matter of factly, "you are going to have a pretty good load."

"Yes," Mason agreed. "A pretty good load."[19]

Although Fidler might have had plans about where he wanted the soldiers from each state placed, a few of the men had different ideas. Cpl. Jeremiah Mahoney (Company I, 2d Michigan Cavalry) followed Fidler up to the hurricane deck but saw that it was much too crowded. Going all the way back down to the main deck, he found a place to lay his blanket near one of the wheel housings. As he claimed his spot, he noticed the many hogs that had been put on the boat at New Orleans and some horses and mules that had been taken on at Vicksburg.[20]

Coming on board the boat with the last party, Cpl. Thomas Sharp (Company F, 2d West Virginia Cavalry) noticed the completion of the work, perhaps the cleanup, being done on the larboard boiler. Wary of curling up next to a potential danger, Sharp avoided the area around the boilers and went up to the second deck to find a spot.[21]

Lt. Simeon W. Dickenson (Company E, 2d Michigan Cavalry) climbed the main stairway to the second deck and found between fifteen and twenty men so sick from chronic diarrhea that they were virtually helpless. Filled with compassion toward his fellow soldiers, the lieutenant left to find some medicine for the ailing men.[22]

Pvt. Samuel F. Sanders (Company I, 137th Illinois Infantry) had been helping the sick in the Vicksburg hospitals and had missed going north with the rest of the Illinois troops. Now, seeing a second chance, he stole on board the *Sultana* to help with the sick until the boat reached Cairo.[23]

Only about one third of the men from the last train had boarded the *Sultana* when the column suddenly came to a halt. The men insisted that they would go no farther. They could see the crowded conditions on the *Sultana* and the empty decks of the *Carroll.* Rising in minor rebellion, they claimed that they were not going to be packed on the *Sultana* "like damned hogs," with no room to lie down or no way to attend to the calls of nature. Some unknown officers, intent on placing everyone on the *Sultana,* told the men that the *Carroll* was infected with smallpox.

Fearing the disease more than the crowded conditions, the men shuffled on board the *Sultana*.[24]

As the decks overflowed, some of the men previously on the boat began to complain. Sgt. David Hites (Company G, 102d Ohio Infantry) protested the overcrowding but to no avail. Although he knew that the men were anxious to go home, he felt that they did not all have to go on one boat.[25]

More and more men kept coming on board. Sgt. William Fies (Company B, 64th Ohio Infantry), when he saw the overcrowding on the second deck, felt that the prisoners were being put on "more like so many cattle than men."[26] It became so crowded on the front half of the hurricane deck that Sgt. Robert Talkington (Company A, 9th Indiana Cavalry) grabbed the only spot available, the top of a coffin that he thought contained a dead Union officer being sent home for burial.[27]

At one point during the loading of the third trainload, Lieutenant Tillinghast went to Captain Mason's cabin in the forward part of the texas deck. Although Tillinghast had repeatedly tried to get the last load of soldiers put on the *Carroll*, Mason believed that Tillinghast was working for the *Sultana* and had helped Colonel Hatch to get all of the men from Camp Fisk put on his boat. Mason told Tillinghast that if he had his measure, it would cost him nothing for clothing for a whole year, but, because he did not have the lieutenant's measure, he had made it all right anyhow.[28] How Mason made it right has never been explained, but perhaps he had worked out some form of compensation with Tillinghast's boss, Colonel Hatch.

Tillinghast said nothing to correct Mason's erroneous assumption. He left the cabin and started back to the wharfboat. Because of the large crowd of prisoners covering almost every available inch of deck space, it took Tillinghast a full fifteen minutes to reach the wharfboat.[29]

When Captain Kerns boarded the *Pauline Carroll*, he found that Captain White was already getting up steam and preparing to leave. Kerns asked White if he would wait until all the prisoners were on the *Sultana*. Once everybody realized how crowded she would be, there was the outside possibility that some of the men would be transferred to the *Carroll*. Although White was doubtful, he agreed to stand by.

From the *Carroll*, Kerns looked down on the overcrowded decks of the *Sultana*. Soldiers seemed to be everywhere: on the main deck, second deck, hurricane deck, and even on top of the texas. Only the rear guards, behind the paddlewheel boxes, were free of soldiers; this space was already occupied by about twenty-five or thirty mules and horses. About one half of the last trainload of men had yet to board.[30]

Also looking at the *Sultana* from the deck of the *Carroll* were passengers William Butler and a Judge Burwell, who agreed that the passengers were "packed thick."

"It is a damned shame to crowd men on a boat in that way," Burwell said. "I do not believe those men will have as much room to lie down as was allowed to slaves on slaveships."[31]

Pvt. Louis Bean, a saddler with Company A, 6th Kentucky Cavalry, boarded the *Sultana* and found the main deck already crowded. He wandered about for a while but was unable to find a spot to bed down. Finally, he happened on a place near the left engine, inside the covered stern cargo area. As he spread out his blanket, he noticed that a number of men, content to sleep on any spot that was dry, had crowded up next to the hogs and horses.

Bean witnessed Major Fidler trying to put a stop to the overcrowding. Fidler approached Captain Mason and told him that the boat was becoming much too crowded. Although Mason might have agreed, he remarked to Fidler that he could not help it.[32] The loading was being done by the government, and he could do little about it.

Perhaps sparked by Fidler's words, however, Mason approached an unnamed officer and, making a formal protest about the overcrowding, said that he had a large enough load already. Cpl. George M. Clinger (Company E, 16th Kentucky Infantry) and Pvt. Levi G. Morgan (Company B, 21st Ohio Infantry) heard the unknown officer, whom they both thought was a quartermaster, swear that he "was loading the boat and would put as many on as he pleased." Clinger added, "We were driven on like so many hogs until every foot of standing room was occupied."[33]

Unfortunately for the soldiers, Mason had almost no power to try to override the actions of the Union officers. Although oceangoing vessels were bound by national and international codes of maritime laws and regulated as to what they carried, how much they carried, and when and where such action took place, inland river vessels were not bound by such laws. As early as 1825, the U.S. Supreme Court had ruled that "admiralty jurisdiction was limited to tidewaters"; maritime laws did not apply to inland river commerce.

In response to this, individual states began passing regulations meant to curb the frequent accidents occurring along America's inland waterways and to bring some culpability to the steamboat captains and their owners. Such regulations could be enforced only within the limits of each state, however, and when a river passed through several states, their application to boats on that river presented difficult jurisdictional problems.[34]

As these problems grew among the states, public demand shifted the focus of regulation to the U.S. Congress. Something had to be done, and it had to be federally controlled. After a number of years of debate, Congress passed the Steamboat Act of 1838 to help provide for "the better security of the lives of passengers." Steamboat boilers now had to be inspected; engineers had to be licensed; and, above all, owners and captains were now held responsible for all disasters unless responsibility was otherwise proved. Although strong on paper, the act was nothing more than a feeble attempt to placate an angry public. Federal inspectors were given no standards by which to inspect the boats, and many proved incompetent in their work. In reality, the owners and captains seemed unaffected by the weak act.[35]

"This is the only country in the world," a legislator protested, "which has not passed stringent laws to regulate the manner in which that powerful agent, steam, is to be employed by individuals; this is the only country in the world where human life would be recklessly and wantonly sacrificed to the cupidity of steamboat proprietors."[36]

Mistakenly acting under the impression that it should not try to interfere too stringently in the management of a rising new branch of enterprise, Congress did little to upgrade the 1838 act or regulate its enforcement. It hoped that the captains and owners would regulate themselves by a "law of discretion" and allow their moral convictions over the loss of human lives to guide them toward better control of their vessels.[37]

By the early 1850s, however, the "law of discretion" obviously had not worked. During each year between 1847 and 1852, the number of explosions, collisions, and fires had increased, and a second Steamboat Act was passed in August 1852. Spurred on by the shortcomings of the 1838 act, the new act called for hydrostatic testing of boilers, among other things, and placed limits on the amount of steam pressure in the boilers. New safety regulations required steamboats to carry life preservers and fire hoses.

Most important, the new act carried two special changes. First, provisions were made for the examination and licensing of engineers and pilots, and the licensed individuals were given exclusive power to override the instructions of steamboat captains if there were perceived dangers in their areas of operation. Second, an adequate system of inspection and enforcement of the laws was established. Inspectors were given the power to prevail over any owner or captain and could order a vessel to remain in port if certain violations of the act were disclosed and left unrepaired.

The new act greatly curtailed steamboat accidents throughout the rest of the 1850s, but, with the coming of the Civil War in 1861, the old law of supply and demand took precedence. Looked on as a means of quick and easy transportation for troops, river steamboats were requisitioned by both the Union and Confederate governments over protests

from owners, captains, and passengers. When either government demanded a vessel, the owner or captain had to supply her.[38]

Suddenly, the Steamboat Acts of 1838 and 1852 were all but discarded. Steamboats were overloaded with troops and supplies, as the
Union Army utilized the natural highways of inland rivers to travel into
the heart of the South. If a steamboat owner or captain protested, he
was informed: "It is a necessity." The number of accidents, both minor
and major, increased. A number of captains were brought before grand
juries by local inspectors, but the court always found that "military necessity exonerated the master." It was as if the two acts had never been
written.

Steamboat captains, seeing a legal way to bypass the acts, again began
using the law of discretion. They crowded as many soldiers and supplies
on their boats as they could carry, collected federal money, and then
placed any subsequent blame for accidents on military necessity. Although the inspectors continued at their jobs and filed numerous protests, the wants and needs of an exasperated government, facing year
after year of vicious warfare, made the acts of 1838 and 1852 moot. Although Captain Mason could ignore the acts and claim that it was a
military necessity to carry as many men as he wanted to on the *Sultana*,
the excuse became a handicap when the overcrowding was too great.
Mason tried to use the steamboat laws to back up his protests, but he
knew all too well that, in the end, the military authorities would deem
the overloading of the *Sultana* to be a military necessity.[39]

Lt. Elbert J. Squire (Company D, 101st Ohio Infantry), who had
boarded with the first trainload from Camp Fisk, found the boat "very
crowded" and the men "very upset" about the crowded conditions. As
the sun set, the men began to think about the evening meal; because of
the packed conditions, they could not get to the rations on the main
deck. Squire noticed that the men had to rely instead on crackers and
pickled vegetables provided earlier by the Sanitary Commission.[40]

The soldiers who were friends of Sgt. Alexander C. Brown fared somewhat better that evening. Because he was in a private stateroom, Brown
had dinner at one of the *Sultana*'s dining tables abundantly supplied
with fine foods and pastries, a marked difference from the scraps he had
received at Andersonville. After cautiously eating a light meal of the
plainest foods, the sergeant gathered up an armful of the leftovers and
carried them to his comrades on deck.[41]

Sergeant Brown left behind at the dining table other paying passengers, including some who had come from New Orleans and several who
had boarded in Vicksburg. Also on board were several traveling musi-
cians who called themselves the Chicago Opera Troupe. They had
booked passage to Memphis.[42]

Lt. Harvey Annis, formerly with the 51st Colored troop, his wife Anna, and their small baby were headed farther north. Boarding during the loading of prisoners, Annis and his wife had expressed great fear about the large number of men placed on one boat. Fearful himself, Chief Clerk Gambrel pointed out to the Annises the condition of the hurricane deck, which was sagging in spite of a number of stanchions put in place to buttress it.[43]

Also boarding the *Sultana* was a Mr. Safford, an agent with the Indiana Sanitary Commission, who had come to Vicksburg to be with his prisoner son, Pvt. George M. Safford (Company H, 10th Indiana Cavalry). Now that the boy was finally going home, the elder Safford no longer had any interest in remaining in the South.[44]

Although not a passenger on the *Sultana,* Joseph S. Nauson of Nauson, Ober and Company had a vested interest in this voyage. His firm had put $15,000 on the *Sultana* at New Orleans for shipment north, and Nauson began to have second thoughts about its safety. He feared that the prisoners might be careless with their smoking pipes and set the thin, dry superstructure of the boat on fire. While he toyed with the idea of taking the money off and placing it on the *Pauline Carroll,* he finally reasoned that it was just as safe on one steamboat as another. Instead of removing the money, he added a little more to it.[45]

Major Fidler's right-hand man, Captain McCown, placed the Kentucky troops on the main deck and went up to the *Sultana*'s main cabin. There, he ran into an excited Gambrel.

"Are you in command of these troops?" Gambrel asked.

"I am not," McCown answered. "Major Fidler is."

"If they place many more on the top of the cabin roof," Gambrel said, "it will give way and fall through!"

Fearing the worst, McCown left the saloon and went up to the hurricane deck to find Fidler. He repeated Gambrel's prediction, and the two men quickly began to redistribute the weight. They moved a number of men from the center of the roof down to the second deck and placed them around the gangway running between the outside wall of the cabin and the paddlewheel boxes.[46]

When the last man from the third trainload finally crossed over the gangplank and onto the wharfboat, Captain Williams went on board the *Sultana* to total up the number of men he had counted. Adding together his figures, he arrived at the unbelievably low total of 1,300 men. In actuality, Williams was adding together the numbers from only the first and third trainloads, the only two he was aware of, but even this number was too low. Those two trainloads, had a combined total of slightly more than 1,600 men. Looking around, Williams must have realized that his total was too low. When an officer told him that someone had placed another 650 men on the *Sultana,* he did not even question the source. He quickly added the number to his total and came to the conclusion that Captain Mason had 1,966 men on the *Sultana.* This was an acceptable figure, as far as Williams was concerned.[47]

Finished with his addition, Williams spotted Captain Speed in the main saloon. He had reconsidered his earlier accusations against Speed. Suddenly feeling a pang of guilt, he called Speed to his side.

"I have an apology to make to you," Williams told a puzzled Speed. "I have done you a great injury. I thought you were bribed and told General Dana but he told me that you had reported someone in the Quartermaster's Department. My authority was an officer that I did not know, but I will hunt him up."

"That must be done," Speed finally said, fearing for his reputation as an upstanding person and dutiful officer. "All I have gained for four years' service is my good name."[48]

Concerned about the welfare of the soldiers, Speed then asked Williams how many were on the *Sultana.* When Williams told him there were more than 1,900, Speed was shocked. He had thought there were no more than 1,400 men at Camp Fisk. He asked Williams if they were comfortable. Williams said that the several men he asked had said yes.[49]

Meanwhile, Captain Kerns entered the *Sultana*'s main saloon and spoke with Captain Mason and First Clerk Gambrel.

"Do you not have a pretty good load?" Kerns asked.

"Yes," both men answered, stating that they had taken as many on previous trips.

Yes, thought Kerns, but not comfortably. Unable to get the men divided, Kerns left the *Sultana* for the last time and headed toward the waiting *Pauline Carroll.* It was 8:00 P.M.[50]

As Kerns departed, Speed turned to Captain Mason.

"Now, Captain," he said, "you will take good care of the men because they are deserving of it, and you know the trouble we had to get them to you."

Mason told Speed that the *Sultana* was a good boat and assured him that the men were in capable hands.

Speed then left Mason and began working his way through the reclining soldiers to the stageplank. Passing down the main stairway, he could not help but notice the large number of men crowded into the wide space in front of the main cabin. On the main deck, he noticed the men passing by the boilers, probably getting hot water for their coffee.[51]

Finally finished with the prisoner exchange and no longer the acting commissioner, Speed departed the *Sultana* with a heavy weight removed from his shoulders. Despite his deep involvement with the prisoner exchange and the loading of the *Sultana,* he had never been informed of the repair work on the *Sultana*'s boiler, information that might have changed his mind about allowing the *Sultana* to take all of the remaining soldiers. Speed met Lieutenant Davenport on the wharfboat and the two confidently turned their backs to the *Sultana*. Slowly, they walked up the levee toward downtown Vicksburg. It was just after 8:00 P.M.[52]

When Captain Kerns arrived at the waiting *Carroll,* he met with agent Jones. Mentally exhausted, Kerns told Jones he had done all he could to get the men divided but "it was no go." Kerns said dejectedly that the *Carroll* could leave; she would get no prisoners from the *Sultana*. As Kerns left and started uptown, the *Carroll* backed away from the Vicksburg wharf. On board were a total of seventeen paying passengers.[53]

It was almost 9:00 P.M. when a runner from the *Sultana* arrived at Kern's office to request the necessary government transportation pass. Although Kerns was not in the office, the pass had been written earlier and signed by Kerns. All that was needed was to write in the total numbers of officers and men going upriver as supplied by Captain Williams. The pass was made out for 33 officers and 1,931 enlisted men. This officially put a total of 1,964 paroled prisoners on the *Sultana*. In addition, a pass was issued for Captain Friesner and the twenty-one guards from the 58th Ohio Infantry. Additional passes were issued to five civilian quartermaster employees, who were going along to help with issuing government rations, and two former soldiers, who were using the *Sultana* for their ride back home.[54]

Finally, a little after 9:00 P.M. on April 24, 1865, the *Sultana* was ready to leave. In spite of a swarm of prisoners buzzing around the boilers to get hot water for their coffee, Chief Engineer Wintringer had the pressure up. The *Sultana* slowly backed into the rushing current of the spring floodwaters.[55]

After twenty-seven hours in port, the *Sultana* was on her way north with Captain Mason's precious load of paroled prisoners—his passport to prosperity.

7 Homeward Bound

After leaving the Vicksburg wharfboat, the *Sultana* crossed the swollen river to replenish her load of coal. An hour later, the heavily laden steamer moved into the strong current of the mighty Mississippi and started northward. "In a short time," recalled 2nd Lt. William

French Dixon (Company A, 10th Indiana Cavalry), "we had lost sight of Vicksburg and were gliding along at a merry rate."[1]

As the boat moved upriver, Captain McCown, by order of Major Fidler, went in search of a civilian doctor to look after the thirty or more extremely sick men on the forward part of the second deck, just in front of the main cabin. Despite the general condition of the paroled prisoners, no doctor had been provided to accompany them to Cairo. Luckily, twelve Sisters of Charity (lay volunteers) of the U.S. Christian Commission, a branch of the Young Men's Christian Association, had taken passage on the *Sultana* to care for the weakened men.[2]

"[A] happier crowd I never saw," remembered Sergeant Brown. "We all felt that a few more hours would land us at home where anxious friends were awaiting our return."[3]

In a conversation with First Clerk Gambrel, Brown asked how many people were on the *Sultana*. "If we arrive safe at Cairo," Gambrel admitted, "it will be the greatest trip ever made on the Western waters." He went on to add that there were more people on the *Sultana* than were ever carried on one boat on the Mississippi River. According to Gambrel, the *Sultana* carried 2,400 soldiers, 100 civilian passengers, and a crew of 80 men and women, a total of more than 2,500 people.[4]

While the two men spoke, the *Sultana* cabin crew were dismantling the long dining tables in the center of the spacious social cabin and replacing them with a number of double-deck cots. The cots were intended for civilian deck passengers, for whom there was no space on the overcrowded main deck, and for the paroled Union officers. There were more passengers and officers than cots, however, and many of the officers slept on the carpeted cabin floor.

Although he did not get a cot, Lt. Joseph Taylor Elliott received assurance that he would get a vacated spot once the boat reached Memphis and some of the civilian passengers disembarked. Satisfied with the arrangement, Elliott found a warm spot on the cabin floor just above the boilers and went to sleep.[5]

Rank had its privilege on the *Sultana*. While the officers slept on cots or the carpeted floor of the main cabin, the enlisted men were packed together on the decks like sardines in a can. A very sick Sgt. Arthur A. Jones remembered, "The nights were quite cold to us bloodless fellows, yet being so closely packed, we managed to keep three sides comparatively warm."[6]

Pvt. Lucius W. Waters (Company H, 125th Ohio Infantry) had a unique bedmate. Somehow, Waters had managed to bring on board a pet greyhound. No doubt, he received some benefit from the warmth of the dog's body as they slept side by side on the forward part of the windswept hurricane deck.[7]

As Captain Friesner walked toward his private stateroom, he noticed that forward of the main cabin "the men were so crowded they couldn't lie down, [and] had to sit up against the racks [railings]."[8]

Corporal Winters felt that the men had been crowded on board the *Sultana* "something like a flock of sheep or a drove of hogs." He did admit: "We prisoners, at least those of us from Cahaba, were used to being crowded, and therefore we did not pay much attention to being crowded." He remembered that the crowding was somehow overlooked as "our minds were filled with thoughts of home, and the loved ones awaiting us there."[9]

Bedded down beside the left-hand engine in the covered area of the engine room, Louis Bean was at least protected from the cold night air. Several times throughout the night, Bean noticed the engineers looking at the patch on the middle larboard boiler. Apparently satisfied with what they saw, the engineers maintained the usual pressure of about 135 pounds of steam and kept the heavily burdened transport moving against the bucking current at the customary rate of nine to ten miles per hour.[10]

Early the next morning, April 25, General Dana met with Captains Speed and Williams and inquired about the prisoner exchange. He asked if the *Sultana* had gotten away all right and then wanted to know the exact number of men she had taken. Dana was astonished at the high number of more than 1,900. Although his specific orders for the prisoners to be sent north in lots of 1,000 had been completely overlooked, perhaps he was satisfied to finally have the prisoner exchange at an end. He made no protest to either Speed or Williams.

Never having seen the *Sultana*—not having deemed it important enough to visit the levee, despite the controversy surrounding her loading—Dana next asked if the *Sultana* was spacious enough to take such a large number and whether the soldiers would be comfortable. Both officers quickly assured him that the load was not too large for a boat the size of the *Sultana*, that very few boats had as much room as the *Sultana*, and that the men were comfortable and not overcrowded. Dana believed his officers and made no more inquiries.[11]

With the coming of daylight on the crowded decks of the *Sultana*, the men began to think about eating. A large quantity of government food had been placed on the main deck, but it had not been distributed. Each officer in charge of one of the newly organized companies was required personally to draw the number of rations required to feed the men under his temporary command.[12]

Sgt. Franklin Barker (Company K, 2d Michigan Cavalry) was one of the noncommissioned officers in charge of a company of 90 men. He and his group had laid claim to a spot on the hurricane deck, just in front of one of the wheelhouses, where Barker found it "very difficult to get about among the men." In the morning, he laboriously made his way down to the main deck to receive the allotment of rations for his company. "Except for this purpose, I rarely left my place," he wrote.[13]

Little or no cooking could be done on the *Sultana.* A small stove on the extreme rear of the main deck, employed primarily for making coffee, was the only appliance available to the soldiers. Many of them crowded around the overworked boilers in the hope of getting hot water or boiling their meat.[14]

For those men on the second (cabin) deck and the pitch-covered hurricane deck, there was no possibility of getting near the boilers or heating coffee on a small stove. Captain McCown recalled: "We had rations of all kinds that the Government issued, but we couldn't cook any of them on account of the crowd." The men were limited to eating dry hardtack and raw salt pork and bacon and washing down the food with water drawn directly from the river.[15]

J. T. Farris of the Indiana Sanitary Commission was on board and noticed that some men were issued pickled hog jowls, a poor-quality meat. "It will furnish an interesting field of investigation to a faithful officer," he wrote, "to ascertain who pocketed the difference between the value of the pork purchased . . . and the cheap jowls furnished by a scoundrelly Quartermaster."[16] The chief quartermaster at Vicksburg was, of course, Col. Reuben B. Hatch.

A large number of men might not have received any rations. Although Captain Kerns had issued a pass for 1,964 prisoners, Friesner remembered hearing that only 1,600 rations had been passed out.[17] McCown reported that "upwards of 1,800" rations had been issued.[18] If the government figure of almost 2,000 men was correct, between 200 and 400 soldiers went without food on the *Sultana.*

Despite the government pass, no one knew for certain how many men were on board the *Sultana.* Farris noted, "Only about 800 soldiers should [have been] taken . . . one third of the prisoners were fit subjects for the care of a physician."[19]

Bean placed the number of ill considerably lower. He estimated that there were probably "about 200" who were not well and another 20 "who were right sick." Many of the men were suffering from dysentery and diarrhea, terrible enough ailments to have at any time but even worse on the crowded decks of the *Sultana.* The only restroom facilities on the boat were located on the second deck, fore and aft of the left wheel housing. The men on the main deck had to improvise by using the areas directly behind the paddlewheels, and those on the hurricane deck were forced to cut holes in the tops of the paddlewheel boxes.[20]

Captain McCown had found a civilian doctor to tend the sick men who were just outside the main cabin and above the boilers, perhaps the warmest part of the boat other than the main cabin itself. To make certain that no other prisoners infringed on this spot, Captain Friesner was ordered to place some of his guards around the area.[21]

Among the soldiers on the *Sultana* were, in some cases, almost entire regiments. Almost 400 troopers of the 3d Tennessee Cavalry; 129 men, 18th Michigan Infantry; 112, 9th Indiana Cavalry; and 108, 102d Ohio Infantry, had been captured at Sulphur Branch Creek and Athens, Alabama, on September 24 and 25, 1864, by Confederate Gen. Nathan Bedford Forrest.[22]

About 350 to 400 soldiers on board the *Sultana* were members of regiments from various states that had been captured by Confederate Gen. John Bell Hood during his autumn 1864 raid through Tennessee. Other soldiers had been captured in the east, at such battles as Gettysburg and Cold Harbor, at the siege of Petersburg and at the clash of cavalry at Trevilian Station, Virginia. Some had languished in Confederate prisons for more than a year; others, including the 79 men of the 6th Kentucky Cavalry on board, had been in captivity for only a few weeks. In all, at least 220 regiments were represented on the *Sultana,* with the numbers per regiment ranging from more than 100 men to only 1 man.[23]

A number of sets of brothers were on board. Among those from Michigan were Privates Orson and Warren Rowley (both Company A, 18th Michigan Infantry) and Wagoner David M. (Company E, 3d Michigan Cavalry) and Pvt. Ransom Aldrich (Company B, 18th Michigan Infantry).[24]

Brothers from Indiana included Isaac and Peacha Bright (both, 24th Indiana Independent Battery, Light Artillery),[25] Privates George and Jonathan R. Downing (both, Company G, 9th Indiana Cavalry),[26] and Privates Alexander and Anderson Hall (both, Company K, 40th Indiana Infantry).[27] Kentucky brothers were Privates James Wallace and Francis Mariam McDonald (both, Company I, 6th Kentucky Cavalry).[28]

With the men from the 3d Tennessee Cavalry accounting for almost one-fifth of the total number of paroled prisoners on the *Sultana,* it would be natural to find a large number of related men in that regiment. Cpl. George C. Davis was on board with his brother, Sgt. James A. ("Hickory Jim") Davis (both, Company B).[29] Other sets of brothers were Pvt. Samuel (Company A) and William Cowan Pickens (Company B),[30] who found places on the hurricane deck, along with brothers Privates John Harrison (Company A) and Pleasant M. Keeble (Company H).[31]

Brothers 1st Sgt. William D. and Cpl. Silas W. Wade (both, Company C) were accompanied by Silas's brother-in-law, forty-seven-year-old Pvt. John Wood, and his nephews, Privates James E. and Landon Wood (all of Company C). Wagoner Byrd Newman McPhail was there with his nephew, Pvt. Garrett Newman; his first cousin, Pvt. Daniel Neill McPhail; and his brother's brother-in-law, Cpl. James Winton Sharitz (all of Company C).[32]

At least three groups of three brothers were also among the Tennessee troopers. The Millsaps family was represented by Cpl. James and Privates Jesse Wallace and William M. (all of Company B)[33]; the Hamilton family by Sgt. Henry C., blacksmith John B. and Pvt. Robert N. (all of Company F),[34] and the Farmer family by Privates Adam and Eli (both, Company A) and Pvt. Elisha (Company H).[35] In some instances, perhaps, almost all of the young males from entire towns and communities, eager to finally be on their way home, were crowded on board the *Sultana*.

That same day, April 25, hundreds of miles up the Mississippi, the *Henry Ames,* laden with the first sizable contingent of 1,315 released Union prisoners, reached Saint Louis, her mission of mercy finally at an end. As the prisoners filed from the steamer and marched through the city streets toward Benton Barracks, hundreds of people stared in disbelief at the drawn faces and the bony arms and legs ill concealed beneath the loose-fitting uniforms issued at Camp Fisk. Although the Gateway City had witnessed hundreds of parades during four long years of war, never had its citizens beheld one like this.[36]

Meanwhile, the soldiers on the *Sultana* were making the best of their homeward trip. Corporal Winters noted that the men "whiled away the time gazing at the shifting scenes along the river, playing little tricks on each other, singing little songs, telling little jokes."[37] Lieutenant Dixon recalled, "We were all talking of home and friends and the many things we would have to eat [hoping to be] home in a few days feasting with our loved ones."[38]

While the soldiers, for the most part, tolerated the trip upriver, the crowding and the precious little deck space per man meant that moving about was almost impossible. Louis Bean stated, "The men generally remained in their places day and night. If a man gave up his place once, he would find it difficult to find another one."[39] Noticeably, the boat ran steadier during the night, when the soldiers were quiet and lying down, than during the day, when some of the men went for rations or to relieve themselves.[40] In spite of more than 240,000 pounds of sugar in the hold, the *Sultana* was undoubtedly top-heavy and a bit unstable with so many men crowded onto the upper decks.

Curiosity being a natural human instinct, the men tended to crowd to one side whenever southbound steamboats passed. Bean noticed that on "several occasions when other boats were passing us, the men would gather en masse to one side . . . which careened [the *Sultana*] over very much and two or three times she was very near dipping, or taking water in her guards."[41]

Fearful that the careening of the boat would cause the water in the boilers to slosh from side to side and add to the possibility of an explosion, Captain Mason and First Clerk Gambrel pleaded with the Union officers to keep their men quiet and in place when other boats were passing or when the *Sultana* was moving up to a landing. Gambrel especially, afraid of the great mass of weight on the hurricane deck, complained constantly, saying that if the men "were not careful, they would break through into the cabin."[42]

Heeding the words of Mason and Gambrel, the officers circulated among the men and cautioned them to stay in their places. In addition, Captain Friesner positioned his guards at various locations around the boat to help keep the men quiet and in their spots. "[The] men did well," noted Lieutenant Elliott.[43]

Although Captain Mason had eagerly sought a large load of prisoners for the *Sultana,* he had never expected this number of men, nor had he wanted that many. Expressly concerned about the shifting of the troops and afraid for his vessel, Mason appeared to be "very uneasy and troubled in mind" and remarked in the presence of Indiana Sanitary Commission agent Farris that "he would give all he was worth if he had [the boat] safely in port."[44]

Perhaps to ease the intense anxiety, Mason turned to the bottle. A man who "drank frequently" from the *Sultana*'s well-stocked bar was pointed out to Lieutenant Squire as Captain Mason. Although Squire "never saw him . . . under the influence of liquor" he was amazed that Mason "could drink so much and not show it."[45]

Capt. Lewis F. Hake (Company B, 115th Ohio Infantry) saw Mason drinking "very frequently" and actually thought that he was one of the passengers. Hake remembered that he "saw the captain under the influence of liquor . . . so much so that it was very difficult for him to balance himself."[46]

Even though he might have imbibed, Mason was apparently able to continue unimpaired in his role as captain of the *Sultana.* Lieutenant Elliott became well acquainted with Mason and found him to be "as congenial a gentleman as I ever met." Elliott initially thought that Mason was "a careful man," but, years after the *Sultana* disaster, he thought that "Captain Mason, one of the owners of the boat, was probably over-anxious for pecuniary reasons to take the large number of soldiers he did."[47]

As the *Sultana* steamed northward throughout the day of April 25, the soldiers, settling into a routine, found ways to keep occupied as they looked forward to reaching Cairo and transferring to the train cars that would carry them to Camp Chase, Ohio.

On the forward part of the hurricane deck, Sgt. Arthur A. Jones celebrated his twenty-first birthday despite his illness. On the same deck, Pvt. George W. Stewart (Company D, 40th Indiana Infantry) was having the time of his life. "I had a jolly trip," Stewart remembered. "Being the son of a steamboat captain I was at home on the river."[48]

Down on the main deck, the men found a couple of distractions, including the Sultana's pet alligator. Poking sticks at the creature, they laughed and jumped back whenever it opened its jaws and snapped and hissed. In time, the crew grew tired of the men teasing their mascot and moved its crate to a closet beneath the main stairway.[49]

Also down on the main deck, members of the Chicago Opera Troupe entertained the soldiers with songs, burlesque, and dancing during several free concerts. Not to be outdone, two friends of Pvt. Charles M. Eldridge did their own song and dance. "My two comrades were jolly fellows and good singers," Eldridge had to admit.[50]

According to Corporal Winters, "We were a merry-hearted, jolly set of men and boys . . . but few of us thought of danger." Instead, Winters found the men "laughing and talking about the happy times we expected to have when we reached our homes . . . [and] the warm and welcome caresses of fathers, mothers, brothers, sisters, wives, sweethearts and friends."[51]

When night descended on the Sultana, the men settled back as best they could to get some rest. A number of soldiers were forced to share blankets because not enough had been issued at Vicksburg. Most of the men slept in the same spots claimed the night before, but others wandered about the boat looking for a better place to lay their heads.

Throughout the night, they continued northward. At 7:00 A.M. on Wednesday, April 26, with the men awake and clamoring for breakfast, the Sultana approached Helena, Arkansas. The streets were awash with floodwaters, and the townspeople were passing through the streets in boats. The soldiers crowded to one side to get a look at the amazing scene.[52]

As the soldiers on the upper decks shifted to one side, the boat began to tilt. Captain Mason, aware of the condition of his boilers and fearful of an explosion, exhorted Major Fidler and Captain Friesner to help in keeping the boat trim. Friesner's guards fanned out among the moving soldiers; Fidler climbed atop the roof of the pilothouse and called for attention. Quickly, he told the men not to change places when the boat was stopped and asked all to keep quiet and still, especially in case of an accident. The soldiers quieted down and settled back to await the short layover at Helena.[53]

The spectacle of such a mass of humanity covering the *Sultana* like "so many insects" likewise aroused the curiosity of the residents of Helena. Almost the entire population of the town came to the river, among them photographer T. W. Bankes, who set up his camera slightly downriver from the *Sultana.*

As he focused his lens, Bankes could clearly see the tightly packed men on the stern of the main deck, on the front of the cabin deck, and covering every inch of the hurricane deck. He could see men on the roof of the texas cabin and on top of the larboard wheel housing. He focused a sharper image to discern the pair of elk antlers, symbol of a swift boat, hanging majestically from the spreader bars between the towering twin smokestacks. Bankes could see laundry hung on the second deck, just in front of the paddlewheel box, and the head of a horse poking over the white railings on the afterguard. In the center of his lens, he placed letters to spell out "S U L T A N A." It was an amazing shot.[54]

The photographer was still setting up for his shot when one of the soldiers suddenly spotted the camera. In an instant "each soldier seemed to be bent on having his face discernible in the picture." Again, the men crowded to one side and the boat tilted. Capt. J. Walter Elliott was sitting on the edge of the hurricane roof dangling his legs, when he suddenly felt the boat going over. He grabbed onto a flotation device and "exhorted and entreated prudence."[55]

Mason and Gambrel again pleaded with the Union officers to control the men. The officers spread out among the prisoners and cautioned them against careening the boat. Within minutes, the boat was back on an even keel and Bankes had his photograph.[56]

After almost an hour in port, the *Sultana* slipped away from Helena and continued upriver toward Memphis, her next stop. The trip was routine on the stretch of water between Helena and Memphis.[57]

The *Sultana*'s engineers kept a watchful eye on the boilers and were pleased to see that there was "not the slightest sign of giving way at the patch or of leaking." Captain Friesner watched the miles roll by. The boat was going "merrily up the river," he remembered, "past homes with wide verandas . . . groups of deserted Negro cabins . . . miles of cottonwood brakes that could only raise their leafy tops above the waters." As day turned to night, Friesner watched "the black pipes spread their dark feathery vapors far down the river until they mingled with the dim sky."

He wrote, "Tonight Memphis, in the morning Cairo."[58]

The steamboat *Luminary* (*center*), twin sister of the *Sultana,* at the Vicksburg wharf. Because of the elongated deck space in front of the two oversized smokestacks, the *Sultana* was considered ideal for the shipment of the paroled prisoners. (Courtesy of Public Library of Cincinnati and Hamilton County, Ohio)

Close-up of a recently discovered photograph, circa 1864, of the *Sultana* on the Saint Louis waterfront. The tall smokestacks gave her trouble with the low bridge at Wheeling, West Virginia, on her maiden trip. (Courtesy of St. Louis Mercantile Library)

Form C Enrollment. The license to operate the *Sultana* from her home port of Saint Louis was issued on March 24, 1865, just one month before the disaster. (National Archives photo)

J. Cass Mason, captain of the *Sultana*. (Courtesy of Ohio State Historical Society)

Camp Fisk Parole Camp, near Vicksburg, Mississippi. Several thousand paroled Union prisoners, some visible among the tents in the background, recuperated at Camp Fisk after their release from Confederate prisons. At center in the foreground is a member of the 66th U.S. Colored Troop, which guarded Camp Fisk. (Courtesy of Old Court House Museum)

Four Mile Bridge at Camp Fisk. (Courtesy of Old Court House Museum)

The steamboat *Henry Ames* (*center*) carried the first load of paroled prisoners, numbering 1,300 men, from Vicksburg to Saint Louis without incident. (Courtesy of Public Library of Cincinnati and Hamilton County, Ohio)

Maj. William H. Fidler, Regimental Command, 6th Kentucky Cavalry, who was in charge of the paroled prisoners on the *Sultana*. He lost his life while trying to save a female passenger.

Capt. William S. Friesner, Regimental Command, 58th Ohio Infantry, survived the disaster. Friesner was in charge of the small guard unit placed on board the *Sultana*. Sixteen of the twenty-two guards perished. (Courtesy of Dennis Kessee)

The grossly overcrowded steamboat *Sultana* at Helena, Arkansas, April 26, 1865. This photograph, by T. W. Bankes, was taken less than twenty-four hours before the *Sultana*'s boilers exploded. (Courtesy of Public Library of Cincinnati and Hamilton County, Ohio)

8 Prelude to Destiny

While the *Sultana* was continuing her journey upriver, the Union picketboat *Pocohontas* pushed into the swollen Mississippi River at Memphis with orders to destroy all watercraft owned by private citizens. Perhaps the orders resulted from fear of some last-ditch attack by Confederate guerrillas. Sailors from the *Pocohontas* spent the entire day of April 25 sinking or breaking apart all the skiffs and canoes they could find at houses and plantations up and down the river.

Shortly after the sailors left the Wooldridge stock farm seven miles north of Memphis on the Tennessee side of the river, overseer Hill sent word to William H. Wooldridge, a mere boy, who was already in Memphis, to attempt to procure a boat. The farm and all the land around were almost totally underwater. Only a few high spots, including the farmhouse, barn, and overseer's house, and some small wooded patches remained above the flooded Mississippi. The Wooldridge livestock had taken refuge on the dry "islands," and Hill needed a skiff to care for the animals. It was imperative that young William find a boat.

After hunting for several hours, the boy finally located a man willing to lend his skiff to Widow Wooldridge. Setting out shortly past noon on April 26, the man and the boy paddled the craft north out of Memphis by way of the Wolf River. They were careful to avoid Union pickets lest the boat be seized and destroyed. Continuing upriver, the two eventually found a spot where they could cut across the flooded fields almost to the front door of the house. Arriving just about sundown, young William went to bed happy with the thought that he had succeeded in procuring a skiff for his mother.[1]

Memphis was known as the "Good Samaritan City." Many disasters had taken place on the Mississippi near the city, and the people always responded with haste and charity. Countless victims had been cared for in the city's hospitals, and graves were given tender care in its cemeteries. Four years of civil war had only added to its reputation for mercy. By war's end, thirteen hospitals, two Soldiers' Homes, and a branch office of the U.S. Sanitary Commission were operating in Memphis.[2]

By the time the *Sultana* approached the high bluffs just south of Memphis, the sun was sinking. As the steamer plowed along, two hundred troopers from the 11th Illinois Cavalry, stationed on the bluffs three miles south of the city, spotted her and sent up a cheer of salute, to which the men on the boat responded with a cheer of their own.[3]

Anticipating the momentary arrival of the boat at the Memphis wharf, the men on board forgot all that they had been told and began to crowd to one side.[4] Instantly, the officers and guards circulated throughout the excited crowd and again cautioned the men to remain quiet and in place.

At 7:00 P.M. on April 26, without further incident, the *Sultana* nosed up to the Memphis levee. Although the soldiers had been warned not to leave the boat, Pvt. Walter G. Porter (Company C, 18th Michigan Infantry) recalled, "The moment the boat touched the wharf . . . the boys began to jump off." Porter had to admit, "I went with the rest."[5] Although the guards of the 58th Ohio Infantry tried to stop the men, a large number managed to slip through their grasp.[6]

Some went into town with a purpose. Pvt. George Downing (Company G, 9th Indiana Cavalry) had a few friends in Memphis whom he was going to look up. Pvt. George Hass (Company A, 102d Ohio Infantry), who had some money, was intent on purchasing a few provisions. He planned to eat them at noon the next day so that he would have at least one good meal on the *Sultana*. Some two hundred soldiers made their way to the Soldiers' Home for a hot meal of pickled onions and curried cabbage.[7]

The *Sultana's* main reason for stopping at Memphis was to discharge 200 to 230 hogsheads of sugar consigned to the Quartermaster Department; the ninety-seven boxes of wine; and, much to the relief of all on board, the lot of hogs. Knowing that the unloading of the huge hogsheads would take some time, Chief Engineer Wintringer, on duty at the time of the boat's arrival, reduced pressure in the straining boilers from the running rate of 135 pounds to a standing rate of 90–100 pounds. Like many steamboat engineers, Wintringer preferred to keep a low pressure while in port, rather than bank his fires completely.[8]

Captain Mason sent out a call for volunteers from among the soldiers to help in the unloading. Pvt. Samuel H. Raudebaugh (Company K, 65th Ohio Infantry) helped with the unloading because of the seventy-five cents per hour that the men were promised.[9] Sgt. Hosea C. Aldrich (Company G, 18th Michigan Infantry) and many others saw it as a means to slip past the guards. Finding that it took about a dozen men to roll one of the hogsheads ashore, Aldrich and others got behind a keg and began pushing. Once the hogshead was on dry land, they wandered off and left "a dozen more to roll the next one."[10]

One of the hogsheads broke open, and 1,200 pounds of sugar spilled onto the Memphis wharf. In seconds, the hungry soldiers descended on the spill like ants at a picnic. Pvt. Andrew Pouder (Company K, 50th Ohio Infantry) filled a bucket with the precious white powder and carried it up to his comrades on the cabin deck, just forward of the twin smokestacks. After eating all they could, Pouder kept some of the sugar for the future; he knew that meals on the *Sultana* could be few and far between.[11]

Another soldier to think of the future was fifteen-year-old musician Stephen M. Gaston (Company K, 9th Indiana Cavalry). Although he did not have a bucket, he recalled that he and a friend "filled everything we could find with sugar, intending to eat the sugar and hardtack while going up the river." Carrying the powder up to their sleeping spot on the roof of the texas cabin in front of the pilothouse, the two ate "about two pounds of sugar each" and stored the rest at their heads. As he turned in, Gaston found that his "evening dreams were sweet."[12]

With the hogsheads removed, more than a few soldiers found new sleeping quarters in the dark hold of the boat. They knew that the heavy cargo hatch would be closed behind them, but they were just glad to be free from the overcrowded upper decks and looked forward to a night of quiet rest.[13]

With the removal of the sugar from the hold and the great mass of human beings still on the cabin and hurricane decks, the *Sultana* undoubtedly became top-heavy, a factor that should have been considered by Captain Mason; Chief Mate Rowberry, who was responsible for the distribution of weight; and Chief Engineer Wintringer. As experienced steamboat men, they should have realized the danger in which they were placing the *Sultana*. The boat had careened before the more than 120 tons of sugar had been unloaded. By not compensating for that ballast, they were setting up the *Sultana* for certain disaster.

During the unloading of the *Sultana,* a small number of passengers were coming and going. Among those disembarking were Colonel Compton and, much to the dismay of the soldiers, the members of the Chicago Opera Troupe.[14]

Among the passengers coming on board was Lucy Ross, the recent bride of Buck Ross, a soldier with the 47th Illinois Infantry stationed in Memphis. The regiment had received orders to march north, and Mrs. Ross had purchased passage to Illinois on the *Sultana* in advance of the boat's arrival at Memphis. She had not known of the *Sultana*'s crowded condition, but she elected to board anyway and arrive in her new home before her husband.[15]

Another passenger boarding for Illinois was Pvt. Epenetus W. McIntosh (Company A, 14th Illinois Infantry). A former prisoner of war, McIntosh had left Vicksburg on April 22 on the *Henry Ames.* Two days later, when the *Ames* reached Memphis, McIntosh had gone into town and missed the boat when she left. With the *Sultana* so heavily crowded, Mc-

Intosh figured that nobody would notice if one more soldier slipped on board.[16]

It was close to 10:00 P.M. when perhaps the last passenger, William Dunham Snow, crossed the *Sultana*'s gangplank. The thirty-three-year-old Snow was on his way to Washington, D.C., to take a seat in the U.S. Senate. He had been recently elected senator from the state of Arkansas under a special proclamation of President Andrew Johnson.[17]

Unloading of the freight was completed shortly before 11:00 P.M. Captain Mason gave the signal to ring the steamer's bell to call the soldiers who had gone into town back to the boat. Afraid of missing their ride to "God's Country," many had already returned, but others seemed intent on waiting until the last minute. Among these was a tall, gangly Tennessean who had wandered into one of the many saloons in Memphis and was rip-roaring drunk. Shouting and cursing, the man was escorted back to the *Sultana* by the guards of the 58th Ohio Infantry who had gone into town to hasten along the stragglers. The inebriated man managed to stumble his way up to the overcrowded hurricane deck, where he drew the attention of twenty-year-old William A. McFarland.

"I was quite young at the time," McFarland later recalled, "and it pleased me very much to tease this fellow." The drunken Tennessean heard McFarland and tried to get at him. As the Tennessean fell over many reclining forms in his way, according to McFarland, he "received a number of hard licks for his trouble" and never did get to McFarland.[18]

Just before midnight, the *Sultana* cast off her lines. Wintringer increased the pressure in her boilers from 100 pounds to about 135 pounds and noticed that all four high-pressure tubular boilers "seemed to be in good condition." After backing away from the Memphis waterfront, the *Sultana* moved upriver to the coaling barges anchored about one-half mile above the city landing near the mouth of the Wolf River.[19]

As was customary, the *Sultana* probably burned wood and coal together in her furnaces. In 1865, it was generally believed that wood and coal used together produced a hotter fire because the wood scattered throughout the coal tended to keep it loose and open and promoted greater combustion. Although the *Sultana* has been generally considered a coal-burning boat, Louis Bean remembered, when he first boarded the boat at Vicksburg: "The main deck was pretty much filled with wood." Now, in addition to some one thousand bushels of coal, the firemen and deckhands took on a large amount of cordwood and placed it around the boilers.[20]

On the way to his cot shortly before midnight, Lieutenant Elliott stopped to speak with Captain Mason. "[I]f I believed in presentiments I would believe that he had one that something dreadful was going to happen," Elliott remembered, "for in our conversation he said that he would give all the interest he had in the boat if it were safely landed in Cairo." (These were almost the exact words that agent Farris had heard Mason speak on leaving Vicksburg.) "I was impressed at the time by what he said," Elliott admitted, "but in a few minutes it wore off." Bidding the captain good night, Elliott retired to his cot just in front of the ladies' cabin.[21]

At midnight, Second Engineer Clemens came on watch to relieve Wintringer. Undoubtedly, Wintringer told Clemens what had transpired with the boilers and the machinery during the past four hours. The boilers were "in good condition" and "all right" and the amount of water was "three cocks," a sufficient amount. Knowing that the second engineer had "been engineering twenty-five years" and regarding him as a "very able engineer," Wintringer retired to his bunk, about midships, on the Arkansas side of the texas cabin.[22]

When the *Sultana* had backed away from the Memphis levee, she left behind a handful of soldiers who had not heard her bell. Privates George Downing and James Payne (Company C, 124th Indiana Infantry) were two of the stragglers. Payne was forced to wait for another boat, but Downing had some money that he had received from home. Finding a man with a skiff, he paid him two dollars to be rowed upriver to the *Sultana*. After making his way up to the crowded hurricane deck, he took his place beside his comrades in front of one of the wheel housings.[23]

"If I had not sent home for that money I would have been left," Downing told them and then quickly went to sleep.[24]

Sometime before the *Sultana* left the coal barges, Captain Mason turned over command of the boat to his good friend, Chief Mate Rowberry, and retired to his room in the forward-most part of the texas cabin. As Mason made his way up from the decks below, Sgt. William Fies noticed that he had a very difficult time, being "compelled to crawl around on the rail, as the deck was so crowded with men lying down that he could not find room to step."[25]

Finally, near 1:00 A.M. on April 27, the coal bins on the *Sultana* were full and pilot Kayton nosed the steamer away from the coal barges. Kayton found that now, with most of the men fast asleep, the boat was "running steadily without careening, . . . on an even keel."[26]

As the *Sultana* started upriver, a low bank of storm clouds settled over the Memphis area and opened up with a light drizzle. In the enclosed area of the engine room, Clemens built up the pressure in the boilers to a running speed of nine or ten miles per hour. High up in the pilot-house, Kayton started to steer the *Sultana* past the first of the submerged Chickens islands, while Rowberry slowly made his way upstairs through the sleeping forms with the intention of spending some time in the relative quiet of the pilothouse.[27]

Fifteen feet from the boilers, next to the guard railing enclosing the main deck, Pvt. Chester D. Berry (Company I, 20th Michigan Infantry) sang a little song that he had found in a hymn book passed out by one of the Sisters of Charity on the boat. Before Berry had joined the army, the song "Sweet Hour of Prayer" had been popular at home and, as Berry remembered, "before darkness had stopped me . . . I had committed those words to memory and sang them for the boys."[28]

Inside the protected engine room behind the bank of boilers, Bean tried to fall asleep beside the left engine. Before dozing off, he watched Engineer Clemens working around the boilers and the engines. Although Bean had noticed the engineer's concern about the boilers on the leg of the trip from Vicksburg to Memphis, as he constantly looked at the newly laid patch, he could not later recall if the engineer had showed the same concern after leaving Memphis.[29]

Pvt. George A. Clarkson (Company H, 5th Michigan Cavalry), suffering from diarrhea and having just visited the rear of the boat, was making his way back to his sleeping spot when he met Clemens. Remarking on how nicely the boat was running, Clarkson continued on and lay down about fifteen feet from the warm boilers. Feeling chilly, he wrapped his blanket around himself and went to sleep.[30]

Inside the cabin, passenger Daniel McLeod, the ex-soldier with the permanently useless leg, settled down at a table in the center of the cabin and decided to read a book.[31]

One deck higher, on the windswept hurricane deck, Sergeant Talkington returned to his favorite spot on top of what he presumed to be the coffin of a dead Union officer. Using his knapsack as a pillow, he told his friends he "was going to hold that officer down for the rest of the night."[32]

It was nearly 2:00 A.M. Kayton had worked the *Sultana* past the rest of the Chickens and the larger Hen islands. She was now about seven miles above Memphis. Even in the darkness, Kayton knew that just ahead of him, on the Tennessee side, was submerged Island No. 40 and behind that was old Fort Harris, an unfinished Confederate fort that had been started in 1862 on the property of Widow Wooldridge's stock farm. He also knew that on his left, under the swirling waters of the Mississippi, was Woppenaughkee Bar, a place to avoid during low water but well beneath the surface now. In fact, Kayton knew that right here, as he began to work the *Sultana* from the Tennessee side of the river to the Arkansas side to pick up the slack water, the river was well over the Arkansas bank and extending back for several miles. Only the tops of the trees that normally edged the riverbank were still above the surface of the cold brown water.[33]

Pvt. Benjamin G. Davis (Company L, 7th Kentucky Cavalry) lit his pipe from the fires of a furnace and finally made his way back to his sleeping place on the hurricane deck. He sat down to enjoy his smoke. After about ten minutes, Davis finished his pipe and reached for a canteen. As he brought it to his lips, the crippled boilers of the *Sultana* suddenly exploded and the canteen blew out of his hands. "I never saw it again," Davis recalled.[34]

In an instant, the *Sultana* sustained a mortal wound, one from which there could be no hope of recovery. Death could be swift and painless or slow and agonizing.

It was then about 2:00 A.M., April 27, 1865. The death of the *Sultana* would be slow and agonizing.

9

The Explosion

An absolute determination of what caused the boilers of the *Sultana* to burst suddenly never has been made. The best speculation involves a combination of factors that included too much pressure, too little water, and a slight careening of the boat.

In relation to the pressure factor, pilot Kayton, at the wheel, and Chief Mate Rowberry, in command at the time of the explosion, both stated that the boat was running at her usual rate of "nine or ten miles per hour."[1] Although mortally wounded, Second Engineer Clemens, who was in charge of the boilers, was able to state that he was "carrying about 135 pounds of steam."[2] To maintain the usual rate of speed against the strong force of the April flood current, the *Sultana* had to be carrying much more pressure than stated and more pressure than the boiler could safely hold.

In 1865, steam gauges were the only means to judge the pressure inside a boiler. They had been required on steamboats only since 1852 and were far from perfect. The gauges were not calibrated and could be adjusted to read any degree preferred by the simple twist of a screwdriver at the back of the gauge. Although a gauge might have read 135 pounds of pressure per square inch, actual pressure could have been higher, depending on the setting of the gauge.[3]

The safety valves in the boilers of 1865 constituted another flaw. Although the valves were installed on boilers from the very beginning, their workings were frequently misunderstood and their maintenance often overlooked by engineers. The valves were designed to open and release steam if the pressure inside the boiler reached a certain degree; however, lack of care generally led to corrosion and sticking of the valve. In addition, to allow for an increase in pressure, many engineers frequently tied weights to the valves, which made release of the excess steam impossible.[4]

It is apparent that Clemens and Wintringer were pushing the boilers beyond their safe limit. By running the *Sultana* at her usual speed, against the strong current, the engineers were putting undue stress on her boilers. This can be compared to maintaining the same speed in an automobile while going up a steep incline as on a level surface. The engine has to work much harder on the incline.

The patch on the middle larboard boiler must have added to the problem, although it would be only speculation to conclude that the patch caused the explosion. Three of the four boilers, including the one with the patch, were involved in the explosion, but there is no way to ascertain which one blew first.[5] Present-day boiler mechanic and expert Donald Cooper of Hayes Boiler & Mechanical, Inc., Chicago, Illinois, was questioned about the patch, which was constructed of metal $5/48$ inch thinner than the surrounding boiler shell. Cooper stated that the patch might have given way first, but the tremendous force of the escaping steam would have ripped and shredded the area adjacent to the patch, much like the explosion of gunpowder, and torn the boiler shell to bits.[6]

Current findings coincide precisely with those of the experts in 1865. The supervising inspector of steamboats, J. J. Witzig, stated that the safety valve on the *Sultana* was regulated to the thickness of the boiler shell, not to the thinner patch. "Had the boiler been reinspected after the repairs," he stated, "the pressure allowed by law would have been 100.43 pounds of working pressure [instead of 135 pounds]." Additionally, he said, "I can only assign one cause [to the explosion]—over-pressure at the time."[7]

Perhaps the type of boilers used on the *Sultana* was also responsible for the higher pressure. Tubular boilers had a tendency to clog because the flues were so numerous and close together. The water in the Lower Mississippi was always filled with sediment, and it was even worse in flood season. One engineer estimated that, during one twelve-day trip, more than two hundred tons of mud were injected into a steamboat's boilers with the feed water. Mud had a tendency to clog the flues, particularly on a tubular boiler, and to keep water away from the clogged part of the boiler, thus allowing the metal to become red hot and to weaken. When the mud clog broke and the water came into contact with the hot metal, it immediately formed into steam, which instantly increased the pressure and the possibility of an explosion.[8]

Regarding the problem of low water, Engineer Clemens stated that there was "plenty of water in the boilers" when the boat left the coal barge. An 1865 boiler maker and engineer stated, however, that the "deficiency of water is sometimes attributable to . . . the careening of the boat, at which time water from the highest boiler runs into the lower ones." The boilers might contain sufficient water when a boat is sitting still, such as at a landing or a coal barge, but when she gets into midstream and tilts, whether from top-heaviness or from the current, or both, the water can become higher in the downstream (lower) boilers and lower in the upstream (higher) boilers.[9]

Although the soldiers were asleep at the time of the explosion and Kayton had stated that the boat was not careening[10] Inspector Witzig followed the *Sultana*'s course in a tugboat shortly after the disaster. After finding that the tug "did careen some," Witzig was asked if "the *Sultana* with 1800 [*sic*] passengers on board, and no ballast or freight in the hold" would careen. "My opinion is," he said, "she ought to careen certainly."[11]

Cooper stated:

Taking the above facts and assumption, the following would be the most likely scenario. The *Sultana,* running with 135 pounds per square inch of steam pressure, top heavy, and slightly low on water, lists thus exposing the portion of the boiler metal that was repaired to direct heat with no water against it. This area of the boiler overheats and the metal fatigues [weakens]. The boat moves out of the main current and rights itself. The water returns to level against the overheated, fatigued metal, causing this area to explode out, the steam and water from the other boilers would be pushed to the opening and explode also.[12]

The weak boilers, either from the patch, from the type of construction, or because they were more than three years old and constantly operated at high pressures so that Captain Mason could collect his precious speed records; the top-heaviness of the vessel; the "usual" pressure in the boilers; and the strong current all added up in the explosion of the *Sultana*'s boilers. The result, as would be expected, was disastrous. A 1903 test demonstrated that the water contained in a high-pressure boiler, heated to 150 pounds of pressure, had "enough energy to hurl the boiler over two miles into the air."[13]

On the *Sultana,* one boiler exploded first. A split second later, the other two ruptured with the force of a ton of explosives. The explosion of a boiler is even worse than the explosion of dynamite. In addition to the force of the blast, an exploding boiler sends out a deadly spray of scalding hot water and steam. People in its path are cooked in seconds.

The force of the blast on the *Sultana* was tremendous, with the three boilers completely shredded. Shards of red-hot metal, ranging in size from larger than a man to a fraction of an inch, flew outward from the center of the main deck. Hundreds of pieces shot out into the water, but others tore through the upper decks, through the railing surrounding the main deck, and through human beings on the crowded decks.

Below the boilers, the furnaces that contained white hot coals and burning pieces of cordwood disintegrated. Coal and wood scattered throughout the flimsy wooden remains of the *Sultana,* with the inevitable result of fire.

The main force of the blast went up and to the rear, almost at a 45-degree angle. The engine room partition wall, behind the boilers, was torn to kindling. A wave of boiling water, hot steam, choking ashes, pieces of the boiler and furnace, and wood from the shattered wall rained down on the occupants of the stern cargo room.

The area on the sides and to the front of the boiler, although out of the main path of the blast, was almost equally affected. Support beams and stanchions holding up the cabin deck blew apart, which left the deck unsupported. Hot coals, boiling hot water and steam, and the debris of the ruptured boilers and furnace shot through the area behind the main stairway.

Above and behind the boilers, the floor of the cabin deck shattered into a thousand pieces. The staterooms and the carpeted floor of the main cabin directly in the path of the explosion disappeared into space. A huge hole replaced the flimsy deck planking and the demolished staterooms. In other rooms, farther back, the wall partitions cracked and splintered, and the occupants were flung about like lifeless rag dolls. What remained of the cavernous social hall, the rear three fourths of it, was filled with scalding, choking steam.

In front of the right wheel housing, a large section of the cabin deck, including the kitchen, blew into the river. Portions of the deck and guards all around the steamboat followed. Large sections of the ornate railing encircling the deck shot out into the cold Mississippi or shattered into splinters. Ornate railing beams, helping to support the hurricane deck, fractured and split.

The flat, pitch-covered hurricane deck immediately above the blast path was torn asunder. All that remained was a gaping hole. Some intact sections of the deck flew far out into the river. Other sections disintegrated completely. A searing cloud, formed by the escaping steam, engulfed everything around and behind the hole.

The texas cabin, the domain of the steamboat crew, was ripped in half. The front half was rocked but stayed together, but practically the entire back half was blown to pieces or sank into the wide hole in the decks.

The pilothouse, atop the texas cabin amidships, was ripped apart. The rear three quarters were torn off and blown into the water. The front section, only a sliver, remained intact and upright.

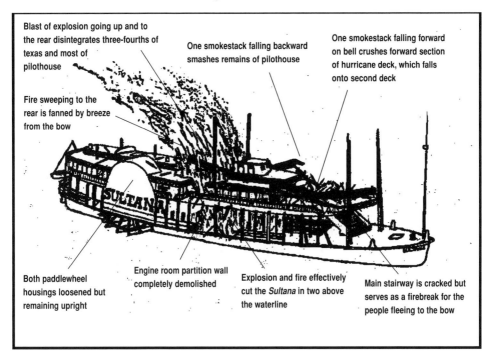

Blast of explosion going up and to the rear disintegrates three-fourths of texas and most of pilothouse

One smokestack falling backward smashes remains of pilothouse

One smokestack falling forward on bell crushes forward section of hurricane deck, which falls onto second deck

Fire sweeping to the rear is fanned by breeze from the bow

Both paddlewheel housings loosened but remaining upright

Engine room partition wall completely demolished

Explosion and fire effectively cut the *Sultana* in two above the waterline

Main stairway is cracked but serves as a firebreak for the people fleeing to the bow

The *Sultana*, after the explosion.

Both of the wheel housings, loosened by the blast, tilted slightly outward from the hull but remained upright. The badly shaken twin smokestacks, left unsupported by the severing of the many guy lines and the destruction of the boilers and furnaces, stood only a few seconds before toppling. The spreader bars between the smokestacks continued to hold them apart momentarily, but, on each end of the bars, the smokestacks twisted and turned in opposite directions. One fell forward and the other backward.

As the stacks twisted, the spreader bars were unable to withstand the pull from both directions and were torn loose. The prized pair of elk antlers, symbol of the *Sultana*'s speed, disappeared forever.

The smokestack twisting backward fell onto what was left of the pilothouse, shattered it to pieces, and forced the remains into the yawning hole. Soot and sparks rained from the top of the stack as it broke through the rear section of the splintered texas cabin and hurricane deck and followed the pilothouse into the hole.

The smokestack twisting forward crashed on top of the forward section of the hurricane deck, directly in the center on top of the bell frame. As it hit the bell, the stack split apart, with sparks and coal dust spraying in all directions. The now unsupported forward section of the hurricane deck, pushed onto the forward end of the cabin deck, was reduced to pieces of shattered wood and broken timbers.

The sturdy railings of the main stairway caught some of the falling hurricane deck and held it aloft, leaving a small cavern-like breathing space between the two decks. Where there was no railing, the two decks slammed together with terrific force. As they shattered and broke, many people were trapped between them and killed. Although the stairs cracked, the main stairway remained intact, an open escape route to the deck below.

Behind the stairway, where the deck was left unsupported by the shattering of the support beams and stanchions on the main deck, the combined decks tumbled down. A pile of rubbish consisting of the splintered remains of the hurricane and cabin decks lay atop hot coals and what was left of the ruptured boilers and furnace.

The center of the *Sultana* was a mass of kindling. With the disintegration of the pilothouse, the tiller rope was severed and there was no way to maneuver the vessel toward either bank. The *Sultana* was now a drifting hulk, left to the whim of the strong flood current of the mighty Mississippi. The men and women still alive on the steamer were on their own.

The explosion was felt by many on board as a tremor running through the boat. Ironically, although people miles away heard the echoes of the explosion, many people on the *Sultana* heard nothing. Perhaps they were asleep or in a secluded area, or they might have been momentarily stunned by the concussion of the blast and could not remember it. Those who heard the explosion and lived to tell about it, however, never forgot the incredible sound.

Corporal Winters thought it "resembled the discharge of a battery of artillery."[14] and Capt. J. Walter Elliott remembered it as "a report as of the discharge of a park of artillery" with the shock "of a railroad collision."[15] Sgt. Henry Tolbert Linginfelter (Company I, 3rd Tennessee Cavalry) suffered "severe deafness" in his right ear from the explosion, as well as injuries to his right hip, back, and hand.[16]

One of the most vivid descriptions of the noise resulting from the explosion comes from Pvt. Benjamin F. Johnston (Company A, 5th Michigan Cavalry): "[The] explosion came with a report exceeding any artillery that I had ever heard," he stated, "and I had heard some that was very heavy, especially at Gettysburg."[17]

Hundreds of soldiers were killed outright by the explosion of the three boilers. Hundreds more were sent hurtling from the *Sultana* into the dark, cold waters of the Mississippi, many not knowing what had happened or how they ended up in the water. Experiences of some of them, specific to their locations on the boat, are detailed below.

Cabin Deck

When the portion of the cabin deck containing the kitchen blew out into the water, a large number of soldiers went with it. Some were dead when they hit the water. Others were badly injured; yet others were left completely untouched by the hot steam and scalding water.

Sgt. James T. Wolverton (Company G, 6th Tennessee Cavalry), asleep beside a leaking icebox, recalled that he "felt a terrible shock followed by a deafening explosion, and before I could think my head struck water and I went down, down struggling for breath." Wolverton tried to keep his head above the surface, "the best I could with my clothes and shoes on." Coming across a few small pieces of the shattered *Sultana,* he tucked them under his arms and legs and floated with the current.[18]

Cpl. Ira B. Horner (Company K, 65th Ohio Infantry) had a dislocated left shoulder, and his left side was severely scalded. At first, he felt that "some poor emaciated comrade" had fallen on him but then awoke "struggling and strangling in the water." A poor swimmer, Horner clutched at a few pieces of wreckage. He panicked when someone grabbed his legs. Fearing for his life, he kicked out at the unseen person. He broke the grip and gladly left behind one of his socks in the hands of the clutching man. Still not sure what was going on, Horner suddenly saw a "brilliant light" and heard other men in the water around him asking what the light was. Some said it was the *Sultana* that had exploded and caught fire; others thought it was a steamer coming to their rescue. In excruciating pain, Horner simply floated along.[19]

Samuel H. Raudebaugh had been sharing the same blanket with Horner when the boat exploded. Awakened under water, Private Raudebaugh felt the pain of a bruised chest and groin but was unaware of what had happened. He broke the surface and found Wolverton's icebox close at hand. As he started toward it, he realized that "so many were trying to get onto it that it would do none of us any good." Swimming toward a clear part of the river, he imagined that the *Sultana* had sunk until he saw the boat on fire. Finding a large rail, he climbed across it and hung on with his remaining strength.[20]

A large group of soldiers from companies D and I of the 102d Ohio Infantry had quartered on the cabin deck guard in front of the left wheel housing. Some of the men were outside the railing, and others were clustered around a small set of inside stairs that ran up to the hurricane deck.

Pvt. George S. Schmutz had been sleeping with his head toward the stairs. He awoke to "a burning and falling sensation," not realizing that he had been badly scalded on his face and body.

"What's the matter?" he shouted as he flew through the cool night air. Seconds later, he landed in the water.

A good swimmer, Schmutz remained calm. He thought that someone had thrown him overboard. Swimming back toward the *Sultana*, he suddenly saw flames erupt from her decks and "came to a full knowledge of the situation." Grabbing a few pieces of wreckage, he recalled, "I now turned down river with the current, knowing my chances of recovery was better down the river than trying to swim ashore . . . [knowing] the river was over its banks." Every so often, as he swam, he dipped his head under the cold waters of the Mississippi to alleviate the pain of his scalded face.[21]

Sleeping to the right of Schmutz was Pvt. Philip L. Horn (Company I). Not knowing whether he was "blown through the stairway or thrust out sidewise," Horn found that his "first consciousness was that of being in the air." Landing uninjured in the water, Horn, a nonswimmer, went down twice before grabbing onto a large floating section of the cabin guard already supporting seven others.[22]

Outside the railing, Pvt. John H. Kochenderfer (Company D) was slightly scalded by the explosion. Thrown outward, he struck a guy rope and injured his back. "The first I realized after the explosion," he wrote, "I found myself 300 feet from the boat, shrouded in total darkness and in what appeared to be an ocean of water. To say I was dumbfounded would but faintly express my condition."[23]

Pvt. William C. Warner (Company B, 9th Indiana Cavalry) thought that he had been thrown a mile from the boat by the explosion. "Without any warning whatever, I found myself floundering about in the water while the screams and cries of the injured and those . . . unable to swim could be heard on all sides." Suffering from a slight contusion, Warner spotted a piece of wreckage with a number of prisoners holding on and swam over to it. "Many of the men were praying and everyone was frantic with fear," he recalled.[24]

Cpl. John Fox, Jr. (Company A, 50th Ohio Infantry), was sleeping with his friends on the cabin deck just forward of the smokestacks when he was shot out into the water. Drenched by the boiling water, Fox's back was a mass of raw flesh from his neck to his hips. Feeling more dead than alive, he endured the pain and let the current carry him along.[25]

Hurricane Deck

Many of the men from the 3d Tennessee Cavalry had found places to sleep on the pitch-covered hurricane deck. Charles M. Eldridge had gone to sleep beside one of the smokestacks and did not feel or hear the explosion.

"I was sound asleep when this happened, waking up while flying through the air . . . whirling over and over." Striking hard upon the water, Eldridge fought his way to the surface, "took a deep breath and struck out for land." A good swimmer, he was swimming along when he came upon a ladder that had been blown off the hurricane deck. "Believe it or not," he said, "my two comrades who had taken care of me ever since I had been in prison had already got hold of it."[26] One of the two men might have been bugler James J. Brock (Company I), who also grabbed hold of a ladder.[27]

Seventeen-year-old Pvt. John H. Simpson, also of Company I, suffered a cut and fractured skull when he was hit in the head by a piece of wreckage before being blown into the water. A poor swimmer, Simpson dog-paddled for a while until he found a few pieces of floating debris. Nonswimmer Pvt. William Marshall ("Marsh") Pryor (Company B) was lucky to land near a horse that had been blown off the *Sultana*. Grabbing onto the horse's tail, Marsh let the animal drag him downriver while he struggled to keep his head above the icy waters.[28]

Samuel Pickens was another Tennessean who was fortunate to land near a horse. Blown thirty feet from the boat, Pickens grabbed hold of a horse, but the panicky animal kept heading back toward the *Sultana*. Spotting the floating bulk of a dead horse, Pickens, who dearly loved horses, felt he made the best trade of his life when he switched rides in the middle of the Mississippi River. As he clung to the warm, dead, animal, he undoubtedly wondered what had become of his brother William.[29]

Another large group from the 102d Ohio Infantry had taken refuge on the hurricane deck. Ten men from Company G were quartered together. Sgt. David Hites was seriously scalded in the explosion and sent flying 50 feet into the air, "without any previous notice of [his] promotion." Sailing out over the bow, he slammed into the *Sultana*'s main gangplank, suspended high above the deck, and fell heavily into the water. Grabbing a piece of debris, he remembered "suffering so from the scalds and my nearly-broken back that I could do no more than hold on for dear life." Of the nine men with Hites, only one was found alive.[30]

Among those thrown from the hurricane deck was Epenetus W. McIntosh of Illinois, who had been left behind at Memphis by the *Henry Ames*. Sent whirling through the air, Epenetus found that, "As I struck the water I heard groans and screams of agony on every side. Oh, the scene! It is impossible to describe." Keeping a clear head, he tried to stay away from the other men in the water but quickly found that "it was not an easy matter, as the drowning were making for any who could swim, and catching at a straw." McIntosh tried to reach the shore but found himself being swiftly carried downriver by the strong current.

Although almost every Union prisoner had cursed the time spent in prison and felt physically unable to endure any such calamity, McIntosh thought that his time at Andersonville probably saved his life. Before entering the prison, he had weighed 175 pounds. On his release, he was down to 80 pounds. He wrote that "being reduced to a mere skeleton was in my favor, as I could never have survived that awful disaster had I weighed as much as I did before my prison experience." He reasoned that his loss of weight left him more buoyant.[31]

Texas Cabin

The section of the texas cabin in front of the pilothouse stayed intact, but the deck area behind the house, which held some men from the 13th Indiana Cavalry, completely disintegrated. The sleeping troopers were sent spinning into the cold night air. Charles J. Lahue (Company D) had bedded down with three other Hoosiers near the stairs leading from the roof into the pilothouse. The explosion sent Lahue and the others flying across the deck. Only quick thinking and quicker reflexes kept Lahue from ending up in the water. Somehow, he managed to catch hold of the small bulwark railing that edged the hurricane deck.[32]

Pilothouse

Pilot Kayton, standing at the pilotwheel, and Chief Mate Rowberry were the only two men in the pilothouse at the time of the explosion. When the main force of the explosion came up through the lower decks, it ripped the back off the pilothouse and Rowberry went with it into the water.

The *Memphis Argus* reported that Rowberry "saw a flash, and the next thing he knew he was falling into the water with a portion of the pilothouse." Rowberry was hurled forty feet into the air and, by the time he hit the water, "the flames [were] bursting up from the furnace and soon enveloping the entire boat in flames." Slightly injured by his flight and the landing, Rowberry grabbed at a plank holding five soldiers. As he floated helplessly down the river, he heard the screams and cries of the wounded, the trapped, and the drowning.[33]

Kayton was blown out of the pilothouse but came straight down through the gaping hole where the pilothouse had stood. Falling to the main deck, he landed amid the wreckage of the pilothouse on top of the boilers and severely bruised his legs. By strenuous effort, he was able to free himself and crawl out from under the wreckage of the pilothouse. When he reached the crowded bow, Kayton tried to get the soldiers to put out the fire, but they had panicked. Seizing a plank, he jumped into the water and started for Hen island.[34]

Main Deck near the Boilers

The explosion threw dozens of men into the air and back down onto the *Sultana,* some landing close to their sleeping spots and others hundreds of feet away. Pvt. William T. Shummard (Company A, 7th Ohio Cavalry) had been sleeping in front of the boilers. Because he was protected by his blanket, the boiling water scalded only his exposed head, face, and feet, but the force of the explosion propelled him across the crowded bow. "The first that I knew, I was holding to a chain at the bow of the boat." How he got there, he did not know.[35]

Feeling ill, and sleeping close to the boiler for warmth, Pvt. Eli Finley Provines (Company A, McLaughlin's Independent Ohio Cavalry) and Pvt. Thomas Horan, as well as a score of other sick men, were killed instantly.[36]

Second Engineer Clemens, who had been standing watch over the boilers, was horribly scalded in the face and chest and blown off the boat.[37] Seven soldiers, including seventeen-year-old Pvt. John W. Lesley (Company K, 3d Tennessee Cavalry), asleep beside the boilers, were severely scalded by the escaping steam and boiling water. Of the seven, only Lesley survived.[38]

Pvt. William Crisp (Company D, 18th Michigan Infantry) had the horrifying experience of waking up with a large rounded piece of red-hot boiler pinning him to the deck. "The heat was so intense I seemed to be nailed to the floor," he recalled. "I could not stir hand or foot [and] I thought I should be roasted alive then and there." Crisp's left shoulder had been broken by the fragment. Still not knowing what had happened, he had to wait for the piece of boiler to cool down a bit before working his way out from under it. "I cralled [*sic*] out from that Hell to the front of the Boat and then it was I saw what happened. I could look into the fire and see hundreds of men burning up among the Timbers." It was only then that he realized the "boiler saved me from being crushed to death." Thinking that the safest place was in the water, Crisp quickly went over the side.[39]

High up on the hurricane deck, Pvt. William P. Madden (Company I, 8th Ohio Infantry) had a similar terrifying experience. Wakened from a sound sleep, he suddenly heard "an upheaval and crashing of timbers." Throwing up his hands, he got them severely burned against an unseen object encasing him. "[I] was horrified to find that my efforts to extricate myself were fruitless and the heat was stifling."

Madden could hear the groans of his wounded comrades and the shrieks of the women cabin passengers, but he still did not know what was happening. Keeping a cool head, he was determined to save himself. He wrapped his blanket around himself to ward off the heat and called out for God to help him. Instead, an unknown soldier heard his cries and removed the debris covering one end of his trap.

"I crawled out as black and begrimed as a coal digger," he wrote. Only then did he realize he had been trapped under a half circle piece of red-hot boiler. "All of this took place in a few minutes," he remembered, "but those few moments were an eternity to me."[40]

10 Panic on the Bow

For a few minutes immediately after the explosion, there was no fire, but the hot contents of the shattered furnaces were scattered about the decks. Had the soldiers organized themselves and worked together, they might have been able to control the fire. Unfortunately, and understandably, a majority of the men panicked. It was every man for himself—the group as a whole ceased to exist.

The blasting force from the boilers, which tore upward and to the rear, left the center of the boat a mass of debris and ruins and cut the *Sultana* in two above the waterline. At first, a slim, rubbish-strewn path along the main deck still connected the bow to the stern, but it was soon closed down by fire. The two sections of the boat were then totally cut off from one another. The fight for life on one section was isolated from the same fight on the other. On both ends, however, at the bow and at the stern, the results were the same. Men were dying by the hundreds.

Main Deck in Front of Explosion

Pvt. Benjamin F. Johnston, who was sound asleep, found the explosion "a rude awakening." As he jumped to his feet, a piece of red-hot coal "as large as a goose egg" shot past his right ear. It landed on the bundle of clothing he had been using as a pillow and set it on fire. While others were "hurrying hither and thither, clasping and wringing their hands; . . . shrieking and groaning, and calling upon God to save them," Johnston sat down and put on his heavy army shoes. Remaining calm, he called for everyone to be quiet, but found that his "remarks were without effect." Although others were "jumping into the river, to rise no more," Johnston stayed cool and waited.[1]

Hundreds of soldiers began shoving and pushing and jumping into the cold, dark water. Weak and emaciated from their long stays in prison and unable to maintain their strength, they began going under by the score. Many clutched at anything that was floating—boards, scantlings, logs, and other human beings. Even the best swimmer, weighted down by the death grip of others, would not last long in the crowded, panic-filled waters of the Mississippi.

Cpl. Simon D. Chelf (Company G, 6th Kentucky Cavalry) was asleep on the bow with his head against one of the cable posts. After a piece of iron glanced off his head, he awoke to find his blanket "covered with ashes, cinders and fragments of timber." Looking around, he saw that the "front part of the cabin and the pilot house were blown to atoms," and heard a man shouting at the top of his lungs, "The boat is sinking!"

"[The] men rushed to the bow of the boat," Chelf recalled, "and jumped overboard as fast as they could, tumbling into the river upon each other and going down into the deep by the hundreds."

Knowing that the boat was doomed, Chelf grabbed a board and waited for the water to clear. As he waited, Pvt. Alfred N. Jacobs (Company G, 6th Kentucky Cavalry) came up to him with a railing post.

Looking for someone to help him, Jacobs told Chelf, "You can swim and I cannot."

"I will help you all I can," Chelf replied, "but a man cannot do much in water."

Jacobs asked Chelf for the board he was carrying in exchange for the railing post as the two went forward to the edge. Though intending to jump overboard, Chelf found "too many men in the water, the water being covered with men's heads. . . . I believe I saw 150 or 200 men sink at once."

The initial stampede off the bow was maddening. Chelf spotted a man, killed in the explosion, whose "clothing had been torn off him by the men running over his body." Chelf and Jacobs delayed their jump until the crowd thinned out and took to the water as flames began licking overhead.[2]

Turning toward the only chance of escape in an otherwise desperate situation, dozens of men suddenly headed for the heavy ironbound main stageplank suspended high above the bow. They considered the huge plank, forty feet long by six feet wide, to be a ready lifeboat.

The stageplank had already saved the life of Cpl. Michael Brunner (Company C, 59th Ohio Infantry). Asleep on the second deck, he awoke at the report of the explosion and instantly jumped onto the suspended plank. Remaining in place as the frightened mob on the bow hacked at the lines securing the heavy staging, Brunner fell off when the plank crashed down on the heads of those below, "crushing many prisoners under it." Gaining his feet, Brunner watched as hundreds of men grabbed the plank and carried it toward the water.[3]

Pvt. Henry B. Gambill (Company B, 14th Kentucky Infantry) had been asleep on the cabin deck at the head of the main stairway. Although he suffered a severe wound to his left leg, he managed to hobble down the cracked stairs in time to help cut down the stageplank and start it toward the water.[4]

Cpl. Erastus Winters also arrived in time to help. Bedded down on the front section of the hurricane deck, he had awakened to find himself, along with hundreds of others, sliding down the slanting deck toward the coal bunkers on the main deck. Winters was only slightly injured in his slide. He worked his way out of the mess and reached the bow just in time to see the heavy stageplank being carried toward the water.

"You men that can't swim better follow this plank," he heard someone shouting. "That appealed to me," he recalled, "for I knew no more about swimming than a year-old child."[5]

At that time, Pvt. James King P. Brady (Company B, 64th Ohio Infantry) and Pvt. David Eddleman (Company I, 64th Ohio Infantry) arrived on the bow. Both had been asleep on the forward end of the hurricane deck until, as Brady remembered, he awoke to find that "fire was all over me and my friend [Eddleman] was trying to brush it off; it already burned most of the hair from the top of my head." Dropping down to the bow by a couple of ropes, the two rushed forward and grabbed hold just as the heavy stageplank went over the side.

"I thought it would never stop going down," Brady remembered, "but it finally did, and slowly rose to the surface." Although the plank had gone into the river with at least three hundred men holding on, it surfaced with only about fifteen or twenty remaining.[6]

Somehow Brady, Eddleman, Winters, and Gambill managed to retain their grip. Then, Winters and some other men felt that the only safe place was on top of the plank. While Brady, Eddleman, and Gambill remained calm and held to the sides of the stageplank, Winters and the others fought each other to get on top. "We only drifted a short distance," Winters recalled, "till the plank was turned completely over." Thrown from the float, Winters was able to grab hold again and, becoming more rational, begged those around him to be careful. "Though the plank was turned over a number of times," Winters wrote, "I always managed to retain my hold on it."[7]

As Brady held on, someone suddenly seized his right foot, "as though it was in a vise." Repeatedly he tried to shake the man loose until finally, he wrote, "I got my left foot between his hands and my foot and while holding onto the plank with both hands, I pried him loose with my left foot." Although Brady lost a sock to the drowning man, he figured "he is welcome to [it]."[8]

At the same time, a man climbing onto the top of the plank grabbed Gambill by the shoulders. Fearing for his life, Gambill fought the man off. Although exhausted, he called to the others to stay off the stageplank, but they ignored him. Each time a few men climbed on top, the plank flipped over and a few more men lost their grip and drowned.[9]

While hundreds of prisoners fought over the main stageplank, one of the smaller stages, about fifteen inches wide by thirty feet long, was generally overlooked. Pvt. Lewis W. McCrory, from his place on the forward area of the cabin deck, was one of the few who noticed the stageplank suspended from a pole. Taking hold of his ironbound pocketbook containing more than a hundred dollars and a valise containing a "good suit of citizen's clothes," McCrory jumped onto the suspended plank. From there, he witnessed the horror that surrounded the launching of the main stageplank.

As the fire grew in intensity, McCrory figured that it was time to leave. "Fearful lest I should need one hand, I put my pocket book between my teeth and hung onto my valise with one hand." Jumping into the river below, he went down deep. Adding to his discomfort, the pocketbook between his teeth forced him to keep his mouth partially open "so that I took in some water." When he finally rose to the surface, McCrory struck out downriver as best he could.[10]

Like the main stageplank, the smaller stage was soon spotted by a number of men and cut down. Sgt. Nicholas Karns (Company B, 18th Ohio Infantry), from the cabin deck, and Pvt. O'Connolly C. Russell (Company C, 3d Tennessee Cavalry), from the hurricane deck, reached the bow in time to help throw the smaller stageplank into the water. Although many men let go when the plank hit the water, the four or five who hung on kept their heads and did not panic. Working together, Karns, Russell, and the others began to guide the plank toward the Tennessee shore.[11]

Pvt. Chester D. Berry, with a board in hand, had avoided the launching of the stageplanks. He spotted a man crying and "wringing his hands as if in terrible agony."

"O dear, O dear," the man kept repeating.

Thinking that the man was seriously hurt, Berry went over to see if he could help.

"I am not hurt at all," the unknown soldier said, "but I can't swim, I've got to drown, O dear."

Berry told the man to calm down and showed him the board he was holding.

"There, do you see that?" he asked. "Now you go to that pile of broken deck and get you one like it, and when you jump into the water, put it under your chin and you can't drown."

"But I did get one," said the man, "and someone snatched it away from me."

"Well then, get another."

"I did and they took that away from me."

"Well then," Berry persisted, "get another."

"Why?" the forlorn soldier exclaimed. "What would be the use? They would take it from me."

Determined that he must perish, he cried, "O dear, I tell you there is no use; I've got to drown, I can't swim."

Berry, thoroughly disgusted with the man's lack of self-preservation, shoved him into the water.

"Drown then, you fool!"

Berry, who would later become a member of the clergy, regretted that impulsive act for the rest of his life.[12]

Cabin Deck in Front of Explosion

When the smokestack that fell forward slammed into the hurricane deck, it smashed that deck onto the forward portion of the cabin deck. Many people were crushed and killed, and dozens more were trapped. Those not caught in the debris of the two decks quickly scrambled down the cracked main stairway or climbed down the wreckage, adding to the panicked mob already on the bow. The cabin deck gave way completely behind the main stairway, and inclined toward the exploded boilers. Hundreds of soldiers slid down into the shattered furnace.

Cpl. Myrum W. Gregory (Company C, 55th Ohio Infantry) awoke to find himself "mixed up with the debris of the wreck," and he had "some difficulty in releasing myself from between the two decks." He managed to slide down to the bow but suddenly encountered another crisis: "The jam of men was so great that after I slid down, it seemed near impossible for me to get a foothold, and I came near being carried overboard by the surging crowd." Fighting to keep his footing, Gregory remained on board as the crush of prisoners on the bow sought the safety of the water.[13]

Pvt. George N. Young (Company A, 95th Ohio Infantry) awoke to find himself pinned under the wreckage of the hurricane deck. Thinking that lightning had struck the *Sultana*, Young and a few of his friends began calling for help. A man from the hurricane deck heard their cries and freed hospital steward William F. Clancy (Regimental Staff, 20th Ohio Infantry). Turning to help his friends, Clancy broke open a space above Young, who instantly scrambled out of his hellhole and onto the top of the crushed hurricane deck.

Pvt. David S. Muller (Company D, 13th Ohio Infantry), still trapped in the wreckage, was pinned tight by a heavy beam. As flames began to shoot up around them, Young and Clancy grabbed at the beam pinning Muller and tried to lift it. Suddenly, the flames spread toward them and forced them to scramble away from the beam. They listened in horror to Muller's torturous screams as the fire reached him. When the flames died down, Young and Clancy rushed forward and grabbed at the beam a second time. Again, the flames came their way and they had to retreat. "It was agonizing to listen to the beseechings of our comrade while we were so helpless," Young found. "We could not escape from his hoarse cries, and, cruel as it seems, we were relieved when death ended his horrible agony." Fearing for their own lives, Young and Clancy scrambled down the debris to the bow.[14]

"When the explosion occurred, we all, except one, rushed out from under the wreck," Pvt. William Boor recalled. Boor and his friends had bedded down at the head of the main stairway after Boor had decided that it was unsafe to sleep on the hurricane deck above the boilers. "Comrade Thomas Brink [Company A, 64th Ohio Infantry] was fastened in the wreck," Boor went on, "[and] I commenced clearing away the broken timbers that were about him and got him out." Both men quickly rushed down the cracked stairs to the bow.

"Can you swim?" Boor asked Brink.

"Yes, I can swim."

Boor admitted that he could not but told his friend that he would somehow meet him on shore. Brink jumped into the water among the struggling mob under the bow of the *Sultana* and was never seen again.

Boor went back to his sleeping spot to retrieve his bundle of clothing and tied it to a length of board. "If the board could carry me," he reasoned, "it also could carry my clothing, for I thought they would come good after having been in the icy water for a few hours." Hurrying back to the bow, he surveyed the water below. "It was a most distressing scene to see hundreds of men in the water pleading for help, clinching one another . . . going down by the dozens."[15]

Pvt. Albert Norris (Company A, 76th Ohio Infantry) fell through the crumbling decks. He later wrote that he landed on the "hot irons of the furnace burning my left shoulder to a crisp." Pinned by men and debris, he required some time to free himself and get to his feet. As others fled toward the bow, Norris and Pvt. James Stone (Company D, 76th Ohio Infantry) grabbed an empty cracker barrel and a coal box and climbed over the protective railing at the center of the boat. Avoiding the frenzied crowd at both the bow and stern, Norris, with the barrel, and Stone, with the box, made their way to safety.[16]

Stunned by the explosion, Pvt. George F. Robinson (Company C, 2d Michigan Cavalry) awoke to hear someone screaming, "For God's sake, cut the deck! I am burning to death!" "I tried to find out where I was and when I did I found I was in the coal in front of the [boilers]. The deck I had laid on was on top of me." Robinson's arms were scalded, and his friend, Pvt. John S. Corliss (Company C, 2d Michigan Cavalry), crushed in the fall of the decks, lay dead across his legs. Pinned under the wreckage, Robinson heard someone calling to a bunk mate just before he passed out again.

Astonishingly, when Robinson awoke a second time, he found that someone had miraculously dragged him out of the coal bunker and placed him on the very tip of the bow.

"What will I do? I cannot swim." Someone was talking to him and tugging at his shoulder.

Still in a stupor, Robinson looked at the men in the river. "My God, what a sight! There were three or four hundred, all in a solid mass, in the water and all trying to get on top." But, while he shivered from the sight in the water, he said that the "most horrid of all was to see the men fast in the wreck and burning to death. Such screaming and yelling I never heard before or since."[17]

A small knot of soldiers from Company A, 102d Ohio Infantry had been sleeping around the head of the main stairway. Only the stair banister kept them from suffering the fate of so many others.

"I sprang to my feet at the noise [of the explosion], and in doing so struck my head against the deck above," Pvt. Wesley Lee said. Crawling to the edge of the deck, he looked up over the fallen hurricane deck and saw the fire starting at the center of the boat. He shinnied down to the main deck and took off his outer clothing. Lee added that he "tore two pine boards from the center of the stairway," and jumped overboard.[18]

Pvt. Joshua S. Patterson (Company F, 104th Ohio Infantry) had been sleeping beside the 102d Ohio soldiers. "I received a blow on the top of my head which caused a severe wound," Patterson recalled. His head bleeding, he jumped down to the main deck and "observed more fully the horrors" of the situation. All about him people were crying out for help when, suddenly, the center of the boat caught on fire. Patterson continued, "The fire broke out in the vicinity of the boilers, which caused the soldiers to rush with tiger-like ferocity to the opposite extremity of the boat . . . without regard to rank, position or life."

Pushed along by the crowd, Patterson, who "was not versed in the art of swimming," suddenly found himself in the water. Struggling along, he grabbed a spar of timber projecting from the hull and hung on for all he was worth. Although two or three drowning men clutched at his clothing, he fought them off and continued holding onto his precious spar with a deathlike grip.[19]

After finding his way to the stairs blocked by the crushed hurricane deck, Cpl. Peter F. Rosselot (Company E, 50th Ohio Infantry) climbed down to the lower deck "by means of ropes and spikes." Amazed at what he found on the main deck, he saw "many men mangled—some with arms and legs broken, others scalded and screaming in their agony, while others would be fighting over a piece of timber or plank." Jumping overboard, Rosselot remembered that he "swam away as fast as I could for a short distance." In time, he came across some pieces of planking tied together with a pair of suspenders and rested while he floated down river.[20]

Knocked unconscious by the explosion, Sgt. William Fies awoke to find the left side of his face bruised and bleeding and his left shoulder dislocated and quite painful. Coming to his senses, Fies wrote that he "took hold of an iron brace rod near me which was so hot that it actually blistered my hands, and scrambled onto the hurricane deck." When he learned that the boilers had exploded, he slid down a rope to the bow.

As Fies stood on the bow, he watched the launching of the main stageplank and noticed a "number of men bringing from the hold empty cracker barrels and jumping overboard with them." Fies soon noted that the barrels "were worse than useless in keeping the heads of the men above water, having only one head in them they would not balance." Looking down at the "struggling mass of humanity," he decided to wait a while before leaving the *Sultana*.[21]

Pvt. William Lugenbeal (Company F, 135th Ohio Infantry) headed for the closet beneath the main stairway. Remembering the *Sultana*'s mascot alligator and the sturdy wooden crate that it was kept in, he broke open the closet door, stabbed the alligator with a bayonet, and dumped the dead reptile on the burning deck. Lugenbeal stripped to his drawers and dragged the crate to the edge of the deck. He pushed it into the water and jumped after it. To his surprise, he missed it and went down deep. "When I came up I got hold of the box, but slipped off and went down again," he said. Coming to the surface again, he worked his way around to the edge of the crate and finally pulled himself in. He used his arms and legs to paddle and kick. "So you see," Lugenbeal said, "I was about as large as an alligator."

The drowning men in the river saw the crate as a means to save themselves and tried to grab it. "When a man would get close enough," Lugenbeal wrote, "I would kick him off, then turn as quick as I could and kick someone else to keep them getting hold of me." Although his actions seemed cruel, Lugenbeal knew that "if they had got hold of me we would both have drowned."[22]

Hurricane Deck in Front of Explosion

A large group of men from the 115th Ohio Infantry were clustered around the large signal bell when the smokestack fell across it.

"What a crash! My God!" recalled Sgt. Arthur A. Jones. "Such a hissing of steam, the crash of the different decks as they came together with the tons of living freight, the falling of the massive smoke stacks, the death-cry of strong-hearted men caught in every conceivable manner, the red-tongued flames bursting up through the mass of humanity."

Pushed completely through the hurricane deck, Jones awoke to find himself pinned in the tangle of wreckage and men on the forward part of the cabin deck. Although sick and weak, Jones made his way to the railing bulwark running around the edge of the deck and climbed down to the main deck. He grabbed a plank and was about to go overboard when an unknown soldier asked him if he could slide down the plank into the water. Jones consented. When the man hit the water, he jerked the board from Jones's hands and started down the river with it.

"I stood wondering what next to do . . . [when] a plank like the first floated from beneath the swell of the boat." Quickly jumping after it, Jones remembered swimming away while trying "to avoid obstacles being thrown on me."[23]

Sleeping on the opposite side of the bell, Pvt. James Stuart Cook (Company C) and his young companion, Pvt. James C. Cook (Company C; no relation) were crushed onto the cabin deck and buried beneath a pile of debris. James Stuart extricated himself and retrieved a board. He then turned back to his young friend. "I looked around . . . but could not see him and never have since," he said. "This was the saddest part of my experience, as he was the only son of his father and I had something to do with his enlisting."[24]

Awakened by the "explosion and the cries of the wounded," Cpl. William H. Norton (Company C) found "men rushing to and fro, trampling over each other in their endeavors to escape." Shinnying down a rope, Norton reached the bow and found men "jumping into the river by the hundreds." After taking off his heavy army shoes and woolen outer clothing, he jumped into the water and was almost immediately jumped on by several other prisoners.

"I despaired of ever reaching the surface again," Norton recalled, "but by a desperate struggle, I succeeded in getting out from under them and reached the surface." As he tried to swim through the mass, someone suddenly caught hold of him and began dragging him under. Fighting free, "and not knowing what to do or which way to go," Norton turned and swam back toward the burning boat. Exhausted, he finally grabbed onto a mooring ring hanging over the side of the boat and hung on for dear life.[25]

A group of friends from the 50th Ohio Infantry was also in front of the signal bell. Pvt. John Lowery Walker was with four of his mates when they were suddenly covered with debris that killed one man instantly. After the others dug themselves out, Walker remembered, "[It] took us some moments to understand just what had happened and to realize fully that we were on a burning boat." Looking around, he noted that the deck had been broken "within three or four feet of us."[26]

Sgt. Jacob Helminger (Company B), told the others to stay put while he went in search of a board large enough to save them all. Fighting his way down to the cabin deck, Helminger found nothing that was not already claimed or being fought over by somebody else, so he quickly made his way back to his friends. Unfortunately, in the confusion, the others had thought that Helminger had already gone overboard and had set out on their own. With his friends gone, Helminger began looking for a means to save his own life.[27]

While Helminger was gone, Walker and his two remaining comrades had worked their way down to the bow where they found "everything in confusion." Joining the crowd that cut down the main stageplank, all three helped to carry it to the edge of the boat but wisely stepped back as it went into the water. "Never in my life have I witnessed such a struggle as there took place," Walker recalled. "I thought the sights on the battle-fields terrible, and they were, but they were not to be compared with the sights of that night when the animal nature of man came to the surface in the desperate struggle to save himself regardless of the life of others."[28]

One of Walker's friends set out on his own. Walker, a nonswimmer, told the other man to save himself, as every man was on his own. As Walker stripped off his clothing "to be better able to swim, or learn to swim," the last of his bunk mates jumped overboard and swam away from the Sultana. Determined to wait until the very last, Walker looked around and estimated that there were only between eighty and one hundred men left on the bow.[29]

Still up on the hurricane deck, Helminger looked down at a "solid mass of men" in the water and suddenly heard the voice of Captain Mason calling out to the men. Mason said that the hull of the boat was not damaged and the Sultana would soon land. The captain had been asleep in his cabin in the forward part of the texas cabin when the explosion occurred. He was now trying to do all in his power to save those entrusted to his care.

Seeing the flames reaching high into the night air, Helminger knew that Mason's words were only rhetoric. "The fire had now become so great," he wrote, "a person could see a considerable distance each way from the boat." Helminger saw a clear spot in the water and jumped overboard from the hurricane deck.[30]

Sgt. John E. Norton (Company A, 5th Michigan Cavalry) awoke under the clutter of the shattered hurricane deck. Wriggling free, he was making his way down to the main deck when a hand shot out from under a pile of wreckage and grabbed him around the ankle.

"Help me out."

By the light of the fire, Norton could see four men trapped between the debris of the hurricane and cabin decks. A heavy beam blocked his way to them. Try as he might, Norton could not budge the beam until another man came along to help. As the trapped men came scrambling out and the flames swept overhead, Norton hurried down to the bow.[31]

Texas Cabin in Front of Explosion

Most of the off-duty steamboat officers were in the texas cabin at the time of the explosion, and the entire top of the texas was covered with soldiers. Only those in or on the forward part of it were spared from the explosion and falling smokestacks.

Chief Engineer Wintringer was in his room about midway back in the texas cabin, on the Arkansas side. Awakened by the explosion, he hurried outside and "stood bewildered for a moment," finding that "most of the [texas] behind my room appeared to have sunk down on the cabin or lower deck." When he realized what had happened and heard the cries, "Put out the fire!" he hurried to the main deck to help fight the blaze. Wintringer knew full well, however, that the *Sultana* was doomed if the fire made any headway.[32]

Because the texas roof was narrow, only a few men were asleep there. They included a small group from the 9th Indiana Cavalry who had found room in front of the pilothouse.

Although Stephen M. Gaston had gone to sleep with "sweet" dreams after eating about two pounds of sugar, he awoke with a feeling of being "raised to a height and then a crash." Trapped in the wreckage with a deep thigh wound, he called for help from his bunk mates but received no answer. The area directly behind him, where the pilothouse had been, suddenly caught fire.

As the smoke and flames swirled up around him, Gaston heard voices from men trapped below. They pleaded with him to break away the debris. "I was helpless and could render no assistance," he recalled. "They soon smothered from the heat and smoke." Frightened by the deaths of the trapped men, Gaston found renewed strength. He wriggled free and stumbled toward the stairs.

"I found my way obstructed and debris scattered everywhere," he said. He was just about to jump from the hurricane deck onto the main deck when he noticed that one of the smokestack breechings reached down to the lower deck. Despite his wounds, he shinnied down the breeching and reached the bow.

"Oh! God, what a sight," he wrote. "Men were crying, praying, swearing and begging." Finding an empty flour barrel, young Gaston stripped off his clothes, tossed the barrel into the water, and leaped after it. Although two or three drowning men tried to grab him, he swam as fast as he could and left them far behind.[33]

Cpl. William H. Peacock and four friends were also on top of the texas roof. Crushed down under the wreckage, Peacock worked his way out in spite of a bruised back, cut shoulder, and scalds along his entire right side. Finding that his four friends had been killed by the explosion, Peacock helped "get a good many of the boys out who were pinned down by [the debris]." Soon, however, "the fire got so hot," he wrote, "that I had to stop and look out for myself." Wearing only his drawers and an army coat, he made his way down to the lower deck and quickly swam away from the rapidly burning *Sultana*.[34]

11 Devastation on the Stern

While hundreds of soldiers were scurrying to the supposed safety of the bow, hundreds more, trapped behind the hole in the center of the *Sultana*, were rushing to the stern.

Main Deck behind Explosion

The engine room partition, directly behind the boilers, was torn to kindling by the explosion and thrown back on the men in the stern cargo room. With it came a rain of debris, scalding hot water, searing steam, and bits and pieces of human bodies.

"First a terrible explosion, then hot steam, smoke, pieces of brick-bats and chunks of coal came thick and fast," Pvt. Otto Bardon (Company H, 102d Ohio Infantry) recalled.[1] Nearby, Commodore Smith "was nearly buried with dead and wounded comrades, legs, arms, heads and all parts of human bodies." He tried to go forward but found that he "could not on account of the wreckage and carnage of human freight which now covered the lower deck."[2]

The force of the blast throughout the cargo room tossed men around like straw scarecrows. Pvt. Jacob L. Slick (Company A, 18th Michigan Infantry) was thrown against one of the wheel housings and knocked unconscious.[3] Cpl. Jesse Martin (Company D, 35th Indiana Infantry) awoke to find that he was "down on my knees by a cow, as though I had got there to milk her." Thrown across the cargo room, Martin said, "If the cow had not stopped me, I guess I would have gone on into the wheel house." Water splashing in from the wheel, which was still turning, had brought him back to his senses. Unable to reach his original sleeping spot because of the rush of people and the clutter of debris, he turned and went out the stern door.[4]

Before the debris had time to settle or the soldiers time to get to their feet, five deckhands jumped into the small sounding yawl tied to the after part of the main deck and began rowing to safety. Left behind was a woman crew member, probably the wife of one of the men in the boat, who pleaded desperately for the men to come back. Her pleas fell on deaf ears.[5]

A cluster of men from the 18th Michigan Infantry were asleep around the rear hatchway to the hold. Pvt. Nathaniel M. Foglesong (Company A) remembered experiencing "a terrible crash and everything coming down upon us." Not knowing what was happening, Foglesong laid still and waited.

"Thaniel, why don't you get up; the boat is all on fire?" one of his comrades asked.

"I cannot swim," Foglesong replied.

"Get ready and go with us."

Fearful of panicking and taking the life of one of his friends, Foglesong told the others to save their own lives. When they would not leave him, he finally rose and followed them out the stern door. Standing on the after guard, he saw that "[the] water was full of men, horses and mules." He heard men "calling on God for help, while others took his name in vain." Out of the tumult, he recognized a familiar voice.

"Come help poor Pat, he is a-drowning."

Unable to swim, Foglesong could only watch as Pvt. Patrick Lackey (Company G, 18th Michigan Infantry) slipped beneath the brown waters of the Mississippi.[6]

Also sleeping near the rear hatchway were Pvt. Ogilvie E. Hamblin, who had only one arm, and his good friend Sgt. Francis M. Perkins (both Company E, 2d Michigan Cavalry). Wounded in the arm at his capture, Hamblin's limb had been removed at the shoulder by a Confederate surgeon. Waking to find "the whole boat in a tremendous tumult and uproar," the two men stood bewildered before hearing cries of help coming from the men trapped in the enclosed hold. Hamblin and Perkins managed to pull away the heavy hatch cover and watched as a large number of men "came rushing out of the hold like bees out of a hive, followed by dense clouds of steam and smoke."[7]

While the majority of men rushed toward the stern door, Pvt. Daniel Allen (Company K, 3d Tennessee Cavalry) pushed his way toward the bow, perhaps wanting to get off the boat in the same way that he had gotten on. Moving forward, he passed by "many wounded sufferers, who piteously begged to be thrown overboard." He remembered seeing men "pitch down through the hatchway that was full of blue curling flames," the same hatchway that Hamblin and Perkins had just uncovered.[8]

Otto Bardon, heading toward the stern door, also noticed the open hatchway. Although many men thought only of themselves, Bardon risked his life and "stood at this hatch-hole to keep comrades from falling in." By his own admission, he "helped several out of this place."[9]

More than anything else in the enclosed cargo room, it was the killing steam that everyone remembered. Sgt. Andrew T. Peery (Company B, 3d Tennessee Cavalry) felt that the steam, "for a few seconds was almost as hot as fire." Thinking that the boat was still at Memphis, Peery and his friends ran out a side door and found "nothing but water." Avoiding the rush to the stern, they made their way along the side of the boat toward the bow. "As we passed," Peery recalled, "the fire was getting a start and we had to pass it." In moving through the wreckage he stepped on what was probably a piece of a shattered boiler and burned the bottoms of his bare feet. Followed closely by his friends, Peery and his group were among the few who went from one end of the boat to the other after the explosion.[10]

In the first mad rush, the men in the cargo room had gone toward the fresh air on the open after deck guard, but no one knew what was happening. Then, with the first flickering light of fire, the rush began anew. Hundreds of men began pushing and shoving to get away from the flames and into the safety of the water. As was happening on the crowded bow, people began to die in droves.

Pvt. Robert N. Hamilton jumped into the water from the side of the boat. At first he had imagined that he "would be crushed to death by the falling timbers." Escaping with only a cut scalp, he had rushed to the stern and witnessed the frightened soldiers "leaping off into the water on top of each other [and] hundreds drowning together." Reasoning that this "was not the place for me" he went to the center of the boat and "climbed down the wheel, and got off into the water without sinking."[11]

Although many of the troopers from the 3d Tennessee Cavalry had found quarters on the windswept hurricane deck, a few had bedded down in the stern cargo room. When the boilers blew, Pvt. Thomas Pangle (Company K) and three of his comrades thought that they had been fired on by a Confederate cannon. After he realized their mistake, Pangle, an expert swimmer, decided to try for shore. In spite of limbs crippled with rheumatism from his long stay in prison, he found a board and plunged into the river. "So cold was the water," he wrote, "that I soon became powerless to swim, and determined to climb up on the deck of the steamer." Of the four bunk mates, only Pangle survived the disaster.[12]

Having reached the safety of the after guard, Cpl. Albert W. King (Company D, 100th Ohio Infantry) and his four friends were amazed by what they saw. "Hundreds of men came rushing out [of the stern cargo room] to get breath." King noticed that jamming and crowding commenced. Those crippled were trampled on. Below them, the water was filled with drowning men. "We could not see how any of us could be rescued. It was an exciting scene."

Pvt. James Adgate Fleming, one of King's friends from Company D, could not swim. He repeatedly asked King and the others what he should do. "Our answer was, to avoid the big crowd and remain close to us," King wrote. He and the others then tried to tear a large piece of siding from the boat, but "a large white horse fastened to the railing" prevented them from doing so. The horse fought and kicked at their every move, and, frightened beyond reason, Fleming "rushed into the crowd going overboard and was never heard of afterward."[13]

Pvt. John F. Hartman (Company K, 102d Ohio Infantry), who had grown a long, luxurious beard while he was in prison, was swimming in the water below the stern. A strong swimmer, he was making his way through the struggling crowd when a drowning soldier suddenly grabbed his beard. Hartman fought in vain to escape, but both men drowned in the cold, dark waters of the Mississippi.[14]

Cabin Deck Midship Gangway

Although it is generally believed that every inch of deck space on the *Sultana* was covered by the soldiers, this might not have been true. The cabin deck guards on the side of the main cabin, just behind the two paddlewheels, was apparently reserved for the paying passengers so that they could have some place to enjoy the trip as best they could. Even with this space off limits, a contingent of Michigan soldiers pressed in as close to it as possible without actually breaking the rules and grabbed sleeping spots in the gangway between the main cabin and the wheel housing.

Sgt. Hosea C. Aldrich was asleep near the starboard wheel housing with a bundle of clothing as a pillow. Pvt. John W. Dunsmore (Company I, 1st Michigan Engineers and Mechanics) was beside him. Aldrich remembered the explosion as a "terrible crash, and everything was coming down." As the floor beneath their heads gave way, taking Aldrich's bundle with it, the two men scrambled back to avoid the smoke and flames that suddenly shot up from the newly created hole.

"What is the matter?" they heard men yelling.

"The boat is on fire!"

Suddenly, they heard the "screams of women and children mingled with the groans of the wounded and dying." In an instant, they realized that the *Sultana* was doomed.[15]

"We must get into the water," Dunsmore said.

"What shall I do? I cannot swim," Aldrich admitted.

"You have got to," Dunsmore said, as a gust of flames came overhead. Tearing two blinds from a window, he handed them to Aldrich.[16]

Clutching the blinds, Aldrich climbed over the railing around the cabin deck and slid down to the main deck. Just as he gained the deck, a panicked soldier knocked into him and threw him backward into the water. Aldrich lost his grip on the blinds as he went under. Sputtering to the surface, he grabbed a large board and a small one. At that moment, an acquaintance from an Ohio regiment seized him.

"Smith, let go of me and take the board," he yelled.

Giving the small board to Smith, Aldrich watched him take hold and float away. He never saw Smith again.[17]

Dunsmore had seen Aldrich head for the lower deck and followed him. Believing that his friend was safe, Dunsmore jumped into the water and began "swimming for dear life." As he swam through the struggling mob, someone suddenly called out to him for a chew of tobacco. Dunsmore, of course, kept on swimming.[18]

Main Cabin behind Explosion

Besides the many paroled officers and noncommissioned officers sleeping on the double-deck cots and the carpeted floor of the main cabin, there were also an estimated eighty to one hundred civilian passengers, more than half of them women and children, in the many staterooms lining either side of the grand saloon.

The shattering blast of the boilers tore through the forward part of the main cabin and disintegrated the first few staterooms and everybody in them. A second later, a thick scalding cloud of steam, rolling down the ornate gingerbread ceiling of the saloon, obscured the dimly lit chandeliers and sent the occupants of the saloon into panic. The first licks of flame were following the choking steam.

Passenger Daniel McLeod, with his useless right leg, was reading a book in the main cabin. Without warning, the floor behind him suddenly erupted, pitching him over a table and slamming him against the wall. As the steam rushed up around him, he checked to make sure he still had his head and temporarily ignored the pain from two broken ankles, the bones protruding through his skin. Relieved that his head was all right, McLeod took off his suspenders, calmly made tourniquets, and slowly began dragging himself away from the gaping hole in the floor.[19]

Waking in an oppressive heat, Lt. Joseph Taylor Elliott found the cabin lights dimmed by the escaping steam. Moving forward, he "did not go far" before discovering that the cabin floor "had dropped down at the front, without breaking off . . . [making] an inclined plane to the lower deck."

Turning around, Elliott rushed back to the curtained-off ladies' cabin. He hoped that he was only dreaming.

"What do you want in here, sir?" a guarding matron, who was shocked that a man would enter the forbidden domain, called out as he entered.

"There is something wrong with the boat," Elliott said and swept past. Climbing out one of the rear transom windows, he pulled himself up across the small, decorative bulwark railing around the hurricane deck and looked toward the bow. He wrote, "The boat's bow was turning towards the Tennessee shore, and . . . one of the boat's chimneys was down, and all the men [on the hurricane deck] were in commotion."

Realizing that he was not dreaming, Elliott started back down to the main cabin. Turning, he looked down at the water below the stern and could already see panicked soldiers from the main deck jumping into the water, "twenty or thirty jumping off at one time."[20]

Capt. James M. McCown was asleep in one of the temporary cots near Maj. William H. Fidler. When the tremendous explosion threw him out of his bunk, he crushed his left thumb and tore off the skin and fingernail. Engulfed in the searing hot steam, McCown suffered excruciating scalds to his right arm and face and, while trying to catch his breath, severely scalded his throat and lungs. The mucous membranes on his tongue and the inside of his lips peeled off. Coughing and spitting blood, McCown called out for Fidler.

"Mac," Fidler called out, "I want you to stay with me."

In spite of his terrible injuries, McCown followed Fidler out of the shattered main saloon and down toward the stern cargo room.[21]

Springing out of his bed at the sound of the explosion, Sgt. John B. Hinckley (Company A, 9th Indiana Cavalry) found the cabin rapidly filling with flames. Everything was in confusion as the passengers fled from their staterooms and rushed toward the rear of the cabin away from the spreading fire. "I never heard such terrible and mournful wailings," he recalled. Tearing off a shutter, Hinckley jumped overboard and started downriver to safety.[22]

Capt. J. Walter Elliott awoke to find his "face, throat and lungs burning as if immersed in a boiling caldron." Springing to his feet before the flames started, he went forward and groped his way "between the stateroom doors and the cots, to learn what happened."

Suddenly, he spotted the "yawning opening in the floor." As the fire broke out below, Elliott saw "mangled, scalded human forms heaped and piled amid the burning debris of the lower deck."

Shocked by the sight, Elliott was turning to leave when he heard, amid the confusion, a calm, cool voice call out politely, "Captain, will you please help me?"

Looking in the direction of the voice, he spotted McLeod, "bruised, cut, scalded in various places, both ankles broken and bones protruding."

"I am powerless to help you," Elliott said, "I can't swim."

"Throw me in the river is all I ask," McLeod pleaded, "else I shall burn to death here."

Elliott called to Capt. William L. Coleman (Company D, 40th Indiana Infantry), and the two officers carried McLeod to the promenade guard and gently set him down to fend for himself. Hurrying back into the swiftly burning main cabin, Elliott went in search of one of the cork-filled life belts so that he could try to save his own life.[23]

Meanwhile, McLeod had been helped to the edge of the second deck guard. He "climbed down on the hog chains to where they had been broken off and let [himself] drop into the water." Getting into the river before the mad rush, McLeod, a good swimmer, carefully avoided other people and headed toward the nearest shore.[24]

Sleeping on the carpeted floor near the ladies' cabin, Lt. William French Dixon recalled, "I was sound asleep and knew nothing until I was awakened by a sudden jar that threw me across the boat." Injuring his chest so that he threw up blood, Dixon rose to his feet and tried to make sense out of the confusion. He thought of the "long months that I had struggled for existence in prison, of the friends at home waiting to receive me" and made up his mind to try to survive. He gathered two small planks and waited until the waters cleared some before jumping overboard. When he hit the water, Dixon lost one of the planks but managed to keep his head above water. As he recalled, he worked along slowly, so as "not to overdo myself" and headed toward what he thought was the nearby shore.[25]

Captain Mason rushed into the steam-filled main cabin from the broken hurricane deck and instantly began to help the people there. While others ran about in fear, Mason began to hand out chairs, stateroom doors, pieces of wreckage—anything that would float—to the cabin passengers and soldiers and tried to pull wounded and scalded people from the burning debris.[26] His dream of the "greatest trip" ever made on Western waters was suddenly a nightmare. His efforts to get the paroled prisoners on board and the deals he had made were suddenly for naught. Now, during the last minutes of his beloved *Sultana,* as she burned around him, he worked to redeem his wrongs.

Lt. Joseph Taylor Elliott was busy tearing pieces of sheeting from the side walls of the main cabin and tossing them down to the men in the water. He was approached by Pvt. George M. Safford, who was looking for his father.

"Have you seen my father?" Safford asked.

"I have not," Elliott replied, "but I know the stateroom he occupied."

As the two men started toward the room, the elder Safford suddenly appeared. Despite badly scalded arms, the father embraced his son. The two looked around for a means to save each other. Quickly, the son gathered up three discarded life belts. He tied two around his injured father and one around himself and, tearing off a stateroom door, led his father to the side of the cabin deck guard. He threw the door into the river. Father and son jumped after it and started away from the crowd. Unexpectedly, a frightened horse, leaping from the flaming boat, landed on the raft and sent father and son into the water in opposite directions. Although he looked frantically for his injured father, the younger Safford could not find him. Brokenhearted, he drifted along in his life belt and let the current carry him downriver.[27]

Elliott wrote that, after helping the Saffords, he glanced up at the ceiling of the grand saloon and saw "the fire jumping along from one cross-piece to another in a way that made me think of a lizard running along a fence." Figuring that it was time to leave, he made his way down to the main deck and jumped into the river. He forced his way through the crowd in the water and eventually grabbed onto a set of steps with three other men. They struck out for the shore.[28]

Unable to swim, Capt. J. Walter Elliott could not find a life belt. Although he felt that death was inevitable, he hoped to cheat it a while longer. He tossed a mattress into the river and was about to follow when a group of men in the water seized the mattress. Learning a valuable lesson, Elliott went back to get another mattress, but he hung onto that one and climbed down to the main deck.

Sliding the second mattress into the water, Elliott jumped on top of it just as four drowning men grabbed hold of it. "Down, down, I went into the chilly waters," he wrote. Caught in a death struggle, he fought free and clawed his way to the surface. Looking about frantically, he saw the mattress nearby with only one occupant; the other three men had drowned. He grabbed hold of the mattress, and he and the other man began kicking as fast as they could to get away from the boat. Instead of the threat of drowning men, the two found that they were in the path of one of the huge wheel housings that was beginning to topple away from the burning boat directly toward their heads.[29]

Passenger Staterooms behind Explosion

Mrs. Perry, the wife of an engineer assigned to a U.S. warship, was alone in her stateroom. Seconds after the explosion, she fastened a life belt around her waist and headed toward the stern. Wasting no time, Mrs. Perry sprang into the river only to find herself "floating in the midst of soldiers, horses, and all the debris incident to the wreck." She seized a floating door, along with a half dozen struggling soldiers. The group forced its way out of the growing mob and slowly started downriver.[30]

Guard Captain Friesner, sleeping in a private stateroom, awoke when he heard "a dull, heavy sound." Not realizing that the boat had already left Memphis, he thought that the deckhands had dropped another hogshead of sugar. Seconds later, however, he heard a "confusion on the deck" that made him think a fight had broken out.

Jumping out of bed, he began pulling on his pants and shouted through the closed stateroom door, "What is the matter out there?"

"I don't know, sir," he heard. "We're all stove in here."

Pulling on his army coat, Friesner opened the door leading into the main saloon. Met by a cloud of smoke and steam, he instantly realized that the *Sultana* was on fire. He was worried about his guard company and pushed his way through the panicking soldiers. Finding the huge hole torn in the center of the boat, he looked across the hole and saw a man, trapped in the wreckage, who was burning to death.

"Help, help for God's sake!" the man cried. Although Friesner wanted to help, he knew he could never reach the man. "There was an impossible gulf between us and I turned from the horrid sight."

He moved to the edge of the cabin deck and looked down at the water, where he saw "a great, confused, frantic crowd of men, perhaps 1,000, struggling and drowning." Not the best swimmer, he later admitted that "this scene convinced me of the hopelessness of my case and I returned to my stateroom to await my fate."

Waiting quietly in his room, Friesner thought of his young wife and his mother and determined to "make all the effort in my power that I at least might die as I thought a man ought to die." Tearing off his stateroom door, he rushed back to the edge of the deck and looked for a place to enter the water.

Suddenly, he saw a pair of legs sticking out from beneath the fallen decks; when he touched them, "they kicked." Although Friesner tried to lift the fallen timbers away from the trapped soldier, they were too heavy. Looking around for help, he spotted Captain Mason throwing pieces of wood into the water for others to grab onto. He called Mason over and asked for help, but Mason was physically exhausted from his efforts to help others. Friesner estimated that Mason "could not lift twenty pounds."

"I can't, I can't," Mason uttered and staggered toward the stern.

Still determined to save the soldier, Friesner managed to lift the decking enough for the man to begin squirming out. Just then, a group of soldiers, fleeing from the fire on the hurricane deck, jumped down and landed on the piece of decking he was lifting.

The man was surely dead. Friesner was about to leave when he saw the legs kick again. Friesner lifted the decking once more, and the man finally crawled out and jumped overboard. To his surprise, Friesner realized that he was Pvt. James Stuller (Company A, 58th Ohio Infantry), one of his missing guards.

Taking up his door, Friesner worked his way down to the main deck and began taking off his clothes. As he put his orders and pocketbook in his shirt pockets, Sgt. William H. Elder, also a guard with Company A, emerged from the water, stripped off his clothes, and jumped back in. As he did, Elder accidentally upset some of the wreckage that Friesner was sitting on. Friesner recalled, "[He sent] me into the water with my pants on."

Although he had managed to hang onto his stateroom door during his plunge into the water, it was quickly seized from his grasp and Friesner was forced to grab at some floating wreckage. "I collected many of these," Friesner said, "hoping to make a raft [but] many of the swimmers, disheartened and weary, seeing me use a float, swam towards me to share it." Knowing that he would surely drown if someone got hold of him, Friesner passed some boards over to the drowning men and struck out for clearer water.[31]

Passenger William Long was sound asleep in stateroom No. 10 when the partition separating his room from the next was suddenly "knocked all to pieces." Rushing out into the main cabin wearing nothing but his shirt, he ran to the stern windows, looked out, and realized that the boat was on fire. He "saw fifty persons jump overboard every minute." Hurrying back to his stateroom, he quickly pulled on his trousers and scurried down to the lower deck. After seeing "three or four hundred people go overboard," he decided to bide his time and wait for the water to clear.[32]

Senator-elect William Dunham Snow was asleep in a rear stateroom when he felt a "sensible tremor or shudder passing over the boat." Getting up, he slowly began to dress when a cloud of steam rolled through the transom window over the door leading into the main cabin. Realizing that there was something wrong, he opened his stateroom door and remembered finding "the pilothouse and at least one third of the cabin roof had fallen to the [main] deck and the boat was on fire, with a fresh breeze carrying the flames with lightning-like rapidity through the balance of the cabin."

Stepping back into his stateroom, Snow grabbed his life belt and rushed back into the main cabin. He headed toward the stern but found "a sea of heads" on the Tennessee side of the boat. As he crossed back through the cabin to try the other side, he witnessed "several husbands fasten life-preservers to their wives and children and throw them overboard into the struggling mass below." Reaching the Arkansas side, Snow found the same sea of heads but glimpsed a clear spot near the left wheel housing. Getting as close to the housing as he could, he tore a piece of wood from the side of the *Sultana* and leaped overboard from the second deck.[33]

Among the last to leave the main cabin were Seth W. Hardin, Jr., and his bride. While the other passengers had rushed headlong into the river, the two had remained close together in the hope of waiting until the last minute before attempting to escape. When the main cabin filled with smoke and fire, the newlyweds took to the water. With hundreds of drowning people clinging to one another and taking each other to the depths of the Mississippi, the two eventually became separated. Severed from his young bride, Seth Hardin tried desperately to find her, but his efforts were useless. Exhausted and brokenhearted, he floated away from the struggling mob and his lost love.[34]

Lt. Harvey Annis and his wife Anna were still awake when the explosion tore through the center of the *Sultana*. Hearing a loud noise, "something like the rattling of iron," Lieutenant Annis opened the stateroom door leading into the saloon and was enveloped in a cloud of steam. Slamming the door shut, he quickly moved to the door leading out onto the promenade guard but found that it would not budge.

Clutching her infant child to her breast, Mrs. Annis heard someone on the outside shouting that the boat was "all stove in." After putting life belts around his wife and himself, Lieutenant Annis took his child in his arms and escorted his wife through the smoke and steam-filled main cabin to the stern. Still holding his child, Annis shinnied down a rope to the lower deck and waited for his wife to follow.

Anna Annis was halfway down the rope when somebody from the hurricane deck jumped overboard and knocked into her. She went sprawling onto the main deck and down the open hatchway leading into the smoke-filled hold. Working frantically, the lieutenant pulled his wife from the hold and moved his family to the stern railing.

With his child in his arms, Harvey Annis jumped overboard. Anna Annis followed behind them, but, when she hit the water, she found that her life belt had been fastened incorrectly. Struggling in her long dress and fighting with the slipping belt, she made her way to the *Sultana*'s rudder and grabbed hold. As she hung on and tried to correct her slipping life belt, she was almost hysterical in her worry about her husband and child.[35]

12 Death on the Hurricane Deck

The rush of people from the open bow and enclosed stern was maddening, but the stampede from the densely occupied hurricane deck was far worse. The men on the flat deck knew immediately that the boat was doomed. They could easily see the wide hole in the deck, which only seconds before had been the pilothouse and texas cabin, and the two fallen smokestacks that had crumpled the forward part of the deck. Their race to the water, some twenty feet below, was almost instantaneous. The crowd was crushing.

Hurricane Deck behind Explosion

A group of men from Company G, 9th Indiana Cavalry, was situated in front of a wheel housing. Many of them, close to the hole, were scalded by escaping steam and boiling water or trapped beneath the wreckage and burned to death in the ensuing fire.

Seventeen-year-old Pvt. Henry J. Kline had gone to sleep between Pvt. George Downing and Pvt. Charles William M. King. Downing, who had caught up with the *Sultana* at the coal boat after being left behind at Memphis, was killed instantly by the explosion. Kline and King sprang to their feet and saw the gaping hole in the deck.

"Oh God, Oh mother! I am lost, I am gone!" King cried and bolted away.

Kline tried to follow him, but King pushed through the panicked mob and jumped overboard. Fortunately for King, his lieutenant, Elihue H. Swain, saw him jump and immediately followed him. Procuring a plank for King and telling him to stay calm, Swain swam behind and pushed him along to escape the crowd.[1]

Pvt. George W. Stewart, the son of a steamboat captain, and Sgt. George D. Kent (both, Company D, 40th Indiana Infantry) were near the Indiana cavalrymen on the deck. Seeing the flames rising from the hole in the center of the deck, they knew that they would have to swim or burn. Stewart urged Kent to stay with him, but Kent was soon gone and never seen again.[2]

In company with Pvt. Jacob W. Rush (Company L, 3d Ohio Cavalry), who had been raised on Lake Erie and was also familiar with boats, Stewart quickly started toward the stern. The two men reached it before most of the other soldiers realized what had happened. They witnessed the cowardly deckhands launching the sounding yawl and leaving behind the pleading wife of one of the men.

Turning toward the *Sultana*'s metallic lifeboat stored on the hurricane deck, Stewart and Rush helped to throw it overboard. "But," wrote Rush, "as soon as the boat struck the water, crowds from each deck jumped into it, striking one another, and the boat was capsized." They abandoned the idea of the lifeboat and tossed floatable objects to the men in the water before making their way to the cabin deck to look for life belts. Finding only a cabin filled with smoke and steam, Stewart and Rush scurried down to the stern cargo room in time to help several other men throw a large stageplank into the river. As had happened on the bow when planks were thrown overboard, dozens of drowning men suddenly grabbed at the floating stage. During the struggling and fighting, many of them died.

Next, Stewart and Rush tried to force a mule overboard. As stubborn as ever, in spite of the licking flames, the mule refused to leave the boat. Abandoning the animal to its fate, Stewart and Rush moved to the stern railing and prepared to jump.

At that moment, Rush recalled, "quite a number of ladies came out of the [stern] cabin, knelt upon the deck, and resting their heads upon the rail of the stern of the boat, prayed for help." Just then, seemingly out of nowhere, Captain Mason appeared. "The captain tried to quiet them by saying that he thought that help would reach us soon," Rush remembered, believing that "Captain Mason did all that any person could do under the circumstances."

With the flames "gradually working to the rear," Rush stripped out of his clothes and dove headfirst into the water. Stewart, still fully clothed, jumped in feetfirst. Breaking the surface, Rush looked back and was amazed to see that many people were still standing on the after guard and braving the flames as they waited until the last second to save themselves.[3]

Cpl. Winfield Scott Colvin (Company F, 6th Kentucky Cavalry) had never learned to swim. He waited for the mad rush to pass before he went to the remains of the texas cabin and tore off a shutter. As he was sliding down the side of the boat, a gust of flames suddenly shot out "with such force," Colvin remembered, "that I let go and fell into the water." Rising to the surface, he grabbed hold of another man and fought to keep his head above the surface, but the two soon separated. "I caught holt [*sic*] of a large trunk over another man's shoulder," he wrote, "and held to it until it floated into the wheelhouse." Grabbing hold of the paddlewheel, Colvin held on and caught his breath.[4]

Pvt. Manly C. White (Company B, 8th Michigan Cavalry) had been asleep beside the left wheel housing. After the explosion, he waited for the crowd on the hurricane deck to pass and then made his way toward one of the stairways leading down to the cabin deck. The stairway was gone, either splintered by the explosion or ripped off for a float. Although weak and sick, White headed down to the stern cargo room and took a hurried glance around. "What a sight," he wrote, "men dead and dying, parts of bodies, arms, legs, and the wreck of the boat, all in one mingled mass!"[5]

Among those responsible for the missing stairs was Pvt. Samuel C. Haines (Company G, 40th Indiana Infantry). Unable to swim, he had rushed down to the cabin deck and helped a group of prisoners tear off the stairs between the cabin and hurricane decks. Although he had intended to use the stairs to save his life, the large number of men going into the water with the stairs persuaded him to seek another means.

Working his way down to a stateroom, Haines grabbed a mattress from one of the beds and jumped into the water with it. The heavy mattress was not the best float and went down twice before Haines let it go, "having swallowed some water and almost strangled." Unable to keep his head above water, he splashed his way over to a plank with two men clinging to it and took hold. Although the men tried to fight him off, Haines was "too strong for them and succeeded in getting a firm hold on it." Finding that the other two men were good swimmers, Haines hung on and let the two unknown men maneuver the plank toward the distant shore.[6]

Just forward of the wheel housing, Alonzo A. Van Vlack was momentarily knocked unconscious by the blast. Regaining his senses, he found that the boat was "all in flames and the water was covered with men." As he stood on the hurricane deck, he looked through the hole and saw "women and children running to and fro and screaming for help" in the main cabin. Although Van Vlack tried to calm the passengers by calling down to them, he remembered that "there was so much confusion that they could not hear me." He finally gave up and decided that it was time to look out for his own life.

Sliding down a post behind the wheelhouse, Van Vlack stood on the lattice work directly in back of the paddlewheel and stripped off his outer clothing. When the water below him was free of men, he jumped in. "I saw some drown so close to me," he wrote, "that I could place my hand upon their heads as they were going down."[7]

Sgt. Joseph Stevens had gone to sleep beside his reunited brother-in-law, Sgt. William H. Finch (Company D, 18th Michigan Infantry). Immediately after the explosion, Finch, who could not swim, began "fretting and crying." Stevens, a poor swimmer himself, tried to encourage Finch by telling him not to give up, that there was always hope. The frightened

Finch, however, seeing men attempting to launch the *Sultana*'s one metallic lifeboat from the stern of the hurricane deck, suddenly ran after them and was never seen again.

Stevens was also frightened, but he stayed away from the lifeboat and jumped into the river near the stern, going down deep and "never expecting to arise again." Finally coming to the surface, he began swimming "dog fashion" and spotted Captain Mason, on the stern after guard, helping a woman and her little girl from the boat. As she hit the water, the girl's life belt slipped too far down and she flipped over. Hours later, she was found miles downriver, drowned and floating with her feet upward.

Unable to keep up his dog-paddling for long, Stevens felt his strength giving out and began calling for help. Pvt. Charles Thayer (Company B, 18th Michigan Infantry), clinging to a floating bale of hay, heard Stevens's frantic pleas and, recognizing his voice, went to the rescue. Grabbing Stevens by the hair, he pulled him back to the bale and, with the help of others who were clinging to the float, pushed him on top of it. Chilled and exhausted, Stevens soon lost consciousness.[8]

Pvt. William A. McFarland also noticed a child having trouble with a life belt. While in the water, he saw a woman "in her night clothes" rush out of her stateroom, throw a little child wearing a life belt into the river, and then rush back into the room. "The preserver had evidently been fastened on too low," McFarland recalled, "for when the little one hit the water it turned wrong end up." As he watched, the mother hurried out of the room, sprang into the water, and righted the infant, "all of which occurred in the space of a couple of minutes."

As he floated along, McFarland suddenly caught sight of the big "seven-foot Tennessean" who had been brought back, drunk and disorderly at the point of a bayonet, to the *Sultana* at Memphis. Having teased the man at the time, and realizing now that "a guilty conscience needs no accuser," McFarland imagined that the man "would drown me if he caught me" so he quickly turned away from the Tennessean and struck out downriver.[9]

Although Pvt. William Lockhart (Company E, 102d Ohio Infantry) had gone to sleep near the texas cabin, the explosion blew him clear to the stern. Getting up and catching his breath, he started forward to find his bunk mates and ran into the company sergeant, Philip L. Holtom, whose face was streaming blood. Linking up, the two were soon joined by Corporals Jacob Irons and Jacob Bierly, also from Company E. The four men agreed to stay together and started forward again to procure a plank large enough to support all of them. Suddenly, the deck gave way beneath their feet. As the others dropped into the roaring flames, Lockhart managed to grab hold of a set of steps and pull himself up and out of the hole. His face and hands were badly burned, and he lost most of his hair to the flames.

Temporarily relieving his pain by pouring a bucket of water over his head, Lockhart next went to help Sgt. Michael H. Sprinkle (Company K, 102d Ohio Infantry), try to save some soldiers injured by one of the fallen smokestacks. "I threw over ten or twelve," Lockhart remembered, "but [only] one survived." After he could do no more, Lockhart retreated to the top of a wheel housing and waited as the boat burned around him.[10]

With Lockhart gone, Sergeant Sprinkle, who estimated that he and Lockhart threw at least "fifty of those who had been wounded" into the water, felt the deck "tottering" and about to cave in. As he turned to leave, he unexpectedly saw Pvt. Charles P. Ogden, who was in his company, standing nearby in a daze. Calling out to Ogden that he would have to leave or burn, Sprinkle ran to the edge of the boat and sprang into the river. "As I came to the surface," he wrote, "the deck had fallen in and I have no doubt Charley perished in the flames."[11]

Scattered about the hurricane deck, a large number of paroled prisoners from Tennessee had found sleeping places wherever possible.

"I thought the boat was being fired upon by the enemy," Pvt. George A. King (Company B, 2d Tennessee Cavalry) recalled. Soon recognizing the cause of the blast, he quickly tore off his clothes and shinnied down a rope to the bow. He jumped overboard but swam only a few feet before being "struck by a piece of timber." Injured and dazed, King tried to get through the drowning crowd but was suddenly grabbed by someone. Fighting the man off, he swam only a short distance before spying four men going past him on one of the smaller stageplanks. King grabbed hold and rested a bit before climbing on top with the others.[12]

Pleasant M. Keeble had been asleep on the crowded hurricane deck, and his brother, John Harrison Keeble, was on the roof of the texas cabin. Waking with a feeling of being strangled by smoke, Pleasant Keeble had time only to rise to his feet before he was swept along by the surge of the crowd rushing for the safety of nearby stairs. Fearing for the life of his brother, Keeble managed to wedge his back against a stair post to stop his downward movement and then work his way up onto the railing. He forced his way onto the top of the mass of humanity and crawled across heads and shoulders until he was back on the hurricane deck. Where his brother John had been sleeping, Keeble found only a gaping hole and one of the collapsed smokestacks. He knew that John was gone forever.

Attempting to save his own life, Keeble, a nonswimmer, located a small box, "too small for much support," and climbed down to the main deck. After stripping naked, he threw the box into the river and jumped after it. Holding the box tightly against him, he avoided the drowning crowd by staying close to the *Sultana* and waited for a large piece of siding to burn away from the side of the boat.

When the siding crashed into the water, Keeble and five other men made their way to it and grabbed hold. Unfortunately, an exhausted mule also spotted the piece of siding and swam straight toward it. The mule got its front feet on the siding and kept trying to get up on it, "almost capsizing the raft." Each time the mule raised itself, Keeble fought it off. Man finally prevailed, and the tired beast either drowned or swam away for easier pickings.[13]

Paddlewheel Housings

Perhaps twenty minutes after the explosion of the boilers, while the waters around the *Sultana* were still teeming with frightened men, women, and children, the twin paddlewheel housings burned away from the superstructure. One after the other, they toppled into the crowd below and crushed to death many people in the water.

The wheel housings had been supported by counterweighting one against the other with a bottom-chord cantilever. The explosion had loosened the cross chains forming the cantilever system, which caused the housings to tilt slightly away from the superstructure, but they were still upright. As the inferno intensified at the center of the boat, the growing flames ate away the wooden posts supporting the cross chains and the truss system was unable to hold up the two huge paddlewheels. Gravity suddenly took over.

The left paddlewheel and housing were the first to fall. Still attached to the base of the hull, the housing fell perpendicular to the *Sultana* and gave her the appearance of a bizarre outrigger canoe. The toppled structure, caught by the strong Mississippi current, suddenly began turning the *Sultana* in a 180-degree circle.

Shortly afterward, the right paddlewheel and housing burned through and fell, but the damage had already been done. The *Sultana* continued to turn completely around until she was facing downstream, which was opposite from her original heading.

Private Lockhart, atop one of the wheel housings, was an expert swimmer and wondered whether he should jump into the congested waters below or wait for the crowd to disperse. Fate stepped in, however, before he could decide. Without any warning, the sidewheel housing suddenly toppled and pitched him far away from the vessel, beyond the reach of the drowning soldiers. Thrown into the river without a float, Lockhart "struck out without anything."[14]

Otto Bardon was inside the stern cargo room and standing guard over the open hatchway leading into the hold when he saw two friends heading toward one of the wheel housings. He decided that it was time to leave his precarious spot. He picked up a thin board and raced after his friends. Reaching a spot near the wheel housing, Bardon was about to go overboard when a young soldier came up to him.

"You jump first," the soldier said, "I cannot swim."

Incredulous, Bardon said, "You must paddle your own canoe. I can't help you."

Then, without another word, Bardon jumped into the cold river. "I went down so far that I let go of my board and paddled to get on top of the water." He strangled twice but finally came to the surface. Just as he gulped a breath of air, the young soldier from the boat jumped next to him and caught hold of him. Taken down, Bardon strangled twice again before breaking free. "By this time I was about played out," he admitted and slowly made his way toward the paddlewheel.

"I clung to it until I tore off all of my clothes," he remembered. At the same time, he looked at those around him who were also clinging to the lifesaving wheel. To his surprise, he found he was next to Pvt. Ignatious Saunders (Company F, 102d Ohio Infantry).

"Saunders," Bardon said, after catching his breath, "here is a door under the wheel. Let us get it out."

Pulling the door from under the wheel, they found that it had a number of glass panels in it and would make a precarious buoy.

"Let this go," Bardon instructed. "Here is a whole door."

They watched the glass-panel door float free and a number of other soldiers on the wheel jump after it. With the attention of the others drawn to that door, Bardon and Saunders pulled the solid door free and set off by themselves. They had gone only a short distance when another man swam up and climbed across the center of the door. Ignoring the uninvited stranger, Bardon and Saunders continued to guide their door toward clear water. Then, Bardon recalled, "I looked back and saw the wheelhouse fall—it had burned off and fell over. If we had remained there one minute longer it would have buried us in the fire."[15]

An exhausted Lt. Elbert J. Squire was clinging tightly to one of the paddlewheel blades as several men on the opposite side tried to climb out of the water. "This excessive weight on one side caused the wheel to make a partial revolution," Squire remembered. "This carried me well out of the water, but the poor fellows on the other side were submerged and the wheel stopped, leaving me well up towards the top." Taking advantage of the situation, he rested a few moments and then peeled off his heavy clothing.

"I feared the fire would soon cause the wheel and the wheelhouse to fall from the boat and sink [so] I determined to reach the outer edge [of the wheel]." Inching his way along, he succeeded in getting only about halfway when the housing suddenly gave way and toppled over. "The rush of water broke my hold, and I was carried along, nearly drowning."

When the wheel housing fell, the outward side with the name *Sultana* was submerged. The inside wall, which remained slightly above the water, became the top.

"Floating on my back in this prison," Squire wrote, he managed to locate a small hole burnt in the upper surface and broke away at the charred edges until he could wiggle his body up and out. "Portions of the wheelhouse were still burning, and the heat of the steamer was such as to make it necessary for me to let myself down into the water to prevent roasting." Knowing that he would either burn with the boat or drown with the slowly sinking wheel housing if he stayed where he was, he found a floating window blind and set off downstream for Memphis.[16]

Sgt. William Carver (Company B, 3d Tennessee Cavalry) was inside the wheel housing when it toppled over. "It broke loose and fell into the water and drew me under," he recalled. As he went down, Carver felt a heavy iron rod in the wheel strike him in the side. Taking hold of it, he rose to the surface and fought to keep his head above the cold water.

"When the flames came towards me I buried myself in the water as long as I could," he said. Despite his best efforts, Carver was severely burned on the right side of his face and his right shoulder. "In some way," he admitted, "I got on a board with a comrade, and we floated to a drift pile on the Arkansas side of the river." As he waited to be rescued, he undoubtedly wondered what had become of his father, fifty-nine-year-old Pvt. James Carver (also of Company B), perhaps the oldest soldier on board the *Sultana*.[17]

High up on the hurricane deck, Pvt. Isaac Van Nuys (Company D, 57th Indiana Infantry) looked down at the fallen wheel housing and concluded that, if he had trouble with the drowning crowd, he would go back toward the housing. Jumping into the water, Van Nuys went down deep and came up sputtering and reaching for the fallen housing. Catching hold, he pulled himself out of the water and surveyed his situation.

"I was so close to the burning boat that I had to let myself down in the water to keep from being burned," he noted. Finding a few pieces of wood, he started to build a raft. Tying the two longest boards together with his army suspenders, Van Nuys recalled that he then "nailed a board across the other end with a chunk of wood; all the time lowering myself into the water every few minutes to keep from being burned." When he completed his raft, he jumped astride it and pushed away from the sinking paddle wheel housing and started downstream.[18]

Swimming on the opposite side of the boat, Pvt. Chester D. Berry suddenly heard a "crash of breaking timbers" and looked back at the *Sultana*. "[T]he wheelhouse or covering for the wheel, . . . had broken away partially from the hurricane deck, and a poor fellow had been in the act of stepping from the hurricane deck onto the wheelhouse." The right wheel housing "reached an angle of about forty-five degrees" and then suddenly stopped, "till it nearly burned up." Watching in horror, Berry could see that the man who had been attempting to step onto it had "got no further, for [the housing] broke and let him part way through, then held him, as in an iron vice, till he burned to death." For the rest of his life, Berry would "hear the poor fellow's screams, as the forked flames swept around him."[19]

13 The Horror of Fire

William H. Wooldridge was sound asleep in his mother's house, about a mile upriver from the *Sultana*, when he was suddenly awakened by the noise of the explosion. "It sounded like a hundred earthquakes," he said. "It rolled and re-echoed for minutes in the woodlands." He thought that the noise was the roar of a cannon and paid little attention to it until his room suddenly lit up with an eerie light. Calling to his mother, William raced out to the front porch. "Quite a distance out in the river we saw the steamer burning," he recalled. "The flame was shooting far up into the sky. It was so light, I could have picked up a pin."[1]

The gunboat USS *Tyler* was tied up at the U.S. navy yard just above Memphis. William H. C. Michael, officer of the deck, was on routine duty when the boat's quartermaster reported that a vessel was on fire upriver. Grabbing his field glasses, Michael could see the burning vessel but she was too far away to identify. Unable to go to the rescue because the *Tyler* was undergoing repairs, Michael could only watch.[2]

William B. Floyd, acting master's mate on the tinclad USS *Grossbeak*, had watched the *Sultana* leave the coal yard at Memphis and steam upriver. "Shortly after she had passed out of sight," Floyd recalled, "I noticed a red glow in the sky, which very soon showed plainly as a fire. I cannot describe the horror I felt at the thought that perhaps it was the

Sultana on fire." Finding the *Grossbeak*'s quartermaster, Floyd asked him what he thought the light was.

Aided by a powerful telescope, the quartermaster was soon able to say, "A large steamer on fire and lying in shore."

Using his own field glasses, Floyd steadied them against an upright post. "I then discovered she drifted past the glass, which showed that she was floating and not lying in shore." Fearing the worst, Floyd ran to awaken the senior master's mate. The senior officer watched the burning boat for a time but "did not seem much excited about it." When Floyd asked him if they should go to the rescue, he said, "No." The *Grossbeak*'s captain was in town, and the senior master's mate did not want to take the responsibility of ordering the tinclad's boilers fired up. His decision made, the senior officer returned to his quarters and left an excited Floyd standing by himself.[3]

Main Deck: Behind the Flames

Even before the twin paddlewheels fell, the soldiers remaining in the stern cargo room and on the crowded after guard had felt the rapidly growing flames licking hard at their heels. Their position was untenable.

Major Fidler and Captain McCown had descended from the main cabin and called for fire buckets, but the buckets had been taken from their racks long before the disaster. The soldiers had used them to obtain drinking water, thus inadvertently helping to seal their own fate.

A young woman suddenly appeared and rushed toward the water. "My mother, oh, my mother!" she cried, looking down at the mob struggling in the river.

Fidler raced to the woman's side and then sprang into the water. Intent on saving the woman's mother, Fidler was caught in the crowd; neither he nor the mother was ever seen again.[4]

In spite of his serious injuries, McCown was suddenly in charge. He could see about "eight hundred men in the water drowning," but he knew that the water was the only safe haven. He successfully calmed a number of soldiers and spread the word for everyone to strip off their heavy woolen uniforms and jump overboard. After waiting until most of the others had left, McCown slipped into the water and swam away.[5]

Chief Engineer Wintringer stayed on the burning boat for about twenty minutes. When he had tried to get close to the fire to determine if it could be brought under control, the panicked soldiers and burning rubbish soon convinced him that fighting the fire was out of the question. Knowing that the *Sultana* was doomed, Wintringer finally grabbed a shutter and went into the cold water.[6]

James Wallace McDonald and his brother Francis had remained on the afterdeck as long as possible.

"We'd better swim for it," James said.

"Jim," Francis answered, "we'll never make it."

Although he was a better swimmer than James, Francis felt that a year and a half in a Confederate prison had left them both too weak to force their way through the maddened crowd.

Trying to inspire his brother by example, James jumped overboard; someone instantly grabbed his coat and pulled him under. Fighting free, he climbed back on board the *Sultana* and took off his clothes. After finding a few planks to help him float, he glanced at Francis. Apparently resigned to whatever fate had in store for him, Francis was kneeling in prayer. James knew that he probably would never again see Francis alive, but he jumped back into the water and fought his way through the clutching, grabbing mob.[7]

After losing the battle with the white horse on the stern after guard, Cpl. Albert W. King and his three friends waited on the stern for things to calm down. Although all four had agreed to stick together, King remembered that his friends "were now with me, but a minute later they had disappeared." Left by himself, King wrote that he "climbed the stern railing and jumped [as] far as I could to avoid the crowd just below me."

Although he started swimming away from the boat, his head suddenly struck the hull of the *Sultana*. "I had got turned in the water by coming in contact with drowning men," he wrote. Turning around, he started back through the drowning crowd again.[8]

Ogilvie E. Hamblin had remained on the boat as long as possible because he knew that he could never survive in the crowded waters with only one arm. "I remained on board the boat until the fire and steam drove me off," he remembered. Taking "every stitch of my clothing off as coolly as though about to take a bath," Hamblin screwed up his courage "to the sticking point," and jumped overboard. "Having but one arm to swim with I found I could do nothing against the strong current, and so let myself float."[9]

"I remained on board the hull of the boat for perhaps twenty or thirty minutes," Pvt. Commodore Smith recalled, "throwing overboard all the loose boards and timbers and everything that would float to assist those in the water. . . . And now occurred the hardest task of my life. [T]he wounded begged us to throw them overboard, choosing to drown instead of being roasted to death."

Smith and a few other men stayed on the stern and performed what Smith said was "the most heart-rending task that human beings could be called upon to perform—that of throwing overboard, into the jaws of certain death by drowning, those comrades who were unable . . . to help themselves." Some of the men, Smith found, "were so badly scalded by the hot water and steam . . . that the flesh was falling from their bones." As carefully as they could, Smith and the others dragged the injured to the edge of the boat and dropped them over. Smith would never forget "the gurgling sounds [and] the dying groans" and seeing the injured men "writhing in the water and finally . . . sink to rise no more."[10]

Pvt. Levi G. Morgan was helping with the wounded when he was approached by Pvt. Harrison Spafford (Company B, 102d Ohio Infantry).

"Morgan," Spafford cried, "what am I going to do?"

"Get a plank," Morgan said.

"I cannot find any," the helpless Spafford responded.

Taking Spafford in tow, Morgan went over to a pile of debris and pulled out a large plank. He threw the board into the water and made Spafford jump after it. Morgan then decided that it was time to get off the boat himself.

A good swimmer, Morgan watched for his chance and jumped in. He took nothing with him. "My only fear was that someone would get hold of me and pull me down," he wrote.

He swam as fast as he could and was able to get through the struggling crowd.[11]

Others who helped with the injured were Sgt. Christian M. Nisley who was himself scalded, burned, and cut after falling through the cabin deck, and Captain Mason, who had done all he could on the hurricane and cabin decks and was now lending a hand on the main deck. As Nisley wrote, "In company with Capt. Mason of the *Sultana*," he tried to "extricate those who were caught fast by pieces of the boat." But, as the fire continued to grow, Nisley decided to save his own life.

Looking down at the water, Nisley noticed that the crowd had dwindled. "A great many had sunk to rise no more," he noted, "and there were but few floating and swimming about that would be liable to drag me down." Grabbing a piece of wood, he said a few words to Captain Mason and went over the edge. "Capt. Mason was the last man I talked with while on board the boat, and he was still on the boat when I left," Nisley wrote.[12] With the stern cargo room of the *Sultana* engulfed in flames, Nisley might have been the last person to see J. Cass Mason alive.

With the fall of the twin wheel housings, the intense flames soon ate through the rear wall of the stern cargo room and threatened the few nonswimmers who still clung to the after guard. As the doomed boat began to turn, the devouring flames finally forced the remaining soldiers into the cold waters of the Mississippi.

One of the very last to leave the stern was Cpl. Perry Howard Alexander (Company G, 115th Ohio Infantry). Alexander had gone to sleep on the hurricane deck but had been shoved off the stern by the panicked crowd. Instead of landing in the water, however, he struck the guard rail surrounding the main deck and fell heavily onto the after guard. Striking the small of his back, "so badly that it was impossible to move," Alexander had been forced to remain in place, trying to regain some of his mobility, while those around and above him continued to plunge into the river.

Now, with the *Sultana* "nearly burned [so] that the heat was unbearable," Alexander summoned enough strength to pull himself up and over the guard rail and gingerly slipped into the water.[13]

The *Sultana*'s huge wooden rudder was the only component of the stern that was still untouched by the roaring flames. Although hundreds of people had died in the water below the stern, a few had found relief by clinging tightly to the rudder.

Nathaniel M. Foglesong, still afraid to jump into the water, had managed to grab the top of the rudder by reaching out from the stern railing. Wrapping his arms and legs around it, he slid slowly below the edge of the main deck.

"Get off from me," Foglesong heard from below him. Looking down, he saw nine other men clinging to the rudder, one atop the other, each calling for those above to get off.

"In a minute," he casually replied. As Foglesong remembered, "being the top one [I] kept quiet."

Although he had no one sitting on his shoulders, he soon found that being on top also had disadvantages: "Soon the coals from above began to fall on my head and shoulders and I began to think that I must get out of there."

Noticing a burnt piece of decking floating nearby, he encouraged those below him to try swimming to it.

"My God," he was told, "if we let go of this we shall drown."

"Let us die like men, helping ourselves," Foglesong answered, "for God helps those who help themselves in this case and I believe in all others."

Still, the other men did not leave, and the hot coals continued to fall on Foglesong.

"The coals came thicker and faster so that I had to brush them off my head and shoulders with one hand and hang onto the rudder with the other," he wrote. Finally, unable to take it any longer, he mustered up his courage.

"Here goes for ninety days!" he shouted and jumped.

Striking the water, Foglesong went down three times before grabbing someone by the heel. Pulling himself up, he gulped a breath of air just before the man kicked him loose. Sinking again, he caught the same man by the ankle and simultaneously grabbed a wire cable hanging down from the *Sultana*. Nearly exhausted, he grabbed a piece of scantling that was floating nearby and then, "kicking and paddling like a dog," finally reached the piece of decking.

"My God, is that you?" he heard as he climbed up.

Holding to the same piece of wreckage was Sgt. Edward Burnes (Company G, 18th Michigan Infantry), who recognized Foglesong.

"Yes," Foglesong choked out, "all that is left of me."

Foglesong crawled onto the float and bumped into the bodies of a deckhand and two women, who had died from scalds. He found a piece of siding and a door caught under the decking and used the siding to shove the door back to those still clinging to the rudder. With his help, "they all got upon the piece of deck."[14]

Anna Annis, distraught with grief over the loss of her husband and infant child, had also sought refuge on the rudder. She stated that she "held onto the rudder till I was obliged to let go by fire." While the others on the rudder went toward the safety of Foglesong's piece of decking, Mrs. Annis took "to a small piece of board." Then, giving in to her sorrow, she began to panic and thrash about wildly, crying out, "My husband and baby are gone."[15]

Albert King was floating in the water near Mrs. Annis. He was turned around in the water and shoved under "by some person jumping upon me." He clawed his way to the surface and, he recalled, found "a lady . . . beside me grasping me and calling for help." Breaking away from the hysterical woman, King swam over to a piece of wreckage, then went back for Mrs. Annis. After helping her onto the debris, he climbed up beside her and "left the burning boat quite a distance [behind.]"[16]

The last man on the stern was gone. Only flaming debris and burning bodies remained on the back half of the *Sultana*. Some thirty or forty minutes after the explosion of the boilers, the rapidly advancing flames had devoured the stern of the sidewheeler. As the *Sultana* slowly rotated, her nose headed downstream and the slight wind from the north changed the direction of the flames. They now threatened the soldiers and passengers on the open bow.

Main Deck: In Front of the Flames

After the explosion, hundreds of men on the bow had pushed and shoved for the safety of the Mississippi. Some were able to avoid the crush and had remained on the bow. Hundreds more, escaping from the forward hurricane and cabin decks, continued to descend on the bow.

After coming down from the cabin deck, Pvt. Jacob Horner (Company A, 102d Ohio Infantry) had been on the bow for about twenty minutes, "looking at the poor boys in the water." Finally deciding that he would "rather drown than burn to death" and being a good swimmer,

Horner slid into the cold water. As he swam along, drowning men called for him to help them. "I thought they might get hold of me, so I swam away," Horner admitted. Finding two small boards, he tucked them under his breast. "You have no idea how they helped me," he reported. "[B]y the light of the [burning] boat," Horner saw the tops of the submerged trees sticking above the surface of the floodwaters and "lit out for the timber."[17]

Sgt. William Fies had remained on the *Sultana* for as long as possible. "[It] was now apparent the fire was fast gaining headway," he wrote, "and would soon burn through the slight barrier formed by portions of the upper decks which had fallen down, and which had up to this time kept most of the flames from reaching those of us who were on the bow of the boat." Glancing about, he spotted Sgt. Robert White (Company I, 64th Ohio Infantry) standing with one arm around the jackstaff.

"Bob, what is to be done?" Fies asked him.

"Billy," White said, "I guess we will all be drowned or burned up."

Although Fies thought White might be correct, he was determined "to at least make an effort for my life."

Turning to look for something to help him in the water, Fies recalled that he found only "splinters of boards; everything else had been taken, even to a box which had contained a live alligator." Finding nothing better, Fies gathered an armload of splinters and tied them together with a length of rope. By now, the two wheel housings had toppled over and the *Sultana* had begun her turn, causing the flames to blow toward the bow. "About this time, the fire had burned through the wreckage, and it became apparent to those of us who were still on board [that we] would either be compelled to jump overboard or burn up." Electing to jump, Fies sprang into the water only to be jumped on by someone whom he thought "must have weighed at least 200 pounds." Coming to the surface, Fies found his bundle of splinters gone and began paddling away from the wreck when a drowning soldier suddenly grabbed him.

"I was just about gone myself," Fies recalled, "but I kicked him loose." Swimming the best he could with his dislocated shoulder, Fies kept his head above water "at least part of the time" until a struggling soldier with a "nice large board" came near. Catching hold, Fies threw his disabled arm over the board and rested.

"For God's sake let go," the other soldier yelled, "I am drowning."

"You fool," Fies said. "Keep cool, this board is large enough to save both of us and several more if managed right."

Panicking, the unknown soldier began spinning the board in an attempt to shake Fies off, but, as Fies remembered, "[I] kept very cool, occasionally putting my hands on it, thus keeping myself afloat," and it was the other man who kept "going over with it at every revolution." In time, the soldier wore himself out and slipped beneath the waters of the Mississippi. Now in full possession of the board, Fies headed in the direction of the riverbank.[18]

Approximately four hundred people were huddled on the bow of the *Sultana* when she began her turn. As the boat started to head south, the northern breeze swept the intense flames toward the bow. For a short time, perhaps only minutes, the cracked main stairway and fallen debris from the upper decks acted as a firebreak, which allowed the people on the bow a few moments to prepare before the flames forced them into the water.

Cpl. Myrum W. Gregory had scavenged a couple of door panels and a large coil of rope while the firebreak withstood the flames. Securing one end of the rope to the boat, he dropped the free end overboard. He recalled that he waited calmly until "the heat was more than I could bear" before climbing down. A good swimmer, Gregory admitted making "good use of [my ability], that is, as good as I could after being six months at Andersonville prison." Using the door panels as floats, he set out downriver for Memphis.[19]

Cpl. Adam Leake (Company B, 3d Tennessee Cavalry) was standing near the jackstaff when the boat swung around. He wrote that this "sent the flames in a solid mass against us, sending us in a body overboard." As he went over, he grabbed hold of a coil of rope and let out the length until he hit the water. He recalled that the rope "kept me above water and thus saved my life, as I could not swim at all."[20]

Most of the men on the bow left the *Sultana* during the turn. John Lowery Walker estimated that there were still "perhaps eighty or one hundred of us on the bow [when the boat] swung around and the wind blew the flames directly on us." Having stripped off his clothes, Walker found that the flames "scorched our naked bodies [as] we all made a frantic rush for the water."

In the middle of the crowd, Walker turned from the fire and pushed those in front. At the same time, those behind turned and shoved him. "I pushed those in front, those behind pushed us, and we all went into the river in a bunch," he wrote. "When I touched the water it was a great relief to my scorched body."[21]

Few men were left on the bow by the time that the *Sultana* had completed the turn. As the flames ate through the main stairway firebreak, they roared out over the open bow and drove the last stalwart survivors into the water. Pvt. Asa E. Lee (Company A, 6th Indiana Cavalry) was among the last to leave the boat. When he jumped into the river, the *Sultana* was entirely wrapped in flames.[22]

The men in the water were fighting one another for the last piece of floating wreckage or the last bale of hay. Suddenly, one of the sisters with the U.S. Christian Commission appeared on the flame-enshrouded bow. Looking down at the struggling mass of humanity "fighting like demons . . . in the mad endeavor to save their lives, [and] actually destroying each other and themselves by their wild actions," she began to call to the men, "talking to them, urging them to be men." Her soothing words, combined with the sight of this angel of mercy standing so bravely against the backdrop of flames, had an effect that "finally succeeded in getting [the men] quieted down, clinging to the ropes and chains that hung over the bow of the boat."

"The flames now began to lap around her with their fiery tongues," and the men pleaded with the woman to jump into the water and save herself.

Shaking her head, she spoke loudly, "I might lose my presence of mind and be the means of death of some of you."

Then, as the men continued with their pleas, the woman "folded her arms quietly over her bosom and burned, a voluntary martyr to the men she had so lately quieted."[23]

An hour after the explosion, it is likely that not a single living person was on board the *Sultana*. As she floated downstream on the current and pierced the night with the brilliance of her flames, a few men hung below the guards. They grasped tightly to ropes or chains or mooring rings to avoid the conflagration overhead. On this last phase of her final voyage, the *Sultana* carried on her decks only the bodies of those killed in the explosion, trapped in the wreckage, or trampled underfoot during the human exodus.

Standing on the front porch of their house, completely surrounded by the flooded river, young Wooldridge and his mother, with overseer Hill beside them, watched the incredible sight of the burning *Sultana*. "We could see timber falling and we heard the cries of hundreds for help," the boy recalled. "We saw many jumping into the water to save themselves from being burned to death. We could see plainly as they struggled in the river. Their cries for help were pitiful. They were indescribable."

As the boat grew into "a massive ball of fire," Hill and William hurried to get the skiff that William had borrowed the day before. Halfway to the skiff, they were hailed by a dozen soldiers clinging desperately to a piece of wreckage. Taking a long pole, Hill held it out to the survivors and pulled them safely to shore. While Mrs. Wooldridge aided the men, Hill and William continued on to the skiff.

"[I] did the most I could for a little fellow," William recalled. Sitting in the bow of the boat, he "occasionally [gave] a lift to a struggling fellow." Carefully avoiding large crowds, for fear that they would grab the boat and cause it to capsize, the two rescuers managed to save some forty-five men. "We took ashore all we could pick up and laying them on the ground, built a big fire," William wrote. With their farm surrounded by water, the Wooldridges had no way to report the disaster to Memphis. As the *Sultana* drifted farther downriver, William, his mother, and overseer Hill could only tend to the men they had rescued and hope for the best for the others.[24]

Miles downriver from the site of the explosion, a "very cold" Pvt. Wesley Lee floated along as he hung tightly to two boards. He recalled that "soon the lights of [Memphis] became visible" and in spite of "getting colder all the time," he worked with renewed vigor and the "thought of home."

"When I came in front of the wharfboat," he wrote, "two men came out with a lantern and I called for help." Pulled into a small skiff, the half-frozen Lee was soon seated by the fire in the wharfboat.

"When I informed them the *Sultana* had blown up and her crew was in the water," Lee wrote, "the telegraph operator went to his instrument and in a few minutes a steamer was moving out and picking up men."[25] Within minutes of the news reaching Memphis, the waterfront was a beehive of activity. The able-bodied people of the Good Samaritan City set out immediately to do all they could for those who had already been through so much.

14 The Cold Mississippi

By the time Wesley Lee was pulled on board the Memphis wharfboat, the majority of the people who had been on the *Sultana* were dead. Those still alive, however, who were floating in the icy waters of the Mississippi, never gave up hope of being delivered from their hell on earth.

Cpl. William A. Hulit (Company A, 64th Ohio Infantry) had kept on his woolen pants while taking to the water. As he swam along unsupported, they became waterlogged and weighed him down. Spotting a "large cottonwood sapling floating down root foremost," Hulit swam over and grabbed hold. As he began to strip off his pants, he was suddenly startled by the sound of a voice.

"[T]o my surprise a man was holding to the branches at the top." Afraid that Hulit's weight would sink the tree, the soldier "objected very much" to Hulit's grabbing hold. "It would have been sufficient to carry both of us," Hulit thought, "but he continued to object to me being a partner."

"Comrade," Hulit said, "as soon as I can get my heavy trousers off, I will let you have your tree to yourself."

After slipping the suspenders off his shoulders and kicking out of his trousers, Hulit was true to his word and continued downriver.

"Almost exhausted and strangling and swallowing much water," he felt relieved when he suddenly spotted a small board in front of him. "This little board was a godsend to me," he felt as he took hold. Chilled and numbed by the cold and icy waters, Hulit lost all track of distance and time. "How long I had been in the water or how far I had traveled I could not tell, but it seemed almost an age."

Only half aware of his surroundings, Hulit unexpectedly ran into something in the dark water. "I put my hand on it to keep it off and it was rough with pitch and gravel." The object turned out to be a large piece of the hurricane deck, and Hulit quickly climbed aboard. Now exposed to both the cold water and the chilling night breeze, he "floated a long time, chilled almost to unconsciousness."[1]

Pvt. Hugh Kinser (Company E, 50th Ohio Infantry) and another man were clinging to a board when they were swept up in a swirling eddy. "As we were going around," Kinser recalled, "a person caught on to our board, who said she was a woman." Spun in the eddy, the three went "around once or twice [before] she let go and floated down on her own."

Shot out of the eddy, Kinser and his companion were making for the semisubmerged trees when Kinser found a discarded pair of pants. "[T]his was a lucky find for me," Kinser wrote, "as I had divested myself of all unnecessary clothing before I jumped into the water." Reaching the trees, the two men grabbed hold and hung on. "When I reached the tree I was too much exhausted to lift myself upon it for some time," Kinser said. Finally summoning enough strength, Kinser climbed into the tree and slipped on the trousers. "My companion was in great distress as soon as he got out of the water," Kinser noted. "He was so badly scalded that his face, hands and whole body began to blister."[2]

Mrs. Perry was clinging tightly to a door with a half-dozen soldiers. Only she and one young soldier kept their heads and spoke encouraging words, while the others "wept aloud" and sent out "shrieks of utter despair." One soldier noticed that Mrs. Perry was wearing a life belt. Intent on getting the belt for himself, he suddenly attacked her.

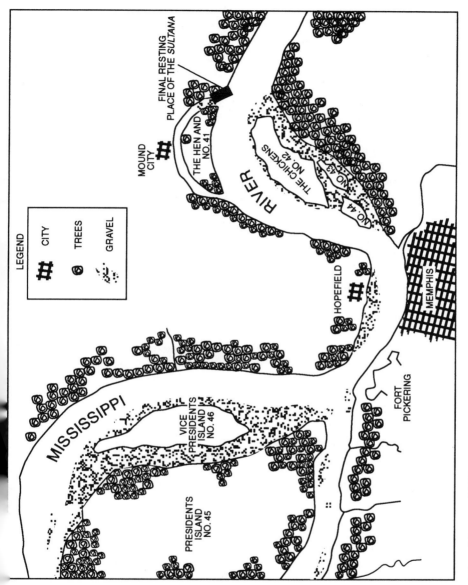

Memphis area, 1865.

Shoved underwater, Mrs. Perry fought back. She managed to break away and regain the door. As she caught her breath, the crazed soldier came at her again. The young soldier shouted that he knew the identity of her attacker and was ashamed for his cowardly act. Unaffected, the crazed man grabbed Mrs. Perry and forced her underwater a second time.

Mrs. Perry was close to drowning, but she fought with a fury and momentarily drove the man away. Breaking the surface, she noticed another floating door not far away and swam toward it. Just as she reached out to take hold, "a soldier that had been clinging to it arose to the surface," and warned her off. Startled, she told the soldier that the first door was too crowded and put out her hands again. The soldier, bolting at her, thrust her back into the water. Cold and tired, she returned to the first door.[3]

Many soldiers, especially those thrown from the *Sultana* by the explosion and those who had jumped overboard immediately afterward, had been in the icy water for almost an hour. Their limbs were numb and beginning to cramp.

Walter G. Porter worked his way over to the riverbank only to find, as he recalled, "when I got to land, or where the land is most of the time, . . . it was covered with water." Climbing into one of the treetops, he wrote that he "had to rub myself considerably to keep warm, as I did not have any clothing on."[4]

Capt. J. Walter Elliott was on a mattress with another soldier when, after floating "nearly five miles," they struck a drift and were able to climb into the top of a large tree. "Chilled and benumbed," he wrote, "I could not sit up." Finding three doses of quinine in his pocket, he took them all and "by vigorous rubbing soon was able to stand and walk." Elliott revived but found that his companion, still on the mattress, was unable to garner enough strength to get into the tree.

"I held the mattress to the drift," Elliott noted, "and with a keen switch I struck the man, . . . striking first one place, then another." Although the man begged Elliott to stop, the beating had the desired effect of circulating the man's blood. Before long, he was able to climb into the tree. Elliott wrote, "I hope he has forgiven me that whipping."[5]

Despite floating downriver with a badly burned and blistered left arm, with his army drawers hanging about his ankles, George N. Young recalled that he felt "happy, for I believed that I was going to get out somewhere." Swimming in close to a cluster of semisubmerged trees, Young was within a few feet of a branch when he was seized with severe cramps in both legs. "[W]ith one hand almost disabled . . . it was impossible for me to keep above the surface," he wrote. Panicking, he began to sink faster. Only after regaining his composure was he able to rise to the surface. "The cramp abating, I paddled with my uninjured hand up to the tree, and, seizing a limb within reach, drew myself from the water. As soon as I was sufficiently rested to make any exertion, I gathered up my drawers . . . and drew on pants I had picked up in the river." He soon found, however, that "the chill night wind pierced my clothing like needles, and feeling a benumbing chilliness creeping over me, I dropped back into the water. Whoever prayed for 'light, more light,' more earnestly than did I . . . clinging to that tree in the darkness and cold!"[6]

Some soldiers, chilled by the cold water and unable to reach shore because of flooded riverbanks, experienced cramped limbs and felt the first sleepy effects of hypothermia.

John Lowery Walker was clinging to a board as he floated in the darkness and listened to the unseen men around him. "While floating down the river many ludicrous, as well as pathetic sounds reached my ears," he recalled. "Some were pleading for help, some praying, some cursing." He heard one man praying incessantly for help; "by this effort he was of course expending much of his strength." Suddenly, out of the enclosing gloom, Walker heard a "good-natured comrade" call back to the praying man to "quit his damned praying and go to swimming—that would do him more good at the time."

Submerged in the icy water, Walker began to feel numb and sleepy. "During the long three and a half or four hours' struggle in the water my greatest difficulty towards the end was in keeping awake. I found myself going to sleep a number of times, and I would then work hard with my arms and legs to arouse myself."[7]

George S. Schmutz, his face badly scalded, was grateful for the cooling effect of the water as he constantly dipped his head beneath the surface to relieve the pain. He realized, however, the trouble that he would face from prolonged immersion in icy water. "[A]s the water was somewhat cool, I began to fear cramp, so I exerted myself to keep up circulation," he wrote. Moving rapidly downriver, he came upon a "moon-eyed" soldier who could not see at night. Linking up, the two swimmers continued toward Memphis.[8]

Lewis W. McCrory was swimming along with his pocketbook containing "over a hundred dollars" gripped between the last two fingers of his right hand and a valise holding "a good suit of citizen's clothes." He switched the valise "from one hand to the other as either arm grew tired." Swimming side by side with McCrory was Sgt. John Cornwell (Company A, 100th Ohio Infantry).

"After awhile [Cornwell] called out to me that he could hold out no longer, but I cheered him up, urging him to try a little longer," McCrory recalled. "He tried awhile longer and then cried out again that it was no use, he must sink." Urging Cornwell to fight on, McCrory wrote, "We had gone about two miles [when] he called out a third time and sank immediately, and I saw him no more." McCrory was "startled a little" by Cornwell's death and let go of the waterlogged valise, but he managed to hang onto the pocketbook.

"Now," McCrory wrote, "what seems strange to me is that in a very short time after throwing away my valise both arms became entirely help-less and I was obliged to turn over on my back and float in order to rest." Unfamiliar with the effects of hypothermia, McCrory was experiencing a numbness in his limbs. "After floating awhile I swam a short distance when my arms gave out again." Forced to turn on his back a second time, McCrory repeated his earlier motions until he was lucky enough to spot a log "upon which I crawled," he remembered, "and where I remained."[9]

Though wet and cold, George F. Robinson recalled that "some amus-ing things transpired." While drifting along, he came across a man on a beer keg. "He would crawl up on it and pray," Robinson wrote, "[but] he got up a little too far and over he went still hanging to it." Coming to the surface the man sputtered, "Damn this thing, it will drown me yet."

Passing the man on the keg, Robinson heard someone calling out to the man in army slang, "Morgan, here is your mule."

"It was a mule that saved my life," Robinson wrote, "and a dead one at that." Chilled through, he thought he was "almost a goner" when he spotted a dead mule floating along because of the air trapped in its lungs. Finding that the dead animal was "not quite cold," Robinson crawled onto it and continued downriver. He eventually lost consious-ness.[10] It was inevitable that a few of the survivors would encounter some of the government's horses and mules from the *Sultana*.

Spitting blood from a blow to the chest caused by the explosion, Pvt. Perry S. Summerville (Company K, 2d Indiana Cavalry) was swimming along on two long rails when he heard a horse nearby. Surrounded by darkness, he tried to get near the horse to grab on, but he recalled that "when he came close enough, I distinguished at least a dozen men clinging to him." Fearing that the men would snatch his rails, he steered clear of the animal and continued on.

Placing one rail under his feet and the other under his arms, Sum-merville wrote that he "lay so near the surface that I suffered extremely from the cold." Although "almost freezing," he worried more about his socks, which had worked partly off his feet and were catching on the rear rail. Despite almost sinking while struggling with his socks, he continued downriver toward Memphis.[11]

Philip L. Horn and several other men were huddled together on a piece of decking when they encountered a mule. As Horn explained, "We were clinging with a death grip to the wreck, when a mule—another floating waif of this disaster—swam along and dumped us all into the river, compelling us all to exert our strength to gain our hold on the wreck." The group regained their piece of decking and floated on.[12]

Holding tightly to the tail of a swimming horse, William Marshall Pryor knew that, if the horse tired and sank, he too would drown. As luck would have it, the horse swam past the warm, floating remains of a horse that had recently died, and Marsh Pryor quickly grabbed hold. Buoyed from the air trapped in its lungs, the dead horse kept Pryor warm with its body heat as he waited patiently to be rescued.[13]

The flood conditions added greatly to the suffering of the soldiers, passengers, and crewmen who had sought safety in the water. An unseen peril of the flood placed sixteen-year-old Pvt. William C. Warner in jeopardy. While floating on a large piece of wreckage with some other soldiers, he suddenly saw a lot of cattle swimming toward the wreckage. Afraid that the cattle would upset the decking, Warner "seized some floating boards and left. [The] cattle swam under the wreckage and the other men went down."[14]

A number of men were greatly concerned about the *Sultana*'s alligator. Unaware that the reptile had been killed for its crate, many men floating in the dark waters feared that any splashing heard behind them was the alligator on its way to eat them.

Benjamin G. Davis guessed that "everyone that was on the *Sultana* knew something about the monstrous alligator that was on the boat." He recalled, "While the boat was burning the alligator troubled me almost as much as the fire."[15] Ira B. Horner wrote, "Although I felt that I would not drown, at the same time I did not feel comfortable from the fact that there was an alligator . . . keeping me company."[16]

Joseph Taylor Elliott recalled "several men who were floating down the river on a log, when a horse that had been on the boat swam up and stuck his nose over the log." In the dark, the long, slender muzzle of the horse must have looked like the nose of the alligator. Elliott said, "Rather than keep company [with this supposed alligator] they let loose and gave him full possession [of the log].[17]

When the boilers blew, some of the bales of hay on the *Sultana* had blown into the river, and the soldiers had quickly shoved others overboard. Densely bundled, the large bales supported countless lives as they floated along with the strong current.

Almost immediately after leaving the *Sultana*, Sgt. John E. Norton had grabbed hold of a bale of hay with a young soldier lying across it. As the two floated along, Norton found that his companion was suffering from hypothermia. "The water was cold and chilly and but for my care the boy would have fallen off and drowned," Norton recalled. "I kept him using his limbs so as to keep the blood in circulation and thus prevent chilling so much."[18]

Sgt. Hiram C. Wells (Company E, 8th Michigan Cavalry) was in the water only a short time and was starting to feel sleepy when he suddenly came upon five soldiers clinging to a bale of hay. "I caught on," Wells wrote, "as they Sed it was a free raft and woul[d] float all that could hang on." Eventually, two more men latched onto the bale. The last, Wells remembered, was crazy with fright and tried to climb on top of the bale. "Wee had all wee could do [to] keep him from climbing up on to the hay," Wells wrote. Fighting to control the panicked soldier while they hung precariously to the bale, Wells and the others let the current carry them downriver.[19]

Around 3:00 A.M., the sidewheeler *Bostona II* was steaming downriver on her maiden voyage from Cincinnati to join the Memphis–Natchez trade.[20] Noticing a light ahead, Chief Mate William B. Alwood, Jr., confessed, "We just thought it was a fire at Memphis. . . . When we first discovered [it was the *Sultana*] it was completely in flames, and the river appeared almost black with persons."

When the *Bostona II* was a little more than a mile from the *Sultana*, her crew realized the horror of what they were seeing and immediately set about doing what they could to help those in distress.

Captain John T. Watson ordered all floatable items thrown into the water to save those who were drowning. Alwood recalled, "Captain Watson directed the stageplank, tables, chairs and anything that would be of assistance to be thrown overboard." With well-earned pride, he said, "The entire crew, officers and deck hands, worked their utmost to save the drowning."[21]

Among those offering assistance was a Mr. Deson of Lake Providence, Louisiana, a passenger on board the steamer. Taking one of the footplanks from the *Bostona II,* Deson went into the water and risked his life among the panicky soldiers. He brought out eight people. The *Memphis Argus* reported: "Such deeds should not go unnoted."[22]

While the *Bostona II* slowed her engines and drifted with the current, her crew shoved bales of hay into the water and tossed out ropes to those with strength enough to catch hold.[23]

Clinging to a little board, James Stuart Cook admitted that he was on the "verge of despair," and that "scenes of my life were passing through my mind and I was about to give up all hope when I saw down stream a dim light; this gave me new hope." Paddling with renewed vigor, he soon found that the light was the *Bostona II,* and he began shouting "with all the strength of a drowning man." The crew of the *Bostona II* heard Cook and quickly threw him a line. Dragging him on board, they helped him to the main saloon and placed him near a stove. A woman gave him dry clothes and two strong drinks of whiskey. "This is the only time that I felt that whiskey did me any good," Cook said.[24]

The *Bostona II,* floating near the *Sultana,* sent out her sounding yawl nine times, and as Chief Mate Alwood noted, "bringing in at each trip from four to nine persons."[25] Fifteen-year-old Stephen M. Gaston was one of those pulled from the river by the men in the yawl. He recalled being taken to the steamboat "in a cramped and exhausted condition."[26]

Albert Norris was holding fast to a cracker barrel when his long drawers came loose at the waist. They slipped down his legs and tangled around his feet. While he was struggling with the garment, which brought him to "near drowning," the *Bostona II* arrived on the scene. "I swam close to her," he wrote, "when three men in a small boat took me in and carried me to the rescuing steamer."[27]

After he found a small board, Jacob W. Rush was swimming along, resting his head, and not looking where he was going when he unexpectedly ran into the edge of a door protruding out of the water. The other end was held under by another person. Quickly taking hold, Rush tried to talk to the man but got no response, so Rush rested on the door and continued paddling downstream.

"All this time," he wrote, "I could hear people calling and praying for help, while others, who were reasonably secure upon state planks [sic], bales of hay, etc., were using their old prison slang and expressions.

"Lie down and keep cool!

"Fresh fish!

"Keep your hands on your pocketbook!"

Amazed that they could jest under such circumstances, Rush attributed it to "men who had been for years accustomed to the hardships of severe campaigns and been inured to misfortunes of all kinds."

Rush was still holding to the door with his silent companion, when the *Bostona II* "came about the time the last of the passengers were leaving the wreck," he wrote. "She did all she could to secure those in the water by putting out her yacht [referring to the yawl] and throwing out her lines, . . . pick[ing] up those who were being carried off by the current, while those who had made the shore and the timber were safe anyway . . . A yawl came near us when I called for help, but as I reached with my right hand for the rope, my companion reached for me and got hold of my hair, which at the time was very long." Pulled underwater, Rush struggled to break away. "His hold soon relaxed," Rush remembered, "[but] as I came up the yawl passed out of sight, and I was again left in the darkness." Rush realized "that I could do nothing but keep above water, so I made no effort only to float in hopes the current would carry me ashore."[28]

Captain Friesner had managed to get away from the *Sultana* by holding onto a stateroom door. He had his vest and army coat in his hands. As he paddled along, he came across a man on a board.

"Stranger, can you swim?" the man asked.

"Not enough to get out of this," Friesner admitted.

"I never swam a stroke before tonight," the unknown man said, as the two continued on together.

The new soldier was very talkative, causing Friesner to recall that "we went on together, talking of what had happened, much as we might have done on a lonely walk."

As the two tried for the Arkansas shore, they met a man going in the opposite direction with eyes "very wide open [that] seemed to glow like living coals of fire."

"Turn to the right," Friesner called, "You are swimming downstream."

"There's a boat," the swimmer shouted back.

Turning to his companion, Friesner said, "That poor fellow has gone crazy and will be drowned."

"Yes," the talkative man assented, "he's crazy."

But, while Friesner continued to look straight ahead, the other soldier turned to watch the swimmer.

"There *is* a boat!" he shouted and began thrashing after the swimmer.

"Another man gone crazy," Friesner thought, but he looked back over his shoulder and saw a "white arch a mile or more below. Across its center in great black letters was 'BOSTONA.' "

Buoyed by the realization that rescue was near at hand, Friesner began kicking his door toward the brightly lit decks of the steamboat. "I started down carefully, but as I perceived I was gaining home and friends and life was nearer and dearer, a sort of delirium seized me." Exhausted from the night's endeavor, Friesner fought to keep his senses as he drew closer to the *Bostona II.*

Still a quarter of a mile away from the boat, he came upon the swimmer with the "glowing eyes" who had stopped swimming and was now "trying to climb an empty water barrel." As the barrel spun and flopped in the water, the swimmer spoke "in most emphatic tones" to the item in an apparent attempt to coax it along. Friesner recognized the voice of Lt. John E. Earl (Company L, 1st Michigan Engineers and Mechanics).

"I felt myself stiffening with incipient cramp," Friesner wrote. "I could not keep my head." Seeing the *Bostona*'s yawl close by, he shouted for help, and the boat turned in his direction. "Oh, such a feeling of gladness—but lo, it crossed some distance in front of me and picked up another man."

Shouting again, he tried to steer toward the yawl but it passed him within fifteen or twenty feet and stopped to rescue his talkative acquaintance. Struggling to keep his wits about him, Friesner repeated his call, but the *Bostona II* crewmen could not find him in the darkness. Instead, they spotted Lieutenant Earl, still struggling with the barrel, and pulled him into the yawl.

"To be lost at the feet of deliverance," Friesner worried, "in the presence of safety and all it means seemed unbearable."

Trying one last time, he shouted, "If you intend to save me, you must do it now. I can't hold out longer."

Chilled and exhausted, Friesner began to lose his grip on the door when, as he wrote, "a brawny hand pulled me on board." Friesner was still clutching his army coat and vest.

"This is a pretty time to be saving clothes," the crewman remarked as he dumped Friesner into the bottom of the yawl atop the other rescued men.[29]

Many half-drowned, half-frozen soldiers were plucked from the Mississippi by the crew of the *Bostona II,* but hundreds of others were less fortunate. To their grievous disappointment, many saw the steamboat but, in their weakened condition, could not reach her. Fighting to keep their heads above water, some were even close enough to witness the valiant efforts of her crew before the *Bostona II* continued on her journey.

Simon D. Chelf was about halfway between the burning *Sultana* and the shore when he saw "a boat down the river with bales of hay, which were dumped into the river." Unable to reach the *Bostona II,* Chelf remembered the "waves overtaking me [and] I was strangled by their slapping me in the face." He was finally able to time them and managed to dive through one and ride out the crest of the next.[30]

With the steamboat's decks filled with survivors, many in need of immediate assistance and all suffering from exhaustion and hypothermia, Captain Watson made the difficult decision to recall his rescuers and set off downriver toward Memphis. By leaving the scene of the disaster with so many victims still struggling in the water, Watson was surely condemning a number of men and women to certain death. Perhaps he felt, however, that his first duty lay with those already saved and that he had the responsibility of reporting the terrible disaster to Memphis so that other vessels could assist in the rescue.

The *Bostona II* rescued about 150 people, some through the valiant efforts of her crew in the yawl; others through individual efforts, such as those of Deson; and, according to Alwood, "perhaps 50 or 60 were brought in by the assistance of our lines."[31]

Captain Watson's timely arrival at the scene of the disaster was a minor miracle that brought well-earned praise. The *Memphis Daily Bulletin* stated: "Captain Watson's heroic efforts in behalf of the sufferers of the ill-fated *Sultana* has made for him a record that will shine forever."[32]

Although Watson had no way of knowing, Memphis had been alerted to the disaster and was already responding. All small skiffs and yawls from the docked steamboats were ordered into the river, and the steamer *Jenny Lind* rushed to the stricken *Sultana* as quickly as possible.[33]

On board the U.S. picketboat *Pocohontas,* tied up at Beal Street, pilot Henry Seman and the crew had been watching the eerie growing light far upriver. Not knowing which boat was on fire or the extent of the disaster, the crew did nothing for more than an hour. Then, they suddenly heard "the cries of the people who were floating in the river."

The commander of the *Pocohontas,* a Lieutenant McDougal, immediately ordered the boilers fired up and, according to Seman, "every yawl belonging to the boat . . . put into requisition." Although hampered by the darkness, Seman and an engineer set out in a yawl and rescued five or six men. The two "heard many cries in the water, but it being very dark, numbers of them could not be reached."[34]

One of those rescued was George S. Schmutz who was "badly scalded, so much so that [his rescuers] wondered that he could swim so far." Floating along with the "moon-eyed" soldier and repeatedly dipping his scalded face into the cold water, Schmutz had refrained from calling for help while going down the river, knowing, "that if I kept on going I would in time come to Memphis." Seeing the lights of the city, he "sent up such a cry that soon brought some small boats."

"There's one!" someone in the boat shouted.

When he was pulled into the yawl, Schmutz found that his injuries did not end with his face. "I then realized that I had been terribly scalded," he said. "My entire left side was one blister, and such agonies I never wish again to experience." Although wearing only a shirt, he quickly pulled it off in an attempt to relieve the pain from his burns.[35]

Unable to get the senior master's mate of the tinclad *Grossbeak* to do anything, Acting Master's Mate Floyd could only stand by helplessly. Suddenly, he heard "faint cries for help," coming from the river. "These cries of distress were too much to bear," he wrote.

Rushing to the stateroom of the pilot, a Mr. Karnes, Floyd shouted, "Mr. Karnes, the *Sultana* is on fire!"

"Great Lord! Is that so?" Karnes exclaimed as he sprang out of his warm berth.

"Shall I call all hands, Mr. Karnes?" Floyd asked.

"Yes."

The pilot's affirmation gave Floyd all the power he needed to arouse the crew of the *Grossbeak.*

"All hands on deck and away all cutters, away!" he ordered.

"[I]n a very few minutes," Floyd recalled, "I was seated with six good oarsmen and a boy in the bow, and we were on our way out in the river in the direction of the cries for help."

Taking the rudder, Floyd guided the boat to a piece of wreckage holding about a dozen men "raising a terrible cry for help." As Floyd neared the wreckage, he heard a "lone voice calling in the most piteous tone for help." The voice struck a cord, but Floyd knew that he could not abandon the many for the few. Although he felt terrible, he "had to leave the poor fellow, . . . to his fate and row towards the raft."

As the cutter neared the wreckage, a sailor in the cutter suddenly cried out, "For God's sake, Mr. Floyd, don't put us alongside that raft or they will swamp us."

Knowing the sailor was right, Floyd set the cutter downriver from the wreckage. "[A]s the occupants dropped off into the water, [we] picked them up and pulled them aboard." When the sailors missed one man, Floyd leaned out "as far as I could, . . . at the risk of being pulled overboard," and caught the man by the hair. After they rescued all twelve men on the raft, Floyd steered the cutter toward the Tennessee shore because it had drifted far below the Memphis wharfboat.[36]

The ironclad USS *Essex* was tied up at the Memphis wharf. Shortly after word of the disaster had reached the city, Quartermaster Thomas G. Love, on watch, "heard the cries of drowning men calling for help" and immediately went to awaken the officers.[37]

In command of the *Essex,* Acting Ensign James H. Berry was informed that "the steamer *Sultana* had blown up and . . . that the river was covered with drowning men." Soon hearing the agonizing cries of the people in the river, Berry recalled later, he "ordered all the boats manned, which was done immediately, and I went in the cutter, which was the first boat ready, and we went out to the middle of the river."[38]

Following the disaster, Berry told the *Memphis Argus,* "The morning was very dark; it was impossible to see twenty feet ahead." He guided the boat by "the shrieks and groans of the wounded and scalded men." Surrounded in darkness, Berry prayed for the morning light as he listened to the cries of the survivors: "Oh, for God's sake save us! We cannot hold out any longer!"[39]

The gunboat *Tyler,* although at a distance from the activity along the Memphis waterfront, was closer to the *Sultana* than the other navy ships. Her crew had spotted the glow of the fire upriver, but the *Tyler* could not respond because of her disabled condition.

"When we first heard the cries of help from the misty bosom of the river," officer of the deck Michael wrote, "I ordered all hands to be called, and the small boats to be lowered away, manned and immediately sent to the rescue."

Commanding cutter No. 1, Michael and a crew of half-clad sailors pulled into midstream. Swept up in the excitement of the moment and knowing that most of the crew were away while the gunboat was under repair, Frances Ackley, wife of the *Tyler*'s executive officer, grabbed a boat hook and jumped into the bow of cutter No. 2.

"Of the many heart-rending tragedies of the war witnessed ... on land and water," Michael wrote, "this one remains the most vivid. I never think of it without a shudder."

The cutters moved quickly about the river, but they were hampered by the darkness and a slight fog that began to rise from the cold water. The *Tyler*'s crew tried desperately, but in vain, to respond to the terrifying cries from those in the water: "Help! help! For God's sake, help! help!" "O! is there no one able to come to us?"

"The wails, cries and prayers could be heard, but the morning fog made it impossible to see any object distinctly," Michael said. "Even when we had reached the nearest to us, it was impossible to see the struggling men from whom the cries for help ascended."

Gripped by a feeling of helplessness, the crews from the *Tyler* and other vessels at Memphis tried their best to find the survivors as they waited for the first gray streaks of dawn.

"What a position to be in," Michael wrote. "Surrounded by piteous prayers for help, and yet unable to save a single soul."[40]

15 Help from Memphis

Few soldiers and civilian passengers on board the *Sultana* could have known the exact location of the vessel at the time of the disaster. Almost all of them had been asleep. They had no way of knowing that the doomed steamboat had been crossing from one side of the river to the other and that her boilers exploded while she was close to midstream. With the flooded Mississippi stretching out several miles on each side of the *Sultana,* the only immediate safety for the hundreds of people jumping into the icy water was in the treetops standing above the submerged islands and riverbanks.

Swimming along almost fully clad, Benjamin F. Johnston had been fortunate to find a floating fence rail and had made his way safely toward the treetops. "I reached what I supposed was the main land," he recalled, "but it proved to be an island, over which the waters poured to the depth of 15 feet."

Grabbing a branch, Johnston tried to pull himself out of the water but ran into problems. "My clothing, which had been a help prior to this time, was now a detriment because of its weight." He found that the branches were "small and dry, and were not strong enough to hold my weight . . . neither was there sufficient strength in my arms to enable me to climb out."

Resigned to holding onto the tree until daylight, Johnston soon found that he was beginning to feel cold and sleepy. "My judgment told me that this would never do—I must not go to sleep—so I concluded to try another tree." Swimming to a second tree, Johnston tried again to get out of the water but had no better luck.

"Having now been in the water for some time, it began to get daylight, and looking around, I saw a tree at a distance whose top was bent down and lay in the water." With renewed vigor, Johnston made his way down to the bent tree and finally dragged his weary body out of the water.[1]

Albert W. King, while holding the distraught Anna Annis on a piece of wreckage, tried to work his way toward the shore. Quiet for the most part, Mrs. Annis occasionally asked, "For God's sake, tell me, do you think we will be saved?"

Not sure himself, King recalled that he "said but little as I was beginning to fear that we were a long distance away from anything on which to rest. All at once, however, my feet came in contact with brush . . . and I worked fast, fearing if it was an island under water we might accidentally miss it."

Seeing that they were among a small grove of half-submerged trees, King tried to touch bottom but could not. Pushed along by the current, the two finally ran up against a "drift lodged against saplings" and grabbed hold. When King climbed onto the log, his weight pushed the log partly underwater, which made it easier to get his frightened companion onto the float.

"Our weight upon the log brought it down and we were in the water to our shoulders," King wrote. Holding onto Mrs. Annis with one arm, he hung onto the trunk of one of the saplings with the other. King recalled that they "became so chilled that we could scarcely speak."[2]

After reaching the trees, Simon D. Chelf counted on "having a good rest" and stretched down his feet. "Not finding bottom, I concluded that was no place to rest and started out in the brush to find land," he wrote. Moving from treetop to treetop, Chelf finally found a leaning willow tree and quickly threw his left arm and foot over the limb. "It held about half of my body out of the water, but I got chilly in that position and again let down for bottom." Still unable to touch land, Chelf went back into the water and wandered around for one or two hours before deciding to give up and swim back toward the main channel of the river where, he thought, "some boat might pick me up."[3]

Floating along in a vest and drawers, George A. Clarkson worked his piece of wood over to a "clump of four or five cottonwood trees." Grabbing hold of a few branches, he bent the limbs down to the surface of the water and climbed on top. "[I] stood on them up to my waist in the water," Clarkson recalled, although he admitted that "once in a while, losing my hold, I would get a ducking."[4]

In the growing light of morning, Levi G. Morgan was swimming along unassisted when he unexpectedly heard his name called.

"Hello, Morgan, is that you?"

"Yes," he quickly replied and discovered that his unseen companion was none other than Harrison Spafford, whom he had helped off the *Sultana.*

Still holding the plank that Morgan had procured for him, Spafford offered him a free end. Morgan snatched it up. "I was nearly used up," he recalled, "for my legs were badly cramped."

Assisted by the long plank, the two men found a pile of driftwood lodged against a tree. By climbed up on it, they were able to get out of the water. "My first landing place was a tree that protruded from the water," Morgan wrote. "I climbed into the branches of this tree, only to find others of the company there." Feeling a bit safer, Morgan, Spafford, and the others awaited eventual rescue.[5]

Although he had suffered from a hernia after his running leap from the hurricane deck, William P. Madden had linked up with three other soldiers holding onto a board. He assisted them downriver by letting one man rest his hands on his shoulders, but Madden slowly began to feel his strength giving out. He wrote, "True to the first law of nature, I released myself [from the board] and our friend went down to be seen no more."

Alone again, Madden continued on until he ran into a pile of driftwood lodged among the sunken timber. "So dark was it that the first intimation that I had of a shore was when I struck my head against a lot of drift, upon which I dragged myself [and] at the same time shouted back to those I had parted with." Though he had "the pleasure of helping [the two surviving men] to a place of safety," he felt guilty for letting the other man drown when they were so close to the trees. He wrote, "Could I have perceived the short distance to the shore I would have saved his life."

Wringing the water from his shirt and pants, Madden began a "vigorous walking" to get his circulation going. One of the other men did the same until both were feeling a little more alive. "But the other [man]," Madden recalled, "we had to pull along between us until a better circulation was obtained for him, after which we got along very well considering our condition."[6]

Clinging to a door, Otto Bardon and Ignatious Saunders were going along nicely when they came upon three men holding tightly to a floating steamer trunk. Bardon and Saunders agreed to aid them and took the trunk in tow in an attempt to steer it toward the timber. "We had not gone far," Bardon recalled, "before these [men] bore too much weight on our door; that put us all under the water." Fearful for his own life, Bardon gave the trunk a good kick.

"Boys," he said, "if you don't keep your weight off of the door, then you must steer the trunk yourselves."

Without any more difficulty, the five men soon reached a stand of partially submerged trees on one of Paddy's Hen and Chickens islands. While Saunders and the others climbed into the treetop, Bardon found that he was too chilled to climb up, so he swam around until he found something better. "I had the good luck of finding saplings under the water," he wrote. "I put my foot in the fork and raised myself out of the water [and] soon got warm and swam to a larger tree."

Bardon climbed into the top of that tree and settled in to await rescue. He watched one of the men break open the trunk. "It contained only ladies' dresses," Bardon noted, "so it was no help to us." After being in the tree for only a short time, Bardon remembered that he became "so cold that I fell from the tree into the water." Scrambling back into the tree, he held on with all his strength and could only watch when one of the men became "so cold that he drowned with his arms around a tree."[7]

Another soldier to reach the safety of trees on Paddy's Hen and Chickens was Pvt. Michael Dougherty (Company M, 13th Pennsylvania Cavalry). Besides being the only soldier from Pennsylvania on the *Sultana*, Dougherty also held the distinction of being the only soldier on board to have received the Medal of Honor. He had been awarded the highest U.S. military honor for his actions during a cavalry skirmish at Jefferson, Virginia, on October 12, 1863.[8]

As word of the disaster spread through the streets of Memphis, scores of people descended on the waterfront to help. Many set out in yawls and rowboats to rescue those who floated past the city. Others remained on the wharf to build fires and pass out blankets and stimulants as they tried to bring back life to the half-frozen survivors.

Amid this beehive of activity, the *Bostona II* nosed up to the Memphis wharf with her load of 100 to 150 *Sultana* survivors. When they had been carried ashore, the *Bostona II* went back to the *Sultana* to continue her rescue efforts.[9]

Holding onto a bale of hay with a young soldier and suffering from a head wound and lacerated right leg, Sgt. John E. Norton was "cold and chilly" from being in the water so long. Fearful that the boy would fall off and drown, Norton had him use "his limbs so as to keep the blood in circulation and thus prevent chilling so much." Norton and the boy floated all the way to Memphis and were rescued by the crew of the *Bostona II* on her second rescue mission.[10]

As the steamer moved slowly upriver and snatched victims from the frigid waters, her crew spotted a board carrying a soldier with two little girls in his arms. The steamer quickly dispatched her yawl while crewmen tossed the soldier a rope. The crew watched in horror as the tired soldier reached for the rope and lost his grip on the girls. Completely forgetting his own safety, he made a desperate attempt to grab the two children, but they were carried out of his reach by the swift current. Disheartened and exhausted, the demoralized man made no further effort to save his own life and was sinking without a struggle when the yawl reached him.[11]

The crew were unable to save the little girls, and the *Bostona II* continued upriver to pick up more survivors. William Rowberry, the *Sultana*'s chief mate, who had been blown out of the pilothouse, was pulled from a plank along with five soldiers. Although wet and chilled, Rowberry refused medical attention and insisted on remaining in the yawl to help others.[12]

Captain J. H. Tschudi of the steamboat *Marble City* also dispatched a yawl. Within minutes, his crew had brought in seventeen people. Later, two more soldiers were found clinging to one of the huge paddlewheels of the *Marble City*. They had been washed in alongside the docked steamboat by the strong current.[13]

The small boats from the U.S. military vessels *Pocohontas, Grossbeak, Tyler,* and *Essex* continued to pick up people from the icy waters. The *Tyler*'s officer of the deck, William Michael, skirted the overflowed trees along the Arkansas shore in cutter No. 1 and plucked soldiers from their precarious perches. "One poor boy clutched to the limb of a tree so tightly that we could not force him to let go his hold," Michael wrote. "We took him and the limb aboard together." They pulled in a soldier who "was so badly scalded that the flesh sloughed off when we pulled him over the [gunwale] of the boat."

A "young lad who had been reduced to a skeleton by his confinement in prison" had been blinded by the escaping steam. One of the sailors in the cutter cradled the boy in his arms until he breathed his last.

"Tell mother . . ." the boy started to say and then died.

Cutter No. 1 soon came upon a drift holding several survivors. At almost the exact moment, cutter No. 2 reached the same drift. "To my surprise," Michael wrote, "I observed the wife of the executive officer . . . standing in the bow of the boat with a boat hook in hand." As Michael watched, Frances Ackley snagged one of the *Sultana* victims with the boat hook and drew him toward the waiting sailors in cutter No. 2.

"Bless your brave and devoted soul," Michael shouted involuntarily, as the men in his boat cried out, "Amen!"

Continuing in their search, the crew of Cutter No. 1 floated opposite the city wharf where they found a woman clinging to a plank as she tried desperately to keep her baby's head above water. Michael guided the cutter alongside the woman and baby and pulled them into the boat. "The babe was dead," Michael noted, "but the half-dead mother did not know the awful truth till hours after she was saved. For days she was a raving maniac."[14]

The boats from the ironclad *Essex* set out at about the same time as those from the *Tyler*. Nothing was left behind on the *Essex* but the captain's gig. "Our six messenger boys took it," Quartermaster Love wrote, "and saved [a] woman." Having spotted a number of people on a drift, the boys in the gig arrived just as the woman "was making her last struggle for life."[15] The woman was Mrs. Perry. A yawl from one of the docked steamboats then came along and saved the other victims. When they were floating on the crowded door, Mrs. Perry and the others had come up against "a few logs, which had caught near a small submerged island."[16]

With Love in charge of one boat and Acting Ensign Berry in charge of another, the *Essex*'s boats swept back and forth across the swollen river as they plucked survivors from their floats. Love's boat came across a bale of hay with "nine trying to hold to it" and, further downstream, "twenty-one men on one log that was drifting in the river."[17]

George M. Safford was also rescued by a boat from the *Essex*. Picked up unconscious opposite Memphis, Safford eventually came to and immediately asked about his missing father. Unable to tell him anything, the *Essex* crewmen could only deposit young Safford at the city wharf so that he could check among the many survivors and numerous bodies being brought ashore.[18]

Messengers went to the various hospitals and surgeons' residences to request help on the waterfront.

First to arrive at the wharf were members of the U.S. Sanitary Commission, who brought clothing and blankets from the Soldiers' Home (or lodge) and immediately began helping the many injured and naked survivors.[19] The Soldiers' Home was the Civil War equivalent of the modern-day United Service Organizations (USO). Soldiers could find everything from a hot meal to a warm cot at a Soldiers' Home.

George W. Signor (2d Illinois Cavalry), a steward at the 1,000-bed Adams Hospital, had just arrived at the hospital. He had visited the *Sultana* while she was unloading sugar. When he learned that the steamer had blown up, Signor rushed back to the river and boarded the steam tugboat *Jenny Lind*. He was soon plucking people out of the river. "The water was very cold," Signor noted. "We found [survivors] floating on staging, furniture, and everything they could get hold of. . . . We saved several, who had their limbs badly injured, from bleeding to death."[20]

C. M. Kendall (29th Wisconsin Infantry), also a steward at Adams Hospital, remembered being awakened "in great haste by our sergent [*sic*] of the guard" and informed that the "*Sultana* had been wrecked." Kendall had also been down to the steamer when she was unloading the sugar and knew in an instant the dire meaning of the sergeant's words. Asked to "get out all Surgeons, nurses and stretchers and report to the landing at once," Kendall did not waste any time.[21]

A guard awakened Dr. Pieto, the surgeon in charge of the 500-bed Webster Hospital, and informed him of the disaster. Gathering up thirty blankets, a case of medicine, and his surgical instruments, Dr. Pieto hurried to the wharf.[22]

Dr. B.J.D. Irwin, medical director and superintendent of U.S. hospitals in Memphis, was awakened and told that "an explosion had taken place up the river, a few miles above the city . . . that a large number of wounded men were floating ashore, and requiring immediate medical assistance." On his way to the wharf, Dr. Irwin stopped at one of the general hospitals to order a number of ambulances and medical attendants to hurry to the river.[23]

People in the city, as well as others north of Memphis, rushed to assist the survivors as they floated downriver. Two employees of a wood yard just above the city heard chilling cries for help and immediately set out in a small boat. Rowing back and forth to some moored ferryboats, the men deposited the living on the boats to wait for rescue and placed the dead on sections of driftwood for later retrieval.[24]

After rescuing a soldier with both legs broken below the knee and another with only one arm, one of the employees was taking the men back to the ferries when they suddenly spotted a young girl struggling in the water. "She had on a life preserver," the *Memphis Daily Bulletin* reported, "but it was on so low that her head was thrown downward." In a desperate attempt to grab her, the men nearly upset the boat and missed the girl. They watched in horror as the child's gaitered feet disappeared beneath the brown waters of the Mississippi.[25]

A few of the survivors ran into an unexpected situation. The high flood waters were creating strong whirlpools that knocked some of the weakened prisoners from their precious floats.

Joseph Taylor Elliott recalled that he and three other men held lightly to a set of steps as they floated toward Memphis, "resting our hands on the steps, with our bodies in the water." They were drawing close to the Tennessee shore when they suddenly "struck a cross-current that came in on the side, and which, on striking the main current, made a whirlpool.

"Into this we went, and such a twisting and turning round, upside down and every other way, was never seen." Tossed about by the strong whirlpool, Elliott "held onto the steps with an iron grip," until the steps were "shot out into the current and on down the river, less one man who was left in the whirlpool and drowned."

Saved for the moment from a watery grave, Elliott and the other two men eventually linked up with a man on a log who agreed to share his float. One of the men from the steps climbed onto the log, and the other threw himself partly across the log and partly across the steps. This allowed Elliott to climb a little higher on the steps, but he was weak and exhausted and soon slipped into a state of semiconsciousness as the four continued downriver.

Elliott became separated from the three men on the log. "I remember passing Memphis, and seeing the gas lights burning in the streets," Elliott wrote. "Then it is all blank until I heard the splash of an oar." Trying to call out for help, he found that his voice had deserted him. "It was some such feeling as when one tries to call out in a nightmare."

By chance, Elliott was noticed by the crewmen in one of the cutters from the *Essex,* and they dragged him into the boat. Cold and exhausted, Elliott "went down in the bottom [of the cutter] in a lump like a wet rag" and, when given a draft of whiskey, felt the strong drink going down his throat "with no more effect than water down a rat hole." When they reached the *Essex,* the sailors removed Elliott's clothing, rolled him in a blanket, and placed him close to the ironclad's boilers to thaw out.[26]

Paddling and kicking along in the crate that had been used for the *Sultana*'s alligator, William Lugenbeal ran into a couple of whirlpools but managed to get out of them. "I would only try to steady my box when I would get in those whirls," he wrote. Moving along downriver, Lugenbeal was passed by a swimming soldier who called out, "Here goes your old tugboat." Fearful of having the soldier take hold of the crate and upset it, Lugenbeal said nothing. He recalled that he "had tug enough of my own."[27]

Lt. Elihue H. Swain, by privilege of his rank, was expected to carry a heavier burden than the enlisted men. True to form, when the *Sultana*'s boilers exploded, Swain had gone to the assistance of Pvt. Charles William M. King when the frightened soldier bolted overboard. As he pushed King on the plank, Swain told him not to cry and promised to get the soldier out of harm's way. On reaching some driftwood lodged against a tree, Swain pushed King up against the wood and told him to climb up. Still afraid and chilled by the cold water, King could not summon enough strength and did nothing to help himself. When Swain let go of King and began to work his way around to the other side of the drift so that he could pull him up, King slipped below the surface of the water and disappeared. Deeply disheartened, Swain climbed onto the drift and waited for rescue.[28]

"Horner, is that you?" Ira B. Horner heard someone calling in the darkness.

"Yes, what there is left of me."

Severely scalded along his entire left side and with a dislocated left shoulder, Horner had felt lucky when he found a small board that would keep his head above water. Finding that his unseen friend was on a piece of the hurricane deck, Horner asked if there was enough room for him on board.

"All right, Horner," the friend answered. "Come along."

Releasing his grip on his own board, Horner swam over to the other man and was disappointed to find that the piece of decking was very small and already carried three other men. Having already released his own board, however, Horner realized that "he had to remain. Now there was a squad of four, two swimmers and two hangers on."

As the four "floated gently and peacefully along," they were unexpectedly fired on by a band of Federal soldiers stationed above the city. Hearing the commotion in the dark waters and not knowing what was the matter, the guards had fired at Horner and his three comrades but, fortunately, had missed.

Successfully eluding the minié balls, the four men continued to float downriver until they "arrived in sight of the city lights." Horner wrote that he shouted out "with all my strength." The sailors from the *Essex* heard the pitiful cries and came to the assistance of Horner and his companions. Pulled from the water and taken to the ironclad, all four were given "something to drink from a canteen which set the blood in circulation."[29]

Truman M. Smith also ran into trouble with the guards above the city. Smith and another man were swimming along when they suddenly heard someone cry, "Halt!" Ecstatic to hear a voice from shore, the two men began to swim toward the voice when they were once again commanded to halt where they were.

"I replied that we could not as we were in the water," Smith recalled. The two continued forward until they could finally feel the river bottom beneath their feet. "[W]e got to shore and we were ordered to get out, but my limbs were so benumbed that I could not." Coming down to the water's edge, the Federal sentry grabbed Smith by the arm and literally dragged him onto dry land. The sentry called to a comrade, and the two carried Smith to a nearby tent and placed him in a cot. After doing the same for Smith's companion, the two guards built a fire, gave the two men some warm clothes, and rubbed their limbs until their circulation was flowing.[30]

After floating seven miles downriver to Memphis, hundreds of cold, exhausted soldiers and passengers were suddenly filled with fear at the thought of being swept past the awakening city by the strong flood current and missing their only chance to get out of the river alive.

Sgt. Arthur A. Jones, "benumbed and cramped," floated along until he was finally opposite Memphis. "When I saw in the gray of the morning the street lamps at Memphis, . . . I was more horrified than at any time," Jones wrote, "for the thought of going beyond that city into the wild region below, in that mad, rushing current, was enough to curdle the blood if any was left in my veins."

Almost powerless to help himself, Jones was fortunate to be noticed by rescuers in a yawl. "I heard the dip of oars and felt a strong hand grasping and raising me from my faithful friend, the plank." Cold and exhausted, the naked Jones was placed in the bottom of the boat and taken to the city wharf. There, he was given a blanket by two women volunteers with the Sanitary Commission and placed alongside the other survivors who were now starting to accumulate.[31]

Passenger William Long, adrift on a cabin door, had decided to let the current carry him downstream. "Pretty soon I saw some lights [and] I then knew I was at Memphis." Coming across a large log, Long transferred to the new float and continued past the city. He recalled that he was soon joined by a tired soldier "and soon after another and another and another until I picked up four." Slipping past the Memphis waterfront, Long wrote that he and the others "would keep quiet for a moment and then halloo; and thus we went on until I was taken into a yawl with the rest whom I had taken aboard of my log."[32]

Sgt. Michael H. Sprinkle had one of the more horrifying experiences of those who survived the disaster. While holding onto a floating cargo door, he had been grabbed around the ankle by a drowning man. Sprinkle had tried to break the man's grip but only managed to lose his hold on the precious float. With the dead man gripping tightly to his ankle, Sprinkle wrote, he was forced "to drag that dead weight until we reached

Memphis." Pulled out of the water above the city wharf, Sprinkle passed out as the many rescuers worked feverishly to pry "the dead man's grip loose from my leg."[33]

While dozens of people were being plucked from the water, scores of others, to their utmost horror, were being swept past the Memphis waterfront.

Pvt. Joseph D. Bringman (Company D, 102d Ohio Infantry) saw the "buildings on the bank of the river at Memphis" and immediately "hallooed for help." Floating along, he heard the "steamers along the wharf . . . ringing their bells" and saw the dozens of small rescue craft. "I was on the opposite side of the river and was not noticed," he wrote. "I soon dropped to sleep, or unconsciousness, with the music of the bells of the steamers ringing in my ears."[34] Unconscious, Bringman drifted past the city.

Holding lightly to a piece of decking from the *Sultana*, Pvt. Jotham W. Maes (Company B, 47th Ohio Infantry) and nine other men managed to keep "evenly divided around the edge and just float along." Coming in sight of the coal barges north of the city, Maes and the others tried to reach them "but the current carried us away." Farther downriver, Maes recalled that they could not "reach the Memphis shore nor make the people on either bank hear us," and were horrified as they were swept past the rescue boats.[35]

Fortunately for them, Acting Ensign Berry's cutter from the *Essex* also had been carried below the town. Spotting Maes and the others, Berry and his crew began to haul the men into the boat. Berry said, "We soon drifted down to Fort Pickering [the installation guarding the southern river approach to the town] when the sentry on shore fired at us."[36]

After living through battlefield and prison pen, surviving the march to Vicksburg and the crowded conditions of the *Sultana*, persevering through the explosion and fire of the steamboat, avoiding the clutching grasp of hundreds of drowning men, and making their way downstream to Memphis, only to see the lights of the city slowly slip from view, the soldiers who had been carried past Memphis now faced another peril: the unseen riflemen guarding the riverfront at Fort Pickering, Tennessee.

16 The *Sultana*'s Last Minutes

Situated three miles south of Memphis, Fort Pickering guarded the southern river approach to the city. The garrison consisted of a small number of Negro soldiers from the 3d U.S. Colored Artillery. All sentries went on duty with orders "to bring to [shore] all small boats passing up and down the river, by discharging their pieces."[1] Because of constant concern about Confederate guerrillas, the sentries had instructions to shoot first and ask questions later.

In the middle of the river, seventeen-year-old Cpl. Samuel W. Jenkins (Company L, 3d Tennessee Cavalry) heard a shot and figured he had been fired on by Confederate guerrillas. Continuing to float downriver, he was eventually rescued and taken to Adams Hospital with a raging fever.[2]

Acting Ensign Berry, in cutter No. 1 from the *Essex,* tried to ignore the warning shot from the fort but was obliged to "come to" for fear of being shot at again. With *Sultana* victims "crying out and imploring us . . . to save them," Berry was forced to ignore their pleas temporarily and instruct his sailors to pull for the shore.

"We . . . hailed the sentry, who ordered me to come on shore, and who," Berry wrote, "it seems, had not hailed me before, or if he had his hail had been drowned by the groans of the men drowning in the river." Perturbed by the actions of the sentry, Berry asked him why he had fired at the cutter. The guard replied that he was only obeying orders. Berry quickly informed him of the *Sultana* disaster and told him that he was in the act of saving drowning men. As the sentry stood mute, Berry climbed into his boat and headed out into the river.

Rowing back into the middle of the swollen river, Berry and his crew fell in with the gig from the *Essex* and moved toward a large drift that was covered with drowning men. So cold and stiff were the victims that Berry's crew were "obliged to handle [them] as if they were dead men."[3]

Among those taken from the drift was Philip L. Horn. Blown from the decks of the *Sultana,* Horn had drifted past Memphis with five or six other men on a piece of the cabin guard. He sounded the "loudest possible alarm" and was pulled into the gig.

At the same moment, he heard a familiar voice from those still on the drift: "For God's sake, help me in!"

Immediately, Horn recognized the voice of Pvt. Joseph M. McKelvey (Company I, 102d Ohio Infantry). "Is that you?" he asked.

"It is."

"Are you hurt?"

"Yes," McKelvey answered, "scalded from head to foot."

Taking hold of him by one arm, Horn and a sailor gently lifted McKelvey out of the water and laid him in the bottom of the boat. When he saw McKelvey's terribly scalded body, the sailor took off his coat and put it around McKelvey's blistered flesh.[4]

Joined by a yawl from one of the steamboats at Memphis, Berry and the others had managed to remove only about half of the men from the drift when "another shot was fired from the fort and came whistling over our heads." Berry recalled that, although it was still not daylight, "our two boats and the steamboat's yawl, . . . made a large mark to shoot at, [but] I would not leave the poor fellows in the water to attend the sentry on shore." Berry's cutter and the yawl continued their work until "the day began to dawn [and] the cries of the sufferers ceased, and all who had not been rescued had gone down." Fearing that he might be shot at again, an angry Berry gave the order to pull to shore and take him face to face with the soldiers who were firing on drowning men.[5]

Meanwhile, having heard what must have been the second shot from the sentry, Lt. Daniel P. Yates, in command of Company A at Fort Pickering, rushed out of his quarters to find out why the sentries were firing. When he heard the cries of the drowning, Yates immediately realized what must have happened upriver. He ordered his thirty or forty men to help the *Sultana* victims.

Whether they came to shore because of the shot from the sentry or because they were full of rescued survivors, two or three small steamboat yawls nosed in at Fort Pickering. Immediately, Lieutenant Yates and his men went to work. While coffee was put to boiling, they handed out blankets and whiskey to the victims. "Three or four of the most suffering [were] carried into the barracks and covered warmly," Yates recalled, "and the remainder provided with blankets and clothing to make all comfortable."[6]

Among the men aided by the soldiers of Fort Pickering were two brothers, Jesse Wallace and James Millsaps. Although separated from each other in the confusion following the explosion, the brothers had floated downriver together, each holding to the opposite end of a plank. Neither knew that his brother was on the other end.[7]

When Acting Ensign Berry drew close to shore, he spotted a sentry with his rifle raised. "I called out to him not to shoot," Berry reported, "and at the same time told [him] that if there was an officer there, I wished to see him." Called over from another area of the fort, Yates encountered a very angry Berry. According to Berry, he only "asked why he had been fired at.[8]

Yates, however, remembered differently. He claimed that Berry spoke "in a manner which approached more to 'slang' " and used "discourteous language." According to Yates, when he told Berry that standing orders required all sentries to "fire on all skiffs," Berry became irate.[9]

Berry told Yates that the rescue boats "were not skiffs [but were a] man-of-war's gig and cutter." Reminding Yates of the disaster and of the drowning men "whose cries he could not help hearing," Berry asked, "For the sake of humanity, why could he not execute his orders with some discretion in a time like this?"[10]

Offended, Yates responded, according to Berry, that "he had as much humanity as anyone" and continued to insist that he was only following orders. Looking at a number of skiffs and yawls lying nearby, Berry pointed to the unused boats and "reminded [Yates] that that did not look much like humanity." Berry reported: "No one at the fort offered to do anything for the suffering men in our boats."[11]

Yates recalled otherwise. "Some of the men," he reported, "said it would be well to put his [Berry's] sufferers (one or two, I believe) ashore that they might be better cared for, but for some reason or other he took no notice of the suggestion."[12]

While the two men argued, the troops at the fort, now fully aware of the situation, were doing all they could for the drowning men. They pulled survivors from the river at four or five different points and lit fires to help warm them. The senior surgeon, called from his bunk, instantly recognized the enormity of the situation and quickly sent a courier to Memphis with an urgent request for a train of ambulances and a supply of blankets. The most seriously injured victims were carried into the barracks buildings and the fort hospital, where their burns were dusted with flour and their injuries dressed.[13]

When Yates left Berry to assist in the care of the survivors, Berry went back to his cutter. With the help of a watchman from some coal barges near the fort, he and his sailors built a huge fire and hauled ashore a few of the rescued prisoners who wished to stay there. The others, too injured or chilled to help themselves, remained in the cutter when it headed back into the Mississippi.[14]

As the rescue continued, more and more men were being plucked from the icy waters in front of Fort Pickering. Lt. William French Dixon was "very cold and numb" and felt his mind wandering. "It was getting light," he recalled, "and there were two men [in a boat] pulling in another man . . . and when they shifted their oars they made quite a noise, and it aroused me." Dixon called out to the two men, and they quickly came to his assistance. Still spitting blood from a blow to his chest, Dixon was soon resting in the bottom of a boat.[15]

Also dazed and bewildered, Robert Talkington believed that he floated "twelve miles below Memphis" and was rescued at "an army post at a small town there." In reality, he was pulled from the Mississippi at Fort Pickering. "I began to cry for help," he recalled, "someone heard and answered back." By the sound of his voice, Talkington guided a rowboat toward him. He soon heard the clink of the oarlocks and the slap of the oars, which, he thought at the time, "was the best sound I had ever heard." He was pulled from the cold waters and taken back to "the little town I had just passed."[16]

The ironclad *Essex* headed downstream to pick up the men who had been carried past the city. Once past the wharf, the ship floated with the current. Periodically, she stopped completely and anchored in mid-stream to take on board all of the victims that her crew could find.

Hiram C. Wells and seven other men, holding tightly to a bale of hay, were rescued by the sailors on the anchored ironclad *Essex*. "We struck the bow of the boat," Wells wrote, before the sailors had time to toss out lines. Pulled on board, Wells admitted that "the moment I struck the deck I fainted." He did not wake up until the *Essex* returned to Memphis.[17]

William Lugenbeal, paddling and kicking along in the crate that was once the home of the *Sultana*'s alligator, was also picked up by the *Essex*. Bruises under both arms and across his chest attested to the tight fit of his makeshift skiff.[18]

Two crewmen from the ironclad rescued Cpl. Stewart Oxley (Company I, 51st Ohio Infantry) and an unknown companion. "While passing near the gunboat anchored in the river," Oxley wrote, "I think one or the other of us must have shouted and given the alarm." Plucked from the water, Oxley was taken to the *Essex*. "As we were put on the deck," he wrote, "the surgeon poured a glass of whiskey down each one and the men of the crew took off our wet clothing, cut down their hammocks for us to lie on, and did everything possible for our comfort."[19]

Rescued by men in a steamboat's yawl and transferred to the *Essex,* Pvt. Daniel Garber (Company E, 102d Ohio Infantry) wrote that "about the last thing I remember was that I was very nearly chilled to death." Garber was given "some stimulants," had his wet clothing cut off, and was then stuffed between two mattresses in an attempt to raise his body temperature.[20]

This treatment was no more strange than other standard remedies of that era. People suffering from burns or scalds were sprinkled with flour and wrapped in wads of loose raw cotton. If a person had apparently drowned but there was a slight possibility that he or she was still alive, the individual was placed atop a barrel and rolled vigorously back and forth in an attempt to expel the water from the lungs.[21]

By dawn, the garrison at Fort Pickering, the crew of the *Essex,* and the men in the small boats downstream from Memphis were picking up the last of the survivors. Acting Ensign Berry wrote, "When the day began to dawn the cries of the sufferers ceased, and all who had not been rescued had gone down." The *Essex* returned to Memphis with sixty men and one woman. Left in the care of the surgeons and soldiers of Fort Pickering were another seventy-six men, all of whom would be sent to Memphis as soon as ambulances arrived.[22]

The old river town of Mound City, Arkansas, two miles north of Memphis on the west bank of the Mississippi, was a cluster of small houses holding a half-dozen families. In January 1863, Union forces had burned a number of houses while searching for Confederate guerrillas, and, in April 1865, sailors from the U.S. picketboat *Pocohontas* had destroyed all watercraft.[23]

In the early morning hours of April 27, John G. Berry awoke "to find the whole premises lightened to almost the brightness of midday." Rushing outside, he spotted the furiously burning *Sultana* and woke up his wife and young son. He then raced outside to rouse his Mound City neighbors.

"Standing on the bank of the river," Berry's son, L. P., recalled, "I could hear the screams, prayers, and cries of a thousand men . . . the flames were leaping and plunging and breaking like the waves of the ocean."

John Berry and his neighbors began making preparations to save anyone they could. While Mrs. Berry started boiling a big pot of coffee, young Berry and his cousin built bonfires on the shore to warm and dry the men as they were brought ashore. Frank Barton, an ex-Confederate officer, ran to fetch a dugout canoe that he had hidden from the sailors of the *Pocohontas.*[24]

Wearing his Confederate jacket, Barton set out in his canoe and immediately began snagging soldiers from the tops of partially submerged trees. Cpl. Pleasant S. Atchley (Company K, 3d Tennessee Cavalry) was among the first to be rescued. From the shore, Atchley watched as the "Confederate soldier worked hard to save the lives of the drowning men, and brought to shore in his little dugout about fifteen of them."[25]

His left hand and wrist badly burned and blistered, George N. Young was clinging to a tree in the darkness when he heard a voice from shore and cried out.

Doing as Barton instructed, Young and another man climbed far out on the limb and then slowly let themselves down in the water. Gingerly walking toward the sound of the voice, they spotted Barton and his canoe. "We waded toward him, at one place falling completely under water, but a few minutes after we were—oh, how thankful our hearts, how cheering the thought!—in his canoe," Young wrote. "We were so stiff from the cold and the long-continued bath that we could only get out of the canoe by his assistance."

They went toward a small cabin, but Young recalled that he and his friend "tried to warm ourselves by exercising for a few minutes, for we saw that there were several persons within, and that the fire around which they were hovering was small." With the cool wind biting into their wet clothing, however, the two men finally gave in and crowded into the cabin.

Inside, Young found two female survivors huddled beside a fire; two soldiers, "badly scalded and burned," lying on a bed; and two other slightly injured men lying on the floor. Feeling the pain of his scalded hand, Young searched for a bandage but instead found a barrel of flour. Putting on a thick layer, he felt the burning sensation "much diminished" and went back outside where he found that a few more men had shown up.[26]

Ogilvie E. Hamblin was naked and afraid to enter the cabin because of the two women inside. Young gave Hamblin his army underwear and kept the pair of pants that he had found floating in the river for himself. When he went inside, Hamblin admitted later, he "never was as cold in all my life; I shook until I thought I would shake down the shanty."[27]

Albert W. King and Anna Annis were among the survivors brought to Mound City. They had been sitting on a drift log lodged against a tree, with the water up to their shoulders. King had held onto the dispirited Mrs. Annis as the sun began to rise. Unseen by the men paddling about the trees, Levi G. Morgan, seated on another drift, called to the rescuers and directed them to the two survivors. "[I]n a few minutes," King recalled, "we were lying in the bottom of the boat."

King and Mrs. Annis were helped to the shanty house, placed in front of the fire, and covered with warm blankets and quilts. A short time later, Mrs. Annis, heartbroken over the loss of her husband and baby but grateful for King's exertion on her behalf, drew a ring from her finger. She gave it to him, King wrote, "saying that all the valuables she had with her on the *Sultana* were lost excepting that ring, and it was all she could at the time offer me as a token of reward."[28]

Also rescued was eighteen-year-old DeWitt Clinton Spikes. Reportedly a veteran of the Confederate Army, Spikes had boarded the *Sultana* at New Orleans with his mother and father, three sisters, two brothers, and a niece. In the confusion after the explosion, Spikes had become separated from his family and was eventually brought to shore at Mound City. Taking only a few minutes to rest, Spikes was soon on his feet and helping with the rescue of others. Undoubtedly, he was searching for his family. He received credit for saving the lives of fourteen people by himself and twenty-four more with the assistance of another man.[29]

A mile or so upriver on the Arkansas side, opposite Hen island, stood a small steamboat landing known as Fogleman's Landing, named after the family that lived there. When they saw the burning *Sultana* and heard the victims' cries, John Fogleman and his two sons, Dallas and Leroy, lashed together a couple of log rails for a makeshift raft. Then, John set out to help those stranded in the treetops on Paddy's Hen and Chickens islands.[30]

William Boor was one of the first to be saved by Fogleman. He wrote that he was "so chilled that I had no recollection of being rescued." Once on land, Boor dragged himself up to the house. "Although it was daylight," he wrote, "with me it was all darkness." Temporarily blinded and about to pass out, he heard a woman tell him to go over to the fire. "How long I was unconscious I know not; but before my sight came to me I began to revive," and he was handed a bottle. "Soon satisfied that I knew what it contained," he handed it back, saying, "I do not drink whiskey."[31]

Among those found by Fogleman was Pvt. William Cruddes (Company F, 1st West Virginia Cavalry). Picked up while "almost in the agonies of death," Cruddes was holding to the limb of a partially submerged tree with such force that Fogleman had to cut the limb before he could get Cruddes onto the raft. Fogleman carried the soldier to his house, but Cruddes died before he could be transferred to a Memphis hospital.[32]

Pvt. Nathaniel M. Foglesong and Sgt. Edward Burnes had floated into the treetops on their piece of decking with the hole in the center. Rescued by Fogleman, the two went up to the huge bonfire to warm themselves while Fogleman's sons carried ashore the scalded bodies of the two women and the deckhand who had shared the deck piece with them.[33]

Even though Fogleman and his sons had already managed to rescue a couple of dozen people, their biggest challenge was yet to come. The wreck of the *Sultana,* still burning, suddenly floated downriver and ran into the treetops on Hen island. As she began to turn slightly in an eddy, the Foglemans were amazed to see a knot of survivors standing on the boat and fighting the flames.

When disaster struck the *Sultana,* hundreds of people fled for the safety of the water, but others, out of ingenuity or by sheer luck, simply lowered themselves over the bow by cables, ropes, or chains and hung on. After much of the superstructure burned away, the billowing flames sweeping over the bow lacked combustible fuel and died down. With the flames receding, the men hanging over the bow saw the unburnt forward section as a safer haven from which to await rescue than their precarious perches. With herculean efforts, the tired, spent soldiers

slowly began pulling themselves up the cables, ropes, and chains to re-
claim the bow of the *Sultana* as she floated downriver.

Sgt. Andrew T. Peery was the first person to climb back on the bow.
Holding onto a rope, he recalled that he "could see the fire but it soon
burned down [and] soon I could not see the blaze." As he clung to the
rope, Peery watched another man try again and again to climb back up,
but the man lost his grip each time and slid back into the water. "I told
him if he would hold tight and let me climb up, I would help him up."
Agreeing to this, the two men worked together until Peery was on the
bow.

"I found a space on the bow of the boat that had not been burned,"
he recalled. "The rest of the boat had burned down except the large
timbers which were still burning. . . . The fire was so hot it caused me to
turn around and around." Pulling on a pair of discarded trousers to
protect him from the blistering heat, Peery remembered the pact he
had made with the other man and tried to pull him up, but he lacked
the strength, Peery wrote that "being chilled in the water and then the
heat of the fire affected me, so for a little while I was very weak." As
Peery waited for his strength to return, other survivors began to climb
back up.

Two long spars from the *Sultana* had fallen on the left side of the bow,
each with one end attached to the deck and the other in the water.
Taking advantage of these natural ramps, two more men climbed up
and joined Peery on the unburnt portion of the bow. Then, fearing that
the discarded piles of clothing on the bow would catch fire, all three
men began throwing the clothes into the river.

"While throwing clothing, I saw two human beings lying on the floor
burned to a crisp," Peery wrote. "I staggered back, overcome by the
sight, but the thought struck me that I must not stop my work." Ignoring
the bodies, Peery grabbed another armload of clothing while his two
companions switched to rescuing a few of the other men hanging below
the bow with the aid of a rope found beneath the clothes.[34]

Seeing that "one of the spars was lying with one end in the water and
the other end on the bow," Robert N. Hamilton, floating nearby on a
small board, swam back to the *Sultana* and climbed up the spar. Reaching the unburnt section of deck, Hamilton was happy to be greeted by
Thomas Pangle, who had been hauled on board just moments before.
The two men were horrified when they saw "the bodies of three men
. . . burned beyond recognition." Turning quickly, Hamilton and Pangle
busied themselves by aiding in the rescue of others.[35]

Two men from the 6th Kentucky Cavalry, farrier Samuel J. Thrasher
(Company G) and Pvt. Abraham Rodes (Company I), clung to a rope
and a chain until "the cabin had burned down," Thrasher wrote that
soon someone "threw down a rope which we put under our arms and

they drew us up." Joining the growing number of men back on the bow, the two turned to helping others who were trying to "put out the fire, so that [the *Sultana*] would not sink so quickly."[36]

Another soldier drawn up by a rope was Joshua S. Patterson. Hanging to one of the projecting spars until his "physical powers were nearly exhausted," he felt relieved when he saw that some men had climbed back onto the bow and were "drawing their fellow victims out of the water by means of ropes." When it was his turn, Patterson remembered that he "grasped one of these in a death-like grip, but feeling my utter exhaustion, I put my arms through the noose of the rope and was thus drawn up."[37]

Cpl. Wilson A. Fast (Company K, 102d Ohio Infantry) had already managed to reach a small tree when he saw the *Sultana* float past with a few men on her bow, but he decided to try to get back on the boat. "I made my way from bush to bush down to it," Fast wrote. "I tried to climb upon it, and only succeeded in doing so after, perhaps, one hour's effort and almost complete exhaustion, narrowly escaping death by drowning two other times by falling back into the water after getting nearly on the boat. . . . It was about sunrise, I think, when I made my first trial, and perhaps half-past seven when I got on the boat."

Finally getting on board, Fast looked around to see where he was. The hull of the boat was then about three fourths of a mile from the Arkansas shore, and from two to four miles from the Tennessee shore, and about five miles from Memphis. Of the boat itself, Fast found that the whole superstructure had burned away "except about twenty feet of the floor nearest the prow." Estimating that there were about twenty able-bodied men and five scalded and maimed men on the bow when he got back on board, Fast reported that within the next few minutes, twelve more were hauled aboard, making a total of thirty-seven men to link "their fortunes, for the time, to the burning boat in its last struggle."[38]

Peery noted, "We pulled up a boat man." (In all probability, this was William Durkin, a deckhand.) He was "terribly burnt in the hands and face, and had a horrid gash on his face, the nose being completely severed."[39] As Robert Hamilton noticed, "His nose was torn off, all except a small particle of skin."[40] Although Durkin was severely injured, his mind continued to function.

"The boat was floating down the river and passing an island," Peery wrote. "The boat engineer [referring to Durkin] told us if we would tie the cable rope to the timber, we could pull the boat and draw it and cause it to swing around on the timber." Hoping to make the boat secure to the partially submerged trees, Fast suddenly spotted Sgt. Michael J. Owens (Company I, 13th Indiana Cavalary) floating nearby on a piece of siding, and Peery spotted Pvt. Riley Moore (Company D, 7th Kentucky Cavalry). Tossing the end of a rope to Owens and Moore, the men on the boat instructed them to paddle over to a stand of trees and make the line secure.[41]

"I tied [the smaller rope] to a big rope," Fast recalled, "and Owens pulled up to an island of brush, hauled the big rope out, and tied it to the limb of the fallen tree." With the larger rope fastened securely to the tree, the men on the bow went to work.[42]

"We began to pull at the rope according to the directions of the engineer [Durkin]," Peery wrote. "We would pull and wrap around a [cable]post, and pull and wrap, and kept working." Slowly, the able-bodied men on the bow drew the *Sultana* closer to the trees. "We saw it was drifting towards timber," Peery noted, "but at last the boat stopped and the boat engineer said it had struck land or something and I don't think it moved any further."[43]

Corporal Fast recalled, "Thus we tied up the hull, and here she burned till she sank."[44]

With the boat tied securely to the tree, the *Sultana* stopped drifting downriver. The men on the bow could now turn to battling the flames that were slowly eating away at their small island of unburnt decking.

"By this time the flooring was getting hot," Peery recalled. Knowing that they would have to get off the boat as soon as possible, the able-bodied men took the two spar poles and dropped them into the river. Peery noted that "one man got down and got on the end [of the poles] farthest from the boat." Then Peery climbed down, getting on the near end. "I finally got up on the poles and one of the citizens came along and pushed us up a log and now the men on the bow of the boat threw us down some small ropes and we tied all three together."[45] The citizen who came to the rescue was John Fogleman on his makeshift raft.

Corporal Fast had also spotted Fogleman. He recalled, "About eight o'clock we saw a man put off from the Arkansas shore with two hewn logs lashed together. The logs were about one foot square and ten or twelve feet long." All eyes were on Fogleman as he poled his makeshift raft toward the burning boat and then, to the amazement of all on board, came to a stop while he was still a good distance away. "He . . . stopped for a parley," Fast noted. "He said that he could carry only six of us and if more got on we would all drown." Fast and a man he knew only as "Indiana" stepped forward and "declared in the most solemn manner" that if Fogleman would come to their rescue, the two of them would make sure that no more than six men left the burning *Sultana* at one time. Fogleman agreed and poled his raft closer to the *Sultana*. Six men quickly climbed down onto the lashed logs.[46]

Isaac Noah Davenport was one of the first soldiers taken off the bow by Fogleman. Davenport had held onto a mooring ring until daybreak, but he transferred to the spar poles when they were thrown over by the men on the bow. Safely on the spar, Davenport had helped a soldier clinging to a rope to keep his head above water. "I puld him up a little on the rope," Davenport wrote. "He did not speke but he was not ded." Although Fogleman was afraid to take more than six men at a time, the men still hanging from ropes quickly increased the number on the raft to close to a dozen. "I was one of the first with nine others that got away from the burning boat," Davenport remembered.[47] Samuel J. Thrasher, however, thought that Fogleman took out "as many as twelve at a time by [the men] lying flat across the log."[48]

Realizing that he did not have enough time to take each load of survivors to the safety of land before the boat sank, Fogleman poled his raft to the partially submerged trees and let the men off among the branches. As they watched the rest of the rescue, one of the men found a twist of tobacco in his pocket and passed it around to his comrades. Davenport admitted that despite the chilling breeze, the men chewed their tobacco and were "as happy a little band as ever set on the limes [limbs] of a sickemore [*sic*] tree above the waves of the Mississppy River."[49]

Meanwhile, Durkin, whose expertise had helped to stop the uncontrolled drift of the *Sultana,* had succumbed to his wounds. His body was placed on Fogleman's raft and carried to shore for burial in Memphis.[50]

Fogleman took two more loads of survivors from the bow and placed them among the trees, but, as Fast recalled, Fogleman soon said that "the men were too much exhausted, and it took too long to climb a tree, so he began taking the remainder to shore, the men always paddling with their hands and feet so as to speed the trip."

Fast was still on the boat. After a while, he noticed that the floor, though saturated, was beginning to burn. "Then, the flames swept clean through under us and up through the large [cargo] hole near the prow. . . . So it was fire on both sides and under our feet," Fast wrote. Threatened with burning to death, and feeling the intense heat, Fast and the others on the bow draped blankets and army coats over their shoulders and soaked them down with water drawn from the river in cups tied to ropes. "We fought the fire," he noted, "and hoped to get the last man off before she sank or burned completely."

In lots ranging from six to twelve, the survivors were taken from the furiously burning steamer and carried to land. "Finally," Fast realized, "it came to the last thirteen men, five of whom were about helpless from wounds or scalds." Afraid the boat would sink before Fogleman could make more trips to dry land, Fast, "Indiana," and the other able-bodied men "hurriedly discussed the situation," considering if they should "take to the raft and leave the helpless." Deciding to save themselves, Fast and the others were about to leave when the "maimed ones took in the situation . . . and begged for the strong ones not to abandon them." Fast recalled, "We did not."

The five injured men were quickly lowered onto the raft, and then, as Fast wrote, "someone said that seven must go that load or the next."

"Seven goes this load," Fast shouted and instantly slid down to the raft, ever mindful that this might be Fogleman's last trip.[51]

Thrasher was among the men left on the bow. The intense flames continued to burn closer to them as Fogleman worked feverishly to pole his raft back to the boat. Almost overcome with smoke and heat, the six men clambered onto the raft and quickly pushed away from the flaming wreck. "The writer," Thrasher wrote, "and one of the 3rd Tennessee Cavalry were the last to leave the boat, and had not been off the hull but a short time when it went down."[52]

"The raft had got only about six rods [about 100 feet] from the burning hull when it sank," Corporal Fast noted from shore, "leaving nothing but the jack-staff sticking above water to mark where she went down."[53]

Farther away, Hugh Kinser was seated in a treetop. He remembered, "Before they landed the last man on their return trip the hull of the *Sultana* went down, its hot irons sending hissing water and steam to an immense height."[54] Pvt. Jacob Horner merely noted, "Finally the boat burned to the water's edge and sank."[55]

At around nine o'clock on the morning of April 27, 1865, close to seven hours after the explosion of her boilers, the steamboat *Sultana* was no longer visible.

Fogleman's efforts continued after the *Sultana* went down. He and his sons began to rescue the survivors in the nearby treetops and retrieve the bodies of the dead. Among the latter were those of Elethia Spikes and her seventeen-year-old daughter Susan.

Robert Hamilton saw DeWitt Clinton Spikes, who had continued to search for his family, "frantic with grief at the sight of his dead mother and sister."[56] Sergeant Peery watched as the body of Susan Spikes was carried ashore. "They . . . brought out a girl; she had a life preserver on. She was dead. She looked as if she was asleep. Her brother got out with us. He cried."[57]

The residents of Mound City and Fogleman's Landing rescued a total of about fifty people. The women tenderly cared for the injured, and a massive bonfire warmed the naked and dried out clothes.

As the survivors stood around the fire, they listened to a cacophony of sounds echoing up and down the river. "From daylight till noon," Corporal Fast wrote, "one could hear the boys, who were scattered up and down the river . . . perched upon trees, rocks, points of islands or hanging to the brush in the water, indulging in their humor in a great variety of ways." In spite of the harrowing ordeal they had just come through, the indomitable spirit of American soldiers continued to shine. "Some [of the men in the trees] were singing old and familiar army songs and patriotic airs; some Negro melodies; some mocking the birds; some sitting upon the rocks, and conscious of their ridiculous plight, raised a laugh among their companions by mimicking frogs."[58]

While the residents of Mound City and Fogleman's Landing were busy rescuing survivors, other boats had finally left Memphis and were making their way upriver in a desperate attempt to save the victims of the *Sultana* disaster.

17 The Final Rescues

The *Jenny Lind* was the first privately owned steamboat to go to the rescue of the *Sultana* survivors. Carrying Dr. Pieto and a supply of medicine and blankets from Webster Hospital, she left the Memphis wharf just before sunup. Her crew soon found a small knot of survivors clinging to one of the long, thin stageplanks used in unloading hogsheads of sugar. After leaving the *Sultana* on a shutter, Chief Engineer Wintringer had came across an empty "gangway plank" and switched floats. Continuing downstream, he eventually picked up about ten more men. "There was just about enough buoyancy in the plank to keep our heads above water," he wrote, "and that was all."[1]

"I came across a stage plank floating as a life preserver for ten or more persons, one of whom was an engineer of [the *Sultana*]," 1st Lt. George B. McCord (Company F, 111th Ohio Infantry) wrote. "An invitation from the engineer to catch on was quickly accepted and I peacefully floated along with them."[2]

Wintringer recalled that the plank floated "about two hours when we lodged against a snag, [although] one poor fellow became so numb with cold that he could hold no longer and sank to rise no more." Fortunately, "a very short time after," they were picked up by the *Jenny Lind*.[3] The steamer continued upriver as her crew looked for more men to save.

When the heavy, ironbound main stageplank, capable of saving perhaps a hundred men, was shoved off the bow of the *Sultana,* a fighting frenzy ensued that, instead, claimed the lives of several hundred. Floating downriver with only a handful of riders, the stageplank eventually snagged on a stand of cottonwoods.

"By this time it was fairly daylight," Erastus Winters, who was saved by the plank, wrote, "and some comrades that had escaped to an old stable that was surrounded by water saw us, and they called to us." Told that the water between the plank and the roof of the stable was somewhat shallow, Winters took a chance. He stepped into the water and found that it was only waist deep. While he waded to the roof, the other men worked the plank over to the side of the stable and scrambled up, "roosting like birds waiting to be rescued."[4]

"We . . . soon had our plank along side of the building," James King P. Brady recalled, "which proved to be a log stable."[5] Brady and David Eddleman climbed onto the roof, while the men already there helped Henry Gambill, suffering from a severe wound in his left leg, from the plank. Gambill wrote, "When we reached that most coveted spot, I was so weak and exhausted that my comrades had to help me to a place of safety."[6]

John Fox, Jr., a close friend of Winters, also had to be helped from the stageplank. While he was still in the water, Winters had heard someone praying over and over, but he had been unable to identify the voice. Only later, when the two men were seated atop the stable roof did he realize that the praying soldier was Corporal Fox.

Taken out of the river "nearer dead than alive," Fox had been severely scalded from his neck to his hips; his back "was a mass of raw flesh." Although terribly injured, he fished into his pants pocket and pulled out a plug of tobacco, "considerably swollen" from being wet. As Winters wrote, "Fox passed his tobacco around among us, and after a few jokes about its swollen condition, we each took a chew, and had quite a social time chewing it."[7]

Brady counted twenty-three men on the stable roof, and, "as far as the eye could see, upon every old snag and every little piece of drift big enough, you would see a man," he wrote. Nearby, an unknown soldier swam over to a drift and pulled himself up. Brady was amazed at the sight of him. "He was scalded almost to pieces . . . [a] sight I hope I may never see again," he wrote. Once out of the chilly waters, the man told them, "Boys, it is going to kill me," and laid back and died.[8]

"We were kept busy fighting the buffalo gnats," Corporal Winters noted, "as they came around us in swarms." Being closer to shore now, they were also attacked by biting gnats that hugged the riverbanks. Most of the men had stripped before going into the water, and the gnats "ate them alive."[9]

"A little after sunrise," Brady wrote, "we could see the smoke of a steamer coming up the river, and in due time she came up to where we were. The steamer came as close as she dared to and sent out little boats to take us in. I had now become so stiff that I could not move . . . some of the boat's crew, carried me down into a little boat and took me over to a large one, which proved to be the *Jenny Lind*."[10] Brady passed out while being carried onto the little steamboat. He woke up seven or eight hours later in a Memphis hospital.

On board the *Jenny Lind,* Winters was given a "large size glass of whiskey," which he drank down without much "coaxing" and then went up to the grand saloon. Although dressed in only an army shirt, long drawers, and one sock, he sat down at a dining table and ate "a good warm breakfast of hot coffee, fried sweet potatoes, biscuits, butter and other things too tedious to mention."[11]

The *Jenny Lind* then continued upriver as her crew snatched up individuals from partially submerged trees and small groups from snags and rooftops of flooded buildings.

Capt. J. Walter Elliott watched from a drift lodged against a tree. "Minutes seemed hours. . . . At last the sun, as if reluctant to light the scene of horror, slowly disclosed to my view . . . some half dozen soldiers on the roof of a cabin above us, and here and there a chilled, half-frozen soldier clinging to the branches of a tree or perched on a bit of floating drift." As Elliott watched, Frank Barton, dressed in his Confederate jacket and seated in his dugout canoe, suddenly appeared and began plucking survivors off their precarious perches. "And now the *Jenny Lind*—a little steamer from Memphis—comes, and 'Johnny' puts his passengers onboard, taking them from cabin roof, drifts and trees," Elliott wrote.

The last man in the area to be rescued, Elliott was surprised when he was helped on board by his friend, Lt. George B. McCord. "[I]n the joy of our meeting," Elliott noted "we for the moment forgot the loss of many of our brave companions."

Elliott had been on the boat only a short time when he noticed another dugout canoe coming toward the *Jenny Lind.* In the bottom of the canoe, Elliott was amazed to see, was Daniel McLeod, the civilian passenger who had broken both ankles in the explosion and had applied tourniquets made from his own suspenders. Elliott had left McLeod on the edge of the cabin deck guard and thought for certain that he had perished. "I helped lift him on board," Elliott recalled, "and lay him on deck and gave him a tumbler of whiskey."[12]

By the time McLeod was rescued, other steamboats were making their way upriver to save the living and retrieve the dead. One of them was

Captain Fenton's *Silver Spray,* after spending the night at Memphis on her way downriver to New Orleans.[13]

John Lowery Walker was among the first survivors to be rescued by the *Silver Spray.* After almost three hours of floating in the cold water, Walker was within a mile of Memphis when he suddenly saw "a large object" directly in front of him. "As it came nearer," he wrote, "I saw it was a steamboat, and a number of men were standing around the bow with ropes in their hands." Thrown a rope and pulled on board the steamer, Walker learned that he was only the third man to be rescued. "As soon as my feet touched the deck I sank into unconsciousness."

Walker was carried upstairs where he awoke "on a mattress in the cabin covered with bedclothes." After a warm breakfast, he watched the rescue of other victims. He noted that some were "in a worse condition than I, some not so bad." Each man was given a "tumbler full of whiskey" and then attended by the crew. "One poor fellow," Walker noticed, "was so badly scalded that he died a terrible death before reaching Memphis."[14]

The *Silver Spray* next sent her yawl to rescue William A. McFarland from a tree. Taken from a nearby drift were the woman and child whom McFarland had seen on the stern of the *Sultana.* Although the baby had been flipped upside down in its life belt before being righted by the mother, both seemed all right when they were rescued.

"The next person the yawl approached was my long Tennessee friend, who was comfortably seated on a log," wrote McFarland, as he recalled the drunken, seven-foot Tennessee soldier he had teased at Memphis. Still intoxicated, the Tennessean asked the men in the yawl how far it was to Memphis. When told that it was only a mile, he said, "Go to hell with your boat; if you couldn't come to help me before now you had better have stayed away." Slipping from the log, he began a slow, steady paddle downstream.[15]

Around 8:00 A.M., the *Silver Spray* picked up several men, including Senator-elect William Dunham Snow and Myrum W. Gregory. Snow had managed, "in about ¾ of an hour" after leaving the burning *Sultana,* to reach a stand of cottonwoods.[16]

Gregory had landed in a tree holding three other men and, as he wrote, became "so chilled and stiff that if I had been forced into the water I could not have helped myself." While waiting for rescue, one of the men in Gregory's tree became chilled. He fell out of the tree and quickly drowned. When he and the others were rescued, Gregory recalled, they were "not far from where the explosion took place."[17]

Weaving in and out among the flooded islands and submerged trees, the *Silver Spray* moved from one side of the swollen river to the other as she traveled upriver toward the scene of the explosion. Her crew rescued a total of about 80 people.[18]

Human beings clutched and clung to every treetop and man-made structure protruding above the surface of the flooded Mississippi. Swollen to three times its normal size, the river stretched out across miles of flat Arkansas farmland. The river's size alone made rescue difficult. Crews of the rescue vessels had to check every treetop in the swollen river to make sure that a drift or snag did not hold a desperate survivor.

The gallant *Bostona II,* having already brought between 100 and 150 people to Memphis, continued to retrieve people. Working without rest, her crewmen pulled on board another 100 victims to save an incredible total of 200 to 250 people.[19] Nine years later, the U.S. Congress would pass a special act granting Captain Watson of the *Bostona II* the sum of $3,962 for the cost of property thrown overboard and lost in his heroic efforts to save the victims of the *Sultana.*[20]

The U.S. picketboat *Pocohontas* did not get up steam before many of the private steamboats had already gone upriver. Her crew began to rescue people from treetops around 9:00 A.M. Thomas Sharp had managed to reach the coal barges just north of Memphis. When the *Pocohontas* came by, he unselfishly waved her past. Because he knew there were hundreds of others more in need of help, Sharp was willing to wait for the boat to return before getting on board.[21]

Around 9:00 A.M., the *Pocohontas* picked up Pvt. Chester D. Berry. Suffering from a fractured skull, Berry had been able to get into the top of a thin sapling. He soon began crying from the overwhelming pain of his injury but, realizing that "crying does not ease pain," Berry stopped his tears and looked around for a safer place. He spotted a large cottonwood tree only a short distance away, closer to "where the shore ought to be," and swam over to it.

"[This] was the most foolish move of all," Berry wrote, "for when I arrived there and pulled myself up . . . I was surrounded by a perfect swarm of buffalo gnats." Naked from the waist up, Berry broke off a small branch and used it to slap the pesky insects from his body. His chest and back were "a solid blotch in less than an hour." To Berry's relief, he recalled, "The steamer *Pocohontas* came along, picking up all the men they could find."[22]

Another soldier fighting gnats was William Fies. "I sat on my perch trying to keep from freezing by fighting buffalo gnats, which was very annoying." Although suffering from a dislocated left shoulder, badly scalded left hand, and a bruised and bleeding face, he worried more about his "intimate friend and comrade," Sgt. Asaph O. Cranmer (Company B, 64th Ohio Infantry). He knew that Cranmer was a family man and could not swim a stroke.

Sergeant Fies was still fighting gnats when he suddenly heard the distant sound of a steamboat engine making frequent stops as it slowed down to pick up survivors. "In a few moments the boat was near me," he remembered, but he was too weak to help himself, and had to be taken from his seat in a cottonwood tree by "willing hands." He was being helped on board the *Pocohontas* when he suddenly spotted Sergeant Cranmer. "To say it was one of the happiest meetings of my life would hardly express it." Picked up just minutes before, Cranmer joined Fies in "hot stimulants and plenty of warm coffee" before being put in a "nice warm bed."[23]

Lewis W. McCrory, who was uninjured, was also rescued by the *Pocohontas*. He recalled seeing a man who was so horribly scalded that "there was not a particle of skin upon his entire body."[24] He might have been referring to the *Sultana*'s second engineer, Samuel Clemens. Cpl. Winfield Scott Colvin positively identified Clemens; he stated, "Every particle of the skin was burnt from his face and breast yet I could see that the heart was beating faintly."[25]

In spite of his condition, Clemens made a statement about the condition of the *Sultana*'s boilers at the time of the explosion before he succumbed to his injuries.[26]

On board the *Pocohontas*, McCrory, who had managed to hang onto his heavy ironbound pocket-book containing more than a hundred dollars, was met by a deckhand "who was dishing out hot sling [rum] unsparingly to the boys." After a drink, McCrory felt that he could still use more and made his way up to the boat's bar. "The bartender set down a bottle and a small glass, but I called for a large one," he recalled. Given a "big beer tumbler," McCrory drank down a full glass and then opened his wet pocketbook to pay for it, but "he refused to take pay," McCrory wrote, "saying 'it is free to *Sultana* survivors.' I told him that when he disposed of it wholesale he ought to charge something."[27]

The *Sultana*'s pilot, George Kayton, and watchman Thomas Butler were also picked up by the *Pocohontas*. Kayton was in a stand of cottonwoods. He suffered only from severely bruised legs, the result of his fall from the pilothouse.[28] Butler had horrible burns on his face and hands and a broken left leg. He died before reaching a hospital.[29]

The *Pocohontas* picked up Pvt. Joseph B. Norris (Company C, 51st Ohio Infantry) around 10:00 A.M. Naked, exhausted, and "peppered by bites of buffalo gnats," he had spent his time on his "good sized sycamore log" listening to the men in the treetops around him. "I could hear the boys that had got into trees . . . crowing like roosters, and crying 'Here's your mule!' " As Norris admitted, "It was about seven o'clock before I was able to crow."

Norris was given a shirt by two U.S. Sanitary Commission volunteers on board the *Pocohontas* and a pair of overalls from one of the boat's firemen. After downing a couple of glasses "of something that did not look or taste altogether like spring water," he sat down at one of the long dining tables to partake of breakfast. "I had not eaten at a table for nearly four years and was rather awkward," Norris remembered, "but got there just the same."[30]

Leapfrogging past the other boats, the *Pocohontas* was the first boat to reach the people rescued by the hard-working citizens of Mound City and Fogleman's Landing. Isaac Davenport remembered that it was near 11:00 A.M., as the survivors warmed themselves before the huge bonfire, when help finally arrived. Her decks teeming with more than 150 victims, all chilled and exhausted and suffering from severe scalds or deep wounds, the picketboat turned her bow downriver and raced back to Memphis. Having done what she could along the river, she was now getting the survivors to the Memphis hospitals as fast as possible.[31]

At least two other vessels went to the rescue of the *Sultana* victims. The small steam ferry *Rosedella,* under the command of Captain Thomas Day, arrived on the scene shortly after most of the survivors had been rescued. Satisfied with reclaiming the bodies of the dead, Captain Day sent out the *Rosedella's* skiff among the bushes. The crew picked up quite a number of bodies, including that of civilian passenger J. D. Fontaine of Dallas City, Illinois. Dressed in two "fine white shirts" embroidered with his name and home city, his body was fished from the swirling waters by employees of the first wood yard above the city and passed along to the *Rosedella* for proper burial.[32]

Perhaps the last steamboat to go in search of survivors was the *Rose Hamilton.* Like the *Rosedella,* she arrived too late to rescue many of the living. As she cruised opposite Fogleman's Landing, her crew recovered bodies and kept vigilance for stray survivors. They found the family Bible of the Spikes family. While in the same area, the steamer was hailed by a man in a skiff bearing the body of a young woman. Dressed in the "night attire of a respectable lady," she was found to be carrying three letters on her person that eventually identified her as Sallie B. Woolfolk of Kentucky.[33]

Only the gunboat *Essex* and the tinclad *Grossbeak* went downstream. They picked up people from the water as they went. After collecting some of the men who had come ashore at Fort Pickering, the *Essex* started back upriver toward Memphis around 8:00 A.M. By then, Lt. Joseph Taylor Elliott, who had been chilled to the bone when he was pulled out of the river, had gotten over his chill and given his blanket to a sufferer who needed it more. Completely naked, Elliott sat in front of the *Essex's* furnace. He sipped coffee with the sailors and talked about his experience.

At 9:00 A.M., when the *Essex* arrived at Memphis, Elliott started to go ashore. He stopped when he saw a crowd of people, "among whom were some Sisters of Charity," coming onto the gunboat. Suddenly conscious of his nakedness, Elliott "made a hasty retreat to the rear" and took refuge behind some machinery. "But here I was protected on only one side," he admitted, "and one of the sisters came in on my flank." Seeing Elliott's nakedness, the woman tossed him a set of red flannel drawers and undershirt; Elliott "soon came out in red apparel."[34]

Sgt. Hiram C. Wells was also on board the *Essex* without any clothing. Each man was given a sheet and a pair of red flannel drawers by the volunteers. Wells and many others felt shy about their nakedness and did not get dressed in front of the women. As Wells recalled, he and the others remained in the sailors' hammocks "like so many natives with our blankets [wrapped] around us," until the women left. Dressed in their new red flannel drawers with the clean white sheets drawn over their chilled shoulders, Wells and the other survivors were taken to Memphis hospitals and treated for a myriad of injuries.[35]

Although the *Essex* went only as far as the bend in the river opposite Fort Pickering, the *Grossbeak* went farther downriver, "going past President's Island and coming up on the other side to see if there were any survivors who had floated by and had not been picked up." The crew found only one man, and he was quickly taken on board to join the other ninety or so rescued men. "The sailors got all their blankets and wrapped them up and made them as comfortable as possible," Acting Master's Mate Floyd recalled. "Most of them were unconscious from cold and it seemed impossible that they could recover, but by the time we reached Memphis, about 11 A.M., most of them were able to go ashore."[36]

The *Grossbeak* missed a number of survivors who had floated downriver beyond President's Island. Unable to rely on the rescue boats, many of these men had to use their own resources to save their lives. A few individuals living along the riverbank below Memphis aided others.

As day was breaking, Epenetus W. McIntosh was exhausted and chilled. He had been floating unassisted for about six hours. Suddenly, he felt sand under his feet. McIntosh recalled, "My strength was so near gone that I even then came near having a watery grave." Managing to crawl onto dry land, he was spotted by a Negro man who immediately came to his assistance. "In twenty minutes," he remembered, "I was bloated so much that I could scarcely see, and believe that if I had not been cared for at once I would have died."[37]

Perhaps the same unknown man helped Pleasant M. Keeble and his six companions. Floating downriver on two separate rafts, they kept the rafts together by holding hands. As they neared a bend in the river, they suddenly saw a tall Negro man, "the tallest I ever saw," Keeble wrote, who was running along the Arkansas bank with a long pole. He directed the survivors to work their way toward shore. They began paddling as the tall rescuer waded into the water up to his neck and held out the pole. "We took hold of the pole," Keeble wrote, "and he swung us into the shore. He saved our lives."[38]

Charles M. Eldridge held onto a ladder with two other soldiers and floated four miles past Memphis. Rescued by an unknown Confederate officer, Eldridge was unconscious for more than an hour before awakening beside a roaring fire. "I was so cold," he recalled, "that I tried to crawl right into it, but the boys held me back." Chilled to the bone, Eldridge did not immediately realize that he was dressed in the uniform of a Confederate colonel.

"How did I get these clothes?" he finally asked. "I am not going to wear them."

A die-hard Unionist, Eldridge began to take off the clothes, but he was convinced by the others to keep them on for warmth. Eldridge kept on the uniform and later said that the unknown Confederate, who rescued between twelve and fifteen victims from a watery grave, had earned his respect. "He was a good man," Eldridge grudgingly admitted.[39]

Wesley Lee, first to report the disaster to the city of Memphis, was "well warmed" by the time other survivors began to arrive at the wharf. While sitting huddled in a blanket on the wharfboat, Lee recalled that the telegraph operator from the steamboat *General Boynton* had approached him and asked if he "cared about being mentioned as the person who gave the information of the disaster, as it would do me no good and the river men would get pay for it." Just glad to be back on dry land, Lee said it made no difference to him who got credit for delivering the news. Thus, he gave up his chance to be officially credited as the first person to bring the terrible news of the *Sultana* disaster to the world.[40]

Even though Memphis, a major Confederate citadel, had been in the hands of the Union army for almost three years, the residents were far from ardent Unionists. However, with few exceptions, the citizens of Memphis and the occupational forces cast aside their differences on the morning of April 27, 1865, as the townspeople flocked to the waterfront to aid the *Sultana* victims. Only one woman, watching the devastated survivors brought ashore, stood by gladly proclaiming that "she was pleased by the disaster," until Union authorities hustled her away.[41] Also, when a Memphis woman, collecting donations for the survivors, approached a Federal officer, he "spoke to her in an insulting manner" and called the guards. Thinking better of it, however, he dismissed the guards and let the woman continue with her activity.[42]

Arriving on the *Silver Spray* long after Lee had brought the first word of the disaster to Memphis, John Lowery Walker noticed that "it seemed that the entire city was at the wharf. . . . Nearly every hack in the city was there to meet us." Given a set of underclothes from the U.S. Sanitary Commission, Walker climbed aboard a hack and was taken to Washington Hospital. He was one of the lucky ones to have escaped without injury, however, and he was soon transferred to the Soldiers' Home.[43]

The members of the Sanitary Commission worked tirelessly to help the *Sultana* victims as they awaited transportation to hospitals. At the end of the day, the commission had given out some 40 quilts, 670 shirts, 720 pairs of drawers, 200 pairs of socks, 200 towels and handkerchiefs, and a large quantity of "other delicacies." The grateful survivors of the *Sultana* would always remember the benevolence and compassion of the Sanitary Commission people, especially the women volunteers.[44]

Many military personnel, along with doctors and stewards from both military and civilian hospitals, joined the Sanitary Commission and the citizens of Memphis in providing aid to the survivors. Soldiers from the 113th Illinois Infantry were detailed to act as guards and escort the victims to the hospitals.[45]

One of the men escorted by the guards to a hospital was the drunk Tennessean, whom Private McFarland kept running into. Brought back to Memphis on the *Silver Spray,* McFarland was amazed to find that the Tennessean had arrived at the landing by the time the *Silver Spray* did and was still under the influence of liquor. The Tennessean refused to climb inside a waiting hack. When the guards tried to force him, he knocked down two or three soldiers. Determined to get the man to a hospital, a detail escorted him through the city streets.

While McFarland rode toward Overton Hospital in a carriage, he watched in amusement as the inebriated Tennessean was marched past a number of secondhand clothing stores where he quickly began "pulling off boots, shoes, hats, caps and other articles from the signs hanging in front." As McFarland watched, a small knot of merchants followed after the drunken man, clamoring for their goods.

"Dot ish my goat!"

"Doze was my shoes!"

"Gif me pack my bants!"

The Tennessean finally turned on his heels and threw the stolen clothing at his feet.

"There, help yourselves," he roared. As the merchants stooped to pick up their wares, he kicked them in the seats of their pants and "knocked them right and left."[46]

There was nothing comical about George S. Schmutz's arrival. Badly scalded on his face and his entire left side, Schmutz ran up and down the wharf so that the cool air could soothe his agonizing pain. "I was urged to lie down," he recalled, "but the cool breeze felt better than lying on a cot." Running back and forth, Schmutz remembered that he "felt easy going against the wind, but [when] returning it was excruciating." Finally talked into putting on a pair of drawers and a shirt, Schmutz lay down on a cot "nearly exhausted," and was soon taken to Gayoso Hospital.[47]

When the hundreds of dead bodies were taken out of the water, volunteers laid them on the Memphis wharf. Some were quickly placed in wooden coffins, but, as the supply of boxes ran out, the bodies were placed in long lines. The burned and scalded bodies were already beginning to stiffen and swell in the aftermath of death.

Arriving at the wharfboat on board the *Jenny Lind,* Capt. J. Walter Elliott and young George M. Safford, who had become separated from his father when the two jumped into the river, began searching for the elder Safford among the many dead bodies. "Together he and I opened up more than a hundred coffins on the wharf," Elliott wrote, but they did not find his body.[48]

Rescued by the *Pocohontas,* Jacob Horner waited by the stageplank as the boat neared Memphis. "Finally they landed," he remembered, "and I walked out on the plank and to my astonishment I saw eight women all in a row on the ground, whom they had taken off the boat, burned and scalded to death."[49]

No one knows exactly how many women were on board the *Sultana* on the night of the disaster. Two survivors stated that there were seventeen women passengers, whereas the *Memphis Argus* reported only twelve. Another survivor added six wives of deckhands, and at least a half dozen sources added the twelve Sisters of Charity who had accompanied the paroled prisoners upriver.[50] The best estimate indicates that between thirty-five and forty women were on board.

Equally as hard to determine is the number of children. No source lists the number of children separately. When a number is given, it is included in the number of women and phrased as "women and children." It was known, however, that the Spikes family from Assumption Parish, Louisiana, included at least one young boy and a young girl of about seven, and that Anna Annis had a toddler with her. A baby was found dead in the arms of her mother, who survived, and at least two other girls, ages seven and nine, slipped from the arms of a soldier just prior to rescue. Another baby was found and buried on one of the islands of Paddy's Hen and Chickens, called Cheeks Island. It was believed that the baby had been killed in the explosion, rather than from drowning or hypothermia. The *Memphis Argus* reported that "the head of it was half blown off, and the body terribly burned."[51] Therefore, of the estimated one hundred cabin passengers on the *Sultana* on April 27,

1865, more than half were women and children, with only four or five women surviving.

Survivor Anna Annis was quickly removed from the deck of the *Pocohontas* and admitted to Gayoso Hospital, "very ill from injuries and exhaustion."[52] Possibly, a few more women survived, but only Mrs. Perry, who was picked up by the gig from the *Essex,* was ever identified in any of the contemporary accounts or newspapers. One of the twelve Sisters of Charity might have survived and been picked up by the *Bostona II.* At least two women, in addition to Mrs. Annis, were rescued by the citizens of Mound City, and an Indiana soldier is known to have brought ashore a woman and her child. He gave the woman "a gentle tap on the ear" to make her senseless and stop her crazed struggling as the trio floated downriver. The child in the woman's arms, if it lived, would have been the only child to survive.[53]

Among the female passengers who perished was the young bride of Seth Hardin of Chicago. Hardin was to follow every possible clue in searching for her body, but her grave, as those of so many other victims, would be forever empty.[54]

Only a few of the bodies of the female passengers were ever recovered and fewer still were identified. Perhaps among the dead women on the wharf were Sallie B. Woolfolk, a Mrs. Hoge, and Elethia and Susan Spikes. In time, three more unidentified female bodies were pulled from the river, including "the nude and putrified body of a lady" washed up on the shore being eaten by hogs, which passengers on a northbound steamboat witnessed with horror.[55]

Heartbroken over the loss of his new bride, Hardin, clad in ill-fitting clothes borrowed from his rescuers, started uptown to find a hotel room. Along with his precious wife, he had lost his trunk of clothing and several thousand dollars that had been in the *Sultana*'s safe. A "third-rate hotel" turned Hardin away with the explanation that "they couldn't board a person who had no baggage and looked as he did." Just when it appeared that he had hit bottom, the Worsham House, a first-rate hotel, heard of his plight and gave him a fine room.[56]

Perhaps the last man to reach shore, and undoubtedly among the last to be brought back to Memphis, was Sgt. Seth Sollenberger of the guard unit (Company A, 58th Ohio Infantry). A rescue boat had picked up Sollenberger four miles below Memphis. He arrived back in the city on April 28th, at least twenty-four hours after the sinking of the *Sultana* and long after most of the victims had been taken to Memphis hospitals or laid out along the wharf for burial.[57]

When daybreak brought a cessation of cries for help from the river, rescuers speculated that either the majority of people already had been saved or had already perished. By noon, it was estimated that only about

Pvt. Christian Boss, Company I, 44th Indiana Infantry, who died in the *Sultana* disaster. (Courtesy of J. Bruce Wagner)

Sgt. Aaron V. Waterbury, Company H, 17th Michigan Infantry, died. (Courtesy of Bene Fusilier)

Pvt. Adam Bahn, Company B, 102d Ohio Infantry, died. (Courtesy of Stewart L. Bennett)

Pvt. John F. Hartman, Company K, 102d Ohio Infantry, died. (Courtesy of Maxine H. Smith)

Pvt. John Lewis Swarm, Company K, 111th Ohio Infantry, died. (Courtesy of Ivadel Gibbs Crowell)

1st Lt. John Eadie, Jr., Company C, 115th Ohio Infantry, died. (Courtesy of Timothy R. Brookes collection)

Pvt. William Lugenbeal, Company F, 135th Ohio Infantry, survived. Lugenbeal escaped by killing the *Sultana*'s alligator mascot and floating downriver in the creature's wooden crate. (Courtesy of Bonnie S. Knox)

Pvt. Robert Gaylord, Company C, 115th Ohio Infantry, died. (Courtesy of Timothy R. Brookes collection)

Pvt. Samuel Pickens, Company A, 3d Tennessee Cavalry, survived. (Courtesy of Pickens family)

Pvt. Adam Schneider, Company C, 183d Ohio Infantry, died. (Courtesy of Pam Newhouse)

Q.M. Sgt. James A. ("Hickory Jim") Davis, Company B, 3d Tennessee Cavalry, survived. (Courtesy of Robert E. Maxey)

Cpl. George C. Davis, Company B, 3d Tennessee Cavalry, survived. (Courtesy of Robert E. Maxey)

Sgt. Samuel A. Dyer, Company C, 3d Tennessee Cavalry, died. (Courtesy of Carolyn Smith Gardner)

Cpl. Silas W. Wade, Company C, 3d Tennessee Cavalry, survived. (Courtesy of Paul Wade)

Pvt. James Wiley Hodges, Company F, 3d Tennessee Cavalry, survived. (Courtesy of John W. Hodges)

Pvt. John Wood, Company C, 3d Tennessee Cavalry, survived. (Courtesy of Charles Martin Ward, Jr.)

The steamboat *Bostona II*. Coming downriver on her maiden voyage on the Mississippi, the *Bostona II* was the first vessel to render service to the victims of the *Sultana* disaster. (Courtesy of Public Library of Cincinnati and Hamilton County, Ohio)

The ironclad USS *Essex*. Longboats from the *Essex* immediately began rescuing survivors of the *Sultana* explosion, while the ironclad built up steam before heading downriver to pick up victims who had floated past the Memphis wharf. (Courtesy of Public Library of Cincinnati and Hamilton County, Ohio)

The gunboat USS *Tyler*. Although she was tied up at the U.S. navy yard above Memphis for repairs, her longboats rescued a number of *Sultana* survivors. (Courtesy of Public Library of Cincinnati and Hamilton County, Ohio)

110 enlisted men, 10 officers, 4 women, and 15 men and crewmen had been rescued from the cold waters. By 2:00 P.M., after most of the rescue vessels had returned, the total had risen to 510 in the hospitals, and "from 200 to 300" of the less seriously injured or uninjured at the Soldiers' Home.[58]

The injured faced days and even weeks of excruciating pain and treatment, while the uninjured searched for relatives and comrades—searches that most often ended in failure.

18 The Living and the Dead

The seriously injured victims of the *Sultana* disaster, a total of 521 people, were taken to five Memphis hospitals. Washington Hospital received 143; Adams, 142; Gayoso, 140; Overton, 90; and Officers Hospital, 6 commissioned officers. A total of 241 people with less serious injuries or who were uninjured went to the Soldiers' Home. From these figures, 762 people were accounted for.[1]

Only a few people did not require hospitalization or did not seek the comforts of the Soldiers' Home. The *Memphis Daily Bulletin* reported on April 28: "Thus far 786 have been found alive," which indicated that 24 people refused assistance and were not included in the above lists.[2] During the next few days and weeks, however, of the 786 rescued individuals, "more than 200 of the hospitalized [would die] of their injuries."[3]

William Fies was taken to the 1,000-bed Adams Hospital. "I was placed in a ward with quite a number who were severely scalded, or otherwise badly injured," he wrote, "and such misery and intense suffering as I witnessed . . . is beyond my power to describe." Although suffering greatly from his scalded hands, dislocated left shoulder, and bruised and bleeding face, Fies waited his turn for treatment. He explained that he "did not murmur or complain, as I saw all around me numbers of poor fellows whose injuries needed attention more than mine." Recalling the "agonizing cries and groans of the burned and scalded," he admitted that "in most cases the suffering was of short duration as the most of them were relieved by death in a few hours."[4]

Although slightly burned on the face and body, Erastus Winters found "others were scalded so much worse than I, and there was such a number of them, [that the staff of Adams Hospital] did not come to dress my wounds until nearly night." By then, however, his burns had become so dry and unpleasant that he remembered with fondness "how cool and nice they felt after they had been dressed." After a few days of convalescing, Winters began walking around the hospital. He looked for familiar faces and made new friends. Among those he came to know was civilian passenger Daniel McLeod, the ex-soldier with the crippled right knee who had suffered two badly broken ankles. McLeod was operated on by army doctors. "The surgeon in charge cut off his right limb above the old wound," Winters noted, and the broken left ankle was reset.[5]

Overton Hospital, with 900–1,000 beds, admitted "one man [who] had his head, face and body almost denuded of cuticle [skin] from steam," according to a news article. It also reported: "Some were badly contused, and a few were cut and lacerated from being hit with fragments of the wreck. All were more or less injured from their long immersion in the cold water, and were only saved by the prompt and judicious medical attention given them."[6]

Pvt. John William Norcutt (Company D, 18th Michigan Infantry) wrote that he was so badly scalded that it was "fourteen days before I could stand alone."[7] Sgt. Martin Frazee (Company C, 2d Indiana Cavalry), scalded on his back, hips, legs and arms, "did not walk for five months after the explosion."[8]

At the 400-bed Washington Hospital, Chester D. Berry suffered severe pain from his fractured skull. "[M]y wound was poorly dressed," Berry complained, "none of the broken pieces of skull being taken out."[9] Somewhat luckier, Pvt. William H. Ross (Company A, 102d Ohio Infantry), who suffered from a similar wound, had "5 pieces of his skull bone . . . taken out by a surgeon," and his broken left ankle set.[10]

Admitted to Washington Hospital with only a slight contusion, sixteen-year-old William C. Warner, wearing a stiff hat that he had found floating in the river, an undershirt, and ill-fitting trousers borrowed from his rescuers, was given brandy and a good meal. Glancing out the window of the dining room, he saw his best friend, Pvt. John Mooney (Company B, 9th Indiana Cavalry), passing by in the company of a guard. Excitedly, Warner called to Mooney, "who left his soldier escort and ran in to embrace" Warner.

"Well, Warner," Mooney said as he stared at his disheveled friend, "we never expected to see you again."[11]

While hundreds of other soldiers experienced such joyous reunions, a much higher number never saw their friends or loved ones again. Taken to Washington Hospital "too nigh chilled to death to stand alone," Samuel Pickens was up on his feet the next day in search of his brother William. After looking all day and night, he was forced to write to his mother and sister: "I must confess that to the best of my knowledge brother William is among the lost. I have not heard of him since the explosion took place and I have no hope of ever hearing of him any more."[12]

Although he started out for the 700- to 800-bed Gayoso Hospital, George M. Safford, in company with Captain Elliott, never arrived there. Stopping at the office of a Memphis newspaper to inquire about Safford's father, the two men met a U.S. scout, named Erwin, who had been on the *Sultana* with the elder Safford. To the great relief of the younger man, Mr. Erwin presented him with "his father's watch, a very valuable one," and told him that his father had been "rescued in an unconscious state by some Negroes on President's Island." Ignoring his own exhausted condition, young Safford "took the first boat for the island where he found his father as had been told."[13]

Six officers were admitted to the small 100- to 120-bed Officers' Hospital. Capt. James M. McCown, in agony from a smashed left thumb and severe scalds to his face, lungs, and hands, recalled, "I was so badly scalded . . . that my eyelids were closed for five days before I saw anything. I also inhaled some steam and I couldn't speak for seven days."[14]

Most of the soldiers taken to the Soldiers' Home were uninjured or slightly injured, but there were exceptions. Cpl. Albert P. Varnell (Company I, 3d Tennessee Cavalry) was taken to the Soldiers' Home unconscious and so badly scalded on the left side of his face that he was nearly blind in his left eye. It was two or three days before he regained his senses.[15]

Another exception was George N. Young, also sent to the Soldiers' Home. After treatment for his scalded left hand and arm, he was put in the lower bunk of a double-tier bunk bed. "I was so nervous that I could not sleep," he wrote. Young reacted violently each time a passing steamboat blew a whistle or let off excess steam. "Night after night would I jump up on hearing any noise, and I had to change my sleeping-place from a bunk to a cot, for I had bumped my head till it was sore."[16]

As the uninjured began visiting the hospitals to collect names and note conditions, the size of the calamity began to sink in. Despite the great loss of life, however, there were a few more happy reunions.

Cpl. Jesse F. Millard (Company G, 3d Tennessee Cavalry) had boarded the *Sultana* with his brother, Pvt. Elkaney Millard (Company G). They were separated by the explosion. Jesse was in Washington Hospital for a short while. He wrote that, after his release, he "went back to the river where most of the troops were, and waited to hear about my brother." Standing on the wharf, he watched both the living and the dead brought ashore. "Over all the noise," he recalled, "I heard someone call his name. They were forming some troops across the way from me and I heard his name above all that was going on and I knew he was alive." Joyously, Jesse rushed over to the ranks and quickly found his lost brother. "He was sore and tired," Jesse wrote, "but he was OK."[17]

Robert N. Hamilton had to wait until the next morning before looking for his two brothers. "Next day I met my brother John and several more of our company," he wrote, but his search for his other brother proved fruitless. "My brother Henry was lost with about twenty others of the company."[18]

Eighteen-year-old DeWitt Clinton Spikes thought that he had lost his entire family on the *Sultana*. Three days after the disaster, the *Memphis Argus* reported that "one of the Spikes family, who was supposed to have been lost, has been rescued by some Confederate soldiers on the Arkansas shore."[19] Young Spikes took the first available steamboat to meet his brother. Unfortunately, none of the Memphis newspapers recorded the results of their meeting.

Although most of the paroled prisoners on the *Sultana* did not have any relatives on board, the bond of friendship forged through the rigors of camp, battle, and prison pen could be even stronger than the bond of kinship.

Taken to the Soldiers' Home, John Lowery Walker could get no information about his best friend, Pvt. William M. Morrow (Company B, 50th Ohio Infantry), until late in the evening of the 27th when he finally found Morrow's name on the list of rescued in Overton Hospital.

Very early the next morning, Walker borrowed a pair of pants and set out for the hospital. "No shoes, hat or coat did I have," Walker recalled, "but I thought nothing of it." He remembered that "people would stop and look, and I could hear such expressions as, 'There goes one of them,' or 'There's a *Sultana* victim.' " Reaching Overton, Walker found that it did not open until 9:00 A.M.

"Seating myself where I could see a clock I waited till the first stroke of nine; then as I pushed the door to enter I found my comrade Billy just coming out in search of me." The two embraced and Walker admitted that it was "indeed a happy meeting; we had been together for so long, had endured the same hardships, and had shared the same joys, that only those whose lives have been so closely attached to each other can fully comprehend just what this reunion meant to us."[20]

Wearing the rank of a noncommissioned officer, Sgt. Arthur A. Jones perhaps felt bound by duty to search for the men from his company. After looking for two days, he posted a letter to his brother:

> Dear Brother—I am now in Washington Hospital and in good health. You may think it strange to get a letter from me post marked Memphis, but this is explained by the fact that I was on board the *Sultana* at the time of the disaster.

> Yesterday I was busy all day visiting Soldiers' Home and different hospitals in search of the survivors of Co. C. Of those I could find but 17 out of the 42. . . . We are still in hopes that more of our boys will yet be found, but it is very doubtful. . . .[21]

Although the casualty numbers were not yet dermined, the soldiers were beginning to see firsthand the results of the disaster. When rolls were taken, more names went unanswered than answered. Visiting the Memphis wharf one day after the explosion, young William Wooldridge, who had helped rescue at least forty-five victims, saw "a stretch of dead bodies four blocks long on the river front."[22]

Thirteen days after the loss of the *Sultana,* signs of the disaster were still vivid. Leaving Overton Hospital on May 9, Sgt. Hosea C. Aldrich recalled that he "went down to the landing where they were boxing up the dead and there I saw two hundred of my comrades lying in rows and in the same shape they were taken out of the water, after raising and floating on top."[23]

Despite the extent of the disaster and the serious injuries suffered by the vast majority of those pulled from the river, the great desire of all of the paroled prisoners was to get home. As incredible as it may seem, almost half of the survivors were sent home on April 29, just two days after their terrible ordeal.

By order of Maj. Gen. Cadwallader C. Washburn, Commander, District of West Tennessee, Capt. William S. Friesner, who had been in charge of the small guard unit on the *Sultana,* was given the task of taking about 300 survivors to their original destination of Camp Chase, near Columbus, Ohio.[24] Approximately 450 of their comrades were temporarily left behind.

Presented with new suits of Union blues and new blankets, the 300 survivors marched to the wharf and boarded the *Belle of St. Louis.* Considering all of the trouble encountered in loading the paroled prisoners in Vicksburg on April 24, the quickness at which this first group of survivors left Memphis was amazing. (In fact, the fast, efficient service of General Washburn's staff showed with glaring detail the inadequacies of General Dana's staff in Vicksburg.)

Leaving Memphis around 5:00 P.M. on April 29, the *Belle* traveled steadily upriver through the night. For many of the survivors, the enclosing darkness brought back frightening memories of a night not so long past. Daniel Garber wrote, "Some of the more timid were springing up at every little noise, thinking there was going to be another explosion."[25]

Despite the survivors' nervousness, the *Belle* reached Cairo without incident around 6:00 P.M. on April 30. Again, with a newfound efficiency, the government quickly placed the men on board a northbound train and started them up the tracks through southern Illinois. To the great relief of every paroled prisoner, the rest of the trip would be made overland in railroad cars.

The next morning, the train stopped in Centralia, Illinois. Word of their coming had preceded the *Sultana* victims, and the citizens of Centralia, turning out en masse, offered them breakfast and patriotic speeches. Afterward, the men reboarded the train and proceeded north to Mattoon, where they arrived around 2:00 P.M.[26] If the survivors had been amazed by the reception in Centralia, they were overwhelmed by the hospitality of Mattoon, Illinois.

"On arriving at Mattoon," Robert N. Hamilton wrote, "we were met by the citizens of the surrounding country with wagon loads of provisions, the best that the country afforded." The men were taken to a hotel and treated like kings while they waited for an eastbound train that would take them to Columbus.[27]

Reaching Terre Haute, Indiana, at 10:00 P.M., the men spent the night in town before starting off again. After stopping in Indianapolis for part of the day, the train pulled into Columbus, Ohio, around 4:00 P.M. on May 3.[28] Finally at their original destination, the survivors thought that their troubles were at an end. But they soon learned otherwise.

At Camp Chase, they had expected an immediate release. The men were incensed when they were forced to wait day after day while the government finished the paperwork on their paroles. Thoroughly disgusted, many of the *Sultana* victims took "French furlough" and went home without permission.[29]

While the first contingent of *Sultana* survivors waited impatiently for their release from Camp Chase, a second group had already left Memphis.

By May 1, almost 100 of the original survivors had died of their injuries and burns, and the number left in Memphis had fallen to 380.[30]

Recognizing Capt. J. Walter Elliott as the most senior able-bodied officer among them, the survivors cornered him. "Captain, they have left us," the men pleaded. "You must get transportation for us and take us home."

Elliott also wanted to get home. He made quick arrangements and, on May 1, placed about 250 men on the *Belle of Memphis,* bound upriver for Cairo. Although there were "a dozen or more scalded men laid on the cabin floor," Elliott was forced to leave behind approximately 130 of the more seriously injured, most who were "so badly scalded, that they were likely to die."[31]

This group of survivors was nervous, too. "On one occasion," John Lowery Walker wrote, "those of us who had just had such a thrilling experience became greatly alarmed when the boat ran aground in a short-cut the captain undertook to make through the woods." Having gone through the hell of the *Sultana* disaster, Walker recalled that the men began to panic until they were assured "that everything was all right and that we should be off again in a few minutes, which we were."[32]

Although Captain Daniel Musselman of the *Belle of Memphis* had caused a temporary fright, his kind actions on the rest of the trip were never forgotten by the men. Having left Memphis in such a hurry, without obtaining supplies from the Quartermaster Department, the men had no food until the captain opened his pantry and gave "the best his abundant larder afforded."[33]

The *Belle* reached Cairo after dark on May 2. Elliott "placed the well in barracks and the wounded in hospitals for the night."[34]

Still unable to obtain food from the army, a number of prisoners slipped away and spent the night at the Cairo Soldiers' Home. There, according to James King P. Brady, they "received the finest of treatment, a good supper . . . and a nice bed. . . . Feeling greatly refreshed," the next morning, the men at the Soldiers' Home ate a breakfast "that was good enough for a king," then joined the rest of the survivors at the railroad depot.[35]

Leaving Cairo on the northbound train, the contingent reached Mattoon just before 11:00 A.M. on May 3. "We had had nothing to eat for 24 hours," recalled Elliott, referring to the men who had slept in the Cairo barracks buildings. The news of this second group's arrival had preceded them, however, and the men were amazed by what greeted them when the train pulled into Mattoon.[36]

"O! what a sight we witnessed!" Brady wrote. "The platform at the depot was crowded, from one end to the other, with the citizens of Mattoon and surrounding country, with baskets filled to over-flowing with every thing you could think of to eat."[37] As William A. Hulit fondly remembered, the baskets were "filled with roast chicken, boiled ham, cake, pies, eggs and steaming hot coffee."[38]

Treated like the men in the first group, these survivors were also taken to a hotel where, Brady wrote, "local speakers of the town made several patriotic speeches . . . [and] about forty ladies, dressed in red, white and blue . . . sang several patriotic songs."[39] Then, according to Hulit, "some comrade would give his experience while a prisoner, or relate the frightful scenes and marvelous escape from the burning boat."[40] Years later, Brady recalled that "during my entire term of service I never received such treatment as while in the state of Illinois."[41]

About 1:00 A.M., a train arrived to take the men east. While in Mattoon, Captain Elliott had telegraphed Indiana Governor Oliver H.P.T. Morton, as well as the mayor of Terre Haute, to announce the impending arrival of the second group of survivors in their cities. When the train reached Terre Haute, a crowd and provisions were there to meet them. A son of Indiana, Elliott wrote, "[They] gave us a dinner worthy of my grand old native State."

Continuing east, the train arrived in Indianapolis and was met by Governor Morton and a throng of people. While the men ate a "good supply of bacon and beans," Morton, one of the most powerful wartime governors, stepped in and exerted his executive powers. Although all of the paroled prisoners were destined for Camp Chase, Morton felt that it was unnecessary and somewhat brutal to subject the Indiana soldiers to the long ride to Ohio, only to have them exchanged and sent back. Wielding his governmental saber to sever the red tape, he put the sick Indiana soldiers into hospitals and sent the healthy survivors home.[42]

The remaining survivors reboarded the train and "in due time," arrived in Columbus. These men were also told that they would have to wait a few days for their release. Having expected an immediate release, they were as incensed as the men in the first group. "Oh, what a change," Ohioan Brady lamented. "Instead of being treated like lords, as we were in Illinois, we were treated more like so many dogs than human beings."[43]

"After spending a week in camp I was anxious to get home to see my wife and baby," Corporal Hulit recalled. "So I took what was called in those days 'a French furlough.' " Although anticipating trouble in getting on train cars without a pass, Hulit found that the "conductors and trainmen were very lenient when I would explain to them that I was an ex-prisoner of war and a survivor of the steamer *Sultana*." Hulit and hundreds of others were home only a few days when word came for all *Sultana* survivors to report back to Camp Chase as soon as possible. The men were to be discharged by a special order.[44]

There were perhaps 130 to 150 victims left in Memphis after the second group of survivors departed. Most of these men were more seriously wounded than those who had already left and required continued hospitalization. A few, however, were able-bodied individuals who elected to stay behind either to wait for different transportation or to work up the courage for another steamboat ride.

William A. McFarland "dreaded getting on a steamboat for fear of another explosion . . . like a burnt child dreading the fire." Wanting "to reach home as soon as possible," however, he made his "escape" from Overton Hospital and boarded a steamboat. "Adopting what I supposed was the safest plan," McFarland recalled, "I crawled into the yawl hanging over the stern of the boat and never left my quarters until I arrived at the wharf at Evansville [Indiana]." Although it rained the entire trip, McFarland "stuck it through," but jumped every time "the boat would escape steam or blow the whistle."[45]

Perhaps even more afraid of steamboat travel was Pvt. Samuel C. Haines (Company G) and his friend, Pvt. Nathan D. Everman (Company F), both of the 40th Indiana Infantry. "[We] stayed in Memphis about two weeks," Haines recalled, "[as] we were afraid to try the boats again and waited for the train to go North." When told that it would be several weeks before a train left Memphis for Camp Chase, the two fearfully climbed aboard a northbound steamer and resumed their trip toward "God's Country."[46]

Almost forgotten among the departure of the paroled prisoners were the *Sultana*'s surviving crew members. In addition to chief engineer Nathan Wintringer, pilot George Kayton, and first mate William Rowberry, perhaps an additional twenty-three crew members survived: eighteen deckhands and five cabin hands, including the five men who fled from the *Sultana* in the yawl.[47]

Also overlooked were the few surviving civilians. One by one, without pageantry or fanfare, the crew members and civilians began to leave Memphis. One of the first was Senator-elect Snow, who arrived in Cairo on the night of April 28. Traveling in the opposite direction, pilot Kayton reached New Orleans on May 1.[48]

Anna Annis was perhaps the most notable civilian survivor to leave Memphis. Tenderly cared for at Gayoso Hospital, she slowly began to improve in both body and mind. On April 30, the *Memphis Daily Bulletin*, aware that Mrs. Annis was destitute of both money and clothing, ran an advertisement "To the Ladies of Memphis" and appealed to their "usual liberality" to come to her aid. The appeal met with "considerable success," and Mrs. Annis left Memphis on the evening of May 11.[49]

By May 15, almost 200 of those rescued had died in Memphis hospitals. Yet, almost miraculously, some of the more seriously injured survived. Three weeks after the explosion, Albert Norris, who had fallen on the exploded boilers and burned his left arm and shoulder to a crisp, was taken home by his brother and a family doctor.[50] A week later, David Hites, although seriously scalded in the explosion, walked out of Gayoso Hospital.[51]

On June 7, forty-one days after being badly scalded, John W. Lesley was the last of the *Sultana* survivors to leave Memphis.[52] Twenty-one days later, Pvt. George Washington Dawson (Company G, 30th Indiana Infantry) died in Overton Hospital from his scalds. He was the last *Sultana* victim to die in Memphis.[53]

First Engineer Nathan Wintringer left Memphis for Pittsburgh, Pennsylvania, shortly after the disaster. Investigations soon revealed that the *Sultana*'s boilers had been inadequately repaired. Supervising Inspector of Steamboats J. J. Witzig of Saint Louis maintained that the boiler had been repaired with an insufficient patch, something that Wintringer never should have allowed. "[T]he engineer alone can be held responsible," Witzig concluded and, as a result, acted to revoke Wintringer's engineering license.[54]

Wintringer fought back. In a long letter of explanation, he argued that, "there was nothing wrong [with the repair] nor was there any sign of a leak or defect." Wintringer felt that he was "entitled to a trial and investigation before a proper court of justice; also the privilege of defending myself, which [Witzig] has given me no chance to do." He concluded, "I want the local Board of Inspectors to investigate my case, and on their decision I am willing to stand. What it may be I do not know."[55]

The Saint Louis Board of Inspectors acted on Wintringer's case. The board consisted of John Maguire and John Schaffer, the two men who had been the last to make an official inspection of the *Sultana*'s boilers on April 12, 1865, and had found everything working and in satisfactory condition. Perhaps fearing censorship themselves, the two overturned the revocation of Wintringer's license and, knowing that dead men tell no tales, laid the blame of the explosion solely on the shoulders of the deceased second engineer of the *Sultana,* Samuel Clemens. Publishing their findings in a Saint Louis newspaper, the two inspectors wrote that Wintringer had been off duty when the boilers exploded and thereby publicly exonerated him.[56] Of course, they had ignored the fact that it was Wintringer who had allowed a patch of a thinner metal to be used and who had run the vessel at a pressure rated for a greater thickness.

News of the *Sultana* disaster had reached the northern states almost immediately. The *Marble City* left Memphis after helping in the rescue of the victims and reached Cairo the next day. Although she carried a few copies of the Memphis newspapers announcing the disaster, Captain Tschudi refused to give them to the Cairo reporters. Instead, he elected to save them for the news hawks in Saint Louis, hometown of the *Sultana* and her crew. Finally, after considerable delay, the Cairo newspapers received details of the disaster from steamers that arrived later and immediately flashed them over the telegraph.[57]

During the next few days, several hundred relatives and friends of the *Sultana* victims arrived in Memphis to seek news of their loved ones. The two daily newspapers ran dozens of personal advertisements from people wanting information. As the realization set in that the vast majority of the paroled prisoners had perished, the requests for information were replaced by advertisements offering rewards for the recovery of bodies.[58]

Among the bodies most frequently mentioned in the advertisements were those of the *Sultana*'s officers. A reward of $200 was offered for the recovery of the body of Captain J. Cass Mason. In addition, $100 rewards were offered for the bodies of the first clerk and part owner, William Jordan Gambrel; the second clerk, William Stratton; and pilot Henry Ingraham. The sister of barkeep James O'Hara, a resident of Memphis, sought desperately to find her brother and give him a Christian burial. In the end, however, no rewards were collected. With the exception of the second steward, George Slater, the bodies of the *Sultana*'s officers were never recovered.[59]

On April 28, the day after the explosion, several small boats were sent to the vicinity of the wreck to start the cleanup. They returned with "several pieces of bodies which had been literally torn to pieces."[60]

During the first weeks of May, as the weather grew steadily warmer and the floodwaters began to recede, hundreds of bodies rose to the surface of the Mississippi. Many steamboat crews and citizens, who had helped to rescue the survivors only a few days before, were now retrieving the dead. Few were ever identified because their bodies either carried no identification or had decomposed beyond recognition.

On May 3, the *Jenny Lind,* hired by Captain William A. Thornburg, part owner of the *Sultana,* went to the site of the wreck and retrieved seven bodies for burial. Among them was Pvt. William A. Baker (Company E, 3d Tennessee Cavalry), identified by a tattoo on his forearm.[61] The next day, the *Jenny Lind* recovered another twenty-eight bodies, and the *Rosedella* found six more. At the same time the *Jenny Lind* reported, "that many more can be recovered." In fact, about thirty additional bodies "had risen" from the remains of the *Sultana,* of which twelve had been snagged by John Fogleman and his sons and tied to the shore for eventual recovery.[62]

On May 5, the Memphis newspapers reported: "Many bodies are now rising from the vicinity of the wreck of the *Sultana,* and a few have drifted down past the landing." Barges were sent out to collect the bodies. One barge returned with thirty-eight bodies, and others retrieved an additional forty-five bodies.[63] At one point during the day, "a rough Government wagon drawn by four horses" was seen carrying eleven "rude coffins piled one on another."[64]

With the Mississippi rapidly falling, Paddy's Hen and Chickens islands began to show above the surface of the river. For reasons of convenience, the men recovering the badly bloated, decomposing bodies buried them on Island No. 42, or Cheeks Island, the largest of the Chickens, opposite the sunken wreck. Fifty bodies were interred on the island on May 6 and another thirty-two, including the body of the *Sultana*'s second steward, George Slater, on May 8. The Stewards' Association immediately collected money from its members and reinterred Slater in a "very nice coffin and a lot in Elmwood Cemetery."[65]

Another sixteen bodies were buried on Cheeks Island on May 9. In time, "two long mounds were to be seen, each marking the resting place of a dozen or more of the victims," and to the side of these mounds was a smaller one, "the size of it indicat[ing] that it was once the darling babe of an affectionate mother."[66] On May 13, a special military detachment buried the last large group of bodies, nineteen in all, on Hen island.[67] By May 19, as the *Memphis Argus* reported, "Very few bodies are to be seen now."[68]

The *Memphis Argus* health report for the week ending May 7 stated: "Number of dead bodies taken from river 133." A week later the report listed "Drowned on steamer *Sultana* 20." Altogether, the Memphis authorities buried "one hundred and ninety-seven of the dead by the *Sultana* disaster."[69] This figure is misleading, however, as it includes only the number of those buried in Memphis cemeteries. Three weeks after the sinking of the *Sultana*, the grim work of recovering the bodies near Memphis was finally at an end.

Although the dead received decent care in Memphis, those that floated downstream did not. Coming upriver soon after the disaster, the steamboat *Arkansas* was nearing Memphis when the river was suddenly "full of bodies floating like cordwood, and all of them were dressed in the uniforms of Union Soldiers."[70] Engineer Phineas D. Parker of the ram *Vindicator* was horrified by what he found as his vessel went upriver toward Memphis: "I wish to say that the most horrible sight I saw during my whole service was immediately after the calamity. When clearing the wheels after the *Sultana* disaster we would find them clogged with dead bodies." Not allowed to bury the dead, the sailors aboard the *Vindicator* "came very near . . . a revolt."[71]

South of Memphis, unfortunately, leaving dead bodies unburied appears to have been the norm rather than the exception. Because of the warm temperatures, the bodies from the *Sultana* were "too much decomposed to be moved." Near the end of April, the gunboat *Exchange* was "about 25 or 30 miles [south] of Memphis" when she came upon what her crew thought was "a large amount of driftwood floating in the river." Moving closer, steersman McClaskey "discovered it to be human bodies [and] was obliged to steer the vessel over the bar to avoid running over the bodies." The steersman recalled, "There was no effort made to bury those bodies."[72]

Left unattended, the decaying bodies soon became fodder for the animals. According to the *Memphis Argus*, as the steamboat *W. R. Arthur* steamed along on May 9, those on board "saw numerous bodies floating down the river, some of which the crows had lighted upon, and were enjoying a feast of putrefied flesh." As far south as 120 miles downriver from Memphis, bodies were being seen eaten by "dogs and hogs and doubtless other animals."[73] Understandably, the animals, perhaps as starved as the rest of the Confederacy, saw the bodies only as food.

Carried along by the floodwaters, the bodies of the *Sultana* victims continued to float far downriver. Eleven bodies were recovered and buried in Helena, Arkansas, while others were found "floating down nearly to Vicksburg."[74] Eventually, the bodies disappeared, either sinking completely, decomposing, or becoming caught in some sluggish backwater when the river fell. As time passed, the cities along the river forgot about the *Sultana* disaster, that is, all except Memphis.

The *Sultana* disaster left a marked scar on the city of Memphis. For more than a month, mention of the disaster rarely slipped from the front pages of the two daily newspapers. Every so often, when enough bodies had been collected, a procession of wagons carrying crude coffins slowly made their way toward Elmwood Cemetery, where most of the bodies were placed in graves marked "Unknown U.S. Soldier."[75]

The Good Samaritan City, living up to its sobriquet, held numerous fund-raisers for the *Sultana* victims. On May 1, the Chicago Opera Troupe, which had traveled to Memphis with the paroled prisoners, gave a benefit concert that raised about $100. The next day, the New Memphis Theatre followed with a benefit performance of its own that netted a total of $312, and Brig. Gen. John Shanks's division of Union cavalry, stationed around Memphis, chipped in an additional $459 for the *Sultana* relief fund.[76]

Two sterling sermons, one at Calvary Church and the other at Second Presbyterian Church, drew another $185, and the fund finally totaled $1,183. Ironically, by the time the money was ready to be distributed, almost all of the survivors had left the city. On May 26, twenty-three people, "whose serious injuries and losses pointed them out as special objects for the bestowal of such assistance," received varying amounts of money. Eighteen of the recipients were surviving soldiers, two were the widows of soldiers, and three had been civilian passengers, including DeWitt Clinton Spikes and Daniel McLeod.[77]

The citizens of Memphis required a long time to recover from the shock of the *Sultana* disaster; the victims and most of their families never would. Although many of the survivors did not suffer permanent debilitating injuries, all of them—every person on board the *Sultana* when her boilers blew—would forever remember the morning of April 27, 1865.

"Strive as I may," George N. Young wrote years after the disaster, "I cannot repress an involuntary fright on hearing in the stillness of the night any unusual noise."[78] Another soldier, Harrison Spafford, only twenty-five years old at the time of the disaster, was so badly affected by the explosion and his experience in the cold water that he was unable to do manual labor for the rest of his life.[79]

Because of the number of soldiers on the *Sultana* and the lack of an accurate count or list of the men on board, many families received inaccurate information relating to the deaths of their loved ones. When Ira B. Horner finally arrived home on a pair of crutches, he recalled that his family "looked on me as one of the dead." Having heard that he was on the *Sultana* and knowing that he could not swim, which was not a popular sport in the 1860s, his family had thought that he had perished. Unknown to them, Horner had learned how to swim while in the army.[80]

Sometime after being informed of her husband's death on the *Sultana,* the wife of Pvt. James H. Brown (Company D, 3d Tennessee Cavalry) was working in the garden when a thin, ragged-looking soldier approached. Taking up a rifle, she told the man to "stop or she would shoot." To her amazement, the man called out her name and said he was her husband. "She said no it isn't, he is dead," came the story through the ages, "but he had a missing finger before he had gone into the army so he showed her this and she knew then it was really her husband."[81]

To the families of the many dead, April 27, 1865, always would be a day to mourn. The death of Pvt. Adam Bahn, Jr. (Company B, 102d Ohio Infantry) came as a crushing blow to his father and sister, especially so soon after the death of his mother in 1857.[82] The death of Pvt. Manuel Harnly (Company D, 102d Ohio Infantry), "a family favorite," would be "deplored as long as his sisters and brothers lived."[83] On every April 27 for the rest of his life, *Sultana* survivor Pvt. Michael Conrad (Company C, 183d Ohio Infantry) would visit the family home of his friend, Pvt. Adam Schneider (also of Company C), who had died, and "cry, cry like a baby."[84]

Forty-two-year-old Pvt. Alexander Sackett (Iowa Infantry, regiment and company unknown), who perished on the steamboat, left behind a wife and six children.[85] Pvt. James C. Cook's father refused to believe that his son would not come home. "At least four or five times a day," the old man went out on the front walk to look for his missing son. "[T]his kept up for years, or while he lived."[86]

Perhaps one of the saddest incidents involving the loved ones of the *Sultana* victims occurred at the home of Eli Finley Provines. When word of Provines's death reached his father, the old man rose from the table, walked slowly over to the daybed, and immediately died from a heart attack.[87]

19 The Investigations

Almost immediately after Wesley Lee brought the first word of the disaster to Memphis, General Washburn began looking into the affair. While the survivors were still being rescued, Washburn issued Special Order No. 109 to commission a three-man court of inquiry headed by Lt. Col. Thomas M. Brown (7th Indiana Cavalry). The other two members were Maj. R. G. Rombauer (1st Illinois Light Artillery) and A. R. Eddy, assistant quartermaster of the Army.[1]

At 11:30 A.M. on April 27, 1865, the Washburn Inquiry took its first statements from the surviving officers of the *Sultana,* including the mortally scalded second engineer, Samuel Clemens, who had been on duty at the time of the explosion. Clemens made a dying declaration that the *Sultana*'s boilers were full of water and working fine just prior to bursting.[2] Colonel Brown and his colleagues next spoke to William G. Alwood, Jr., first mate of the gallant *Bostona II,* before taking statements from a number of surviving soldiers.

On April 28, General Washburn sent a wire from Memphis to Secretary of War Edwin M. Stanton in Washington D.C. Washburn had learned from the sworn statements that the paroled prisoners had been crowded on board the *Sultana* while "two other large steamers [the *Lady Gay* and the *Pauline Carroll*] were in port at the same time." Washburn asked Stanton to "please order an inquiry to be made at Vicksburg to ascertain why 2,000 released Federal prisoners were crowded on board the ill-fated *Sultana.*"[3]

On Sunday, April 30, the steam tug *Little Giant* went to the wreck of the *Sultana* and found "about three or four yards of the starboard guard of the wreck" above the waterline. Upon further inspection, "a piece of shell [or cannonball]" was found among a pile of "fire brick, pieces of coal and etc." This discovery started a rumor that there might have been some fiendish plot by Confederate guerrillas to smuggle a live artillery shell into the coal bunkers of the *Sultana.* Investigating all aspects of the disaster, the Washburn Inquiry took testimony on May 2 from steamboat agent William C. Postal and Quartermaster Department agent John Curlic, who had been aboard the *Little Giant.*[4]

Then, after soliciting the testimony of former transportation quartermaster Capt. J. O. Lewis and Pvt. Jacob W. Rush, a survivor of the disaster, Colonel Brown suspended the Washburn Inquiry and, pursuant to Special Order No. 114, adjourned to Vicksburg. The members had learned all they could from the people at Memphis and had raised a number of questions concerning the loading of the *Sultana*. Now, General Washburn hoped to find the answers to the growing mound of questions in Vicksburg.

On the morning of April 29, Secretary Stanton received a telegram from Gen. Charles Thomas, acting quartermaster general in Washington, that requested "a thorough investigation into the cause and extent of this terrible disaster, in order to ascertain upon whom the blame . . . rests."[5] Coming one day after General Washburn's telegram, the request had a profound effect on Stanton. On April 30, he issued Special Order No. 195. Part 3 of the order instructed Brig. Gen. William Hoffman, commissary general of prisoners, to "proceed without delay to Memphis . . . to investigate and report upon the circumstances connected with the destruction of the steamer *Sultana*."[6] On May 1, Hoffman left Washington for Cairo and points south.

General Hoffman was en route to Cairo on May 2 when Maj. Gen. Montgomery C. Meigs, quartermaster general in Washington, directed the issuance of a circular:

> As it is probable a large number of troops will be returning to their homes the strictest attention should be given to prevent the use of any but perfectly safe Transports under experienced and careful masters, provided with everything necessary for the safety and comfort of troops. Especial care should be taken to see that they are thoroughly clean and that they are not overloaded.
>
> The late calamity to the Steamer *Sultana* shows the need of extreme caution which will be expected from all officers in the management of River Transportation.[7]

Although the circular was too late to help the victims of the *Sultana,* the army was showing that it had learned a valuable lesson from the disaster. No longer would troops be subject to the horrendous conditions and overcrowding that the paroled prisoners had faced on the *Sultana.*

When he reached Memphis during the first week in May, General Hoffman learned of General Washburn's inquiry and removal of the court to Vicksburg. Because most of the survivors had already left Memphis, Hoffman had missed the opportunity to conduct his own interviews. Availing himself of the information gathered by the Washburn Inquiry, he also decided to go to Vicksburg.[8] In Vicksburg, at least, he could still find most of the people who had played some major part in the *Sultana* disaster.

Downriver in Vicksburg, General Dana had seated a commission of his own, which began hearing testimony on May 5. The Washburn Inquiry began its investigation in Vicksburg that same day and worked in tandem with the Dana Commission. In fact, the questions to the commission's first two witnesses, Capt. William F. Kerns and L. G. Mitchell, an experienced steamboat captain, and their answers were copied word for word into the records of the Washburn Inquiry.

It is possible that General Dana convened his own five-man commission only after feeling the heat of the Washburn Inquiry. During the next few days, the Dana Commission interviewed just five witnesses, only one of whom (Kerns) could be considered a major witness.[9] Brig. Gen. Morgan L. Smith headed the commission. Smith had been a leading actor in the *Sultana* drama, and he had done nothing to alleviate the overcrowding of the vessel. As head of the commission, he could structure questions in such a way as to elicit answers that completely kept his name from public notice.

For some unknown reason, Smith's first witness, Kerns, was not even present at the hearing. Perhaps this was an intentional move on Smith's part. Kerns had been the only officer to remonstrate against the overloading of the vessel, and he had repeatedly gone to Smith for help in the hope of preventing it. Instead of being interviewed in person, Kerns submitted a written affidavit containing his statement of events and a half-dozen questions and answers, which were "received after being read as a part of the testimony as if taken before the Court."[10]

After Captain Kern's statement and answers were read into testimony before both investigating bodies, General Smith presented four minor characters as witnesses. One was asked to give his impression of the "abilities, caution and etc." of Captain Mason. The others were questioned about possible bribes taken by any officer connected with the transportation of prisoners, especially any offered to Capt. Frederic Speed, senior assistant adjutant general at Vicksburg.[11]

Suspicion had come to focus on Captain Speed through the continued investigation by the Washburn Inquiry. Aside from testimony taken by General Smith, the Washburn inquiry questioned nine additional witnesses, including a number of major participants. When Lt. William Tillinghast was interviewed, he stated that Captain Speed had personally selected the *Sultana*. Incredibly, Tillinghast informed the court that he himself had agreed to take a bribe from a rival steamboat line.[12] By his own testimony, Tillinghast, who had been up to his ears in bribery, not only implicated himself but suggested that bribery was widespread throughout the loading of the *Sultana*.

Other major witnesses in the Washburn Inquiry were Capt. George A. Williams, Captain Speed, and Col. Reuben B. Hatch. Each man answered questions concerning the loading of the *Sultana* and possible bribery. Captain Speed said that he was subordinate to Captain Williams during the prisoner exchange, whereas the other two officers said that they thought Captain Speed was in charge.[13]

Perhaps the most probing question was the one put to Colonel Hatch, who had led Captain Mason to believe that he not only controlled the selection of transportation but also the paroled prisoners. When asked if he considered himself under the orders of Captain Speed "as to matters of business in your department," Hatch answered, "I do."[14] Cool as a cucumber, Hatch did not panic as the heat began to rise. He did what he did best: he lied.

The last major witness was General Smith. He testified that Captain Kerns had made repeated requests for him to come down to the waterfront and see firsthand the overloading of the *Sultana*. Smith admitted that he was on his way to the boat when he met someone from the Quartermaster Department who informed him that there were "only three hundred to go." Relying on the word of the quartermaster, Smith said, "I concluded that they would be very comfortable on the *Sultana* and immediately returned to my office."[15]

Smith's testimony on May 7 might have resulted in the adjournment of the Dana Commission on May 8. By that date, General Hoffman was in Vicksburg and possibly saw Smith's involvement in the investigation as a clear conflict of interest. Meanwhile, the Washburn Inquiry was making great progress, and Hoffman, availing himself of the material from both the inquiry and the commission, was soon ready to begin his own investigation.[16]

On the morning of May 8, Hoffman, wanting to narrow his investigation and focus on a guilty party, asked General Dana to submit his report on the *Sultana* investigation. In a long-winded statement, Dana danced all around the problem and avoided the two main questions: (1) *Who* was responsible for selecting the *Sultana?* and (2) *who* was responsible for overloading her?[17]

Exasperated by the footwork, Hoffman sent a telegram to Dana:

> Will General Dana please state what officer or officers he considers responsible for the shipment of the paroled troops within referred to, and for the proper character of transportation?[18]

Pressed to submit an answer, Dana wrote, "Captain Speed was intrusted with the transfer and shipment of the prisoners," and "Captain Kerns, quartermaster in charge of transportation, responsible for the character of it."[19] Of the two scapegoats selected by Dana, one had spent almost the entire day at Camp Fisk and the other had repeatedly protested the overcrowding.

With General Hoffman now on the scene, the officers of the Washburn Inquiry concluded their work and returned to Memphis. Now the sole investigator, Hoffman began gathering information in earnest. On May 9, he brought back Captains Kerns, Speed, and Williams to clarify some of their earlier testimony. After interviewing Capt. William B. Wells, assistant quartermaster at Vicksburg, and Edward D. Butler, superintendent of military railroads at Vicksburg, Hoffman started his long journey back to Washington, D.C.[20]

Between May 11 and May 17, as Hoffman traveled cross-country by river and rail, he conducted additional interviews whenever possible. He elicited further testimony on the loading of the *Sultana* and the crowded conditions from a number of paroled prisoners recuperating in the Memphis hospitals and at Camp Chase. In Memphis, he also interviewed Anna Annis on her last day in the Good Samaritan City. Seeking to gather professional opinions as to the cause of the disaster, Hoffman spoke to Isaac West, an expert boilermaker, and to W. B. Richardson, the chief engineer of the steamboat *Marble City*, who had examined a salvaged piece of boiler from the *Sultana*.

Perhaps Hoffman's most interesting interview was with the *Sultana*'s chief engineer, Nathan Wintringer. Catching Wintringer in Pittsburgh, Hoffman elicited a lengthy and detailed statement that covered the patching of the *Sultana*'s boiler and the functioning of the vessel on her last trip upriver.[21] He then gathered up his testimony and reached Washington sometime before May 17.[22]

Arriving at his office, Hoffman found a telegram from General Washburn in Memphis that had been sent on May 14. According to Washburn's calculations, "Twelve commissioned officers and 757 enlisted men make the total of paroled prisoners saved from the steamer *Sultana*."[23] Curiously, Washburn made no mention of the number of people who had since died in Memphis hospitals.

Pressed by Stanton to determine the parties responsible for the disaster and to submit his report, Hoffman wrote up his document and gave it to Stanton on May 19. It told the confused story of the loading and gave a brief account of the hardships of the crowded prisoners. Although Hoffman tried to explain the cause of the explosion, he eventually admitted that "the testimony I have been able to collect does not enable me to form a positive opinion." He placed the number of paroled prisoners on board the *Sultana* at "1,866" and the number of civilians at "70 cabin passengers and 85 crew" and concluded that there were 783 surviving prisoners, passengers, and crew and a loss of 1,238 lives. After weeks of investigation, Hoffman had come up with an unbelievably low figure of people carried on the *Sultana*. He also determined that the number of survivors was the same as the number of people rescued from the Mississippi, thus disregarding the fact that more than 200 soldiers had died after they were rescued.

In answering the all-important question of who was responsible for the overcrowding, Hoffman concluded that it was a combination of the actions of four men: Captains Kerns, Speed, and Williams and Colonel Hatch—"Colonel Hatch and Captain Speed being the most censurable." The general wrote, "It was their duty [Hatch and Speed] especially to see that the service was properly performed." He felt that Williams was "assisting Captain Speed," but added that "there was a manifest propriety in his [Williams] knowing the number embarked, and if there was a deficiency of transportation he should have reported it." As for Kerns, Hoffman found that "Captain Kerns made no inspection of the steamer to see that she was properly fitted [and] made no report of the repairing of her boilers."

Hoffman also mentioned General Smith in the report. He wrote that "it was proper that he [Smith] should have satisfied himself from good authority" whether or not the *Sultana* was overcrowded. In addition, Hoffman did not overlook Lieutenant Tillinghast. He noted that "by his [Tillinghast's] own testimony . . . a bribe was proffered to him," and, although Tillinghast did not say that he accepted the money, General Hoffman was sharp enough to realize that "at least he did not reject it."[24]

With Hoffman's report in hand, Stanton had only to wait for the results from the Washburn Inquiry before making a final decision as to what should be done to the guilty parties. On May 23, four days after Hoffman's report, Stanton received a copy of the findings from Memphis.

The findings of the Washburn Inquiry started out, like the others, with a brief background on the loading of the *Sultana*. Using the same figures as did Hoffman, the inquiry found that a total of 2,021 people had been on board the *Sultana* at the time of the explosion, of which "only about eight hundred persons were saved." Although the inquiry found that "the safety of the boat was not particularly endangered by the number of men onboard," it admitted that there was "no military necessity for placing them all on one boat." Without mentioning any names, the inquiry reported that "the quartermaster's department at Vicksburg [Hatch and Kerns] is censurable for not insisting on its rights, and for permitting others . . . to do its duties." It also found "the Adjutant General [Speed] is censurable for taking upon himself duties not properly belonging to him." Having stated its findings, the Washburn Inquiry concluded, "There was no intention, however, on the part of the officers referred to, to do injustice to the soldiers on board the *Sultana*."[25]

The nation's newspapers published the report. The *Chicago Tribune* added this editorial comment: "This report reads very much like a studied attempt to conceal the guilty, and whitewash those who crowded

2,400 souls on a boat that ought not have received one-fourth of that number."[26]

Following soon after the inquiry report was a summarizing report to Secretary Stanton by General Washburn himself. After stating that he believed the explosion had been caused by "want of water in the boilers," he said he thought that the inquiry's censure of the Quartermaster Department in Vicksburg was "not deserved." In his opinion, Hatch and Kerns had "said all that was necessary for them to say" to try and get the prisoners divided, "to such an extent as to draw upon themselves the accusation of receiving bribes." Washburn continued, "The business was taken out of their hands . . . by the assistant adjutant-general [Speed]."[27] So, with just a few lines, Washburn exonerated Hatch and Kerns and placed the blame squarely on the shoulders of Captain Frederic Speed, who had been four miles away at Camp Fisk during most of the day when the *Sultana* was being loaded.

On May 25, 1865, two days after submitting his comments, General Washburn resigned from the army. Two days later, General Dana followed suit.[28] On June 16, after reviewing all of the reports, Quartermaster General Meigs sent a letter to the adjutant general of the U.S. Army. Finding that both the Quartermaster Department and the adjutant general at Vicksburg were "censurable," Meigs "respectfully recommended that the officers . . . to have been concerned in the matter, be ordered before a Court Martial for trial." He mentioned by name both Colonel Hatch and Captain Kerns.[29]

Although not specifically listed, but certainly implied, was the name of Capt. Frederic Speed. Eager to have his name cleared and feeling that he had had almost no control over the selection of the *Sultana* and very little control over the loading of the vessel, Speed "desired a trial immediately" in order to get the matter cleared up as soon as possible.[30]

Captain Kerns's attitude after the disaster is unknown, but he was the least culpable of the officers involved and, like Speed, might not have feared the consequences of a court-martial. Kerns had tried repeatedly to get the paroled prisoners divided. His only fault might have been, as General Hoffman pointed out, not reporting the repairing of the *Sultana*'s boilers.

Colonel Hatch, of course, had faced inquiries and court-martial charges before, but his political connections and influential friends had always come to his aid (see chapter 3). On June 3, however, for an incident totally unrelated to the *Sultana*, General Meigs finally acted on the results of an investigation into Hatch's qualifications as a quartermaster. Finding Hatch mentally unqualified to hold the position, Meigs relieved him of his duties as chief quartermaster of the Department of Mississippi.

Hatch was involved in one more scandal before leaving the army. In late June, he decided to safeguard a shipment of more than $14,000 in government funds to Saint Louis. Sometime during the trip, the steamboat's safe was robbed and the funds stolen. Although a diligent search eventually turned up the thief, only $6,000 of the funds was recovered. More than $8,000 had mysteriously disappeared.

In early July, a special military board looked into the missing funds. Although the $8,000 was never recovered, the board reasoned that Hatch, by transporting the funds without a bonded messenger, had made himself personally responsible. Because the transporting steamboat was insured against loss of items kept in its safe, the government was reimbursed for the lost funds. Although again censured, Hatch was honorably discharged from the service on July 28, 1865.[31]

Two weeks previously, on July 12, General Smith had resigned from the Army. On August 20, Lieutenant Tillinghast, perhaps fearing prosecution for his part in the *Sultana* disaster, also resigned.[32]

Captain Speed was informed on August 28 that he would face a military court-martial. He was the only officer singled out for such action.[33] On November 1, the assistant adjutant general issued Special Order No. 89, appointing a court to meet in Vicksburg "for the trial of Captain Frederic Speed."[34]

On December 11, while waiting for the trial to begin, Speed sent a letter to Col. Adam Badeau, a member of General Grant's staff, who had helped General Hoffman in his investigation. In the letter, Speed addressed his problems in trying to obtain witnesses who had been present during the loading of the *Sultana*. Convinced that Colonel Hatch had selected the *Sultana* for transport, Speed wrote:

> I am now in possession of a list of persons, who, at various times, were present at the several consultations I had with [Colonel] Hatch, upon the subject of transportation for the paroled prisoners and can fully establish the fact . . . that I complied with the customs and regulations of the service in securing transportation for these men. But I greatly fear that some of these persons cannot be found and that others will not obey the summons of the court. . . .[35]

In explanation, Speed pointed out to Badeau that General Dana was living in Nevada and Speed thought it doubtful that he would return for the trial. He added: "Tillinghast, the fellow who started all the stories about the bribery, and, as it proved, was the only one who was offered a bribe is now in jail, at Chicago, charged with forgery. You can judge of the likelihood of his coming."[36]

Another important witness, Captain Kerns, was honorably mustered out of the service on December 13. He returned to his home state of Minnesota.[37]

On January 9, 1866, the court-martial convened in Vicksburg. Captain Speed stood accused of one charge, "Neglect of duty to the prejudice of good order and military discipline," with two specifications. The first stated that he "did *neglect* to avail himself of the services" of Colonel Hatch and Captain Kerns, and "did himself assume to discharge the duties" of those two officers "in *overloading* said steamer *Sultana.*"

Specification No. 2 stated that Speed "did assume unwarrantable authority, in directing the arrangements for the transportation . . . and did (without authority) load and cause to be loaded" the paroled prisoners "on *one* boat, the steamer *Sultana* . . . when at the same time, other (and better conditioned) steamboats . . . were ready and anxious to take a portion" of the men. The second specification went on to claim that Kerns had informed Speed that other boats were willing to take some of the prisoners, but that Speed, "against the remonstrances of the said Captain W. F. Kerns," did, "with criminal neglect and carelessness," place all the men on the *Sultana,* which eventually contributed to its destruction.[38]

As expected, Speed entered a plea of not guilty to all charges.[39] Speed and his counsel, Capt. L. W. Perce, an assistant quartermaster at Vicksburg, who had been a witness before the Washburn Inquiry, must have seen that the government was using Speed as a scapegoat. Speed had consistently penned, "The Quartermaster's Department will furnish the necessary transportation" at the bottom of each order, and all the earlier boats had been selected by Colonel Hatch. Speed *had* availed himself of the services of the Quartermaster's Department, and he was not personally responsible for the overloading of the *Sultana.* In fact, he did not even arrive at the *Sultana* until almost 1,300 prisoners were already on board.

When the *Sultana* first arrived in Vicksburg, Speed had been reluctant to give her any men because, as he said, the rolls were not yet prepared. Only after a meeting with Captain Williams and Colonel Hatch did he agree to ship the men. Also, he mistakenly assumed that there were only 1,400 prisoners at Camp Fisk. He had left the meeting with the understanding that all of the men at the parole camp would be sent on one boat, the *Sultana,* which had been selected by Colonel Hatch.

On the day of the loading, when Captain Williams elected to go to the waterfront and personally see to the loading of the prisoners, Speed had felt that Williams, the officer originally in charge of the prisoner exchange, was taking charge again. After the rumors of bribery began to fly, it had been Captain Williams who had insisted that all the men, no matter the number, go on one boat. He ignored all pleas from Captain Kerns to do otherwise.

Armed with these facts, Captain Speed and his counsel went into the court-martial with high hopes.

Exactly six months later, on June 9, 1866, a verdict was announced. Captain Speed was found guilty on all three counts and faced a dishonorable discharge from the service.[40] From the beginning, the trial had gone against him. Of the several important witnesses who could have shed light on the selection and loading of the *Sultana,* only Captains Williams and Kerns testified. All other major witnesses, including Generals Dana and Smith, Colonel Hatch, and Lieutenant Tillinghast, failed to appear. Minor witnesses were brought forward by both sides, but they could not answer the questions that could be put only to the major witnesses.

Perhaps the most important person who could have been brought before the court was Colonel Hatch (although he certainly would have said nothing to incriminate himself). Ignoring subpoena after subpoena, Hatch refused to come to Vicksburg. Although the court requested Secretary of War Stanton to have Hatch arrested and forced to testify, even Captain Perce knew that it was a useless gesture. Hatch could not be compelled to testify before a military tribunal. "He is not in the Military Service," Captain Perce had argued, "and is not within the jurisdiction of the Court. He is a citizen of the State of Illinois and as such is entitled to all the rights and immunities of a citizen of that State and cannot be forced to leave it."[41]

Maj. Gen. Thomas J. Wood, General Dana's replacement, approved the findings of the court and sent the information to Secretary Stanton. In accordance with regulations, Stanton forwarded the case to Brig. Gen. Joseph Holt, judge advocate general of the U.S. Army and top man at the Bureau of Military Justice. Judge Holt had the last word on dispensing the recommendations of every court-martial. The fate of Captain Speed rested in his hands.

On June 21, 1866, after reviewing the case, Judge Holt ruled:

> It is the opinion of this bureau, after a careful study of the record, that Captain Speed took no such part in the transportation of the prisoners in question as should render him amenable to punishment; that his connection with the events which preceded the disaster to the *Sultana* was a wholly subordinate one; and that the facts developed in the evidence point out with distinctness other officers, whose indifference to the comfort of those placed temporarily in their charge resulted in, though without causing, the death of over 1,100 of their number.[42]

Although the first specification had suggested that Speed had not "availed himself" of the services of Colonel Hatch and Captain Kerns, Judge Holt found that Speed "did not fail to avail himself of the services of [Colonel] Hatch, . . . but only of the services of Captain Kerns, who held a very subordinate position under [Colonel] Hatch." He found that Speed had learned of the overcrowding only late in the day when it was impossible under the circumstances to divide the men. In a bold statement, Judge Holt declared: "The evidence shows that the *Sultana* was selected by [Colonel] Hatch . . ." and that Captain Williams "was present when the men were put on the *Sultana,* counted them as they went aboard, declared them to be comfortable, and insisted . . . that none should go on any other boat."[43]

Because Speed *had* consulted with Hatch, Judge Holt found that the accusation in the first specification, that Speed "did neglect to avail himself of the services" of Hatch and Kerns, "manifestly fails to be sustained." To the second specification, suggesting that Speed had "without authority" overloaded the *Sultana* "against the remonstrances" of Kerns and that his criminal neglect caused the explosion of the *Sultana,* Judge Holt found that "the accused did act with authority"; that Kerns "did not remonstrate with him"; and that the overloading of the boat, by whomever, did not cause the destruction of the *Sultana;* rather, it was caused by an imperfectly repaired boiler.[44]

One of the more interesting questions to come out of the trial was whether or not the *Sultana* had been overloaded. Pilot George Kayton stated, "I do not think [the *Sultana*] was overloaded. It was overcrowded. She was not overloaded in amount of tonnage, but she was overcrowded in my opinion." Kayton confirmed that the *Sultana* was licensed to carry more than 600 tons even with the combined weight of some 2,300 people, their total weight would not have equaled 600 tons.[45]

Judge Holt echoed Kayton when he wrote:

> It is further shown, by abundant evidence, that the boat, though overcrowded, was not overloaded; that in shipment of troops by steamer no attention was ever paid, throughout the war, to the legal carrying capacity of the ship; . . . and finally, that the explosion was owing, not to the excess in the number of men she was conveying, but to the fact that since her last official survey . . . her boilers had been burned, through the probable carelessness of her engineer, and had been repaired imperfectly with a patch of thinner iron.[46]

In summation, Judge Holt wrote: "Whoever should be regarded as meriting punishment for his connection with the event, it is believed that it is not Captain Speed." He also wrote that he did not want to "cast censure upon the conduct of Captain Williams." The judge realized that

Williams had arrived back in Vicksburg just prior to the *Sultana*'s loading and that Williams had been confused by reports of bribery and the total number of paroled prisoners to be shipped. As for Hatch, however, Judge Holt did admit that he must have "felt a consciousness of some responsibility for the disaster" by repeatedly ignoring court subpoenas and refusing to obey each summons. "It is recommended," the judge finalized, "that the sentence [against Captain Speed] be disapproved and that Captain Speed be publicly exonerated from charges which have been made against his character as an officer."[47]

Secretary of War Stanton confirmed Judge Holt's reversal of the charges. On September 1, 1866, Speed was honorably mustered out of the U.S. Army with his record wiped clean and his reputation intact.[48]

Captain Speed's greatest fault in connection with the *Sultana* might have been that he was too ambitious and energetic. He was an efficient adjutant and quick to please, but, when he volunteered to take over the job of commissioner of exchange, perhaps he took on a task larger than he could handle. In carrying out his assignments as quickly as possible, Speed did not allow himself enough time to gather all of the facts, such as how many prisoners had been turned over by the Confederates and how many men were left at Camp Fisk on the date of the loading of the *Sultana*. In an army plagued by lackluster performances and lackadaisical attitudes, it is odd that Speed should have been censured for being too quick and ambitious.

After releasing Speed from blame, Judge Holt took the case no farther. Although he had named Hatch and Williams as the officers whom he felt were most responsible for the events that led to the overcrowding, he did not recommend court action, and none was forthcoming. A year after the event, the interest among the general public and in Washington had waned. The Civil War was over. The people who died in the explosion of a Mississippi steamboat, far removed from the Eastern seaboard and its news network, were all Westerners and not of sufficient interest for additional consideration. The country was in the throes of Reconstruction, and nobody wanted to be reminded about the *Sultana* disaster.

Hatch was now a private citizen living in Illinois and, as witnessed by the lack of strength behind the military subpoenas during Captain Speed's trial, beyond the reach of the military. Even with the death of President Lincoln, Hatch still had highly placed and influential friends and relatives in Washington and Illinois. No one was going to touch Reuben B. Hatch.

Williams was a graduate of West Point, a career military man, still in the service of his country, and certainly within easy reach of a military court-martial. Judge Holt undoubtedly remembered that Williams had faced dismissal from the service in 1864, but the decision was overturned at the personal urging of General Grant, now the most powerful man in the U.S. Army. Rather than endure the wrath of General Grant and others, Judge Holt was apparently satisfied to let the matter die. After the farcical trial of Captain Speed, the case of the *Sultana* was closed. No one would be tried again, and no one would ever be punished for the tremendous loss of life.

20 Too Soon Forgotten

News of the *Sultana* disaster spread rapidly when the *Marble City* arrived at Cairo on April 28. As word went out immediately over the telegraph wires, towns throughout the Midwest—the hometowns of many of the men and boys on the *Sultana*—splashed the information across the front pages of their newspapers. Farther east, the story was less personal but equally as newsworthy.

Most newspapers reprinted stories from the two Memphis dailies, the *Argus* and *Daily Bulletin*. Some, however, sent reporters to Memphis or received special dispatches from reporters already in the field. As word spread that the vast majority of soldiers on board were from Ohio, Indiana, Michigan, Kentucky, Tennessee, and West Virginia, the Midwestern newspapers clamored for more information, whereas East Coast newspapers reduced their coverage.

The *New York Times,* perhaps the leading newspaper of the day, ran its first item on the *Sultana* on April 29. It consisted of a few small dispatches from Saint Louis and Cairo and was followed by similar articles on May 1 and May 2. The disaster finally hit the front page of the *Times* on May 3, when it printed a few words from ex-Congressman John Covode of Pennsylvania. After a short investigation, Covode concluded that the *Sultana* "was overloaded" and that "other good boats" were at Vicksburg while the *Sultana* was being loaded. To the eastern papers, however, Covode's most important contribution was his statement: "No troops belonging to States East of Ohio were lost."[1] With those few words, the *Sultana* disaster all but faded from East Coast newspapers. It was mentioned once more, on May 4, before a final article, a small sidebar, appeared on May 28. The sidebar contained the whitewashed findings of the Washburn Inquiry.

Harper's Weekly, a leading illustrated journal published in New York

City, carried a short account of the disaster in its May 13th edition, with articles from the Memphis newspapers as the basis for its story. A week later, *Harper's* reproduced a vivid, yet highly inaccurate, woodcut of the *Sultana* wreathed in flames that depicted hundreds of soldiers leaping from her decks or struggling in the water. The only mention of the disaster was in the caption to the picture. To those readers who either had missed the previous article or had not heard about the disaster, the picture must have been indeed puzzling.[2]

The Midwest papers, on the other hand, sought every available tidbit of information about the disaster. The *Chicago Tribune*, perhaps the most influential paper in the region, ran its first article on April 29 and kept up a running commentary with short articles and small bits of information for the next two weeks. Finally, on May 24, the *Tribune* last mentioned the *Sultana* when it published the findings of the Washburn Inquiry.

Saint Louis, home port of the *Sultana*, gave the disaster full front-page coverage for several weeks. At first word of the disaster, the two major newspapers, the *Daily Missouri Republican* and *Daily Missouri Democrat*, reprinted the Memphis articles in toto. As the scope of the disaster spread and the people of the city demanded firsthand accounts, both papers dispatched field reporters to Memphis. Trying to outsell each other, the two papers printed every word their reporters wired to them. On May 1, the *Daily Missouri Democrat* scooped its rival by reporting the arrest of the five *Sultana* crewmen who had left their wives behind on the stricken boat.[3] No less concerned than the river towns along the Mississippi were the native states of the paroled prisoners.

Ohio, with the largest contingent of troops on the *Sultana*, covered the calamity extensively. In Cincinnati, most of the early material was reprinted from the Memphis articles, but as interest grew, each of the three city newspapers, the *Daily Gazette, Daily Commercial,* and *Daily Enquirer,* also sent special correspondents to Memphis. Starting with the April 29th edition, the news of the burning and sinking of the *Sultana* was rarely out of the Cincinnati papers for the next three weeks.

In Columbus, Toledo, and other cities and towns throughout Ohio, especially in areas where regiments had been recruited, the story was front-page news.

In Ashland County, which had contributed heavily to the 64th and 102d Ohio Infantry regiments, and only slightly less to the 65th Ohio Infantry and McLaughlin's Independent Ohio Cavalry Squadron, the news was riveting. News of the *Sultana* "cast a gloom over the county, as the lost soldiers were all residents and were soon expected home."[4] Whenever information could be gathered, the names of the living and dead were printed.

In Michigan, Kentucky, and Tennessee, the story was basically the same. Newspapers in the larger towns concentrated on reprinting stories from the Memphis newspapers, but newspapers in the smaller towns that had regiments on board sought more specific information. In Knoxville, one published a list of the known living and dead from the 3d Tennessee Cavalry, the largest single body of troops on the *Sultana,* that had been recruited from the surrounding counties.[5]

The *Louisville Daily Journal* first broke the appalling news on April 30 and, by May 3, was able to publish a list of the Kentucky soldiers who were rescued from the *Sultana.* The *Indianapolis Daily Gazette* ran a number of accounts of the disaster, including an article on May 3 that listed the Indiana soldiers who had been rescued. The Detroit *Free Press* covered the disaster with similar interest but waited until June 15 to print a list of the Michigan soldiers on board the *Sultana.*

Newspapers in small towns and some large midwestern cities clung tenaciously to each word about the *Sultana,* but many newspaper editors quickly forgot about the disaster. This resulted more from the story's being overshadowed, rather than being overlooked. The month of April 1865 was one of the most dramatic times in American history. Beginning with a number of battles in Virginia that eventually forced the surrender of Robert E. Lee's Confederate Army at Appomattox Court House on April 9, it reached a peak with the assassination of President Lincoln on April 14.

As the nation mourned and the military searched for Lincoln's assassin, newspapers across the North provided complete coverage of the assassination details and the hunt for the killer. Every detail, from Lincoln's body lying in state in the nation's capital, through the slow procession beginning there on April 19, to its arrival at Lincoln's final resting place in Springfield, Illinois, on May 3, was printed in the nation's newspapers.

On April 26, as Lincoln's funeral train continued to move back and forth across the eastern and midwestern states, John Wilkes Booth was caught and gunned down in Virginia. That same day, after more than a week of haggling, Gen. Joseph E. Johnston surrendered the last large Confederate Army in the East to Union General Sherman at Durham Station, North Carolina. By all reasoning, the American Civil War was over, and the northern newspapers rejoiced at the triumph of the North over the South.

Wedged into the middle of this sorrow and joy came word of the *Sultana* disaster. After four years of war, the nation had become calloused toward the horrors of constant death and slaughter. Unless the news affected someone personally, it was soon forgotten, swept aside by some new, equally traumatic event. As April turned to May, the newspapers concentrated on Lincoln's funeral, the surrender of Gen. Richard Taylor, and the capture of Confederate President Jefferson Davis.[6] Except for its survivors and the families of its dead and disabled, the *Sultana* disaster became just another footnote in the history of the Civil War.

No one could be certain how many lives were lost on the *Sultana*. The official government tally of paroled prisoners was placed at 1,866, but the actual count was probably closer to 2,050–2,100, with another 22 members of a guard unit from the 58th Ohio Infantry. The government also placed the number of civilian passengers at 70 and the number of crew members at 85. The number for the civilian passengers, again, was too low; it was probably closer to 100. This brought the total number of people on board closer to 2,250–2,300.[7] The *Sultana* was registered to carry legally 376 passengers and crew.

It might be a bit easier to start with the known survivors and work backward. The *Daily Bulletin* reported on April 28 that 786 people had survived the disaster and General Hoffman, in his report to the Secretary of War, stated that there were 783, virtually the same figure. The numbers, however, did not reflect the actual number of survivors. More than 200 people pulled from the river died from their injuries during the following weeks, thus leaving the actual number of survivors closer to 550. In fact, the U.S. Sanitary Commission, which took an active interest in the victims from the beginning, reported that only 507 survivors went home in the first two contingents carried upriver to Cairo, although it is almost certain that a few trickled home after that.[8]

Of the estimated 783 to 786 survivors, it is generally believed that about 18 of those were civilian passengers or crew members. The most recent evidence (see Appendix B), however, indicates that there might have been as many as 35 to 40 passengers and crew who lived. But, because the civilian numbers were never separated from the military numbers, the number of surviving civilians should be considered part of the 550 estimated *Sultana* survivors.[9] Consequently the total number of deaths would have been between 1,700 and 1,750 men, women, and children.

The government, probably trying to lessen the extent of the disaster, placed the number of dead at 1,238 (1,101 soldiers and 137 passengers and crew, out of a total of 2,021 on board); the U.S. Customs Department in Memphis placed the total at 1,547.[10] The latter figure is based on the assumption that there were 2,051 people (1,866 soldiers, 100 civilian passengers, and 85 crew members) on board the *Sultana* on April 27, 1865. If the Customs Department figure is used, it would suggest that 504 people survived and would raise the total number of dead to between 1,746 and 1,796, numbers almost identical to the earlier total.

Years later in 1902, when a number of survivors met at a reunion in Fort Wayne, Indiana, the question was put to them concerning the number of people on board the *Sultana* as she traveled upriver from Vicksburg and how many they thought survived. "To a man," according to the *Fort Wayne Sentinel,* "the survivors say that not less than 2,200 persons [were] on board the boat at the time of the explosion and that of that number not 400 were saved."[11]

Many paroled prisoners known to have perished on the *Sultana,* but whose bodies were never found, were mustered out under General Order No. 77, a wide-sweeping order that tried to disband the army and reduce expenditures. Because many of the paroled prisoners from Camp Fisk left Camp Chase without orders or never reached there at all, government officials had no idea how many people from the *Sultana* were still alive. For example, Sgt. David Nahum Sanders (Company E, 3d Tennessee Cavalry) perished in the disaster, yet he was officially mustered out of the army on August 3, 1865. Later, when his widow applied for a pension, he was listed as having died on May 15, 1865, from "exposure from shipwreck."[12]

Not only did government officials not know who was dead, but they did not know who was alive. Pvt. Chester D. Berry was back home recovering from his fractured skull when "two or three months afterward my mother received official notice from Washington that her son was killed upon the *Sultana*."[13] Pvt. James Stuart Cook came home a week after his mother had learned of his death. And, years later, when the survivors applied for government pensions for their injuries, they first had to prove that they had been on the *Sultana* and then had to prove that their injuries occurred at that time. Because of the shoddy paperwork in compiling the rolls of the men who went on board and of those who actually survived, proving those two facts was almost impossible for many survivors.[14]

When asked why the government would try to downplay the extent of the *Sultana* disaster, many of the survivors, according to the *Fort Wayne Sentinel,* felt that "there was a fear that the knowledge of the fact that the *Sultana* was criminally overcrowded; that she was scandalously out of repair and notoriously unseaworthy [*sic*] might result in the presentation of enormous claims against the government for damages by the heirs of the slaughtered soldiers." The survivors further felt that the government "was in no mood to incur additional liabilities by acknowledging that the drowning of 1,800 loyal soldiers was due to either carelessness, incompetency or avarice of its own responsible officers and agents." The survivors felt the investigations into the disaster had been "whitewashed."[15]

Although the government chose to ignore the *Sultana* disaster, rather than bring it to a satisfactory conclusion, others did not. Or, more correctly, they could not. For the men and women who worked on the Mighty Mississippi, there was a constant reminder of the danger of steamboat travel. Every time they boarded their vessels, constructed of flimsy, highly flammable materials and carrying a potentially dangerous set of boilers, they knew that they risked life and limb. Fatal explosions on the steamboats *W. R. Carter* and *Missouri* later in 1865 and in 1866, respectively, accentuated this fact.

Investigation of the three explosions revealed that the *Sultana, W. R. Carter,* and *Missouri* each carried high-pressure tubular boilers (see chapter 1 for description). When this boiler was first introduced in 1848, it had been considered the most efficient type, but it was proving to be a detriment in the silty waters of the Lower Mississippi. After the loss of the three steamboats, many insurance companies refused to insure goods shipped on boats with tubular boilers. Also, steamboat inspectors issued statements criticizing the boilers. Steamboat owners and officers began to recant their previous faith in tubular boilers. By 1866, almost all tubular boilers were replaced with the more conventional flue boilers as a result of the three disasters.[16]

Another positive outcome of the *Sultana* disaster was the founding of the Hartford Steam Boiler Inspection and Insurance Company, which became one of the most powerful and efficient inspection and insurance companies of its day. Two Hartford, Connecticut, businessmen, who had been members of the Polytechnic Club, established in 1857 to study "scientific phenomena and its practical utilization," acted on earlier club discussions of ways to "anticipate and prevent explosions." They incorporated the company in June 1866. According to the Hartford Insurance Company, it is still committed to the development and promulgation of safety standards.[17]

Several vessels visited the site of the *Sultana,* which was lying charred and mangled in about twenty feet of water at the head of Paddy's Hen island, immediately after the disaster. Some of the first vessels to arrive were the rescue boats. They reached the remains shortly after the *Sultana* sank beneath the rushing brown waters of the Mississippi in the early morning of April 27. Throughout the next few days, vessels constantly searched the area for the bodies that slowly began to rise from the burnt decks.

On April 30, when the steam tug *Little Giant* returned from the site with a "piece of shell" (see chapter 19), a rumor immediately began to circulate that the destruction of the *Sultana* had been a Confederate plot. Many of the survivors believed that a Confederate agent had concealed a torpedo or shell inside a lump of coal and that, when the coal was shoveled into the *Sultana*'s furnace, the boilers exploded.[18] In 1888, a Confederate blockade runner added fuel to this theory by claiming that he had spoken to the very man who had smuggled the lethal lump of coal on board.[19] Although this rumor was believed by many survivors and mentioned at numerous reunions, no proof of such an action exists. To the contrary, the explosion resulted from a number of factors, none of which was a concealed Confederate torpedo.

About a week after the *Little Giant* visited the wreck, the Mississippi had fallen so that some of the *Sultana*'s remains were slightly above the brown water. "She is in fifteen feet of water," the *Memphis Daily Bulletin* reported. "Her jackstaff and part of her ribs are visible above the water. The water is too high and muddy for anything to be seen of the body of the wreck. Pieces of her guards and some of her chains are lying about the island."[20]

The *Sultana* was a complete loss to her owners. According to the *Daily Missouri Republican,* she carried insurance "against sinking and the usual casualties of navigation" but carried none against fire or boiler explosion, ". . . insurance does not cover losses of such an accident."[21]

Much of the *Sultana*'s machinery was recovered from the wreck. For days following the disaster, salvagers piled the loose debris on barges and carted it to the middle of Hen island, now high and dry above the falling Mississippi. There, the machinery and debris were examined and, if reusable, kept for resale; if not, they were discarded on the island. Pieces of firebrick and decking, hog chains, and small potbellied stoves from the texas cabins soon littered the crest of Hen Island, mute testimony to one of the worst marine disasters in history.[22]

Two weeks after the disaster, a portion of the boilers was recovered for inspection in an attempt to determine the cause of the explosion. Six months later, on October 20, 1865, one entire intact boiler was recovered from the wreck, "the only one unharmed, . . . the other three blown to atoms," Supervisor Witzig testified. The intact boiler was one of the inside boilers and showed positive signs that both outside boilers and the other inside boiler had exploded. At the time of recovery, it was full of sand and dirt.[23]

Gradually, the muddy waters of the Mississippi buried the charred remains of the *Sultana* and put her forever to rest away from prying eyes. Silt and sand filled every pore and crevice and eventually covered her completely. In time, the mighty river, forever changing its course and shortening its waterway, moved to the east of the *Sultana*'s location. The once elegant, sleek, and swift steamboat, the pride of Captain J. Cass Mason, was finally entombed beneath twenty feet of mud.

The *Sultana*'s safe, containing at least $32,000, more than half in gold coins, was never recovered. When the explosion tore upward through the main cabin, it completely obliterated everything in front of stateroom No. 10, including First Clerk William Gambrel's office. The safe was probably shot out into the river, covered by silt and mud, and buried forever in some unknown location.[24]

For more than a hundred years, the remains of the *Sultana* lay undisturbed. In the early 1980s, Memphis attorney Jerry O. Potter, utilizing an 1874 map from the Army Corps of Engineers and a magnetometer that locates large pieces of metal buried underground, began a search for the wreck. After numerous frustrating attempts, Potter located the remains under the fertile soil of an Arkansas soybean field. The high cost of excavation and the real possibility that nothing of the *Sultana,* except charred timbers and twisted, rusted metal, will be found preclude the idea of ever bringing her to the surface. Thus, perhaps for all eternity, the last remains of the *Sultana* will lie nestled under a blanket of soil.[25]

Although the remains of the *Sultana* would soon be buried, the memory of the disaster had a long and profound impact not only on those who survived the disaster, but also on the hundreds of regiments with representatives on board. Most of them had only a small number of men; a few had more than 100. In fact, the soldiers from six regiments totaled over one half of the paroled prisoners on board.

The 18th Michigan Infantry boarded the *Sultana* with 129 men and lost 71, a 55 percent loss. The 9th Indiana Cavalry put 112 men on her decks and lost 59, about 53 percent. The 102d Ohio Infantry lost 71 of 108 men, or 66 percent; the 115th Ohio Infantry lost 45 of 85 men, or 53 percent; and the 6th Kentucky Cavalry, recently captured that April, lost 48 out of 80 men, or 60 percent, including Maj. William H. Fidler.

The 3d Tennessee Cavalry, which had the largest contingent on the *Sultana,* also suffered one of the highest losses, both in number and percentage. Diligent research has revealed that some 398 cavalrymen from the 3d Tennessee boarded the *Sultana* at Vicksburg, and only 185 came home. The regiment left behind in the swirling waters of the Mississippi or in Elmwood Cemetery about 213 men, 54 percent of those on board. Because of the government's poor record keeping related to the loading of the *Sultana* and the deaths of men in the Memphis hospitals or after they returned home, many survivors of the 3d Tennessee believed that only 84 of their comrades lived. This figure suggests that the percentage of dead was actually about 79 percent.[26]

When word reached the camp of the 3d Tennessee Cavalry, the men were devastated by the news. "On the 27th of April," Maj. Will A. McTeer, the regimental adjutant, wrote, "the news came to us that the *Sultana* had blown up on the Mississippi River with our prisoner comrades on board, and many of them were lost. This brought bitter sorrow into the camps of the Third. Some of us slept none that night. It appeared as if death was eagerly preying upon those dearest [to] us while the skeleton of the confederacy was tottering and falling to pieces."[27] The numbers, the percentages, and the reactions were similar among the smaller units.

The losses within all of the regiments were lamentable, but perhaps one of the saddest was that sustained by the 58th Ohio Infantry. Against the wishes of Capt. William S. Friesner, the commanding officer, he, three noncommissioned officers, and eighteen privates of the 58th Ohio were ordered to board the *Sultana* and guard the emaciated prisoners upriver to Cairo and cross-country to Camp Chase. The soldiers believed the detail to be a lark. They would be the first of their regiment to get back to Ohio, the first to get home. The 58th's members left behind were quite vocal about favoritism regarding those who had been selected to go, but criticism turned to sorrow on April 29 when word of the disaster reached their camp.

"One day every heart is rejoiced," Sgt. William A. Pontious (Company C) wrote to a friend. "The cup of joy is filled ready to run over. The next the bitter drop of sorrow is mingled with the joy and makes every drop bitter." Reviewing a list of survivors from the 58th Ohio, Pontious failed to find the name of his good friend and comrade, Pvt. William Wells (Company A). "We have learned since," Pontious continued, "that six of our regt. was saved, but Willy Bill is not in that number, but numbered with the dead. . . . It was too bad to think of. I loved Billy almost as I love my own brothers. . . . I can hardly believe that he is dead." Overcome with grief, he knew that he had a hard job ahead of him. "I must write to his friends tomorrow, but it will be a hard task for me to perform. . . . He promised me when he left here that if he got to go home that he would call and see all of my friends and give all my respects, but now he is gone. I can sympathize and do deeply feel sorry for his afflicted Parents, Brothers, and Sisters. But then life is uncertain. There is no telling when death will claim it."[28]

The guard unit of the 58th Ohio Infantry lost 16 of its 22 men on board, a 73 percent loss (see Appendix B).

Indiana was the only state that tried to compile a cumulative number of its soldiers on board the *Sultana* and the number lost. The report listed 413 Indiana soldiers who were on board and 247 who lost their lives, for a total loss of almost 60 percent.[29] This maritime disaster was like no other before or since. Ordinarily, it would have made national headlines for a long time, but the nation was too calloused by war and too eager to forget death.

As the Civil War came to a close, units on both sides of the fighting were disbanded. In time, feeling a camaraderie that could be felt only by someone who had experienced the shot and shell of battle or the horror of prison camp, the veterans began to band together and participate in annual reunions; sometimes, the reunions commemorated certain units or battles. It was only fitting that survivors of the *Sultana* would want to meet and recount their experiences, attempt to educate the populace about the fateful morning of April 27, 1865, and petition the U.S. government for some form of recognition.

The survivors were generally separated into two camps, those in the Northern camp from Indiana, Ohio, and Michigan and those in the Southern camp from Kentucky and Tennessee. The first reunion of the Northern camp took place in December 1885 to mark the twentieth anniversary of the disaster. Meeting in Fostoria, Ohio, the men voted to call themselves the National *Sultana* Survivors' Association and elected Samuel H. Raudebaugh, a former private with the 65th Ohio Infantry, as president and honorary colonel.[30]

Word of the meeting soon spread. Over the next few years, more survivors attended the annual reunions. By 1889, they were meeting each April, close to the date of the disaster. Colonel Raudebaugh was still the president of the association and, with the support of the other survivors, petitioned the government for a "suitable monument, . . . somewhere along the Mississippi River near the place of the disaster in memory of the poor heroes who lost their lives in that most fearful disaster," and for "a special pension of $50 a month . . . to the suffering survivors."[31]

In a letter to the *National Tribune,* a Washington, D.C.–based soldiers' newspaper, Raudebaugh wrote:

> Let me ask, should they not have as good a monument as any General? . . . The Government asks the sworn statement of a commissioned officer or two comrades who were eyewitnesses to the injury.
>
> I was blown off the boat when sound asleep and injured in the breast and groin, and am suffering from it every day I live, but I cannot tell how it was done, nor what did it, much less can anyone else. When the explosion occurred we were sound asleep. . . . hence we cannot help one another as we could had we been injured in battle, in camp, or on the march. . . . [T]his Government will never do its duty to its suffering defenders until a respectable monument is erected in memory of the *Sultana* dead and a special pension is given every survivor.[32]

Perhaps inspired by Colonel Raudebaugh and the Northern camp, the first meeting of the Southern camp took place in 1889. Unfortunately, almost nothing is known of the event, and the meeting place is lost to posterity. By 1892, however, the meeting had become an annual event held in and around Knoxville, home to so many members of the 3d Tennessee Cavalry. John H. Simpson, a former private with the 3d Tennessee Cavalry, was elected Colonel of the southern camp. Simpson also began to petition the government for a national monument and a special pension.[33]

That same year, former Pvt. Chester D. Berry, now a gospel minister, published *"Loss of the Sultana and Reminiscences of Survivors."* He had collected the personal recollections of 134 survivors for his book. Set down on paper, many for the first time, were the experiences of those men on that fateful night so many years ago. A member of the Northern camp, Berry was undoubtedly trying to make a statement to the nation, in general, and to the government, in particular, regarding the devastation of the *Sultana.* Containing an "Official List of Exchanged [*sic*] Prisoners on the Boat," Berry's book was intended to help the survivors to apply for pensions and to urge the government to take notice and erect a suitable monument.[34]

Year after year, the two camps continued to meet separately. At times, each camp sent delegates and speakers to the other camp, although the two reunions apparently were never combined. Letters and minutes of the meetings were exchanged, and work on the monument and special pension was updated and compared. For the most part, the Northern camp met in northern Ohio, with an occasional foray into lower Michigan or eastern Indiana. By 1910, as the ranks began to thin and it became harder for the aged survivors to attend meetings in small towns, the gatherings took place in the Soldiers Memorial Hall in Toledo, Ohio. The Southern camp established itself in the Knoxville area from the start and met at various churches.[35]

The meetings hit their peak around the turn of the century. Almost fifty survivors attended the Knoxville reunions, and up to eight hundred people from the surrounding area came to hear the men tell of their adventures on the *Sultana.* The reunions were grand affairs, with picnic lunches, choral programs, and serenading bands, but the high point of every meeting consisted of the survivors' stories. Although the attendees, both survivors and civilians, had heard the tales over and over, they always listened with awe and respect.[36]

By 1912, the survivors had given up any idea of getting a special pension. Most of them were getting the same $8 per month pension as every other Union soldier. They turned their efforts solely toward the erection of a national monument honoring the *Sultana* disaster. "I believe that the government of this land should erect a monument to these men who were lost in the Mississippi," an honored speaker, Judge Austin, told the assemblage at the 1912 reunion of the Northern camp. "The association has been trying for years to get the U.S. to do this, but without avail."[37]

Facing the reality that a national monument was not forthcoming, Colonel Simpson and the Southern camp took matters into their own hands and, on July 4, 1912, erected a beautiful marble monument in Mount Olive Cemetery on the southern outskirts of Knoxville. Measuring 5 feet 7 inches tall, 6 feet wide, and 2 feet thick, the memorial contained a chiseled replica of the *Sultana* and the names of 365 Tennessee prisoners, both victims and survivors, listed on the sides.

An audience of about one thousand people, including four aging survivors, attended the unveiling of the monument. A message of "sincere congratulations" was read from the "few remaining survivors of the *Sultana* disaster who lived in the state of Ohio," to the "loyal and brave boys from the volunteer state of Tennessee."

The main speaker at the event, Judge Henry R. Gibson, a former East Tennessee congressman, recounted the loading of the *Sultana* and the events of her demise. He then turned toward the monument and said:

> This monument here at Mt. Olive . . . is the only one erected to the
> memory of the survivors of this tremendous catastrophe. [In] the years
> to come, young men will journey to this monument from far and near,
> and when asked why they want to see it, they will answer, "I am told my
> grandfather's name or my great grandfather's name is inscribed
> thereon," and when they search through the names, and find that of
> their ancestors, their hearts will swell with emotion and their eyes fill
> with tears, to know that of a very truth, the man whose blood flows in
> their veins was a soldier on the *Sultana*.[38]

By the mid-1920s, only a few survivors were able to participate in the reunions. Only two survivors, Colonel Simpson and Pleasant M. Keeble, also a former private with the 3d Tennessee Cavalry, attended the 1929 Southern Camp reunion in Rockford, Tennessee, near Knoxville. A year later, only Keeble attended.

"Alone he will attend what would have been a reunion had another of his comrades lived," the *Knoxville Journal and Tribune* lamented. "There will be speeches—and he will make them; dinner, and he will eat it; he will then call the roll, close the meeting, and return to his home."[39] On March 5, 1931, Keeble died at the age of eighty-five.[40]

In August 1931, the *Chattanooga Daily Times* reported that another survivor from the Knoxville area was living in a California Soldiers' Home. Former Pvt. Charles M. Eldridge, who had been with the 3d Tennessee Cavalry, was then eighty-six years old and somewhat disabled.[41] His death shortly afterward left only one remaining *Sultana* survivor from East Tennessee. Former Cpl. Samuel W. Jenkins of the hard-luck 3d Tennessee Cavalry still lived in the Knoxville area and had occasionally attended the Southern camp reunions. Outliving Eldridge by a year and a half, he died on January 19, 1933, at the age of eighty-four.[42]

In the Northern camp, some survivors held on a tad longer. Former Pvt. Henry J. Kline of the 9th Indiana Cavalry died on December 16,

1931, at age eighty-four, in Upland, Indiana. He was the last-known *Sultana* survivor to die on Indiana soil.[43] A year and a half later, on May 18, 1933, Kline's comrade in the 9th Cavalry and the last-known survivor from Indiana, former Pvt. William C. Warner, died in Wellington, Kansas, at the age of eighty-five.[44]

The following year, on April 1, 1934, former Pvt. Philip L. Horn of the 102d Ohio Infantry, died in Wooster, Ohio, at the age of eighty-nine.[45]

Almost seventy-one years after the burning and sinking of the *Sultana*, the last-known survivor of the disaster, ninety-four-year-old former Pvt. Albert Norris of the 76th Ohio Infantry, died in his home in Granville, Ohio, on January 9, 1936.[46]

No national monument was ever erected. (In May 1990, Jerry O. Potter would have a State of Tennessee marker placed beside the old levee in Memphis to mark the last stopping place of the ill-fated *Sultana*.) No special pension was ever delivered. The *Sultana* disaster was now just a forgotten footnote in a few of the better Civil War histories and the subject of several curious articles in periodicals relating to the Civil War.

Major Will A. McTeer, adjutant of the 3rd Tennessee Cavalry, penned these lines shortly after the regiment received word of the *Sultana* disaster:

> Many were killed while others were drowned. There in the bosom of the Mississippi they found their last resting place. No stone or monument marks the spot where their ashes lie. There is no tablet marked with their name, or even "unknown" for them. There is not even a hillock to which friends and survivors can go and drop a tear of remembrance of these noble defenders of the Union. . . . [F]lowers are strewn over the graves in the cemeteries of our dead, but there are no flowers for the dead of the [people], who went down on the *Sultana*. But let us remember them.[47]

Afterword

At the 1912 *Sultana* Survivors' Association meeting of the Northern Camp in Toledo, there had been much talk of another enormous maritime tragedy, the sinking of the RMS *Titanic* after she hit an iceberg in the North Atlantic on April 14, 1912. A total of 1,517 passengers and crew went down with the *Titanic*. In word and print, this disaster was much compared with the loss of the *Sultana*. Both vessels had carried about the same number of people—the *Titanic*, 2,223, and the *Sultana*, between 2,250 and 2,300. A rescue vessel saved 706 people from the *Titanic*, whereas 783 to 786 people initially had been saved from the *Sultana*. Percentages of saved to lost were roughly the same, about 68 percent for the *Titanic* and 65 percent for the *Sultana*.[1] More than 200 people from the *Sultana* died after rescue, however, which resulted in the percentage of dead approaching 75 percent, much higher than the loss on the *Titanic*.

The newspapers pointed out that the month of the disasters, April, was the same and that the time of the disasters was very similar: 2:00 A.M. when the boilers of the *Sultana* exploded and 2:20 A.M. when the *Titanic* sank. "But here the similarity ends," the Toledo *Daily Blade* proclaimed. "The contrast is almost as striking as the similarity."[2]

Although both vessels had carried roughly the same number of people, the *Titanic* dwarfed the *Sultana* in size. The *Sultana* had been 260 feet long, 42 feet wide, and perhaps three or four stories tall from the bottom of her keel to the top of her chimneys. The *Titanic* was 882.5 feet long, 92.5 feet wide, and eleven stories high from her keel to the top of her four huge funnels.[3]

"The *Titanic* represented the wealth and pride of the world," the *Daily Blade* editorialized, "and carried in its passenger list people of great wealth who were enjoying the voyage as a pleasure trip. On the other hand, the *Sultana* was loaded down with Union soldiers who had been confined in Andersonville and [Cahaba] Prisons. Weakened and exhausted from their imprisonment and lack of proper food and shelter they were en route home at the close of the war."[4]

The paroled prisoners who had been shoe-horned onto the *Sultana*, along with her forgotten civilian passengers and crew, were not important enough to be remembered. No Astors or Strauses or Guggenheims were on the *Sultana*. Her victims were just ordinary citizens and common soldiers on their way home to their loved ones after doing their part for their country.

Appendix A
Known Number of People on Board the *Sultana,* April 24–27, 1865

Paroled Prisoners	
Ohio	652
Tennessee	463
Indiana	407
Michigan	274
Kentucky	185
West Virginia	18
Unknown	6
U.S. Colored Troop	3
Illinois	2
Alabama	1
Iowa	1
Missouri	1
Nebraska	1
Pennsylvania	1
Total	2,015
Passengers	100
Crew	85
Guard Unit	22
Grand Total	2,222

NOTE. The figures given for passengers and crew are approximate. Also, the total number of paroled prisoners was probably a little higher, for a grand total of between 2,250 and 2,300 people on board the *Sultana* on her trip upriver from Vicksburg to Memphis.

Individuals Known to Be on Board the *Sultana,* April 24–27, 1865

Because no accurate records were kept of the people on board the *Sultana* during her fateful voyage from Vicksburg to Memphis, and eternity, no one is certain as to the total number of people and their identities. Fifteen years of research have produced the following four lists of the known crew, passengers, members of the guard unit, and paroled prisoners who were on board the *Sultana* at the time of the disaster. Each list indicates the known fate of these individuals; the hospitals to which they were transported, where applicable; and the injuries they suffered.

The crew and passenger lists were compiled mainly from newspapers of the period, as well as from a few regimental histories and personal accounts. The listing of the members of the guard unit is from Memphis newspapers, personal reminiscences, and reports of the Ohio adjutant general.

By far, the most difficult list to compile was that of the paroled Union prisoners. The starting point was a list of known soldiers found at the back of an 1892 book by the Reverend Chester D. Berry. Although filled with misspellings and inaccuracies, it provided a foundation.

The author perused many regimental histories, newspaper lists of survivors and casualties, and personal reminiscences in order to correct many of Berry's misspellings and, where possible, to clarify the errors. The addition of hundreds of names also resulted from checking these sources. Names of the prisoners from each state were then cross-referenced with reports of the adjutant general for that state, as well as other reference works containing listings of soldiers. Through the generous help of hundreds of the prisoners' descendants, other relatives, and people with an interest in the topic, the author was able to add many additional names and correct more spellings.

The lists, in the author's opinion, are the most complete and accurate available. Each of 95 percent of the names on the paroled prisoners' list have been found in at least two other reference works, thereby verifying that these individuals were on the *Sultana.* The names of the remaining 5 percent are found in at least one source and, consequently, warrant inclusion in the list unless subsequent research proves otherwise.

Of course, it is inevitable that such a list, compiled more than a century after the occurrence, will contain some inaccuracies. For example, if a prisoner who died in the disaster was the sole representative of his regiment, his name is likely to be forever lost to history. On the other hand, some individuals who were listed as victims might not have been on the *Sultana* at the time of the disaster.

Many of the paroled prisoners, whose fate is indicated by "Lived," were actually listed by the U.S. government as "mustered out," but their actual fate is unknown. They might have perished on the *Sultana*. Because many of the surviving paroled prisoners took "French leave" and left Camp Chase, Ohio, before being officially mustered out, the government had no way of knowing how many people had survived the disaster and who the survivors were. Where doubt existed, the government issued the necessary paperwork. The soldier was then mustered out, even if his body was still floating in the muddy Mississippi or buried in a Memphis cemetery under a headboard reading "Unknown."[1] In this way, the government was able to minimize the extent of the disaster, but, in so doing, it made accurate research almost impossible. Only through the help of regimental histories, personal reminiscences, and family records can the work of the government be undone.

Key to Abbreviations

RANK

Artif	Artificer
Blksm	Blacksmith
Capt	Captain
Cpl	Corporal
Farr	Farrier (veterinarian)
Hos S	Hospital Steward
Lt	Lieutenant
1st Lt	1st Lieutenant
2d Lt	2nd Lieutenant
Maj	Major
Musc	Musician
Pvt	Private
Sadlr	Saddler
Sgt	Sergeant
C Sgt	Commissary Sergeant
Sgt M	Sergeant Major
OSgt	Ordinance Sergeant
QMSgt	Quartermaster Sergeant
1st Sgt	First Sergeant
Tmstr	Teamster
Wagon	Wagoner

UNIT

AL Cav	Alabama Cavalry (Union)
IA Inf	Iowa Infantry
IL Inf	Illinois Infantry
IN Bat	Indiana Artillery Battery
IN Cav	Indiana Cavalry
IN Inf	Indiana Infantry
KY Cav	Kentucky Cavalry (Union)
KY Inf	Kentucky Infantry (Union)
KY L Art	Kentucky Light Artillery (Union)
KY MI	Kentucky Mounted Infantry (Union)
MI Cav	Michigan Cavalry
MI Eng	Michigan Engineers and Mechanics
MI Inf	Michigan Infantry
MI L Art	Michigan Light Artillery
MI SS	Michigan Sharpshooters
MO Cav	Missouri Cavalry
NEB Cav	Nebraska Cavalry
OH L Art	Ohio Light Artillery

UNIT (*continued*)

OH Cav	Ohio Cavalry
OH Inf	Ohio Infantry
McL OH Cav	McLaughlin's Ohio Cavalry Squadron
PA Cav	Pennsylvania Cavalry
TN Cav	Tennessee Cavalry (Union)
TN Inf	Tennessee Infantry (Union)
TN MI	Tennessee Mounted Infantry (Union)
USCT	U.S. Colored Troop
WV Cav	West Virginia Cavalry (Union)
WV Inf	West Virginia Infantry (Union)
WV L Art	West Virginia Light Artillery (Union)
X	Unit unknown

Key to Fate

Adams	Rescued and taken to Adams Hospital
Gayoso	Rescued and taken to Gayoso Hospital
Lived	Known to have lived or to have been mustered out
Officers	Rescued and taken to Officers Hospital
Overton	Rescued and taken to Overton Hospital
Soldiers'	Rescued and taken to the U.S. Sanitary Commission Soldiers' Home
Washington	Rescued and taken to Washington Hospital

NOTE. A date in the last column indicates the date of death. If no date is given for those who died, the date of death was April 27, 1865. This column might include several listings. For example, "Died June 28, 1865, Overton, severe scalds" indicates that the individual died on that date from severe scalds after being taken to Overton Hospital following the disaster.

Crew

Name	Rank/Rating	Fate
Barnes, William	Crewman	Lived
Butler, Thomas	Watchman	Died
Clemens, Samuel	Second engineer	Died
Cross, Henry	Steward	Died
Durkin, William	Deckhand	Died
Gambrel, William Jordan	First clerk	Died
Hunt, Thomas	Deckhand	Died, Gayoso; severe scalds
Ingraham, Henry	Pilot	Died
Kayton, George J.	Pilot	Lived
McGinty, Thomas	Barkeep	Died
Mason, J. Cass	Captain	Died
McQueene, Sam	Pantryman	Lived
Murphy, James	Pantryman	Lived
O'Hara, James	Barkeep	Died
Rowberry, William	First mate	Lived
Sigismond, Dan	Crewman	Lived
Slater, George	Second steward	Died
Smith, Walter B.	Deckhand	Died
Stratton, William	Second clerk	Died
Welsh, Thomas	Deckhand	Lived, Soldiers'
Wintringer, Nathan	First engineer	Lived

NOTE. The wives of five deckhands were reported to be on board; all were lost. Five unknown crewmen left the *Sultana* in the sounding yawl and were later arrested in Saint Louis, Missouri. No further information is available.

Passengers

Name	Classification	Fate
Annis, Lt. Harvey	Citizen (ex-soldier)	Died
Annis, Anna	Citizen	Lived, Gayoso; exhaustion
Annis, infant	Citizen	Died
Bent, Enoch	Citizen	Died
Butterfield, J.A.B.	Citizen (ex-soldier)	Died
Compton, Lt. Col. Charles E.	53d USCT	Disembarked at Memphis
Erwin, Mr.	U.S. Scout	Lived

Passengers, continued

Name	Classification	Fate
Farris, J. T.	Indiana Sanitary Commission agent	Lived
Fontaine, J. D.	Citizen	Died
Hardin, Seth W., Jr.	Citizen	Lived
Hardin, Mrs. Seth W., Jr.	Citizen	Died
Hoge, Mrs.	Citizen	Died
Long, William	Citizen	Lived
McEvan, Thomas	Government employee	Died
McKerner, Thomas	Government employee	Lived, Soldiers'
McLeod, Daniel	Citizen (ex-soldier)	Lived, Adams; left ankle, broken; right leg, amputated above knee
Moroney, John	Government employee	Lived, Soldiers'
Perry, Mrs.	Citizen	Lived
Safford, Mr.	Indiana Sanitary Commission agent	Lived
Smith, Pvt. George	87th IL Inf	Died
Smith-Ross, Lucy	Citizen	Died
Snow, William D.	Citizen, senator-elect	Lived
Spikes, Samuel B.	Citizen (husband)	Died
Spikes, Elethia	Citizen (wife)	Died
Spikes, Elizabeth	Citizen (daughter)	Died
Spikes, Susan	Citizen (daughter)	Died
Spikes, female	Citizen (daughter)	Died
Spikes, DeWitt Clinton	Citizen (son)	Lived
Spikes, male	Citizen (son)	Lived (?)
Spikes, male	Citizen (son)	Died
Spikes, Adeline	Citizen (niece)	Died
Walker, John	Government employee	Lived, Soldiers'
Witherspoon, William	Government employee	Lived, Adams; left leg, severe contusion
Woodcock, Michael	Government employee	Lived, Gayoso; exhaustion
Woolfolk, Sallie B.	Citizen	Died

NOTE. Also on board were twelve Sisters of Charity, volunteer laywomen whose names are with the U.S. Christian Commission. One of the sisters might have survived.

The Chicago Opera Troupe, a traveling minstrel band, was on the *Sultana* from Vicksburg to Memphis. Its members (number unknown) should be added to the total passengers on board.

Guard Unit, 58th Ohio Infantry

Company	Rank	Name	Fate
A	Capt	Friesner, William S.	Lived
A	Sgt	Elder, William H.	Lived, Soldiers'
A	Sgt	Sollenberger, Seth	Lived, Gayoso; exhaustion
A	Pvt	Branum, Robert	Died
A	Pvt	Elick, John	Died
A	Pvt	Hines, James	Lived, Gayoso; slight scalds
A	Pvt	Keistler, Jacob	Died
A	Pvt	Kinser, Christopher	Died
A	Pvt	Sanderson, John	Lived
A	Pvt	Stuller, James	Died
A	Pvt	Wells, William	Died
A	Pvt	Willson, Samuel	Died
B	Corp	Hawken, John	Died
B	Pvt	Campbell, Hiram	Died
B	Pvt	Kens, George	Died
B	Pvt	Mowry, John	Died
B	Pvt	Neustadt, David	Died
B	Pvt	Wolfkamer, John	Lived, Soldiers'
B	Pvt	Young, Frederick	Died
C	Pvt	Baada, Phillip	Died
C	Pvt	Bauer, John C.	Died
D	Pvt	Bresan, Peter	Died

Paroled Union Prisoners

Unit	Company	Rank	Name	Fate
1 AL Cav	M	Pvt	Reach, Jonathan	(?)
14 IL Inf	A	Pvt	McIntosh, Epenetus W.	Lived, Overton
137 IL Inf	I	Pvt	Sanders, Samuel F.	Lived, Adams, back contusion
6 IN Bat		Pvt	Heinrich, Anton L.	Died
24 IN Bat		Sgt	Williard, Frank L.	Died
24 IN Bat		Cpl	Hughes, William Henry	Lived, Washington, uninjured
24 IN Bat		Pvt	Appenseller, John S.	Died
24 IN Bat		Pvt	Bright, Isaac	Died
24 IN Bat		Pvt	Bright, Peacha H.	Died
24 IN Bat		Pvt	Denny, William	Died
24 IN Bat		Pvt	Hubbell, Albert	Died
24 IN Bat		Pvt	Maxwell, Alonzo	Died
24 IN Bat		Pvt	Shagley, Robert	Died
24 IN Bat		Pvt	Slonebrock, Joseph	Died, St. Louis, Mo.
2 IN Cav	B	Pvt	Brown, Isaiah	Died
2 IN Cav	C	QMSgt	Frazee, Martin	Lived, Overton, serious scalds: back, head, arms, legs
2 IN Cav	C	Pvt	McCutcheon, W.	(?)
2 IN Cav	C	Pvt	Phillips, William	Lived, Adams, slight scald
2 IN Cav	D	Cpl	Harter, Lucas T.	Died
2 IN Cav	D	Pvt	Stevens, William	Died
2 IN Cav	D	Pvt	Tidd, Leonard G.	Died
2 IN Cav	K	Pvt	Summerville, Perry S.	Lived, Gayoso, slight scald, back; badly bruised breast
3 IN Cav	B	Pvt	Conyers, William	Lived, Overton, scald, back
3 IN Cav	C	Pvt	Dilander, Joseph R.	Lived, Soldiers'
3 IN Cav	C	Pvt	Kaney, William	Died
3 IN Cav	F	Pvt	Norman, James	Died
4 IN Cav	C	QMSgt	Renchan, William	Lived
4 IN Cav	C	Pvt	Simkins, Charles E.	Lived
4 IN Cav	F	Pvt	Franklin, B.	(?)

Paroled Union Prisoners, continued

Unit	Company	Rank	Name	Fate
4 IN Cav	F	Sgt	Trimble, Arthur	Lived, Overton, slight contusion
4 IN Cav	H	Pvt	Cook, W. A.	(?)
4 IN Cav	K	Pvt	Smith, J.	(?)
5 IN Cav	A	Pvt	Nutt, James W.	Died
5 IN Cav	B	Pvt	Williams, Nathan Samuel	Lived, Soldiers', double hernia
5 IN Cav	C	Sgt	Dean, Joseph T.	Died, Adams, severe scalds
5 IN Cav	D	Cpl	Mallott, Richard A.	Died
5 IN Cav	E	Cpl	Thevenin, Anthony	Died
5 IN Cav	F	Pvt	Milton, Jesse	(?)
5 IN Cav	G	Pvt	Lawson, Hiram	Lived, Washington, slight contusion
5 IN Cav	H	Sgt	McCullough, Simon A.	Lived, Washington, ankle contusion
5 IN Cav	H	Pvt	Barton, Thomas	Died
5 IN Cav	H	Pvt	Grubbs, Isaac W.	Lived, Soldiers'
5 IN Cav	L	Wagon	McBride, George	Died
5 IN Cav	L	Pvt	Evans, David W.	Died
5 IN Cav	L	Pvt	Humbard, Isaac	Died
5 IN Cav	L	Pvt	Mullen, Jesse	Lived, Adams, back contusion
5 IN Cav	L	Pvt	Richardson, Autebridge	Died
5 IN Cav	L	Pvt	Scott, Louis	Lived, Soldiers'
6 IN Cav	A	Pvt	Lee, Asa E.	Lived, Soldiers'
6 IN Cav	A	Pvt	Parker, D. D.	(?)
6 IN Cav	C	Pvt	Applegate, John S.	Lived, Gayoso, exhaustion
6 IN Cav	C	Pvt	Potterfield, William	Lived
6 IN Cav	D	Pvt	Scole, R.	(?)
6 IN Cav	E	Pvt	Lee, E. C.	(?)
6 IN Cav	F	Sgt	Hobi, A. P.	(?)
6 IN Cav	G	Pvt	Sahal, F.	(?)
6 IN Cav	I	Pvt	Davis, Jasper N.	Lived
6 IN Cav	K	Pvt	Roon, J.	(?)
6 IN Cav	L	Sgt	Clary, Edward D.	Lived, Overton, contusion
7 IN Cav	C	Pvt	Gathman, John Henry	Lived, Soldiers'
7 IN Cav	C	Pvt	Nemire, James	Lived

Paroled Union Prisoners, continued

Unit	Company	Rank	Name	Fate
7 IN Cav	C	Pvt	Rowe, David P.	Lived, Soldiers'
7 IN Cav	C	Pvt	Sohly, Christian	Lived
7 IN Cav	D	Cpl	Farl, John	Lived, Adams, chilled
7 IN Cav	D	Pvt	Frederick, George H.	Lived, Adams, chilled
7 IN Cav	D	Pvt	Hall, John F.	Died June 6, 1865
7 IN Cav	E	Pvt	Ames, Sanford P.	Lived, Gayoso, exhaustion
7 IN Cav	E	Pvt	Blackburn, Joseph	Lived
7 IN Cav	E	Pvt	Donner, Daniel W.	Died
7 IN Cav	E	Pvt	Paxton, John Q.	Died
7 IN Cav	E	Pvt	Porter, Costan	Died
7 IN Cav	G	Pvt	Corbin, William S.	Died
7 IN Cav	G	Pvt	Nichols, C.	(?)
7 IN Cav	I	Pvt	Armstrong, Robert B.	Lived, Gayoso, exhaustion
7 IN Cav	I	Pvt	Barrack, William	Died
7 IN Cav	I	Pvt	Swords, Elisha	Died
7 IN Cav	K	Pvt	Barrett, Augustus	Died
7 IN Cav	K	Pvt	Elkins, Francis M.	Died
7 IN Cav	K	Pvt	Gard, John W.	Lived, Overton, chilled
7 IN Cav	K	Pvt	Schmidt, Joseph	Lived, Washington, uninjured
7 IN Cav	K	Pvt	Scott, William W.	Died June 21, 1865, Delphi, Ind.
7 IN Cav	M	Pvt	Johnston, Henry A.	Lived, Gayoso, exhaustion
7 IN Cav	M	Pvt	McCann, Adam	Lived, Soldiers'
7 IN Cav	M	Pvt	Smith, Charles	(?) Soldiers'
7 IN Cav	M	Pvt	Thompson, William F.	Died
8 IN Cav	A	Pvt	Berry, Willard N.	Lived
8 IN Cav	C	Pvt	Milliken, Erskine	Died
8 IN Cav	D	Pvt	Markland, William	Lived
8 IN Cav	F	Pvt	Fory, Alexander	Lived, Washington, uninjured
8 IN Cav	F	Pvt	Stites, John M.	Lived, Washington, uninjured
8 IN Cav	H	Pvt	Maddox, John C.	Lived, Soldiers'
8 IN Cav	H	Pvt	Tolbert, Romulus	Lived, Adams, chilled

Paroled Union Prisoners, continued

Unit	Company	Rank	Name	Fate
8 IN Cav	I	Pvt	Demoss, Thomas	Died, Gayoso, exhaustion
9 IN Cav	A	1st Sgt	Hinckley, John B.	Lived, Gayoso, exhaustion
9 IN Cav	A	Sgt	Curtis, Daniel	Died
9 IN Cav	A	Sgt	Spades, Jacob	Lived
9 IN Cav	A	Sgt	Talkington, Robert	Lived, Soldiers', slight scalds
9 IN Cav	A	Cpl	Day, Elias R.	Lived, Soldiers'
9 IN Cav	A	Bugle	Evans, Charles	Lived, Gayoso, exhaustion
9 IN Cav	A	Pvt	Day, Patrick	Died
9 IN Cav	A	Pvt	Paul, Arthur H.	Died, May 6, 1865, Indianapolis, Ind., Adams, slight scald
9 IN Cav	A	Pvt	Riley, William R.	Lived, Adams, bruised right arm
9 IN Cav	B	Cpl	Blessinger, Frederick	Died
9 IN Cav	B	Cpl	Lyons, Virgil H.	Lived
9 IN Cav	B	Pvt	Church, Charles E.	Died
9 IN Cav	B	Pvt	Gray, Joseph H.	Lived, Soldiers'
9 IN Cav	B	Pvt	Mooney, John	Lived, Soldiers'
9 IN Cav	B	Pvt	Parman, Ephraim B.	Died
9 IN Cav	B	Pvt	Read, William P.	Lived, Soldiers'
9 IN Cav	B	Pvt	Scott, Robert S.	Lived, Soldiers'
9 IN Cav	B	Pvt	Sears, Christopher H.	Lived, Soldiers'
9 IN Cav	B	Pvt	Steward, John	Died
9 IN Cav	B	Pvt	Waller, Benjamin F.	Lived, Soldiers'
9 IN Cav	B	Pvt	Warner, William C.	Lived, Washington, slight contusion
9 IN Cav	B	Pvt	Wilson, George P.	Lived, Adams, chilled
9 IN Cav	C	Pvt	Englehart, John M.	Died May 9, 1865
9 IN Cav	C	Pvt	Huckins, Warren A.	Died
9 IN Cav	C	Pvt	Kammer, Thomas K.	Died
9 IN Cav	D	Pvt	Wood, Edward	Died
9 IN Cav	E	Pvt	Gilbreath, Robert W.	Lived, Adams, acute diarrhea
9 IN Cav	E	Pvt	Laboyteaux, Thomas	Died June 7, 1865

Paroled Union Prisoners, continued

Unit	Company	Rank	Name	Fate
9 IN Cav	E	Pvt	McCormick, Andrew	Lived, Washington, uninjured
9 IN Cav	F	Sgt	Bonner, John	Died
9 IN Cav	F	Pvt	King, John Henry	Lived, Soldiers', back injury
9 IN Cav	F	Pvt	Penion, Anderson	Lived, Adams, chilled
9 IN Cav	G	1st Lt	Swain, Elihue H.	Lived, Gayoso, exhaustion
9 IN Cav	G	Sgt	Graves, William H.	Died
9 IN Cav	G	Sgt	Rodepouch, Martin V.	Died
9 IN Cav	G	Cpl	Allison, Hiram	Lived, Overton, scalp contusion, scalded legs
9 IN Cav	G	Cpl	Nation, Enoch K.	Died
9 IN Cav	G	Cpl	Peacock, William H.	Lived, Soldiers', scalds, right side, hip; cut shoulder; bruised hip
9 IN Cav	G	Pvt	Clevenger, Charles W.	Died
9 IN Cav	G	Pvt	Downing, George	Died
9 IN Cav	G	Pvt	Downing, Jonathan R.	Died
9 IN Cav	G	Pvt	Hanna, Horton H.	Lived, Soldiers'
9 IN Cav	G	Pvt	Hoover, William C.	Died
9 IN Cav	G	Pvt	Johnson, Lewis	Lived, Gayoso, exhaustion; neck and shoulders, bad burns
9 IN Cav	G	Pvt	King, Charles William M.	Died
9 IN Cav	G	Pvt	Kline, Henry J.	Lived, Gayoso, exhaustion; neck and ears, burns
9 IN Cav	G	Pvt	Maynard, John M.	Died
9 IN Cav	G	Pvt	Ollom, James C.	Died
9 IN Cav	G	Pvt	Reasoner, John R.	Died
9 IN Cav	G	Pvt	Thornburg, Nathan	Died
9 IN Cav	H	CSgt	Mavity, Uriah J.	Lived, Soldiers'
9 IN Cav	H	Pvt	Ballenger, Franklin	Died
9 IN Cav	H	Pvt	Bell, James	Died
9 IN Cav	H	Pvt	Delano, George W.	Died
9 IN Cav	H	Pvt	Dunham, Alonzo	Died

Paroled Union Prisoners, continued

Unit	Company	Rank	Name	Fate
9 IN Cav	H	Pvt	Hardin, William H.	Lived, Soldiers'
9 IN Cav	H	Pvt	Pratt, Josiah	Died
9 IN Cav	H	Pvt	Shull, John W.	Died
9 IN Cav	H	Pvt	Stoops, Hermon B.	Lived
9 IN Cav	I	Pvt	Hawthorn, Darius F.	Lived
9 IN Cav	K	Sgt	Shuler, Thomas D.	Lived
9 IN Cav	K	Cpl	Folderman, Barnett	Lived, Washington, skull fracture
9 IN Cav	K	Cpl	Hartley, Franklin	Died July 28, 1865, Jefferson Barracks, Mo.; Soldiers
9 IN Cav	K	Musc	Gaston, Stephen M.	Lived, Adams, badly scraped, incised thigh wound
9 IN Cav	K	Wagon	Stokes, James	Lived
9 IN Cav	K	Pvt	Bailey, Hiram	Died
9 IN Cav	K	Pvt	Baker, Oleo O.	Lived, Washington, uninjured
9 IN Cav	K	Pvt	Block, William	Lived, Washington, slight contusion
9 IN Cav	K	Pvt	Dorman, Henry	Died
9 IN Cav	K	Pvt	Emmons, John W.	Died
9 IN Cav	K	Pvt	Fisher, George S.	Died
9 IN Cav	K	Pvt	Green, Seth J.	Lived, Overton, head and neck scalds
9 IN Cav	K	Pvt	Harald, Jacob	Died
9 IN Cav	K	Pvt	Kessler, Phillip	Lived, Gayoso, exhaustion
9 IN Cav	K	Pvt	Laughlin, Thomas B.	Lived
9 IN Cav	K	Pvt	Newton, Henry O.	Died
9 IN Cav	K	Pvt	Rea, William F.	Died
9 IN Cav	K	Pvt	Shockley, George H.	Died
9 IN Cav	K	Pvt	Stevens, Darius	Died
9 IN Cav	K	Pvt	Survant, Joseph	Died
9 IN Cav	K	Pvt	Windhorst, Jonathan	Lived
9 IN Cav	K	Pvt	Zix, Matthew	Died
9 IN Cav	L	Sgt	Addington, George W.	Lived, Soldiers'
9 IN Cav	L	Cpl	Collins, William J.	Lived, Washington, uninjured

Paroled Union Prisoners, continued

Unit	Company	Rank	Name	Fate
9 IN Cav	L	Cpl	Moorhouse, Robert A.	Died
9 IN Cav	L	Pvt	Christian, James R.	Died
9 IN Cav	L	Pvt	Daggy, George W.	Lived, Soldiers'
9 IN Cav	L	Pvt	Glaze, William Perry	Lived
9 IN Cav	L	Pvt	Johnson, William T.	Lived
9 IN Cav	L	Pvt	Johnston, James M.	Lived, Adams, chilled
9 IN Cav	L	Pvt	Kelly, Grandison	Lived
9 IN Cav	L	Pvt	McCartney, Leander	Died
9 IN Cav	L	Pvt	Miller, Elias	Lived, Adams, slight scald
9 IN Cav	L	Pvt	Reed, Archibald	Died
9 IN Cav	L	Pvt	Winsor, William Henry	Lived, Washington, slight scald
9 IN Cav	M	Sgt	Gaskill, David	Lived, Overton, contusion
9 IN Cav	M	Cpl	Armstrong, John M.	Died
9 IN Cav	M	Cpl	Brigg, William	Died
9 IN Cav	M	Cpl	Gruell, Nathan E.	Died
9 IN Cav	M	Farr	Watson, Josiah	Lived, Overton, chilled
9 IN Cav	M	Pvt	Alexander, Joseph D.	Died
9 IN Cav	M	Pvt	Blake, George W.	Died
9 IN Cav	M	Pvt	Brigg, John M.	Died
9 IN Cav	M	Pvt	Chance, William H.	Died, Gayoso, severe scalds
9 IN Cav	M	Pvt	Halloway, Enos	Died
9 IN Cav	M	Pvt	Huffman, William H.	Died
9 IN Cav	M	Pvt	Isentrager, William L.	Died
9 IN Cav	M	Pvt	King, Samuel	Died
9 IN Cav	M	Pvt	McGinnis, Samuel S.	Lived, Washington, uninjured
9 IN Cav	M	Pvt	Ridley, Franklin	Died
9 IN Cav	M	Pvt	Smith, Lorenzo	Lived, Soldiers'
9 IN Cav	M	Pvt	Spacey, Oscar F.	Lived, Overton, chilled
10 IN Cav	A	2d Lt	Dixon, William French	Lived, Officers, breast, slight injury
10 IN Cav	A	Pvt	Barlow, Jeremiah	Died
10 IN Cav	A	Pvt	Redman, James B.	Died
10 IN Cav	B	Pvt	Cooper, John	(?)

Paroled Union Prisoners, continued

Unit	Company	Rank	Name	Fate
10 IN Cav	C	2d Lt	Reeves, Thomas B.	Died
10 IN Cav	G	Pvt	Graham, John	Lived
10 IN Cav	G	Pvt	McCleland, James A.	Lived, Soldiers'
10 IN Cav	G	Pvt	McKenzie, John W.	Lived
10 IN Cav	H	Bugle	Prindle, Romeo W.	Lived, Adams, chilled
10 IN Cav	H	Hos S	Crawford, Emerson T.	Lived
10 IN Cav	H	Pvt	Kelly, George W.	Died
10 IN Cav	H	Pvt	Safford, George M.	Lived, Gayoso, exhaustion
10 IN Cav	H	Pvt	Smith, William B.	Died
10 IN Cav	K	1st Lt	Twigg, Alexander	Died
10 IN Cav	K	MSgt	Jolley, Van B.	Lived, Soldiers'
10 IN Cav	K	Sgt	Mills, Cleveland W.	Lived, Soldiers'
10 IN Cav	K	Pvt	Bradley, Francis M.	Lived, Washington, uninjured
10 IN Cav	K	Pvt	Jones, James T.	Died
10 IN Cav	L	Capt	Gaffney, Matthew	Died
10 IN Cav	L	Sgt	Farrell, William	Died
10 IN Cav	L	Pvt	Crawler, Jacob	Died
10 IN Cav	L	Pvt	Tressel, William	Died
11 IN Cav	B	Pvt	Mackabee, William	Died
11 IN Cav	E	Pvt	Long, Henry M.	Died
11 IN Cav	F	Pvt	Morgan, Francis M.	Died
11 IN Cav	F	Pvt	Morgan, James M.	Lived
12 IN Cav	F	Pvt	Clansville, G.	(?)
13 IN Cav	A	Pvt	Mitchell, James	Died, July 23, 1865, Saint Louis, Mo.
13 IN Cav	A	Pvt	Sutton, William	Lived, Soldiers'
13 IN Cav	B	Pvt	Baker, Madison Theodore	Died
13 IN Cav	D	Pvt	Johnson, T. B.	(?)
13 IN Cav	D	Pvt	Lahue, Charles J.	Lived, Overton, contusion
13 IN Cav	G	Pvt	Brothers, Hiram	Died
13 IN Cav	G	Pvt	Holmes, Wyman	Died
13 IN Cav	I	Sgt	Owens, Michael J.	Lived, Soldiers'
13 IN Cav	M	Wagon	Watson, William	Died
13 IN Cav	M	Pvt	Haybour, George	Died
13 IN Cav	M	Pvt	Witsil, John	Died
6 IN Inf	D	Pvt	O'Brien, Patsy	Died
9 IN Inf	H	Pvt	Brown, William V.	Lived, Adams

Paroled Union Prisoners, continued

Unit	Company	Rank	Name	Fate
9 IN Inf	K	Pvt	Lewis, John B.	Lived, Gayoso, slight scald
12 IN Inf	A	Cpl	Reynolds, James M.	Died
14 IN Inf	F	Pvt	Kiar, Stephen	Lived, Overton, slight chill
16 IN Inf	E	Pvt	Lewis, William	(?)
17 IN Inf	A	Pvt	Thahbonger, J. W.	(?)
17 IN Inf	G	Pvt	Evens, George L.	Died
17 IN Inf	G	Pvt	Lockman, Beam	Died
17 IN Inf	I	Cpl	Sampson, Richard H.	Lived, Soldiers'
17 IN Inf	I	Pvt	Tantlinger, James H.	Died
18 IN Inf	I	Pvt	Lehman, T. S.	(?)
19 IN Inf	I	Pvt	Simpson, R. H.	Lived
22 IN Inf	H	Pvt	Patrick, Moses	Lived, Washington, scalded hand
23 IN Inf	D	Pvt	Smith, David	Died June 17, 1865
26 IN Inf	K	Pvt	Vesser, Samuel	Lived
29 IN Inf	C	Sgt	Bowen, J.	(?)
29 IN Inf	H	Cpl	Kemp, Martin V.	Died
30 IN Inf	D	Pvt	Aldfant, S. M.	(?)
30 IN Inf	D	Pvt	Morris, S.	(?)
30 IN Inf	G	Pvt	Dawson, George Washington	Died June 28, 1865, Overton, severe scalds
31 IN Inf	I	Pvt	Beard, Otterbine G.	Died
32 IN Inf	A	Pvt	Huber, Evan	Lived, Soldiers'
32 IN Inf	A	Pvt	Schirmeyer, Aloisious	Lived, Adams, slight scald
32 IN Inf	B	Pvt	Shoemaker, Philip	(?)
34 IN Inf	A	Pvt	Rass, C. P.	(?)
35 IN Inf	B	Sgt	O'Garra, Michael	Died
35 IN Inf	B	Pvt	Lynch, Thomas	Lived, Overton, contusion
35 IN Inf	B	Pvt	Mulvany, Peter	Died
35 IN Inf	B	Pvt	O'Donnel, Edward	Lived, Overton, chilled
35 IN Inf	D	Cpl	Martin, Jesse	Lived, Soldiers'
35 IN Inf	G	Pvt	McGuire, Michael	Lived, Soldiers'
35 IN Inf	K	Pvt	Crumbo, Albert	Died
36 IN Inf	B	Pvt	Beal, W.	(?)

Paroled Union Prisoners, continued

Unit	Company	Rank	Name	Fate
36 IN Inf	B	Pvt	Janney, John H.	Died
36 IN Inf	E	Pvt	Hunt, Harrison P.	Lived, Soldiers'
37 IN Inf	G	Cpl	Taylor, Squire A.	Died
38 IN Inf	A	Pvt	Cleveland, Uriah	Died
38 IN Inf	F	Pvt	Nash, Thomas	Died, Soldiers'
38 IN Inf	G	Pvt	Statlings, James W. H.	Died
38 IN Inf	H	Pvt	Veatch, Columbus W.	Died, Adams, chilled
38 IN Inf	K	Pvt	Kellams, Martius	Lived, Soldiers'
40 IN Inf	A	Cpl	McPhonicia, James	Lived, Washington, uninjured
40 IN Inf	A	Pvt	Thorn, Thomas J.	Lived, Soldiers'
40 IN Inf	C	Pvt	Christie, Jacob	Lived, Overton, slight contusion
40 IN Inf	C	Pvt	Howard, John	Died
40 IN Inf	C	Pvt	Welsh, John	Lived
40 IN Inf	D	Capt	Coleman, William L.	Died
40 IN Inf	D	Sgt	Kent, George D.	Died
40 IN Inf	D	Sgt	Nisley, Christian M.	Lived, Soldiers', slight burns; back injury
40 IN Inf	D	Pvt	Benson, Charles	Died
40 IN Inf	D	Pvt	Stewart, George W.	Lived, Soldiers'
40 IN Inf	F	Cpl	Franklin, Benjamin	Died
40 IN Inf	F	Pvt	Everman, Nathan D.	Lived, Soldiers'
40 IN Inf	F	Pvt	Hayer, Stephen	Died
40 IN Inf	G	Pvt	Haines, Samuel C.	Lived
40 IN Inf	G	Pvt	May, Charles	Died
40 IN Inf	G	Pvt	Rose, Josiah N.	Lived, Soldiers'
40 IN Inf	G	Pvt	Thompson, John	Died
40 IN Inf	H	Pvt	Couk, William A.	Lived, Washington, uninjured
40 IN Inf	H	Pvt	Jackson, James H.	Died
40 IN Inf	H	Pvt	Mayes, Joseph H.	Lived, Soldiers'
40 IN Inf	I	Pvt	Ellenboogen, John C.	Died
40 IN Inf	I	Pvt	Sloan, Tildon W.	Died, Overton, contusion
40 IN Inf	K	Capt	Haxelrigg, Henry L.	Died
40 IN Inf	K	Cpl	Benson, Felix	Lived, Gayoso, slight bruises
40 IN Inf	K	Pvt	Hall, Alexander	Died
40 IN Inf	K	Pvt	Hall, Anderson	Died

Paroled Union Prisoners, continued

Unit	Company	Rank	Name	Fate
42 IN Inf	A	Cpl	Moushart, Rening	Died
42 IN Inf	A	Pvt	McFarland, William A.	Lived, Overton, chilled
42 IN Inf	A	Pvt	Smith, Joseph	Died
44 IN Inf	I	Pvt	Boss, Christian	Died
47 IN Inf	C	Pvt	Crabb, Jacob	Died
47 IN Inf	C	Pvt	Ganze, Wilson	Lived, Soldiers'
47 IN Inf	C	Pvt	Marvin, William	Died
52 IN Inf	C	Pvt	Prince, John W.	(?)
52 IN Inf	C	Pvt	Young, John	Lived, Soldiers'
53 IN Inf	D	Pvt	Sturdevant, James	Died
53 IN Inf	D	Pvt	Veazy, John	Lived, Soldiers'
57 IN Inf	A	Pvt	Fletcher, James M.	Died
57 IN Inf	B	Pvt	Zeek, James A.	Died
57 IN Inf	C	Pvt	Beeler, George W.	Died, Adams, severe scalds
57 IN Inf	C	Pvt	Channing, John L.	Died
57 IN Inf	C	Pvt	Lamb, Martin	Died
57 IN Inf	C	Pvt	May, John T.	Died
57 IN Inf	C	Pvt	Newbern, Elam	Died
57 IN Inf	C	Pvt	Smith, Andrew	Lived, Overton, slight contusion
57 IN Inf	D	Pvt	Kibbin, James H.	Lived
57 IN Inf	D	Pvt	Van Nuys, Isaac	Lived, Washington, slight scalds
57 IN Inf	F	Pvt	Chenoweth, John F.	Died
57 IN Inf	F	Pvt	Ginn, Thomas J.	Lived, Gayoso, slight scalds
57 IN Inf	F	Pvt	Wade, Gabriel	Lived
57 IN Inf	F	Pvt	Watkins, Thornton T.	Died
57 IN Inf	G	Cpl	Douglas, David H.	Died, Gayoso, serious scalds
57 IN Inf	G	Cpl	Learner, Benjamin F.	Died, Washington, severe scalds
57 IN Inf	G	Cpl	Pike, Lewis M.	Died
57 IN Inf	G	Pvt	Smith, Frederick	Died
57 IN Inf	G	Pvt	Smith, William	Died
57 IN Inf	H	Pvt	Bridgewater, Jackson	Died
57 IN Inf	H	Pvt	Morrill, Oliver O.	Lived, Soldiers'
57 IN Inf	H	Pvt	Smith, Frederick G.	Died

Paroled Union Prisoners, continued

Unit	Company	Rank	Name	Fate
57 IN Inf	I	Cpl	Hackenburg, August	Died
57 IN Inf	I	Pvt	Norris, Daniel	Died
60 IN Inf	H	Pvt	Jackson, John F.	Died
65 IN Inf	F	Pvt	Gardner, James W.	Lived, Washington, uninjured
65 IN Inf	H	Pvt	Horan, Thomas	Died
65 IN Inf	K	Pvt	Dicky, Jacob K.	Died, Overton, contusion
65 IN Inf	G	Sgt	Milligan, Theophilus W.	Lived, Gayoso, exhaustion
79 IN Inf	A	Pvt	Medsker, Jacob	Lived, Gayoso, exhaustion
79 IN Inf	B	Pvt	Winkle, Samuel L.	Lived, Washington, uninjured
79 IN Inf	C	Pvt	Chappel, Isaac	Died
79 IN Inf	E	Pvt	West, Alleson	Died
80 IN Inf	E	Pvt	Decker, Jefferson	Lived
84 IN Inf	K	Pvt	Naler, T. H.	(?)
86 IN Inf	C	Pvt	Dixon, George	Died
86 IN Inf	C	Pvt	Hashur, Aaron	Lived, Soldiers'
86 IN Inf	C	Pvt	Heglin, James	Died
86 IN Inf	C	Pvt	Reynolds, Marcelus	Died, Adams, wrist wound
86 IN Inf	C	Pvt	Simmerman, Martin V.	Died, Overton
86 IN Inf	G	Pvt	Rollick, John	Died, Washington, bruised breast
88 IN Inf	H	Cpl	Lawrence, Henry K.	Died
89 IN Inf	K	Pvt	Riley, George	Died
91 IN Inf	G	Pvt	Hebbler, Henry	Died
93 IN Inf	A	Pvt	Linson, Samuel	Died
93 IN Inf	A	Pvt	Patterson, Matthew	Lived, Adams, incised wound, right hand
93 IN Inf	C	Pvt	Alexander, John T.	Lived
93 IN Inf	C	Pvt	Franklin, Morgan S.	Died
93 IN Inf	C	OSgt	Petree, David	Died, Overton, slight scalds
93 IN Inf	D	Sgt	Buchanan, William	Lived, Adams, chilled
93 IN Inf	D	Cpl	Pouster, J.	(?)
93 IN Inf	D	Pvt	Grow, James	Lived, Gayoso, exhaustion

Paroled Union Prisoners, continued

Unit	Company	Rank	Name	Fate
93 IN Inf	E	Pvt	Gilmore, John	Died
93 IN Inf	E	Pvt	McGinley, John	Died, Soldiers'
93 IN Inf	E	Pvt	Stockdale, Lindsey	Lived, Washington, uninjured
93 IN Inf	E	Pvt	Willard, Charles	Lived
93 IN Inf	F	Pvt	Alton, Robert	Died
93 IN Inf	H	Sgt	Gass, Nathan J.	Lived, Washington, uninjured
93 IN Inf	H	Cpl	Gass, Jesse M.	Lived, Adams, chilled
93 IN Inf	I	Pvt	Higgins, Earl T.	Died
99 IN Inf	B	Pvt	Cass, James W.	Died
99 IN Inf	C	Pvt	Vanover, James	Died
99 IN Inf	G	Cpl	Rogers, Thomas	Lived, Gayoso, exhaustion
99 IN Inf	G	Pvt	York, Andrew J.	Lived, Soldiers'
99 IN Inf	H	Pvt	Slifer, George	Died
99 IN Inf	I	Cpl	Lindley, Henry C.	Lived, Overton, chilled
99 IN Inf	K	Sgt	Morrell, Henry O.	Died
124 IN Inf	C	2d Lt	Elliott, Joseph Taylor	Lived, Gayoso, exhaustion
124 IN Inf	C	Sgt	Kimberlin, James H.	Lived, Soldiers'
124 IN Inf	C	Cpl	Beardon, Barton S.	Died
124 IN Inf	C	Cpl	Espy, Joseph M.	Died
124 IN Inf	C	Cpl	Hickerson, James A.	Died
124 IN Inf	C	Cpl	White, Thomas A.	Lived, Soldiers'
124 IN Inf	C	Pvt	Brown, Daniel V.	Died
124 IN Inf	C	Pvt	Bryant, Charles F.	Lived, Soldiers'
124 IN Inf	C	Pvt	Donahue, Levi	Died
124 IN Inf	C	Pvt	Galbreath, John W.	Died
124 IN Inf	C	Pvt	Harrington, Patrick	Died
124 IN Inf	C	Pvt	Miller, Henry	Lived
124 IN Inf	C	Pvt	Morton, James A.	Died
124 IN Inf	C	Pvt	Payne, James	Left the boat at Memphis
124 IN Inf	C	Pvt	Ryman, William H. H.	Died
124 IN Inf	C	Pvt	Shinnyfield, Sydney	Lived, Soldiers'
124 IN Inf	C	Pvt	Tahan, James	Died
124 IN Inf	C	Pvt	Thompson, John W.	Lived, Soldiers'
124 IN Inf	K	Pvt	Hall, Luther M.	Died

Paroled Union Prisoners, continued

Unit	Company	Rank	Name	Fate
124 IN Inf	K	Pvt	Palmer, David	Lived
129 IN Inf	I	Pvt	Meagher, Dennis	Lived, Soldiers'
(?) IN			Peachin, Edward	Lived
(?) IOWA Inf		Pvt	Sackett, Alexander	Died
1 KY L Art	A	Cpl	Lewis, William	Died
1 KY L Art	A	Pvt	Cook, John	Died
1 KY L Art	A	Pvt	Elmore, Robert	Lived
1 KY L Art	A	Pvt	Razor, William R.	Lived
1 KY Cav	G	Pvt	Cummings, Charles A.	Lived, Soldiers'
1 KY Cav	L	Pvt	Ashley, James King	Lived, Adams, severe face contusion
1 KY Cav	L	Pvt	Cox, William H.	Died
2 KY Cav	A	Pvt	Elkin, James	Lived, Washington, scalds
2 KY Cav	C	Pvt	Hall, Roland T.	Lived, Washington, scalded hand
2 KY Cav	C	Pvt	Marshall, James T.	Died May 19, 1865, Soldiers'
2 KY Cav	E	Cpl	Cook, William H. H.	Died
2 KY Cav	H	Pvt	Johnson, Nicholas W.	Lived, Washington, scalded arms, legs
3 KY Cav	A	Pvt	Marslin, F.	(?)
3 KY Cav	F	Pvt	Banfield, John P.	Lived
3 KY Cav	M	Pvt	Davidson, Milton M.	Lived, Overton, contusion
4 KY Cav	A	Pvt	Bolin, Alexander T.	Lived
4 KY Cav	B	Cpl	Bender, Nicholas	Died
4 KY Cav	B	Pvt	Breckett, B.	(?)
4 KY Cav	B	Pvt	Foods, A. H.	(?)
4 KY Cav	B	Pvt	Marcum, N.	(?)
4 KY Cav	D	Pvt	Gallagher, J.	(?)
4 KY Cav	E	Pvt	Papers, J.	(?)
4 KY Cav	F	Pvt	Boneur, Matthew	Lived, Soldiers'
4 KY Cav	G	Pvt	Jackson, G.	(?)
4 KY Cav	H	Pvt	Hogan, Edward	Lived
4 KY Cav	I	Pvt	Currey, Michael	Died
4 KY Cav	I	Pvt	Rigney, Michael	Lived, Soldiers'

Paroled Union Prisoners, continued

Unit	Company	Rank	Name	Fate
4 KY Cav	L	Pvt	Gallener, Joseph	Lived
4 KY Cav	L	Pvt	Patterson, Thomas	(?)
5 KY Cav	B	Pvt	Jackson, James	Lived, Washington, scalded feet
5 KY Cav	B	Pvt	Jackson, John W., Jr.	Lived, Washington, scalded hand
5 KY Cav	K	Sgt	Favre, James H.	Died
6 KY Cav		Maj	Fidler, William H.	Died
6 KY Cav	A	Sgt	Cuney, Charles C.	Died, Adams, severe scald
6 KY Cav	A	Sgt	Foley, Richard Jourdan	Died
6 KY Cav	A	Sgt	Green, Alexander	Lived, Washington, uninjured
6 KY Cav	A	Sgt	Wheatley, Lucien C.	Died
6 KY Cav	A	Cpl	McMurtry, David	Lived, Adams, slight scald
6 KY Cav	A	Sadlr	Bean, Louis	Lived, Adams, severe scald
6 KY Cav	A	Pvt	Allen, Robert	Died
6 KY Cav	A	Pvt	Bonhage, Henry	Lived, Overton, scalded left hand, leg
6 KY Cav	A	Pvt	Elliott, William	Died
6 KY Cav	A	Pvt	Gauph, Louis	Died
6 KY Cav	A	Pvt	Hammonds, John	Died
6 KY Cav	A	Pvt	McKinney, Robert	Lived, Adams, slight scald
6 KY Cav	A	Pvt	Sewill, George W.	Died
6 KY Cav	B	CSgt	Zoler, George C.	Died
6 KY Cav	B	Sgt	Woodruff, Stephen B.	Died
6 KY Cav	B	Pvt	Braughton, James W.	Died
6 KY Cav	B	Pvt	Coleman, David	Died, Overton, severe scalds, hands, arms, back, face
6 KY Cav	B	Pvt	Lay, George W.	Died
6 KY Cav	B	Pvt	Littral, John A.	(?)
6 KY Cav	B	Pvt	Schauman, Louis	(?)
6 KY Cav	B	Pvt	Steward, Perry A.	Died
6 KY Cav	C	Capt	Parrish, Edmund H.	Died

Paroled Union Prisoners, continued

Unit	Company	Rank	Name	Fate
6 KY Cav	C	Sgt	Fluke, Arthur W.	Died
6 KY Cav	C	Sgt	Root, Uriah O.	Died
6 KY Cav	C	Cpl	Elliott, Uriah	Lived
6 KY Cav	C	Cpl	Watts, Stephan J.	Died, Adams
6 KY Cav	C	Bugle	Tyre, Jackson	Died
6 KY Cav	C	Pvt	Bartlett, Charles M.	Lived, Soldiers'
6 KY Cav	C	Pvt	Hamilton, Richard	Lived, Soldiers'
6 KY Cav	C	Pvt	Merritt, Baxter	Died
6 KY Cav	C	Pvt	Mofford, Joseph T.	Lived
6 KY Cav	C	Pvt	Moppin, John T.	Lived, Adams, severe scald
6 KY Cav	C	Pvt	Pierce, William	Died
6 KY Cav	C	Pvt	Polley, William	Died
6 KY Cav	C	Pvt	Taylor, John	Lived
6 KY Cav	C	Pvt	Vanoy, William D.	Died
6 KY Cav	D	Pvt	Allison, R. C.	(?)
6 KY Cav	D	Pvt	Dabney, George	Died
6 KY Cav	D	Pvt	Hale, Nathan H.	Died, Washington, scalded face
6 KY Cav	D	Pvt	Haydiman, Thomas H.	Died
6 KY Cav	E	Pvt	Evansberry, H.	(?)
6 KY Cav	F	Cpl	Colvin, Winfield Scott	Lived, Soldiers'
6 KY Cav	F	Pvt	Cammack, James	Lived
6 KY Cav	F	Pvt	Cheatman, George H.	Lived, Adams, diarrhea
6 KY Cav	F	Pvt	Colvin, James	Lived
6 KY Cav	F	Pvt	Montgomery, William	Died, Gayoso, severe scalds, fractured femur
6 KY Cav	G	1st Lt	Surber, James J.	Died
6 KY Cav	G	Sgt	Munday, William H.	Died May 28, 1865, Adams, severe scald
6 KY Cav	G	Cpl	Chelf, Simon D.	Lived, Soldiers', head contusion
6 KY Cav	G	Farr	Thrasher, Samuel J.	Lived, Adams, chilled
6 KY Cav	G	Pvt	Davenport, Seth H.	Died
6 KY Cav	G	Pvt	Hobbs, Levi A.	Lived, Overton, contusion
6 KY Cav	G	Pvt	Jacobs, Alfred N.	Lived, Overton, chilled

Paroled Union Prisoners, continued

Unit	Company	Rank	Name	Fate
6 KY Cav	G	Pvt	Jacobs, John A.	Died
6 KY Cav	G	Pvt	Saddler, Matthew	Died
6 KY Cav	G	Pvt	Stephens, Thomas M., Jr.	Died
6 KY Cav	G	Pvt	Winstard, John	Died
6 KY Cav	H	Sgt	Wright, David	Died, Gayoso, severe scalds, severe head cuts
6 KY Cav	H	Pvt	Daugherty, Thomas	Lived, Washington, slight scald
6 KY Cav	H	Pvt	Hogland, John B.	Died
6 KY Cav	H	Pvt	Morris, James	Died
6 KY Cav	H	Pvt	Thompson, John B.	Lived, Gayoso, exhaustion
6 KY Cav	H	Pvt	Wilson, Thomas P.	Died
6 KY Cav	I	Sgt	Hall, James T.	Died
6 KY Cav	I	Sgt	Johnson, Henry	Died, Overton, severe scalds
6 KY Cav	I	Cpl	Tucker, George W.	Lived, Washington, uninjured
6 KY Cav	I	Pvt	Jones, Stephen	Lived, Gayoso, slight scald
6 KY Cav	I	Pvt	McDonald, Francis Mariam	Died
6 KY Cav	I	Pvt	McDonald, James Wallace	Lived, Soldiers'
6 KY Cav	I	Pvt	Moary, Charles R.	Died
6 KY Cav	I	Pvt	Parker, James R.	Lived, Gayoso, exhaustion
6 KY Cav	I	Pvt	Rodes, Abraham	Lived, Soldiers'
6 KY Cav	I	Pvt	Wooley, William	Died
6 KY Cav	K	Capt	McCown, James M.	Lived, Officers, severe scalds, face, neck, lungs, and hands; crushed left thumb
6 KY Cav	K	Sgt	Elder, John L.	Died
6 KY Cav	K	Pvt	Burns, Patrick	Died
6 KY Cav	K	Pvt	Huges, Henry	Died
6 KY Cav	K	Pvt	Martin, James A.	Died
6 KY Cav	K	Pvt	McCabbins, J. B.	Lived, Gayoso, exhaustion
7 KY Cav	A	Farr	Hargett, Whitfield	Lived

Paroled Union Prisoners, continued

Unit	Company	Rank	Name	Fate
7 KY Cav	A	Pvt	Bradley, George W.	Died
7 KY Cav	A	Pvt	Goodpastur, George W.	Died
7 KY Cav	B	Cpl	Cayton, William A.	Lived
7 KY Cav	C	Pvt	Cardeirlle, W. M.	(?)
7 KY Cav	C	Pvt	Moss, Joseph	Died
7 KY Cav	D	Pvt	Moore, Riley	Lived, Washington, uninjured
7 KY Cav	F	Cpl	Handorf, John C.	Lived, Adams, back contusion
7 KY Cav	F	Pvt	Esginn, W.	(?)
7 KY Cav	F	Pvt	Ragsdale, Robert	(?)
7 KY Cav	F	Pvt	Riley, John	(?)
7 KY Cav	F	Pvt	Willhelm, C. C.	(?)
7 KY Cav	G	Sgt	Malaley, Morris	Died
7 KY Cav	L	Sgt	Creen, A. W.	(?)
7 KY Cav	L	Pvt	Davis, Benjamin G.	Lived, Soldiers'
7 KY Cav	L	Pvt	Roberts, J. R.	(?)
7 KY Cav	L	Pvt	Scott, Thomas	(?)
10 KY Cav	F	Pvt	Mattlinger, J.	(?)
11 KY Cav	B	Cpl	Arnold, William T.	Lived, Soldiers'
1 KY Inf	K	Pvt	Miller, Robert	Lived, Adams
3 KY Inf	A	Sgt	Banks, Jacob W.	Died, Gayoso, serious scalds
3 KY Inf	A	Pvt	Penticuff, John	Died May 1, 1865
3 KY Inf	B	Pvt	Branon, John	Died
3 KY Inf	C	Pvt	Van Hoosier, Thomas	Died, Adams, severe scalds
3 KY Inf	D	Pvt	Banon, George E.	Lived
3 KY Inf	E	Pvt	Wallace, Arthur F.	Lived, Overton, face scalded
4 KY Inf	A	Pvt	Gray, George W.	Died
4 KY Inf	A	Pvt	Hope, Thomas W.	Lived, Soldiers'
4 KY Inf	A	Pvt	Johnson, William	Died
4 KY Inf	A	Pvt	Pope, James A.	Lived, Washington, uninjured
4 KY Inf	A	Pvt	Royalty, Daniel B.	Died
4 KY Inf	B	Pvt	Seymor, George B.	Lived, Adams, chilled
4 KY Inf	C	Sgt	Carey, John	Died
4 KY Inf	C	Sgt	Spencer, Allen	Died

Paroled Union Prisoners, continued

Unit	Company	Rank	Name	Fate
4 KY Inf	C	Pvt	Gillen, Henry	Died
4 KY Inf	C	Pvt	Higdon, Charles T.	Lived, Overton, scalds, hands and feet
4 KY Inf	D	Pvt	McQueen, Abner	Died
4 KY Inf	D	Pvt	Webster, Peter	Died
4 KY Inf	G	Cpl	Phillips, Joel W.	Lived, Soldiers'
4 KY Inf	G	Pvt	Harper, Edward L.	Lived, Adams, chilled
4 KY Inf	H	Pvt	Harley, John N.	Died
4 KY Inf	H	Pvt	Humphrey, Benjamin	Lived, Soldiers'
4 KY Inf	H	Pvt	Redman, William	Died
4 KY Inf	H	Pvt	Vincent, H.	(?)
4 KY Inf	K	Pvt	Coulter, M.	(?)
4 KY Inf	K	Pvt	Edwards, William H.	Died
4 KY Inf	K	Pvt	Folwell, Marcus B.	Died
4 KY Inf	K	Pvt	Kennedy, Elias R.	Lived, Gayoso, slight scald
4 KY Inf	K	Pvt	Murrell, Stocky D.	Died June 5, 1865, Soldiers'
4 KY Inf	K	Pvt	Williams, William T.	Lived, Overton, chilled
4 KY Inf	K	Pvt	Woolum, John	Died
4 KY Inf	L	Pvt	Collins, William	(?)
4 KY Inf	L	Pvt	McKnight, John	Lived, Washington, scalded arm
10 KY Inf	I	Pvt	Brown, Phillip M.	Died, Gayoso, severe scalds
10 KY Inf	I	Pvt	Noe, Henry H.	Lived, Soldiers'
11 KY Inf	G	Pvt	Smith, J.	(?)
12 KY Inf	A	2d Lt	Barnett, James T. W.	Lived, Officers, slight bruise
12 KY Inf	K	Musc	Monday, Joseph P.	Died
14 KY Inf	B	Pvt	Gambill, Henry H.	Lived, Adams, chilled, severe wound, left leg
14 KY Inf	G	Pvt	Curnutt, Elisha	Died
15 KY Inf	F	Pvt	Davis, Milton P. W.	Lived, Washington, uninjured
16 KY Inf	E	Cpl	Clinger, George M.	Lived, Soldiers'
16 KY Inf	E	Pvt	Springler, S. A.	(?)
16 KY Inf	E	Pvt	Wilson, Henry B.	Died

Paroled Union Prisoners, continued

Unit	Company	Rank	Name	Fate
17 KY Inf	A	Pvt	Carter, Thomas E.	Lived, Overton, uninjured
18 KY Inf	L	Pvt	Emerick, J.	(?)
27 KY Inf	B	Pvt	Wade, James	(?)
27 KY Inf	D	Musc	Smith, James A.	Lived
27 KY Inf	D	Pvt	Colwell, H. C.	(?)
27 KY Inf	D	Pvt	Smith, C.	(?)
28 KY Inf	B	Sgt	Clark, Milton C.	Died
28 KY Inf	B	Cpl	Foley, Patrick W.	Lived, Overton, slight scald
28 KY Inf	C	Pvt	Nailor, Peter	Died
1 MI L Art	E	Sgt	Gardner, David	Died
1 MI L Art	K	Pvt	Green, Amos	Lived, Adams, chilled
1 MI Cav	D	Pvt	Royal, Robert	Died
1 MI Cav	M	Pvt	Castice, Myron	Lived, Washington, uninjured
1 MI Cav	M	Pvt	Phillips, Francis M.	Lived, Washington, uninjured
1 MI Cav	M	Pvt	Watson, Joseph H.	Lived
2 MI Cav	A	Pvt	Maxmon, Marshman	Lived, Washington, uninjured
2 MI Cav	A	Pvt	Albeck, Fred	Lived, Washington, uninjured
2 MI Cav	B	Pvt	Tubbs, Hiram	Lived, Overton
2 MI Cav	C	Sgt	Brooks, Lemuel E.	Lived, Soldiers'
2 MI Cav	C	Pvt	Corliss, John S.	Died
2 MI Cav	C	Pvt	Doddard, James	Lived, Soldiers'
2 MI Cav	C	Pvt	Robinson, George F.	Lived, Adams, chilled, scalded arms
2 MI Cav	D	Pvt	Gleason, George G.	Lived, Washington, uninjured
2 MI Cav	D	Pvt	Hill, Daniel	Died
2 MI Cav	D	Pvt	Johnston, John	Died
2 MI Cav	E	1st Lt	Dickenson, Simeon W.	Lived, Officers, slight puncture wounds, hands and feet
2 MI Cav	E	Sgt	Parker, Jerry	Lived
2 MI Cav	E	Sgt	Perkins, Francis M.	Lived, Soldiers'
2 MI Cav	E	Cpl	Keating, James	Lived, Soldiers'

Paroled Union Prisoners, continued

Unit	Company	Rank	Name	Fate
2 MI Cav	E	Cpl	Olney, John	Lived, Adams, chilled
2 MI Cav	E	Cpl	Petitt, Martin	Lived, Soldiers'
2 MI Cav	E	Pvt	Blakely, Jacob	Lived, Soldiers'
2 MI Cav	E	Pvt	Byron, Joseph	Died
2 MI Cav	E	Pvt	Dingman, McKenzie	Lived, Washington, uninjured
2 MI Cav	E	Pvt	Hamblin, Ogilvie E.	Lived, Soldiers'
2 MI Cav	E	Pvt	Hennich, Charles	Died
2 MI Cav	E	Pvt	Herren, David	Lived, Soldiers'
2 MI Cav	E	Pvt	Kendricks, James	Died
2 MI Cav	E	Pvt	Langley, William F.	Lived, Adams, slight scald
2 MI Cav	E	Pvt	Lindsay, William L.	Died
2 MI Cav	E	Pvt	Mason, Frank	Lived, Washington, uninjured
2 MI Cav	E	Pvt	Nolan, O.	Died
2 MI Cav	E	Pvt	Scudding, James	Died
2 MI Cav	E	Pvt	Thomas, J. P.	Died
2 MI Cav	F	Pvt	Monroe, Francis	Died
2 MI Cav	G	Pvt	Rex, Alfred	Died
2 MI Cav	H	Bugle	Worden, David C.	Lived, Adams, head contusion
2 MI Cav	H	Pvt	Haller, R.	Died
2 MI Cav	H	Pvt	Olmstead, Charles H.	Lived, Gayoso, exhaustion
2 MI Cav	I	Cpl	Gage, Joseph	Lived, Gayoso, exhaustion
2 MI Cav	I	Cpl	Mahoney, Jeremiah	Lived, Overton, chilled
2 MI Cav	K	Sgt	Barker, Franklin	Lived, Soldiers'
2 MI Cav	K	Pvt	Strouser, Louis	Lived, Gayoso, slight scald
2 MI Cav	L	Cpl	Libarker, Porter A.	Lived, Soldiers'
2 MI Cav	M	Pvt	Free, M. C.	Died
3 MI Cav	D	Pvt	Ranks, F.	Died
3 MI Cav	E	Wagon	Aldrich, David M.	Lived
3 MI Cav	I	Pvt	Thompson, Martin	Lived
4 MI Cav	D	Cpl	Baker, Murry S.	Lived, Overton, contusion
4 MI Cav	I	Pvt	Devendorf, John C.	Lived, Soldiers'

Paroled Union Prisoners, continued

Unit	Company	Rank	Name	Fate
5 MI Cav	A	Sgt	Norton, John E.	Lived, Overton, head contusion; laceration, right leg
5 MI Cav	A	Pvt	Johnston, Benjamin F.	Lived, Soldiers'
5 MI Cav	B	Pvt	Finch, William B.	Died
5 MI Cav	D	Pvt	Quirk, James E.	Lived, Soldiers'
5 MI Cav	G	Sgt	Warren, Henry F.	Lived, Overton, chilled
5 MI Cav	G	Pvt	Russell, Adam	Lived, Gayoso, slight scald
5 MI Cav	H	Sgt	Carhart, James L.	Lived, Soldiers'
5 MI Cav	H	Pvt	Brown, William	Died
5 MI Cav	H	Pvt	Clarkson, George A.	Lived, Washington, uninjured
5 MI Cav	I	Pvt	Burlingham, E. J.	(?)
5 MI Cav	M	Pvt	Busley, Levi	Died
6 MI Cav	B	Pvt	Fornier, Schofield B.	Lived, Washington
6 MI Cav	C	Pvt	Peck, Charles	Died
6 MI Cav	D	Pvt	Barnes, Augustus M.	Died
6 MI Cav	I	Pvt	Hertz, John	Lived, Soldiers'
6 MI Cav	K	Pvt	Hulet, James H.	Died
7 MI Cav	H	Pvt	McNeal, David	Lived, Gayoso, slight scald
7 MI Cav	K	CSgt	Zacharias, Alexander K.	Lived, Soldiers'
7 MI Cav	M	Pvt	Finkle, Benjamin R.	Lived
8 MI Cav	B	Pvt	Fort, Lewis R.	Died
8 MI Cav	B	Pvt	Lebray, C. G.	Died
8 MI Cav	B	Pvt	Noble, John A.	Died
8 MI Cav	B	Pvt	Norton, Henry	Died
8 MI Cav	B	Pvt	Seabury, Charles G.	Lived, bad burns, face and hands
8 MI Cav	B	Pvt	Smith, Truman M.	Lived, Adams, chilled
8 MI Cav	B	Pvt	White, George	Lived
8 MI Cav	B	Pvt	White, Manly C.	Lived, Adams, chilled
8 MI Cav	C	Sgt	Gheen, T. P.	Died
8 MI Cav	C	Pvt	Snyder, Henry F.	Died
8 MI Cav	C	Pvt	Vent, W.	Died
8 MI Cav	D	Cpl	Dubay, Antone	Lived, Adams, slight scald

Paroled Union Prisoners, continued

Unit	Company	Rank	Name	Fate
8 MI Cav	D	Pvt	Luttenbacher, Laurence	Lived, Gayoso, exhaustion
8 MI Cav	E	QSgt	Wells, Hiram C.	Lived, Gayoso, slight scalds, burns
8 MI Cav	F	Pvt	Kinney, John A.	Died
8 MI Cav	G	Pvt	Wade, Marion F.	Died
8 MI Cav	H	Pvt	Meeker, Clark T.	Died
8 MI Cav	H	Pvt	Snyder, F.	Died
8 MI Cav	H	Pvt	Spencer, Ezra E.	Lived, Washington, slight contusion
8 MI Cav	I	Pvt	Cartwright, Charles	Died
8 MI Cav	I	Pvt	Cory, Oliver	Died
8 MI Cav	K	Cpl	Gier, Rylan	Died
8 MI Cav	K	Pvt	Farmer, Julius M.	Died
8 MI Cav	L	Cpl	Day, John P.	Lived, Soldiers'
8 MI Cav	L	Pvt	Wendt, William	Lived, Washington, uninjured
8 MI Cav	M	Pvt	Brasham, D.	Died
8 MI Cav	M	Pvt	Mellville, Zacharias	Died
9 MI Cav	E	1st Lt	Patterson, W. J.	(?)
9 MI Cav	H	Pvt	Warner, Harvey D.	Died June 25, 1865
1 MI Eng	D	Pvt	Ives, Edward H.	Died
1 MI Eng	E	Pvt	Johnson, Henry H.	Died
1 MI Eng	E	Pvt	Johnson, William F.	Died
1 MI Eng	F	Cpl	Hatch, Absalom N.	Lived, Washington, uninjured
1 MI Eng	G	Pvt	Bremer, J. L.	Died
1 MI Eng	I	Pvt	Dunsmore, John W.	Lived, Gayoso, strain, right foot
1 MI Eng	L	1st Lt	Earl, John E.	Lived, Officers, uninjured
1 MI Eng	L	Sgt	Bunn, Job T.	Died
1 MI Eng	L	Pvt	Decker, Jasper R.	Died
1 MI Eng	L	Pvt	Wait, Henry	Died
1 MI Inf	D	Pvt	Sheppard, L.	Died
4 MI Inf	C	Pvt	Thompson, J. Wesley	Lived, Overton, slight scald
4 MI Inf	G	Pvt	Eastick, Newman A.	Died
14 MI Inf	E	Pvt	Morse, Valoise	Died

Paroled Union Prisoners, continued

Unit	Company	Rank	Name	Fate
14 MI Inf	F	Pvt	Fitzgerald, Thomas	Lived, Gayoso, serious scalds
15 MI Inf	A	Pvt	Butler, John E.	Lived
15 MI Inf	A	Pvt	Ward, Artemus	Lived, Gayoso, exhaustion
15 MI Inf	E	Cpl	Duquette, Duffy A.	Lived, Adams, face contusion
15 MI Inf	F	Pvt	Wright, Homer	Lived, Soldiers'
15 MI Inf	G	Pvt	Barr, George J.	Lived, Soldiers'
15 MI Inf	H	Pvt	Wells, Willard D.	Died
17 MI Inf	B	Pvt	Doan, Thomas R.	Died
17 MI Inf	F	Cpl	Peckham, T. J.	Died
17 MI Inf	H	Sgt	Waterbury, Aaron V.	Died
17 MI Inf	H	Pvt	Smith, Delavan	Lived, Gayoso, exhaustion
17 MI Inf	K	Sgt	Briggs, Samuel C.	Died
18 MI Inf	A	Cpl	Braddish, James W.	Died
18 MI Inf	A	Cpl	Knapp, Andrew J.	Died
18 MI Inf	A	Cpl	Spring, Jeremiah	Died
18 MI Inf	A	Pvt	Doney, Napoleon	Lived, Overton, contusion
18 MI Inf	A	Pvt	Foglesong, Nathaniel M.	Lived, Adams, diarrhea
18 MI Inf	A	Pvt	Hale, Oliver P.	Lived, Adams, chilled
18 MI Inf	A	Pvt	Hindes, Elias E.	Lived, Gayoso, exhaustion
18 MI Inf	A	Pvt	Johnson, George J.	Lived, Washington, uninjured
18 MI Inf	A	Pvt	Koon, Henrich	Lived, Adams, fever
18 MI Inf	A	Pvt	Ludlam, Benjamin F.	Died
18 MI Inf	A	Pvt	Myers, John L.	Lived, Soldiers'
18 MI Inf	A	Pvt	Propper, George W.	Died June 20, 1865, Camp Chase, Ohio
18 MI Inf	A	Pvt	Robbins, Jonathan	Died
18 MI Inf	A	Pvt	Rowley, Orson B.	Died
18 MI Inf	A	Pvt	Rowley, Warren	Died
18 MI Inf	A	Pvt	Slick, Jacob L.	Lived, Soldiers'
18 MI Inf	B	Sgt	Wright, Francis	Lived, Washington, scalded feet

Paroled Union Prisoners, continued

Unit	Company	Rank	Name	Fate
18 MI Inf	B	Cpl	Cornell, Albert W.	Lived, Adams, chilled
18 MI Inf	B	Pvt	Ainsworth, John L.	Died
18 MI Inf	B	Pvt	Aldrich, Ransom D.	Died
18 MI Inf	B	Pvt	Darrow, Samuel Marvin	Lived, Adams, chilled
18 MI Inf	B	Pvt	Jones, Alanson	Died
18 MI Inf	B	Pvt	Smith, Orson W.	Died
18 MI Inf	B	Pvt	Sprague, Franklin	Died
18 MI Inf	B	Pvt	Thayer, Charles	Lived
18 MI Inf	B	Pvt	Welch, Edmund C.	Lived, Soldiers'
18 MI Inf	C	1st Sgt	Baker, Jerome D.	Died
18 MI Inf	C	Sgt	Greenfield, Levi	Lived
18 MI Inf	C	Sgt	Horton, Charles E.	Died
18 MI Inf	C	Sgt	Moore, Jacob	Died
18 MI Inf	C	Pvt	Daly, Michael	Lived, Soldiers'
18 MI Inf	C	Pvt	Deline, Orville	Died
18 MI Inf	C	Pvt	Huyck, George B.	Died
18 MI Inf	C	Pvt	Oakly, Eli J.	Died
18 MI Inf	C	Pvt	Parker, Jacob	Died
18 MI Inf	C	Pvt	Porter, Walter G.	Lived, Soldiers'
18 MI Inf	C	Pvt	Potter, James B.	Died
18 MI Inf	C	Pvt	Southwick, Eugene	Died
18 MI Inf	C	Pvt	Thayer, William	Lived, Soldiers'
18 MI Inf	C	Pvt	Zeidler, Frank	Died
18 MI Inf	D	Sgt	Finch, William H.	Died
18 MI Inf	D	Sgt	Lawrence, Albert W.	Died
18 MI Inf	D	Cpl	Ford, Edwin	Died
18 MI Inf	D	Cpl	Wood, Henry C.	Lived, Overton, bruised left leg
18 MI Inf	D	Musc	Young, William	Died
18 MI Inf	D	Pvt	Bird, John E.	Died
18 MI Inf	D	Pvt	Crisp, William	Lived, scalds, burns, broken left shoulder
18 MI Inf	D	Pvt	Duesler, George W.	Lived, Soldiers'
18 MI Inf	D	Pvt	Eddy, William	Lived, Soldiers'
18 MI Inf	D	Pvt	Mann, Washington	Died
18 MI Inf	D	Pvt	Nelson, Lemon	Died
18 MI Inf	D	Pvt	Norcutt, John William	Lived, Overton, severe scalds
18 MI Inf	D	Pvt	Smith, Goshener F.	Lived
18 MI Inf	D	Pvt	Van Court, Harrison	Died

Paroled Union Prisoners, continued

Unit	Company	Rank	Name	Fate
18 MI Inf	D	Pvt	Watkins, James	Died
18 MI Inf	E	Cpl	Brewer, George H.	Died
18 MI Inf	E	Pvt	Barnum, John P.	Died
18 MI Inf	E	Pvt	Branigan, Patrick	Died
18 MI Inf	E	Pvt	Goodrich, William N.	Lived, Soldiers'
18 MI Inf	E	Pvt	Jones, Josias W.	Lived
18 MI Inf	E	Pvt	Mason, George K.	Died
18 MI Inf	E	Pvt	Millspaugh, David	Died
18 MI Inf	E	Pvt	Randall, Anson	Lived, Overton, chilled
18 MI Inf	E	Pvt	Smith, Thomas S.	Lived, Adams, severe scalds
18 MI Inf	E	Pvt	Sprague, F. S.	Died
18 MI Inf	E	Pvt	Thage, William	Lived
18 MI Inf	F	Sgt	Voglesong, Nelson D.	Lived, Adams, chilled
18 MI Inf	F	Cpl	Cole, Orlando M.	Lived, Soldiers'
18 MI Inf	F	Pvt	Abbaduska, Christian W.	Lived
18 MI Inf	F	Pvt	Carell, E. Abraham	Died
18 MI Inf	F	Pvt	Fuller, Alexander	Died
18 MI Inf	F	Pvt	Gale, Orris	Died
18 MI Inf	F	Pvt	Hinds, William H.	Died
18 MI Inf	F	Pvt	Hines, Y. F.	Died
18 MI Inf	F	Pvt	Holmes, Morgan L.	Died
18 MI Inf	F	Pvt	Lackler, George	Died
18 MI Inf	F	Pvt	Nevins, Joel Frank	Lived, Soldiers'
18 MI Inf	F	Pvt	Smith, Commodore	Lived, Soldiers'
18 MI Inf	F	Pvt	Stubberfield, Samuel B.	Lived, Washington, contusion, right foot and ankle
18 MI Inf	F	Pvt	Van Vlack, Alonzo A.	Lived, Adams, head contusion
18 MI Inf	F	Pvt	Vangorden, George W.	Died
18 MI Inf	F	Pvt	Williams, William H.	Lived, Soldiers'
18 MI Inf	G	Sgt	Aldrich, Hosea C.	Lived, Overton, chilled
18 MI Inf	G	Sgt	Burnes, Edward	Lived, Soldiers', thigh wound
18 MI Inf	G	Cpl	Fanrat, William F.	Died
18 MI Inf	G	Cpl	Palmer, George W.	Died
18 MI Inf	G	Pvt	Burns, Michael	Died

Paroled Union Prisoners, continued

Unit	Company	Rank	Name	Fate
18 MI Inf	G	Pvt	Calwell, James	Died
18 MI Inf	G	Pvt	Hampton, Frank Henry	Died
18 MI Inf	G	Pvt	Haven, Lyman	Lived, Washington, slight contusion
18 MI Inf	G	Pvt	Lackey, Patrick	Died
18 MI Inf	G	Pvt	Merrifield, Edwin G.	Lived, Adams, bruise, left leg
18 MI Inf	G	Pvt	Thompson, Henry	Died
18 MI Inf	G	Pvt	Vanatta, Jason	Died
18 MI Inf	G	Pvt	West, Charles A.	Died
18 MI Inf	G	Pvt	Zeeley, Frederick D.	Died
18 MI Inf	H	Cpl	Plank, Harrison D.	Died
18 MI Inf	H	Musc	Haight, George C.	Lived, Soldiers'
18 MI Inf	H	Pvt	Barrett, Edward P.	Died
18 MI Inf	H	Pvt	Frink, Miles S.	Died
18 MI Inf	H	Pvt	Mallison, Simeon	Died
18 MI Inf	H	Pvt	Nichols, Conant	Died
18 MI Inf	H	Pvt	Smith, Freeman	Lived
18 MI Inf	H	Pvt	Snyder, David S.	Died
18 MI Inf	I	Pvt	Hampton, Frank	Died
18 MI Inf	I	Pvt	Main, Seymour H.	Died, Gayoso, serious scalds, fractured femur
18 MI Inf	I	Pvt	Patterson, Robert	Died
18 MI Inf	I	Pvt	Shafer, Delascus B.	Died
18 MI Inf	I	Pvt	Upton, Harvey W.	Lived
18 MI Inf	I	Pvt	Upton, Warner S.	Died
18 MI Inf	K	CSgt	Harmon, Daniel	Lived
18 MI Inf	K	Sgt	Hinds, Thomas J.	Died
18 MI Inf	K	Cpl	Deland, Charles G.	Lived, Adams, head contusion
18 MI Inf	K	Musc	Countryman, George A.	Lived, Washington, scalds, head and shoulder
18 MI Inf	K	Pvt	Hines, Theodore N.	Died
18 MI Inf	K	Pvt	Hoy, Alexander	Lived, Soldiers'
18 MI Inf	K	Pvt	Lattin, Lemuel H.	Lived, Adams, chilled
18 MI Inf	K	Pvt	Mann, James H.	Lived
18 MI Inf	K	Pvt	McEldowney, Andrew J.	Died

Paroled Union Prisoners, continued

Unit	Company	Rank	Name	Fate
18 MI Inf	K	Pvt	Mette, Anthony R.	Died
18 MI Inf	K	Pvt	Poupard, Alexander	Lived, Soldiers'
18 MI Inf	K	Pvt	Poupard, Samuel	Lived, Gayoso, bruised hip
18 MI Inf	K	Pvt	Russell, James	Lived
18 MI Inf	K	Pvt	Shettleroe, Isadore	Lived, Soldiers'
18 MI Inf	K	Pvt	Shettleroe, John	Lived, Soldiers'
18 MI Inf	K	Pvt	Stump, George	Lived, Soldiers'
18 MI Inf	K	Pvt	Sullier, Levin C.	Lived, Adams, slight scald
18 MI Inf	K	Pvt	Wiecard, Abram B.	Lived, Washington, uninjured
18 MI Inf	K	Pvt	Wright, Nelson D.	Lived, Soldiers'
20 MI Inf	I	Pvt	Berry, Chester D.	Lived, Washington, fractured skull
21 MI Inf	F	Pvt	Meade, George	Died
21 MI Inf	F	Pvt	Smead, Reuban	Died
22 MI Inf	C	Pvt	Lane, James H.	Died
22 MI Inf	H	Pvt	Peer, Richard	Lived, Overton, chilled
22 MI Inf	K	Sgt	Smith, Alonzo K.	Died
22 MI Inf	K	Pvt	Boyce, Edward	Died
23 MI Inf	B	Pvt	Cole, David	Died
23 MI Inf	C	Pvt	Westrip, George	Died
23 MI Inf	E	Pvt	Froeland, George	Lived, Soldiers'
23 MI Inf	E	Pvt	Ludlum, Albert E.	Lived, Soldiers'
23 MI Inf	E	Pvt	Van Couver, A.	Died
24 MI Inf	H	Pvt	Harris, Israel	Lived
24 MI Inf	I	Pvt	Innes, James	Died
25 MI Inf	F	Sgt	Bement, George	Lived, Soldiers'
25 MI Inf	F	Pvt	Luchane, D.	Died
29 MI Inf	A	Pvt	Hershey, Moses B.	Lived, Soldiers'
1 MI SS	E	Sgt	Stevens, Joseph	Lived, Overton, contusion
1 MI SS	E	Pvt	Wells, Daniel A.	Died
1 MI SS	K	Pvt	Miskoquon, Louis	Lived, Overton, contusion
(?)MI			Tabor, Charles	Lived
4 MO Cav		Capt	Hencke, Theodore W.	Lived

Paroled Union Prisoners, continued

Unit	Company	Rank	Name	Fate
1 NE Cav	L	Pvt	Stafford, Seth D. L.	Lived, Washington, uninjured
22 OH L Art		Sgt	Rinehart, J.	(?)
22 OH L Art		Pvt	Musselman, John	Lived, Adams, bruised right side
1 OH Cav	B	Pvt	Barnes, Thomas N.	Lived, Adams, slight scald
1 OH Cav	D	Pvt	Anderson, James	Lived, Gayoso, slight scald
1 OH Cav	D	Pvt	Evans, Edward W.	Lived
2 OH Cav	A	Pvt	Lockwood, Darius	Died
2 OH Cav	K	Sgt	Hailey, Christopher C.	Lived, Soldiers'
2 OH Cav	K	Pvt	Brammer, David E.	Lived, Overton, slight scald
3 OH Cav	D	Pvt	Hawk, Marion	Lived, Soldiers'
3 OH Cav	K	Pvt	Gustin, William A.	Died
3 OH Cav	K	Pvt	Peckins, Ira	Lived, Adams, slight scald
3 OH Cav	K	Pvt	Pouch, Asa	Died
3 OH Cav	L	Pvt	Green, Charles	Lived, Gayoso, exhaustion
3 OH Cav	L	Pvt	Rush, Jacob W.	Lived, Soldiers', slight puncture to chest
3 OH Cav	M	1st Lt	Lewis, Daniel C.	Died
3 OH Cav	M	Sadlr	Kerstetter, Benjamin	Died
3 OH Cav	M	Pvt	McWethy, Charles H.	Lived, Soldiers'
3 OH Cav	M	Pvt	Webster, La Fever	Lived
4 OH Cav	H	Pvt	Nolan, Joseph	Lived, Gayoso, slight scald
4 OH Cav	K	1st Sgt	Smith, William H.	Lived, Adams, chilled
4 OH Cav	L	Pvt	Brown, Benjamin	Lived, Adams, slight scald
4 OH Cav	M	Pvt	Lautmeyer, John B.	Died
5 OH Cav	K	Pvt	Donley, Marion	Died, Soldiers'
5 OH Cav	L	Sgt	Barkley, Nathan	Died
6 OH Cav	I	Pvt	McMannis, Miles	Died
7 OH Cav		Hos S	Saffin, James	Lived, Overton, severe scalds
7 OH Cav	A	Capt	Ketterman, William D.	Died

Paroled Union Prisoners, continued

Unit	Company	Rank	Name	Fate
7 OH Cav	A	Sgt	Hannum, Thomas	Lived, Soldiers'
7 OH Cav	A	Sgt	Leisure, Andrew J.	Lived, Adams, chilled
7 OH Cav	A	Sgt	Moyer, Phillip	Died
7 OH Cav	A	Cpl	Baldwin, Jonas K.	Died
7 OH Cav	A	Cpl	Brickett, James	Died
7 OH Cav	A	Cpl	Gilb, Frederick	Died
7 OH Cav	A	Cpl	McGlincey, William	Died
7 OH Cav	A	Farr	Morganthaler, Jacob	Died
7 OH Cav	A	Pvt	Aubrey, Francis	Died, Gayoso, severe scalds
7 OH Cav	A	Pvt	Baker, William	Died
7 OH Cav	A	Pvt	Bell, John K.	Lived, Soldiers'
7 OH Cav	A	Pvt	Botts, Thomas	Died
7 OH Cav	A	Pvt	Burbrink, August	Died
7 OH Cav	A	Pvt	Cameron, Benjamin B.	Lived, Soldiers'
7 OH Cav	A	Pvt	Dorna, Jacob	Lived, Gayoso, exhaustion
7 OH Cav	A	Pvt	Drainer, Jacob	Died
7 OH Cav	A	Pvt	Drumm, Charles	Died
7 OH Cav	A	Pvt	Faulkner, John S.	Lived, Soldiers', broken leg
7 OH Cav	A	Pvt	Fanning, Albert	Died
7 OH Cav	A	Pvt	Foltz, Peter	Died
7 OH Cav	A	Pvt	Hill, George	Died
7 OH Cav	A	Pvt	Lewis, David	Died
7 OH Cav	A	Pvt	McAllister, Calvin	Lived, Soldiers'
7 OH Cav	A	Pvt	McDaniel, Isaac E.	Lived, Soldiers'
7 OH Cav	A	Pvt	McGlincey, Patrick	Lived
7 OH Cav	A	Pvt	Reibel, William	Died
7 OH Cav	A	Pvt	Robb, Robert D.	Died
7 OH Cav	A	Pvt	Sherrick, Samuel A.	Died
7 OH Cav	A	Pvt	Shummard, William T.	Lived, Soldiers', head contusion; bad scalds, face, head, hands
7 OH Cav	A	Pvt	Trenol, T.	(?)
7 OH Cav	A	Pvt	Woodward, Theodore	Died
7 OH Cav	B	Pvt	Carr, Richard A.	Lived, Washington, uninjured
7 OH Cav	B	Pvt	Harrison, Longshore D.	Died

Paroled Union Prisoners, continued

Unit	Company	Rank	Name	Fate
7 OH Cav	B	Pvt	Klippstein, Leymier	Lived
7 OH Cav	B	Pvt	Maxwell, John W.	Lived
7 OH Cav	D	Pvt	Longhouser, Andrew	Lived
7 OH Cav	E	Pvt	Brofford, John	Lived
7 OH Cav	E	Pvt	Dixon, Archie C.	Died
7 OH Cav	E	Pvt	Waits, Anthony W.	Lived, Washington, uninjured
7 OH Cav	F	Cpl	Starritt, John H.	Died
7 OH Cav	F	Farr	Kurtz, John J.	Died, Gayoso, serious scalds; multiple cuts, bruises
7 OH Cav	F	Pvt	Duzan, William R.	Lived, Soldiers'
7 OH Cav	G	Pvt	Sharp, John R.	Lived, Soldiers'
7 OH Cav	H	Sgt	Bean, James T.	Died
7 OH Cav	H	Pvt	Hoyd, Jeremiah	Lived, Soldiers'
7 OH Cav	M	Pvt	Blane, Henry	Lived
8 OH Cav	I	Pvt	Madden, William P.	Lived, Soldiers', hernia; severe burns on hands
9 OH Cav	A	Pvt	Lawhead, George W.	Lived
9 OH Cav	C	Pvt	Grim, William	Died
9 OH Cav	D	Sgt	Davis, Milton J.	Died, Adams, severe scalds
9 OH Cav	E	Pvt	Hanson, Thompson	Lived, Soldiers'
9 OH Cav	E	Pvt	Hartman, Amon	Lived
9 OH Cav	F	Pvt	Brubaker, Jacob	Lived
9 OH Cav	F	Pvt	Moulton, William P.	Died
9 OH Cav	H	Pvt	Mankin, Silas	Died
9 OH Cav	I	Cpl	Jopp, Joseph	Died
9 OH Cav	K	Sgt	Hedges, George	Lived, Soldiers'
9 OH Cav	K	Pvt	Brown, Isaac	Lived, Washington, uninjured
9 OH Cav	K	Pvt	Kirker, William J.	Lived, Soldiers'
9 OH Cav	M	Pvt	Carter, Morris J.	Lived
9 OH Cav	M	Pvt	Wright, Benjamin F.	Died
10 OH Cav	A	Pvt	Taylor, Charles	Died
10 OH Cav	B	QSgt	Bader, Phillip H.	Lived, Adams, bruised right hand
10 OH Cav	B	Pvt	Jennings, Ira	Died, Gayoso, severe scalds

Paroled Union Prisoners, continued

Unit	Company	Rank	Name	Fate
10 OH Cav	B	Pvt	Morgan, Job	Died
10 OH Cav	G	Pvt	Offit, Albert	Died
10 OH Cav	G	Pvt	Taylor, A.	(?)
10 OH Cav	K	Pvt	White, William H.	Lived
10 OH Cav	M	Pvt	Burnett, Isaac	Died May 5, 1865, Gayoso, serious scalds
10 OH Cav	M	Pvt	Hunter, Albert E.	Died
McL OH Cav	A	Cpl	Steinaur, John W.	Died
McL OH Cav	A	Pvt	Crawford, John L.	Died May 2, 1865
McL OH Cav	A	Pvt	Irvine, James H.	Died
McL OH Cav	A	Pvt	Jesson, Robert	Died
McL OH Cav	A	Pvt	Peterson, Isaac	Died, Overton, severe scalds
McL OH Cav	A	Pvt	Provines, Eli Finley	Died
McL OH Cav	A	Pvt	Terrell, Henry	Lived
McL OH Cav	A	Pvt	Tidball, Charles B.	Died
McL OH Cav	A	Pvt	Wagner, John	Died
McL OH Cav	B	Pvt	Donald, Hosea	Died
McL OH Cav	B	Pvt	Horner, James	Lived
McL OH Cav	B	Pvt	Wescott, Samuel W.	Died, Washington, severe scalds
OH Inf		Pvt	Menenger, George	(?)
1 OH Inf	K	Pvt	Wade, William H.	Died
2 OH Inf	A	Cpl	Graham, John W.	Lived, Overton, slight scalds
2 OH Inf	A	Pvt	Allman, James	Died
2 OH Inf	D	Cpl	Peese, James B.	Lived, Gayoso, exhaustion
2 OH Inf	G	Pvt	Russell, C. G.	Lived, Overton, scalds
2 OH Inf	G	Pvt	Snodgrass, William P.	Died
2 OH Inf	I	Sgt	Brown, Alexander C.	Lived, Overton, chilled
4 OH Inf	G	Pvt	Sorgen, Edward	Lived, Gayoso, exhaustion
9 OH Inf	A	Pvt	Schultz, Ernest	Lived, Gayoso, slight scald
11 OH Inf		Pvt	Lampsell, H.	(?)
12 OH Inf	A	Pvt	Hayner, Enoch	Died

Paroled Union Prisoners, continued

Unit	Company	Rank	Name	Fate
12 OH Inf	K	Cpl	Collins, Patrick	Lived
13 OH Inf	C	Sgt	Longshore, Jeremiah	Died
13 OH Inf	D	Pvt	Muller, Davis S.	Died
13 OH Inf	K	Cpl	McCluray, James	Lived, Washington, uninjured
14 OH Inf	G	Pvt	Bice, Joseph	Died
14 OH Inf	I	Pvt	Van Fleet, Henry C.	Lived, Gayoso, severe scalds
15 OH Inf	D	Pvt	Carter, Francis M.	Died
15 OH Inf	E	Pvt	Etzler, Martin Luther	Lived
15 OH Inf	G	Pvt	Myers, Charles W.	Died
15 OH Inf	H	Cpl	Hamilton, Simon H.	Lived
18 OH Inf	B	1st Sgt	Karns, Nicholas	Lived, Soldiers', chilled
19 OH Inf	H	Pvt	White, William H.	Lived, Washington, uninjured
20 OH Inf		Hos S	Clancy, William F.	Died
20 OH Inf	E	Cpl	Long, George M.	Died
20 OH Inf	E	Pvt	Linstead, Henry P.	Died
20 OH Inf	K	Pvt	Bolenbaugh, Irwin M.	Died
21 OH Inf	B	Sgt	Shively, William H.	Died, Soldiers'
21 OH Inf	B	Pvt	Cassel, Abraham	Lived, Washington, uninjured
21 OH Inf	B	Pvt	Engle, John	Lived, Gayoso, exhaustion
21 OH Inf	B	Pvt	Morgan, Levi G.	Lived, Soldiers'
21 OH Inf	B	Pvt	Morquerat, Phillip V.	Died
21 OH Inf	B	Pvt	Uhler, Nelson M.	Died
21 OH Inf	E	Sgt	Dunafin, Isaac	Died
21 OH Inf	E	Pvt	Kimmell, Rinaldo	Lived, Washington, slight contusion
21 OH Inf	K	Pvt	Forest, Thomas	Lived
22 OH Inf	A	Pvt	Davidson, John	(?)
22 OH Inf	E	Pvt	Murshern, George	(?)
23 OH Inf	D	Pvt	Field, Gilbert G.	Died
23 OH Inf	F	Pvt	Barnes, William C.	Lived, Washington, badly bruised
23 OH Inf	I	Pvt	Gray, William	Lived, Gayoso, exhaustion
23 OH Inf	K	Pvt	Roberts, Charles A.	Died

Paroled Union Prisoners, continued

Unit	Company	Rank	Name	Fate
24 OH Inf	K	Pvt	Babcock, John	Died
26 OH Inf	D	Cpl	Miller, John R.	Died, Gayoso, severe scalds
26 OH Inf	H	Cpl	McClintock, William G.	Lived, Soldiers'
26 OH Inf	I	Pvt	Seahl, Benjamin	Lived
28 OH Inf	D	Pvt	Koch, Lewis	Lived, Washington, breast contusion
30 OH Inf	D	Pvt	King, Lakins	(?)
31 OH Inf	D	Pvt	Shields, Payton	Lived, Adams, slight scald
33 OH Inf	B	Cpl	Lang, James B.	Lived, Washington, scalded hands and arms
33 OH Inf	C	Pvt	Nelson, William	Died
33 OH Inf	I	Pvt	Lyman, Irwin J.	Died
34 OH Inf	E	Pvt	Shepard, William Henry	Died
34 OH Inf	E	Pvt	Skeon, William	(?)
34 OH Inf	G	Pvt	Scott, H.	(?)
37 OH Inf	A	Pvt	Braum, Adam	Died
37 OH Inf	C	Pvt	Abeler, William	Died
37 OH Inf	C	Pvt	Augenbacke, Gustave	Died
37 OH Inf	C	Pvt	Siemer, Frederick	Died
37 OH Inf	C	Pvt	Webler, John	(?)
37 OH Inf	D	Pvt	Hensinger, John	Died
37 OH Inf	D	Pvt	Sessler, Conrad	Died
37 OH Inf	E	Pvt	Hess, John	Lived, Soldiers'
40 OH Inf	I	Cpl	Edwards, Jacob	Died
40 OH Inf	I	Pvt	Kearns, John	Died
41 OH Inf	A	Pvt	Gamber, John	Lived
41 OH Inf	D	Pvt	Mathews, Orlo C.	Lived, Gayoso, exhaustion
41 OH Inf	F	Pvt	Clary, James K.	Died
44 OH Inf	B	Sgt	Ditmore, Aaron	Lived, Soldiers'
45 OH Inf	B	Sgt	Cline, Henry M.	Lived
45 OH Inf	F	Pvt	Sands, William H.	Lived
46 OH Inf	E	Pvt	Thatcher, John	Lived, Gayoso, bruises
46 OH Inf	K	Pvt	Clutter, Loran K.	Died
47 OH Inf	B	Pvt	Maes, Jotham W.	Lived, Washington, uninjured
47 OH Inf	H	Pvt	Bechtolsheimer, Anton	Died

Paroled Union Prisoners, continued

Unit	Company	Rank	Name	Fate
47 OH Inf	K	Pvt	Hesser, Louis	Died
49 OH Inf	B	Pvt	Fesler, John M.	Lived
49 OH Inf	B	Pvt	Huffey, John	Lived, Washington, uninjured
50 OH Inf	A	Cpl	Fox, John, Jr.	Lived, Soldiers', bad back scalds, neck to hips
50 OH Inf	A	Cpl	Price, Alfred E.	Died
50 OH Inf	A	Cpl	Roberts, John	Died
50 OH Inf	A	Pvt	Haskins, Perry	Died, Soldiers'
50 OH Inf	B	1st Sgt	Helminger, Jacob	Lived, Soldiers'
50 OH Inf	B	Pvt	Humphrey, Wilson C.	Lived, Soldiers'
50 OH Inf	B	Pvt	Morrow, William M.	Lived, Overton, chilled
50 OH Inf	B	Pvt	Shearer, George W.	Died
50 OH Inf	B	Pvt	Walker, John Lowery	Lived, Soldiers', slight injuries
50 OH Inf	C	Cpl	Austin, David B.	Died
50 OH Inf	C	Pvt	Ray, Christian	Lived, Gayoso, exhaustion
50 OH Inf	D	Cpl	Pickett, Eugene	Died
50 OH Inf	D	Pvt	King, Lawrence	Died
50 OH Inf	D	Pvt	McClevy, Hugh	Lived
50 OH Inf	E	1st Sgt	Lee, William H.	Died
50 OH Inf	E	Cpl	Rosselot, Peter F.	Lived, Adams, chilled
50 OH Inf	E	Cpl	Vananda, Albert H.	Died
50 OH Inf	E	Pvt	Carr, John W.	Died
50 OH Inf	E	Pvt	Coulter, William S.	Died
50 OH Inf	E	Pvt	Kinser, Hugh	Lived, Adams, chilled
50 OH Inf	E	Pvt	Pettijohn, Cyrus	Died
50 OH Inf	F	Cpl	Moore, Thomas Dunn	Lived, Washington, scalded hands
50 OH Inf	G	Sgt	Green, William	Died
50 OH Inf	G	Cpl	Kruse, Charles T.	Died
50 OH Inf	H	Pvt	Gilmore, Michael	Died
50 OH Inf	H	Pvt	Jordan, Henry	Died
50 OH Inf	H	Pvt	Mottier, Fafor Z.	Lived, Overton, bruised chest
50 OH Inf	H	Pvt	Murphy, Christopher C.	Lived, Washington, uninjured

Paroled Union Prisoners, continued

Unit	Company	Rank	Name	Fate
50 OH Inf	I	Cpl	Griffin, James O.	Died
50 OH Inf	I	Pvt	White, George W.	Lived, Soldiers'
50 OH Inf	K	Cpl	Winters, Erastus	Lived, Adams, slight scalds, face, neck, left arm, hands, feet
50 OH Inf	K	Pvt	Culp, Jackson	Lived, Soldiers'
50 OH Inf	K	Pvt	Pouder, Andrew	Lived, Adams, slight scald
50 OH Inf	K	Pvt	Shilling, Peter	Died
50 OH Inf	K	Pvt	Vernard, Henry	Lived
51 OH Inf	C	Pvt	Norris, Joseph B.	Lived, Washington, uninjured
51 OH Inf	D	Pvt	DeMoss, John	Lived, Gayoso, slight scald
51 OH Inf	D	Pvt	Phillips, William	Lived, Overton, contusion
51 OH Inf	D	Pvt	Smith, William R.	Died
51 OH Inf	F	Sgt	Belknap, Charles M.	Died
51 OH Inf	F	Pvt	Alltop, George W.	Died
51 OH Inf	F	Pvt	Lahr, Jacob	Died
51 OH Inf	H	Sgt	Sayer, Samuel K.	Lived, Washington, uninjured
51 OH Inf	I	Cpl	Hale, Elwood	Lived
51 OH Inf	I	Cpl	Oxley, Stewart	Lived, Overton, broken ribs; back injury; scalds, right side of face, head
52 OH Inf	C	Pvt	Miller, Jerome	Lived, Washington, eye contusion
52 OH Inf	F	Pvt	Flint, Thomas	Died
54 OH Inf	G	Cpl	Christopher, William H.	Lived
54 OH Inf	G	Pvt	Pottle, Winfield Scott	Lived, Adams, chilled
54 OH Inf	G	Pvt	Shaw, William W.	Lived
55 OH Inf	C	Cpl	Gregory, Myrum W.	Lived, Washington, chilled
55 OH Inf	C	Pvt	Niles, Albert G.	Lived, Washington, slight scald
55 OH Inf	D	Pvt	Whyler, Sebastian E.	Lived, Adams, bruised right arm
55 OH Inf	E	Cpl	Sharp, Edward	Died

Paroled Union Prisoners, continued

Unit	Company	Rank	Name	Fate
55 OH Inf	E	Pvt	Pease, Benjamin	Lived
56 OH Inf	F	Pvt	Githens, Lafayette	Lived, Overton, contusion
57 OH Inf	B	Pvt	Waltermier, James T.	Lived, Adams, chilled
58 OH Inf	B	Pvt	Klein, Jacob	Lived
59 OH Inf		MSgt	Blair, Thomas Quinn	Lived, Adams, bruised right shoulder
59 OH Inf	A	Pvt	Jones, Thomas F.	Lived
59 OH Inf	A	Pvt	Meyers, H.	(?)
59 OH Inf	C	Cpl	Brunner, Michael	Lived, Soldiers'
63 OH Inf	F	Pvt	Bridgeman, Austin A.	Died
63 OH Inf	G	Sgt	Wible, Levi	Died
64 OH Inf	A	Cpl	Hulit, William A.	Lived, Gayoso
64 OH Inf	A	Cpl	Vanscoyce, J. W.	Lived, Gayoso, bad chest bruises
64 OH Inf	A	Pvt	Brink, Samuel	Died
64 OH Inf	A	Pvt	Brink, Thomas	Died
64 OH Inf	B	Sgt	Cranmer, Asaph O.	Lived, Adams, scalds
64 OH Inf	B	Sgt	Fies, William	Lived, Adams, contusion, left side of face; burned hands; dislocated left shoulder
64 OH Inf	B	Pvt	Brady, James King P.	Lived, most of hair burned off
64 OH Inf	B	Pvt	Zimmer, Casper	Died
64 OH Inf	D	Sgt	Bratton, Hugh W.	Died
64 OH Inf	D	Cpl	Landon, Simeon	Lived, Gayoso, slight scald
64 OH Inf	D	Pvt	Boor, William	Lived, Overton, chilled
64 OH Inf	D	Pvt	King, Barzilla	Lived
64 OH Inf	E	Cpl	Carmack, Thomas J.	Lived, Soldiers'
64 OH Inf	G	Cpl	Wagner, Joseph	Died
64 OH Inf	I	Sgt	White, Robert	Died
64 OH Inf	I	Pvt	Eddleman, David	Lived, Washington, uninjured
64 OH Inf	I	Pvt	McKinley, Daniel	Died
64 OH Inf	I	Pvt	Stuckey, John	Died

Paroled Union Prisoners, continued

Unit	Company	Rank	Name	Fate
64 OH Inf	K	Pvt	Kennedy, Edward J.	Lived, Adams, severe scalds
64 OH Inf	K	Pvt	Ryan, John	Died
65 OH Inf	C	Sgt	Gregory, Edgar W.	Died
65 OH Inf	D	Sgt	Long, Robert W.	Lived, Washington, uninjured
65 OH Inf	E	Sgt	Nickerson, Charles H.	Died
65 OH Inf	E	Pvt	Kelley, Thomas	Died
65 OH Inf	G	Pvt	Geeseman, David	Died
65 OH Inf	G	Pvt	Grubaugh, David	Died
65 OH Inf	G	Pvt	Hudson, John	Died
65 OH Inf	K	Sgt	Mathias, Ephram	Lived, Soldiers'
65 OH Inf	K	Cpl	Horner, Ira B.	Lived, Adams, dislocated left shoulder; scalds and bruises, left side
65 OH Inf	K	Pvt	Bishlen, John	Died
65 OH Inf	K	Pvt	Davis, John G.	Lived
65 OH Inf	K	Pvt	Emerine, Eli	Lived, Soldiers'
65 OH Inf	K	Pvt	Fairchild, Amos W.	Died
65 OH Inf	K	Pvt	Raudebaugh, Samuel H.	Lived, Gayoso, slight bruises, breast and groin
70 OH Inf	C	Pvt	Brown, John	(?)
70 OH Inf	D	Pvt	Shoemaker, Joseph	Died
70 OH Inf	K	Pvt	Black, John C.	Died May 13, 1865, Overton, slight scald, contusion
71 OH Inf		Maj	Carlin, James W.	Died
71 OH Inf	B	1st Lt	Davis, John L.	Lived, Overton, chilled
72 OH Inf	A	Pvt	Brandt, Jacob	Died
72 OH Inf	A	Pvt	German, Andrew	Lived
72 OH Inf	B	Sgt	McIntyre, William F.	Died
72 OH Inf	B	Pvt	Fisher, Austin T.	Lived
72 OH Inf	B	Pvt	McIntyre, Byron E.	Died
72 OH Inf	C	Pvt	Shoe, Emmanuel	Died
72 OH Inf	C	Pvt	Tearne, Charles	Lived

Paroled Union Prisoners, continued

Unit	Company	Rank	Name	Fate
72 OH Inf	D	Sgt	Duke, William W.	Lived, Gayoso, bad bruises and scalds
72 OH Inf	E	Pvt	Shoemaker, Alexander	Lived, Soldiers'
72 OH Inf	E	Pvt	Shoemaker, W.	(?)
72 OH Inf	E	Pvt	Stotler, Michael	Died
72 OH Inf	E	Pvt	Trimmer, William	Lived, Gayoso, slight scald
72 OH Inf	F	Cpl	Kirk, William H.	Died
72 OH Inf	F	Pvt	Crane, Ira	Died
72 OH Inf	F	Pvt	Hague, Samuel	Died
72 OH Inf	H	Pvt	Aubrey, Morris	Died
72 OH Inf	K	Pvt	Ollendick, John	Lived, Soldiers'
75 OH Inf	A	Sgt	Andrews, William H.	Died
75 OH Inf	A	Pvt	Kelley, John	Died
75 OH Inf	B	Pvt	Washburn, George	(?)
75 OH Inf	G	Pvt	Thomas, Nathan	(?)
75 OH Inf	H	Pvt	Waltz, Moses	Died, Gayoso, severe scalds
76 OH Inf	A	Pvt	Norris, Albert	Lived, Washington, severe burns, left arm and shoulder
76 OH Inf	A	Pvt	Thompson, James	Lived, Soldiers'
76 OH Inf	D	Pvt	McCarty, James W.	Lived, Gayoso, exhaustion
76 OH Inf	D	Pvt	Stone, James	Lived, Soldiers'
76 OH Inf	G	Cpl	Yeisley, Emanuel H.	Lived, Gayoso, slight scald
76 OH Inf	H	Pvt	Thomas, Thomas	Died
76 OH Inf	K	Pvt	Ream, Joseph H.	Lived
78 OH Inf	C	Pvt	Crowell, George W.	Died
78 OH Inf	E	Pvt	White, Joshua	Died
78 OH Inf	H	Pvt	Clipner, John	Died
79 OH Inf	A	Pvt	Low, C. W.	(?)
79 OH Inf	F	Pvt	Mark, Charles	Died
80 OH Inf	E	Pvt	Rummell, Adolphus W.	Died
80 OH Inf	G	Pvt	Sampsell, Henry	Lived, Washington, fractured arm
81 OH Inf	D	Pvt	Shaw, Charles M.	Lived, Soldiers'
82 OH Inf	B	Pvt	Davidson, John	(?)
83 OH Inf	E	Pvt	Snyder, Jacob	Lived

Paroled Union Prisoners, continued

Unit	Company	Rank	Name	Fate
89 OH Inf	H	Pvt	Kerns, William	Lived
90 OH Inf	F	Pvt	Ecord, Aaron H.	Died
90 OH Inf	F	Pvt	Archa, John	Died, Adams, severe scalds
90 OH Inf	G	Hos S	Nihart, Addison	Lived, Washington, uninjured
92 OH Inf	F	Pvt	Pryor, Francis	Lived
93 OH Inf	A	Sgt	Beatty, James	Lived, Soldiers'
93 OH Inf	E	Pvt	Sharettz, Zebulon	Died
95 OH Inf	A	Pvt	Reed, Oliver H.	Lived, Gayoso, exhaustion
95 OH Inf	A	Pvt	Young, George N.	Lived, Washington, scald, left hand
95 OH Inf	B	Pvt	McMillen, D. M.	(?)
95 OH Inf	B	Pvt	McMillen, David E.	Lived, Soldiers'
95 OH Inf	E	Pvt	Miller, Peter	Died
95 OH Inf	E	Pvt	Owen, Warret	Lived, Soldiers'
95 OH Inf	E	Pvt	Poysell, Samuel W.	Died
95 OH Inf	E	Pvt	Poysell, William W.	Died
95 OH Inf	E	Pvt	Rollins, George H.	Died
95 OH Inf	E	Pvt	Shaul, William R.	Lived, Overton, slight contusion
95 OH Inf	F	1st Sgt	Litle, John W.	Died
95 OH Inf	F	Cpl	Leas, Joseph W.	Died
95 OH Inf	F	Pvt	Allen, Morris	Died
95 OH Inf	F	Pvt	Van Horn, Burriss	Lived, Soldiers'
95 OH Inf	F	Pvt	Wilcox, Marvin	Died
95 OH Inf	F	Pvt	Wilson, Robert S.	Lived, Overton, uninjured
95 OH Inf	G	Cpl	Jackson, Truman	Died
95 OH Inf	G	Pvt	Parker, Isaac W.	Lived, Soldiers'
95 OH Inf	H	Pvt	Hammel, Samuel	Died
95 OH Inf	K	Pvt	Allen, Benjamin F.	Lived
96 OH Inf	B	Pvt	McClary, Daniel	Died
97 OH Inf	A	Cpl	Gay, Asa	Died
97 OH Inf	B	1st Sgt	Poland, James L.	Died
97 OH Inf	B	Pvt	Bishard, Charles J.	Lived, Adams, chilled
97 OH Inf	B	Pvt	Johnson, Salem	Lived, Gayoso, exhaustion
97 OH Inf	C	1st Sgt	Emerson, Albert G.	Lived, Adams, chilled

Paroled Union Prisoners, continued

Unit	Company	Rank	Name	Fate
97 OH Inf	C	Pvt	Stevens, William	Lived, Overton, contusion
97 OH Inf	C	Pvt	Mills, C.	Died
97 OH Inf	C	Pvt	Milner, Reason	Died
97 OH Inf	D	Pvt	Hess, Alexander	Died
97 OH Inf	E	Pvt	Watts, George W.	Lived, Gayoso, slight scald
97 OH Inf	H	2d Lt	Larkin, Milton H.	Lived, Gayoso, slight scald, sprained ankle
98 OH Inf	F	Pvt	Gross, M.	(?)
100 OH Inf	A	Sgt	Cornwell, John	Died
100 OH Inf	A	Pvt	McCrory, Lewis W.	Lived, Soldiers'
100 OH Inf	D	Cpl	King, Albert W.	Lived, Soldiers'
100 OH Inf	D	Pvt	Davis, John	Lived, Washington, uninjured
100 OH Inf	D	Pvt	Fleming, James Adgate	Died
100 OH Inf	D	Pvt	Hill, George	Lived, Soldiers'
100 OH Inf	D	Pvt	Lambert, Velmore	Died
100 OH Inf	D	Pvt	Wheeler, William	Lived, Washington, uninjured
100 OH Inf	E	Pvt	Stockwell, Eleazor B.	Died
100 OH Inf	F	Sgt	Heller, Ranatus R.	Died, Adams, severe scalds
100 OH Inf	K	Pvt	Donmire, John	Died
100 OH Inf	K	Pvt	Fleagle, John	Died
100 OH Inf	K	Pvt	Hoofnagle, Abraham	Died
101 OH Inf	D	1st Lt	Squire, Elbert J.	Lived, Officers, uninjured
101 OH Inf	H	Pvt	Rohrer, Jacob	Lived, Soldiers'
101 OH Inf	I	Capt	Taggart, Henry A.	Lived
101 OH Inf	I	Pvt	Shafer, John A.	Lived
101 OH Inf	K	Pvt	Dilling, Adam	Died
102 OH Inf	A	Sgt	Crawford, Ezra	Lived
102 OH Inf	A	Sgt	Wade, Benjamin F.	Died
102 OH Inf	A	Pvt	Fabra, David	Died
102 OH Inf	A	Pvt	Guard, James Watt	Died
102 OH Inf	A	Pvt	Guib, Jacob	Died
102 OH Inf	A	Pvt	Haley, John	Lived, Adams, incised scalp wound

Paroled Union Prisoners, continued

Unit	Company	Rank	Name	Fate
102 OH Inf	A	Pvt	Hall, George L.	Died
102 OH Inf	A	Pvt	Hass, George	Lived, Soldiers'
102 OH Inf	A	Pvt	Henderson, Wesley	Died
102 OH Inf	A	Pvt	Horner, Jacob	Lived, Soldiers'
102 OH Inf	A	Pvt	Lee, Wesley	Lived, Washington, uninjured
102 OH Inf	A	Pvt	McGinnes, Luther	Died
102 OH Inf	A	Pvt	Merchand, Leander	Died
102 OH Inf	A	Pvt	Mitchell, Joseph R.	Died
102 OH Inf	A	Pvt	Peckham, Paul R.	Lived, Soldiers'
102 OH Inf	A	Pvt	Potot, Joseph	Lived, Soldiers'
102 OH Inf	A	Pvt	Ross, William H.	Lived, fractures, skull and left ankle
102 OH Inf	B	Sgt	Richards, Reuben H.	Died
102 OH Inf	B	Cpl	Krebbs, Henry	Died
102 OH Inf	B	Cpl	McCrea, John	Died
102 OH Inf	B	Pvt	Bahn, Adam, Jr.	Died
102 OH Inf	B	Pvt	Fisher, Daniel, Jr.	Died
102 OH Inf	B	Pvt	Mercer, James M.	Died
102 OH Inf	B	Pvt	Potter, Silas R.	Lived, Adams, slight scald
102 OH Inf	B	Pvt	Spafford, Harrison	Lived, Soldiers'
102 OH Inf	B	Pvt	Stacker, Samuel	Lived
102 OH Inf	B	Pvt	Webster, Asa	Lived, Gayoso, exhaustion
102 OH Inf	B	Pvt	Wells, Joseph W.	Lived
102 OH Inf	B	Pvt	Whisemore, Abraham	Lived, Overton, head contusion
102 OH Inf	B	Pvt	Woods, Matthew	Lived, Overton, chilled
102 OH Inf	C	Sgt	Hornbugher, William C.	Died
102 OH Inf	C	Pvt	Flint, Lysander L.	Died
102 OH Inf	C	Pvt	Simons, James	Died
102 OH Inf	D	Sgt	Corts, Joseph B. F.	Died
102 OH Inf	D	Pvt	Baker, John	Died
102 OH Inf	D	Pvt	Bringman, Joseph D.	Lived, Gayoso, fractures, arm and three ribs; face scald
102 OH Inf	D	Pvt	Burt, John H.	Died
102 OH Inf	D	Pvt	Earich, William	Died

Paroled Union Prisoners, continued

Unit	Company	Rank	Name	Fate
102 OH Inf	D	Pvt	Greenfield, Reuben	Lived
102 OH Inf	D	Pvt	Grice, David	Died
102 OH Inf	D	Pvt	Harnly, Manuel	Died
102 OH Inf	D	Pvt	Kochenderfer, John H.	Lived, Gayoso, slight scald; lumbar spine injury
102 OH Inf	D	Pvt	Strawsbaugh, Samuel	Died
102 OH Inf	D	Pvt	Uhlich, George W.	Died
102 OH Inf	D	Pvt	Underwood, James	Died
102 OH Inf	D	Pvt	Williams, James T.	Died
102 OH Inf	E	Sgt	Holtom, Philip L.	Died
102 OH Inf	E	Cpl	Bierly, Jacob	Died
102 OH Inf	E	Cpl	Divelbiss, John	Died
102 OH Inf	E	Cpl	Irons, Jacob	Died
102 OH Inf	E	Pvt	Beal, Amos	Died
102 OH Inf	E	Pvt	Couter, Elias	Died
102 OH Inf	E	Pvt	Garber, Daniel	Lived, Gayoso, face scald
102 OH Inf	E	Pvt	Lockhart, William	Lived, Soldiers', face and hand scalds
102 OH Inf	E	Pvt	Oyster, Simon	Died
102 OH Inf	E	Pvt	Stuff, Frederick	Died
102 OH Inf	E	Pvt	Wheeler, Daniel	Died
102 OH Inf	E	Pvt	Willis, William W.	Died
102 OH Inf	E	Pvt	Yeisley, William	Lived, Soldiers'
102 OH Inf	F	Pvt	Anderson, George C.	Lived, Washington, scalded breast; bruised left shoulder
102 OH Inf	F	Pvt	Keeler, William	Died
102 OH Inf	F	Pvt	Saunders, Ignatious	Lived, Soldiers'
102 OH Inf	F	Pvt	Shepperly, George	Died
102 OH Inf	F	Pvt	Shoup, Charles S.	Died
102 OH Inf	F	Pvt	Sidle, Henry	Died
102 OH Inf	F	Pvt	Stine, David G.	Died
102 OH Inf	F	Pvt	Torbet, Robert	Died
102 OH Inf	G	Sgt	Hites, David	Lived, Gayoso, serious scalds
102 OH Inf	G	Cpl	Frazier, Squire	Lived
102 OH Inf	G	Cpl	Johns, Dixon W.	Died

Paroled Union Prisoners, continued

Unit	Company	Rank	Name	Fate
102 OH Inf	G	Pvt	Price, Simon P.	Died
102 OH Inf	G	Pvt	Rennington, Lucius	Died June 7, 1865
102 OH Inf	G	Pvt	Rose, Jacob S.	Died
102 OH Inf	G	Pvt	Schrader, John	Died
102 OH Inf	G	Pvt	Sleggle, Ezra K.	Died
102 OH Inf	G	Pvt	Stephens, Samuel S.	Died
102 OH Inf	G	Pvt	Tetters, Washington W.	Died
102 OH Inf	G	Pvt	Wallace, William H.	Lived, Soldiers'
102 OH Inf	H	Cpl	Crow, William	Died
102 OH Inf	H	Cpl	Harrington, Gideon	Died
102 OH Inf	H	Cpl	Huntsberger, Jonas	Died
102 OH Inf	H	Cpl	Musser, Benjamin	Died
102 OH Inf	H	Pvt	Bahl, Henry	Died
102 OH Inf	H	Pvt	Baney, John	Died
102 OH Inf	H	Pvt	Bardon, Otto	Lived, Soldiers'
102 OH Inf	H	Pvt	Brenzier, Amos	Died
102 OH Inf	H	Pvt	Brenzier, David T.	Died
102 OH Inf	H	Pvt	Christine, Harmon A.	Lived, Gayoso, slight scald
102 OH Inf	H	Pvt	Smith, Cyrus	Died
102 OH Inf	H	Pvt	Tracey, Wilson S.	Lived, Soldiers'
102 OH Inf	H	Pvt	Wells, Miles	Died
102 OH Inf	H	Pvt	Wynn, Thomas Jefferson	Died
102 OH Inf	I	Sgt	Omweg, Godfred H.	Died, Adams, severe scalds
102 OH Inf	I	Pvt	Horn, Philip L.	Lived, Washington, slight injury, left side
102 OH Inf	I	Pvt	McKelvey, Joseph M.	Died, Adams, severe scalds
102 OH Inf	I	Pvt	Schmutz, George S.	Lived, Gayoso, severe scalds, face and left side of body
102 OH Inf	K	Sgt	Fast, William N.	Lived, Gayoso, exhaustion
102 OH Inf	K	Sgt	Sprinkle, Michael H.	Lived, Soldiers'
102 OH Inf	K	Cpl	Fast, Wilson A.	Lived, Adams, chilled
102 OH Inf	K	Pvt	Burnside, Robert	Lived, Gayoso, exhaustion
102 OH Inf	K	Pvt	Cassel, John, Jr.	Died

Paroled Union Prisoners, continued

Unit	Company	Rank	Name	Fate
102 OH Inf	K	Pvt	Hartman, John F.	Died, Gayoso
102 OH Inf	K	Pvt	Kauffman, John F.	Lived
102 OH Inf	K	Pvt	Kissell, Jacob	Lived
102 OH Inf	K	Pvt	Leidig, Reuben	Died
102 OH Inf	K	Pvt	Ogden, Charles P.	Died
102 OH Inf	K	Pvt	Singer, Jeremiah	Died
102 OH Inf	K	Pvt	Steinmetz, George	Died
103 OH Inf	A	Pvt	Depmer, Aaron	Lived
103 OH Inf	E	Pvt	Shaw, Delos	Died
103 OH Inf	H	Pvt	Jarrett, John	Died
104 OH Inf	B	Pvt	Smith, William W.	Lived, Washington, slight scald
104 OH Inf	F	Pvt	Patterson, Joshua S.	Lived, Washington, severe head contusion
104 OH Inf	H	Pvt	Winkleman, John	Lived, Gayoso, exhaustion
104 OH Inf	I	Pvt	Hulett, George W.	Lived, Washington, uninjured
104 OH Inf	I	Pvt	Moulton, Dallas	Lived, Gayoso, exhaustion
111 OH Inf	E	Pvt	Joseph, Michael	Died
111 OH Inf	F	1st Lt	McCord, George B.	Lived, severe contusion
111 OH Inf	H	Pvt	Humbarger, Samuel	Died
111 OH Inf	K	Pvt	Swarm, John Lewis	Died
114 OH Inf	C	Pvt	Long, Bartholomew	Died
115 OH Inf		Musc	Garrett, Edwin W.	Died
115 OH Inf	B	Capt	Hake, Lewis F.	Lived, Soldiers'
115 OH Inf	B	Pvt	Bair, Martin V. Buren	Died
115 OH Inf	C	1st Lt	Eadie, John, Jr.	Died
115 OH Inf	C	1st Sgt	Ely, John Clark	Died
115 OH Inf	C	Sgt	Boody, Levi B.	Lived, Washington, uninjured
115 OH Inf	C	Sgt	Jones, Arthur A.	Lived, Washington, fever
115 OH Inf	C	Sgt	Way, Charles W	Died
115 OH Inf	C	Cpl	Davis, John J.	Lived
115 OH Inf	C	Cpl	Eadie, James W.	Died
115 OH Inf	C	Cpl	Eatinger, Gillis W.	Died

Paroled Union Prisoners, continued

Unit	Company	Rank	Name	Fate
115 OH Inf	C	Cpl	Nickerson, Henry N.	Lived, Overton, slight scald
115 OH Inf	C	Cpl	Norton, William H.	Lived, Washington, uninjured
115 OH Inf	C	Cpl	Stephens, Charles S.	Died
115 OH Inf	C	Cpl	Tyson, Charles S.	Died
115 OH Inf	C	Pvt	Cochran, Horace H.	Lived, Soldiers'
115 OH Inf	C	Pvt	Cody, Thomas	Died
115 OH Inf	C	Pvt	Conley, Barney	Lived, Gayoso, exhaustion
115 OH Inf	C	Pvt	Cook, James C.	Died
115 OH Inf	C	Pvt	Cook, James Stuart	Lived, Washington
115 OH Inf	C	Pvt	Cover, Henry	Lived
115 OH Inf	C	Pvt	Cross, George F.	Died
115 OH Inf	C	Pvt	Dickerson, Riley	Died
115 OH Inf	C	Pvt	Dolan, James	Died
115 OH Inf	C	Pvt	Dosenberry, George A.	Lived
115 OH Inf	C	Pvt	Doty, Nathan	Died
115 OH Inf	C	Pvt	Ellis, Edward	Died
115 OH Inf	C	Pvt	Garrison, John J.	Died
115 OH Inf	C	Pvt	Gaylord, Robert	Died
115 OH Inf	C	Pvt	Greenover, John G.	Lived, Adams
115 OH Inf	C	Pvt	Harris, George	Died
115 OH Inf	C	Pvt	Harris, John	Lived, Washington, uninjured
115 OH Inf	C	Pvt	Herberth, Charles H.	Lived, Gayoso, exhaustion
115 OH Inf	C	Pvt	Hume, Freeman	Died
115 OH Inf	C	Pvt	King, Edward	Died
115 OH Inf	C	Pvt	Maley, Christopher	Died
115 OH Inf	C	Pvt	Malone, Vincent A.	Lived, Adams, chilled
115 OH Inf	C	Pvt	Moon, Washington	Lived, Washington, uninjured
115 OH Inf	C	Pvt	O'Neil, John A.	Lived
115 OH Inf	C	Pvt	Post, Christopher C.	Lived, Gayoso, exhaustion
115 OH Inf	C	Pvt	Price, William D.	Died
115 OH Inf	C	Pvt	Ririe, John	Lived
115 OH Inf	C	Pvt	Smathers, William	Died
115 OH Inf	C	Pvt	Squires, Albert	Lived

Paroled Union Prisoners, continued

Unit	Company	Rank	Name	Fate
115 OH Inf	C	Pvt	Stephens, William	Died
115 OH Inf	C	Pvt	Stout, Charles	Died
115 OH Inf	C	Pvt	Truby, Abram	Lived
115 OH Inf	C	Pvt	Watson, Robert F.	Lived
115 OH Inf	C	Pvt	Weaver, Peter W.	Died
115 OH Inf	C	Pvt	Whetmore, Alson A.	Lived, Soldiers'
115 OH Inf	C	Pvt	Whetmore, Charles H.	Died
115 OH Inf	C	Pvt	Wilcox, Lemuel N.	Lived
115 OH Inf	C	Pvt	Wood, Isaac J.	Died
115 OH Inf	C	Pvt	Zimmerman, Jacob	Lived, Washington, uninjured
115 OH Inf	F	2d Lt	Shaffer, Jacob N.	Lived, Gayoso, exhaustion
115 OH Inf	F	Sgt	Rue, Thomas	Died
115 OH Inf	F	Sgt	Smith, William H. H.	Died
115 OH Inf	F	Cpl	Crew, Benjamin H.	Died
115 OH Inf	F	Cpl	Deitrick, Charles W.	Died
115 OH Inf	F	Pvt	Clappsaddle, Frank A.	Lived, Washington, uninjured
115 OH Inf	F	Pvt	Fogle, John	Lived, Washington, burned arm
115 OH Inf	F	Pvt	Hendricks, Adam M.	Died
115 OH Inf	F	Pvt	James, John Henry	Lived, Washington, uninjured
115 OH Inf	F	Pvt	Laugheter, Alexander	Died
115 OH Inf	F	Pvt	Roach, Robert W.	Died
115 OH Inf	F	Pvt	Rutman, Adam	Lived, Soldiers'
115 OH Inf	F	Pvt	Spencer, Thomas	Died
115 OH Inf	F	Pvt	Thomas, Linnaus A.	Lived, Washington, uninjured
115 OH Inf	F	Pvt	White, Lewis K.	Died May 16, 1865
115 OH Inf	F	Pvt	Zaizer, John J.	Lived
115 OH Inf	G	Capt	Lowrey, Deming Norton	Died
115 OH Inf	G	1st Sgt	Thompson, Eli	Died
115 OH Inf	G	Sgt	McKinney, William	Lived
115 OH Inf	G	Cpl	Alexander, Perry Howard	Lived, Adams, bad scalds, back and face
115 OH Inf	G	Cpl	Evans, Thomas	Died
115 OH Inf	G	Cpl	Patterson, James	Died

Paroled Union Prisoners, continued

Unit	Company	Rank	Name	Fate
115 OH Inf	G	Musc	Goldswood, Charles B.	Lived
115 OH Inf	G	Pvt	Cox, Robert	Died
115 OH Inf	G	Pvt	Culnon, John	Died
115 OH Inf	G	Pvt	Darrow, James M.	Lived, Washington, uninjured
115 OH Inf	G	Pvt	Davis, William, Jr.	Lived, Adams, head contusion; slight scald
115 OH Inf	G	Pvt	Myers, Daniel	Died
115 OH Inf	G	Pvt	Napp, Charles	Lived, Washington, scalded hands
115 OH Inf	H	Pvt	Dean, William	Lived
115 OH Inf	K	Musc	Everhart, John	Lived, Washington, uninjured
116 OH Inf	F	Pvt	Okey, Emanuel	Died
120 OH Inf	B	Pvt	Pettinger, William	(?)
121 OH Inf	B	Pvt	Robinson, John A.	Died May 3, 1865, Overton, slight scald, left foot
124 OH Inf	A	Pvt	Wallace, Henry B.	Lived, Soldiers'
124 OH Inf	I	Pvt	McDonal, Granville M.	Lived, Soldiers'
125 OH Inf	G	Pvt	Adams, John	Lived
125 OH Inf	H	Pvt	Jackson, James H.	Died
125 OH Inf	H	Pvt	Waters, Lucius W.	Lived, Soldiers', slight burns, bruises
135 OH Inf	F	Pvt	Lugenbeal, William	Lived, Gayoso, bruises, breast and under arms
153 OH Inf	C	Pvt	Test, Josephus	Died
174 OH Inf	C	Pvt	McDaniel, George R.	(?)
175 OH Inf	A	Pvt	Moore, James	Lived, Soldiers'
175 OH Inf	A	Pvt	Rice, Martin L.	Died
175 OH Inf	B	2d Lt	McKeehan, Thomas J.	Lived
175 OH Inf	B	Pvt	Conover, George W.	Lived
175 OH Inf	D	1st Lt	Harover, Francis M.	Lived
175 OH Inf	D	Pvt	Bayne, James	Died
175 OH Inf	D	Pvt	Bybee, Wesley	Lived
175 OH Inf	D	Pvt	Carroll, William	Died
175 OH Inf	D	Pvt	Holmes, Samuel A.	Died
175 OH Inf	D	Pvt	Myers, William O.	Died

Paroled Union Prisoners, continued

Unit	Company	Rank	Name	Fate
175 OH Inf	D	Pvt	Richmond, William	Died
175 OH Inf	D	Pvt	Shelton, William	Died
175 OH Inf	E	Pvt	Gray, Thomas J.	Died
175 OH Inf	E	Pvt	Hendrixon, George W.	Died
175 OH Inf	E	Pvt	Meeker, Timothy	Died
175 OH Inf	E	Pvt	Staton, George W.	Died
175 OH Inf	F	Capt	McCoy, William H.	Died
175 OH Inf	F	Sgt	Conover, James	Died
175 OH Inf	F	Musc	Barnes, Edward	Died
175 OH Inf	G	2d Lt	Barrer, William	Died
175 OH Inf	G	Sgt	Van Eman, Matthew T.	Died
175 OH Inf	G	Pvt	Badgley, Benton	Died
175 OH Inf	G	Pvt	Bercaw, Norman	Died
175 OH Inf	G	Pvt	Boyd, George W.	Died
175 OH Inf	G	Pvt	Cotton, W. S.	(?)
175 OH Inf	G	Pvt	Hudson, Henry	Lived
175 OH Inf	G	Pvt	Hudson, James	Died
175 OH Inf	G	Pvt	Lemons, Nathan	Lived, Gayoso, slight exhaustion
175 OH Inf	G	Pvt	Morris, Stacy	Died
175 OH Inf	I	Pvt	Smith, Henry	Died
178 OH Inf	C	Pvt	Sherwood, Silas	(?)
183 OH Inf	B	Cpl	Piller, George W.	Lived, Overton, bruised back
183 OH Inf	C	Pvt	Conrad, Michael	Lived, Soldiers'
183 OH Inf	C	Pvt	Rohland, Peter	Lived, Soldiers'
183 OH Inf	C	Pvt	Sanker, August	Lived
183 OH Inf	C	Pvt	Schneider, Adam	Died
183 OH Inf	D	Sgt	Miller, Joseph	Lived, Washington, uninjured
183 OH Inf	E	Musc	Gunther, John	Died
183 OH Inf	E	Pvt	Caddy, Charles	Lived
183 OH Inf	F	Pvt	Getterman, John	Died
183 OH Inf	G	Pvt	Minier, Darius	Lived, Gayoso, exhaustion
183 OH Inf	H	Sgt	Zehfuss, Gustave	Died
183 OH Inf	H	Pvt	Bahn, John	Died
183 OH Inf	H	Pvt	Lickleitner, Joseph	Lived
183 OH Inf	K	Pvt	Baumgardiner, W. J.	Died
183 OH Inf	K	Pvt	Oliver, Thomas	Died

Paroled Union Prisoners, continued

Unit	Company	Rank	Name	Fate
183 OH Inf	K	Pvt	Sulcer, Lucius B.	Lived
(?) OH			Talentine, J.	Lived
(?) OH			Tift, H.	Lived
13 PA Cav	M	Pvt	Dougherty, Michael	Lived
1 TN Cav	B	Sgt	Trent, Robert A.	Lived, Washington, head contusion
1 TN Cav	B	Pvt	Taylor, H.	Lived, Soldiers'
1 TN Cav	C	Pvt	Carns, Samuel	Died
1 TN Cav	E	Pvt	Meeks, Rheuben	Died
2 TN Cav	A	Pvt	Powell, John	(?)
2 TN Cav	B	Pvt	King, George A.	Lived, Soldiers'
2 TN Cav	C	Pvt	Atchley, Thomas	Lived, Soldiers'
2 TN Cav	C	Pvt	Magett, Robert	Died May 4, 1865, Adams, severe scalds, face, both arms and feet
2 TN Cav	D	Cpl	Anderson, Isaac T.	Lived, Adams, chilled
2 TN Cav	G	Pvt	Lost, D. M.	(?)
2 TN Cav	H	1st Lt	Prosser, Abijah Sidney	Lived
2 TN Cav	K	Bugle	Pilkington, Elbert	Lived, Soldiers'
2 TN Cav	K	Pvt	Potter, Peter E.	Lived, Soldiers'
2 TN Cav	M	Pvt	Henry, George W.	Died
3 TN Cav		Sgt	Hickox, John E.	Died May 9, 1865, Adams, severe scalds
3 TN Cav		Pvt	Curtes, J.	(?)
3 TN Cav		Pvt	Maddies, William F.	(?)
3 TN Cav		Pvt	Williams, Robert	Lived
3 TN Cav	A	1st Sgt	Cowan, Samuel A.	Lived, Soldiers'
3 TN Cav	A	CSgt	Franklin, James H.	Died
3 TN Cav	A	Sgt	Kidd, Louis M.	Lived, Soldiers'
3 TN Cav	A	Sgt	Rule, Andrew McBath	Lived
3 TN Cav	A	Cpl	Bell, Francis M.	Died
3 TN Cav	A	Cpl	Donaldson, Driden D.	Lived
3 TN Cav	A	Cpl	Kidd, Alexander	Lived, Washington, uninjured
3 TN Cav	A	Cpl	Rogers, Madison H.	Died
3 TN Cav	A	Blksm	Campbell, John H.	Died
3 TN Cav	A	Wagon	Finley, Rice N.	Died

Paroled Union Prisoners, continued

Unit	Company	Rank	Name	Fate
3 TN Cav	A	Wagon	Plemons, Thomas J.	Lived, Soldiers'
3 TN Cav	A	Pvt	Curtis, James M.	Lived, Soldiers'
3 TN Cav	A	Pvt	Dunlap, Hiram B.	Died
3 TN Cav	A	Pvt	Dunlap, Samuel P.	Lived, Soldiers'
3 TN Cav	A	Pvt	Evans, Samuel H.	Died May 1865
3 TN Cav	A	Pvt	Everett, James R.	Died
3 TN Cav	A	Pvt	Farmer, Adam	Died
3 TN Cav	A	Pvt	Farmer, Eli	Lived, Soldiers'
3 TN Cav	A	Pvt	Farmer, John A.	Died
3 TN Cav	A	Pvt	Gamble, Moses	Died
3 TN Cav	A	Pvt	Headrick, Daniel A.	Lived, Washington, uninjured
3 TN Cav	A	Pvt	Houser, Alexander	Died June 19, 1865, Overton, contusion
3 TN Cav	A	Pvt	Houser, Elias	Lived
3 TN Cav	A	Pvt	Houser, Henry	Died
3 TN Cav	A	Pvt	Houser, William	Died
3 TN Cav	A	Pvt	Jeffries, William M.	Died
3 TN Cav	A	Pvt	Keeble, John Harrison	Died
3 TN Cav	A	Pvt	Kidd, James W.	Died
3 TN Cav	A	Pvt	Kuble, John	Lived
3 TN Cav	A	Pvt	Linginfelter, George Thomas	Lived, Soldiers'
3 TN Cav	A	Pvt	McPherson, John A.	Died
3 TN Cav	A	Pvt	Noe, William H.	Died
3 TN Cav	A	Pvt	O'Sullivan, Richard T.	Died
3 TN Cav	A	Pvt	Pain, James Y.	Lived, Gayoso, fractured clavicle
3 TN Cav	A	Pvt	Patta, Josiah A.	Died
3 TN Cav	A	Pvt	Phelps, John M.	Lived, Soldiers'
3 TN Cav	A	Pvt	Phelps, Thompson W.	Died
3 TN Cav	A	Pvt	Pickens, Samuel	Lived, Washington, uninjured
3 TN Cav	A	Pvt	Ragan, James T.	Lived
3 TN Cav	A	Pvt	Rule, Robert	Lived, Gayoso, exhaustion
3 TN Cav	A	Pvt	Russell, Calvin W.	Lived, Adams, chilled
3 TN Cav	A	Pvt	Russell, Nicholas R.	Lived, Soldiers'
3 TN Cav	A	Pvt	Spilane, John A.	Died
3 TN Cav	A	Pvt	Summey, James A.	Died

Paroled Union Prisoners, continued

Unit	Company	Rank	Name	Fate
3 TN Cav	A	Pvt	Thomas, Noah	Lived, Washington, uninjured
3 TN Cav	A	Pvt	Vinyard, William T.	Died
3 TN Cav	A	Pvt	Wilson, Andrew	Lived, Adams, scabies
3 TN Cav	B	QSgt	Davis, James A.	Lived
3 TN Cav	B	CSgt	Davis, George W.	Lived, Adams, chilled
3 TN Cav	B	Sgt	Carver, William	Lived, Gayoso, severe burns, right side of face and shoulder
3 TN Cav	B	Sgt	Cowden, John	Died
3 TN Cav	B	Sgt	Davis, John C.	Lived
3 TN Cav	B	Sgt	Haren, Michael	Died
3 TN Cav	B	Sgt	Peery, Andrew T.	Lived, Overton, burned feet
3 TN Cav	B	Sgt	Tipton, Andrew	Died
3 TN Cav	B	Cpl	Davis, George C.	Lived, Overton, contusion
3 TN Cav	B	Cpl	Houser, James	Died
3 TN Cav	B	Cpl	Leake, Adam	Lived
3 TN Cav	B	Cpl	McClanahan, David B.	Lived, Overton, chilled
3 TN Cav	B	Cpl	Millsaps, James	Lived
3 TN Cav	B	Blksm	Barbra, William E.	Died
3 TN Cav	B	Pvt	Baley, Wyatt	Lived, Soldiers'
3 TN Cav	B	Pvt	Brown, John M.	Died
3 TN Cav	B	Pvt	Brown, William L.	Died
3 TN Cav	B	Pvt	Carver, James	Died
3 TN Cav	B	Pvt	Carver, Jesse	Died
3 TN Cav	B	Pvt	Davis, William M.	Lived, Adams, neck contusion
3 TN Cav	B	Pvt	Ellenburg, Joseph	Died
3 TN Cav	B	Pvt	Finger, Jacob	Died
3 TN Cav	B	Pvt	Lackey, Joseph B.	Lived, Soldiers'
3 TN Cav	B	Pvt	Leak, James	Died
3 TN Cav	B	Pvt	Manies, Riley J.	Died
3 TN Cav	B	Pvt	Millsaps, Jesse Wallace	Lived, Soldiers'
3 TN Cav	B	Pvt	Millsaps, William M.	Lived
3 TN Cav	B	Pvt	Pickens, William Cowan	Died
3 TN Cav	B	Pvt	Pryor, James	Lived, Soldiers'

Paroled Union Prisoners, continued

Unit	Company	Rank	Name	Fate
3 TN Cav	B	Pvt	Pryor, Wm. Marshall	Lived, Adams, chilled
3 TN Cav	B	Pvt	Rogers, Tedford W.	Died
3 TN Cav	B	Pvt	Roling, Robert W.	Lived, Soldiers'
3 TN Cav	B	Pvt	Swaggerty, William S.	Lived
3 TN Cav	B	Pvt	Tipton, Caswell C.	Lived, Gayoso, exhaustion
3 TN Cav	B	Pvt	Tipton, James	Lived, Soldiers'
3 TN Cav	B	Pvt	Tipton, Peter H.	Lived, Overton, slight contusion
3 TN Cav	C	1st Sgt	Wade, William D.	Lived, Adams, severe scalds
3 TN Cav	C	Sgt	Courtney, Joseph S.	Died
3 TN Cav	C	Sgt	Dyer, Samuel A.	Died
3 TN Cav	C	Sgt	Fry, Joseph M.	Died
3 TN Cav	C	Sgt	Matlock, George W.	Died
3 TN Cav	C	Cpl	Brown, Peter H.	Died June 9, 1865, Gayoso, slight scald
3 TN Cav	C	Cpl	Courtney, William S.	Died
3 TN Cav	C	Cpl	Cox, Jesse	Died
3 TN Cav	C	Cpl	Luttrell, William	Lived, Adams, breast contusion
3 TN Cav	C	Cpl	Sharitz, James Winton	Lived, Washington, uninjured
3 TN Cav	C	Cpl	Wade, Silas W.	Lived, Adams, severe scalds
3 TN Cav	C	Wagon	McPhail, Byrd Newman	Died, Gayoso, fractured clavicle
3 TN Cav	C	Pvt	Beckner, Houston	Lived, Adams, chilled
3 TN Cav	C	Pvt	Bishop, John	Died
3 TN Cav	C	Pvt	Bishop, William	Died
3 TN Cav	C	Pvt	Branum, Elijah John	Died, Adams, chilled
3 TN Cav	C	Pvt	Dixon, John	Died
3 TN Cav	C	Pvt	Goulden, James	Lived
3 TN Cav	C	Pvt	Graham, Landon	Lived, Gayoso, exhaustion
3 TN Cav	C	Pvt	Hampton, Jacob	Lived, Washington, uninjured
3 TN Cav	C	Pvt	Hankins, Joseph P.	Died
3 TN Cav	C	Pvt	Hann, Winfield S.	Died

Paroled Union Prisoners, continued

Unit	Company	Rank	Name	Fate
3 TN Cav	C	Pvt	Hickman, Robert L.	Lived, Washington, uninjured
3 TN Cav	C	Pvt	Hoback, George W.	Died
3 TN Cav	C	Pvt	Johnson, William R.	Died
3 TN Cav	C	Pvt	Kennedy, George W.	Died
3 TN Cav	C	Pvt	McPhail, Daniel Neill	Died
3 TN Cav	C	Pvt	Miller, John F.	Died
3 TN Cav	C	Pvt	Myers, Jacob	Lived, Soldiers'
3 TN Cav	C	Pvt	Nealy, William L.	Lived, Soldiers'
3 TN Cav	C	Pvt	Newman, Garrett	Died
3 TN Cav	C	Pvt	Palmore, William N.	Died
3 TN Cav	C	Pvt	Richter, H.	(?)
3 TN Cav	C	Pvt	Riddle, John M. D.	Died
3 TN Cav	C	Pvt	Roberson, Hiram	Lived, Adams, chilled
3 TN Cav	C	Pvt	Roberson, James C.	Lived, Adams, chilled
3 TN Cav	C	Pvt	Russell, O'Connelly C.	Lived, Gayoso, exhaustion
3 TN Cav	C	Pvt	Scott, James R.	Lived, Soldiers'
3 TN Cav	C	Pvt	Skirnisha, George S.	(?)
3 TN Cav	C	Pvt	Stroud, James	Lived
3 TN Cav	C	Pvt	Trobaugh, Allen	Died
3 TN Cav	C	Pvt	Trobaugh, John	Died
3 TN Cav	C	Pvt	Vickery, Joseph	Died
3 TN Cav	C	Pvt	Weese, Stewart	Lived, Soldiers'
3 TN Cav	C	Pvt	Wood, James E.	Lived, Gayoso, slight scald
3 TN Cav	C	Pvt	Wood, John	Lived, Adams, slight scald
3 TN Cav	C	Pvt	Wood, Landon	Died
3 TN Cav	D	1st Sgt	Mansfield, William E.	Lived, Washington, slight burn
3 TN Cav	D	CSgt	Mansfield, Thomas Monroe	Died
3 TN Cav	D	Sgt	Harin, William	(?)
3 TN Cav	D	Sgt	Hines, O. E.	(?)
3 TN Cav	D	Sgt	Hooper, James H.	Died
3 TN Cav	D	Sgt	Knight, James D.	Died
3 TN Cav	D	Sgt	Long, John	Died
3 TN Cav	D	Cpl	Douglas, Edward M.	Died
3 TN Cav	D	Cpl	Douglass, James E.	Lived, Soldiers'

Paroled Union Prisoners, continued

Unit	Company	Rank	Name	Fate
3 TN Cav	D	Cpl	Harris, William B.	Died
3 TN Cav	D	Blksm	Hinchey, Larkin E.	Died
3 TN Cav	D	Bugler	Reneau, Thomas	Lived, Gayoso, exhaustion
3 TN Cav	D	Sadlr	Rice, Jonathan H.	Died
3 TN Cav	D	Pvt	Boles, James	Died
3 TN Cav	D	Pvt	Brown, James H.	Lived, Soldiers'
3 TN Cav	D	Pvt	Cooper, Joseph	Lived, Overton, head bruise
3 TN Cav	D	Pvt	Copeland, Joseph	Lived
3 TN Cav	D	Pvt	DeArmand, Thomas Jefferson	Died
3 TN Cav	D	Pvt	Ellison, James M.	Lived, Overton, slight contusion
3 TN Cav	D	Pvt	Fergerson, John Henry	Died
3 TN Cav	D	Pvt	Hancock, William B.	Died
3 TN Cav	D	Pvt	Henry, John Wesley	Died
3 TN Cav	D	Pvt	Huffaker, Jesse Marshall	Lived, Soldiers'
3 TN Cav	D	Pvt	Long, Abner	Lived
3 TN Cav	D	Pvt	Pierce, Richard M.	Lived, Gayoso, exhaustion
3 TN Cav	D	Pvt	Reneau, James	Died
3 TN Cav	D	Pvt	Saylor, John	Lived, Overton, severe contusion
3 TN Cav	D	Pvt	Smith, John Robinson	Died
3 TN Cav	E	CSgt	Sanders, David Nahum	Died
3 TN Cav	E	Sgt	Rice, John	Lived, Gayoso
3 TN Cav	E	Cpl	Anderson, James M.	Lived, Soldiers'
3 TN Cav	E	Cpl	Elza, Robert M.	Lived, Overton, contusion
3 TN Cav	E	Cpl	Griffin, Holston	Died
3 TN Cav	E	Cpl	Meinsel, C.	(?)
3 TN Cav	E	Cpl	Williams, Spencer Harrison	Died
3 TN Cav	E	Sadlr	Thomas, Marian	Lived, Washington, uninjured
3 TN Cav	E	Pvt	Anderson, James C.	Died
3 TN Cav	E	Pvt	Baker, William A.	Died
3 TN Cav	E	Pvt	Burley, William J.	Lived, Adams, chilled
3 TN Cav	E	Pvt	Burnett, Edmund M.	Died

Paroled Union Prisoners, continued

Unit	Company	Rank	Name	Fate
3 TN Cav	E	Pvt	Burnett, Hugh A.	Died, Soldiers'
3 TN Cav	E	Pvt	Burnett, William B.	Lived
3 TN Cav	E	Pvt	Cruse, William R.	Died
3 TN Cav	E	Pvt	Haun, Joshua A.	Died
3 TN Cav	E	Pvt	Hickey, William J.	Lived
3 TN Cav	E	Pvt	Hickman, Peter	Died
3 TN Cav	E	Pvt	Hines, James	Lived, Soldiers'
3 TN Cav	E	Pvt	Hughs, John J.	Lived, Overton, contusion
3 TN Cav	E	Pvt	Johnston, James M.	Lived, Soldiers'
3 TN Cav	E	Pvt	Kidd, James F.	Died
3 TN Cav	E	Pvt	May, Martin V.	Lived, Soldiers'
3 TN Cav	E	Pvt	Miller, John W.	Lived
3 TN Cav	E	Pvt	Murphy, Ebenezer A.	Died
3 TN Cav	E	Pvt	Murphy, John M.	Died
3 TN Cav	E	Pvt	Ottinger, Morgan	Lived, Adams, bruised abdomen
3 TN Cav	E	Pvt	Simpson, Joseph A.	Died
3 TN Cav	E	Pvt	Smith, John	Died
3 TN Cav	E	Pvt	Swaggerty, Claiborne	Died
3 TN Cav	E	Pvt	Whittenbarger, Drewey A.	Lived, Soldiers'
3 TN Cav	E	Pvt	Wrinkle, Andrew J.	Died
3 TN Cav	F	1st Sgt	Lee, Edward	Died
3 TN Cav	F	QSgt	Maxwell, George W.	Lived, Overton, slight contusion
3 TN Cav	F	CSgt	Allen, Thomas J.	Died
3 TN Cav	F	Sgt	Bailey, Rufus M.	Lived
3 TN Cav	F	Sgt	Hamilton, Henry C.	Died
3 TN Cav	F	Sgt	Harris, Dewitt E.	Lived
3 TN Cav	F	Cpl	Estes, James K.	Died
3 TN Cav	F	Cpl	Jones, Harlen C.	Lived, Adams, bruised right leg
3 TN Cav	F	Cpl	Pierce, Joseph J.	Lived, Washington, uninjured
3 TN Cav	F	Blksm	Fergerson, William H.	Died
3 TN Cav	F	Bugler	Norwell, Elijah M.	Died
3 TN Cav	F	Farr	Hamilton, John B.	Lived
3 TN Cav	F	Tmstr	Bogart, Soloman F.	Lived, Adams, bruised left foot

Paroled Union Prisoners, continued

Unit	Company	Rank	Name	Fate
3 TN Cav	F	Tmstr	Missimer, Henry M.	Died
3 TN Cav	F	Pvt	Bedwell, Charles	Died
3 TN Cav	F	Pvt	Bogart, Charles H.	Died
3 TN Cav	F	Pvt	Bookout, Jesse L.	Died
3 TN Cav	F	Pvt	Cochran, Harvey	Died
3 TN Cav	F	Pvt	Collins, James R.	Lived, Washington, slight scald
3 TN Cav	F	Pvt	Davis, Elisha	Died
3 TN Cav	F	Pvt	Elliott, Jason M.	Died
3 TN Cav	F	Pvt	Elliott, Jasper W.	Died
3 TN Cav	F	Pvt	Elliott, John C.	Died
3 TN Cav	F	Pvt	Finger, Frank	Died
3 TN Cav	F	Pvt	Fisher, Emanuel L.	Died
3 TN Cav	F	Pvt	Fulfer, James	Died, Washington, severe scalds
3 TN Cav	F	Pvt	Hamilton, Robert N.	Lived, Adams, scalp contusion
3 TN Cav	F	Pvt	Harris, David D.	Lived, Gayoso, exhaustion
3 TN Cav	F	Pvt	Hicks, James H.	Died
3 TN Cav	F	Pvt	Hodges, James Wiley	Lived
3 TN Cav	F	Pvt	Howell, E.	(?)
3 TN Cav	F	Pvt	Kinnamon, James M.	Died
3 TN Cav	F	Pvt	Leonard, Thomas J.	Lived, Soldiers'
3 TN Cav	F	Pvt	Long, Melvin P.	Lived
3 TN Cav	F	Pvt	Marr, Benjamin L.	Lived, Overton, scalded face
3 TN Cav	F	Pvt	McClure, Marcus D.	Lived
3 TN Cav	F	Pvt	McMurry, Bartley R.	Lived, Adams, slight scald
3 TN Cav	F	Pvt	Melton, William	Died
3 TN Cav	F	Pvt	Reed, Robert	Died
3 TN Cav	F	Pvt	Rue, Andrew John	Lived, Gayoso, exhaustion
3 TN Cav	F	Pvt	Skaggs, Ishom	Died
3 TN Cav	F	Pvt	Skaggs, James C.	Died, Adams, severe scalds
3 TN Cav	F	Pvt	Spangle, G.	(?)
3 TN Cav	F	Pvt	Stone, William M.	Lived, Washington, uninjured

Paroled Union Prisoners, continued

Unit	Company	Rank	Name	Fate
3 TN Cav	F	Pvt	Usry, John R.	Died
3 TN Cav	F	Pvt	Wayland, Samuel A.	Died
3 TN Cav	G	Sgt	Beard, James O.	Died
3 TN Cav	G	Sgt	Turner, Robert C.	Lived, Washington, uninjured
3 TN Cav	G	Cpl	Millard, Jesse F.	Lived, Washington, uninjured
3 TN Cav	G	Cpl	Williams, David M.	Lived, Washington, uninjured
3 TN Cav	G	Bugler	Cantrell, John	Lived, Adams, diarrhea
3 TN Cav	G	Wagon	Hambrick, Andrew John	Lived, Soldiers'
3 TN Cav	G	Pvt	Badget, B.	(?)
3 TN Cav	G	Pvt	Baker, Cleaver	Lived, Soldiers'
3 TN Cav	G	Pvt	Baker, Jacob	Lived, Adams, bruised right side
3 TN Cav	G	Pvt	Baker, James	Lived, Gayoso, exhaustion
3 TN Cav	G	Pvt	Baker, John	Lived, Adams, bruised left side
3 TN Cav	G	Pvt	Brooks, James	Died
3 TN Cav	G	Pvt	Campbell, Hugh S.	Died
3 TN Cav	G	Pvt	Collins, Joseph H.	Died
3 TN Cav	G	Pvt	Curten, Richard David	Died
3 TN Cav	G	Pvt	Eldridge, Charles M.	Lived, Adams, chilled, badly confused
3 TN Cav	G	Pvt	Everett, Thomas	Died
3 TN Cav	G	Pvt	Gross, Alexander	Died
3 TN Cav	G	Pvt	Hamilton, James	Lived, Gayoso, slight scalds
3 TN Cav	G	Pvt	Hudson, Peter	Died
3 TN Cav	G	Pvt	Jordan, Montgomery	Lived, Soldiers'
3 TN Cav	G	Pvt	Lee, James	Died
3 TN Cav	G	Pvt	McClanahan, James G.	Died
3 TN Cav	G	Pvt	McClanahan, John M.	Lived, Washington, uninjured
3 TN Cav	G	Pvt	Millard, Elkaney	Lived, Overton, contusion
3 TN Cav	G	Pvt	Monger, Gillen	Died

Paroled Union Prisoners, continued

Unit	Company	Rank	Name	Fate
3 TN Cav	G	Pvt	Myers, Leslie	Died
3 TN Cav	G	Pvt	Pendergast, Nathaniel A.	Died, Adams, severe scalds
3 TN Cav	G	Pvt	Smith, William B.	Lived, Adams, bruised left side
3 TN Cav	G	Pvt	Travis, Benjamin B. O.	Lived, Washington, slight scald
3 TN Cav	G	Pvt	Walker, Daniel B.	Died
3 TN Cav	H	1st Sgt	Williams, John W.	Lived, Soldiers'
3 TN Cav	H	QSgt	Everett, William F.	Died
3 TN Cav	H	Sgt	Brown, Miles E.	Died
3 TN Cav	H	Sgt	Jones, James M.	Died
3 TN Cav	H	Wagon	Hysinger, Madison B.	Died
3 TN Cav	H	Pvt	Barrett, Henry	Lived, Washington, uninjured
3 TN Cav	H	Pvt	Cunningham, James	Lived, Gayoso, exhaustion
3 TN Cav	H	Pvt	Cusic, David	Died
3 TN Cav	H	Pvt	Fan, Greenburg	Died
3 TN Cav	H	Pvt	Farmer, Elisha	Died
3 TN Cav	H	Pvt	Farmer, Joseph O.	Died
3 TN Cav	H	Pvt	Farrett, William	Lived, Soldiers'
3 TN Cav	H	Pvt	Fisher, Elisha	Died
3 TN Cav	H	Pvt	Gamer, Calaway	Died
3 TN Cav	H	Pvt	Johnson, Andrew	Died
3 TN Cav	H	Pvt	Keeble, Pleasant M.	Lived, Adams, chilled
3 TN Cav	H	Pvt	Lock, John H.	Lived
3 TN Cav	H	Pvt	Massey, John J.	Lived, Gayoso, exhaustion
3 TN Cav	H	Pvt	Mills, William	Died
3 TN Cav	H	Pvt	Shaver, John M.	Died
3 TN Cav	I	QSgt	Linginfelter, Henry Tolbert	Lived, Washington, severe deafness, right ear; injured back, right hip, hand
3 TN Cav	I	Sgt	DeArmand, Henry Harrison	Died, Gayoso, May 31, 1865, exhaustion
3 TN Cav	I	Sgt	Frazier, Jacob	Died
3 TN Cav	I	Sgt	Howard, Tilmon A.	Died

Paroled Union Prisoners, continued

Unit	Company	Rank	Name	Fate
3 TN Cav	I	Sgt	Rhea, Patterson	Lived, Washington, slight contusion
3 TN Cav	I	Cpl	Ellison, Josiah S.	Lived
3 TN Cav	I	Cpl	Russell, Richard T.	Died
3 TN Cav	I	Cpl	Varnell, Albert P.	Lived, Soldiers', severe scalds, left side of face
3 TN Cav	I	Cpl	Ward, Jonathan	Lived, Washington, uninjured
3 TN Cav	I	Cpl	Webster, Charles H.	Died
3 TN Cav	I	Blksm	Rogers, William I.	Died
3 TN Cav	I	Bugler	Brock, James J.	Lived, Gayoso, exhaustion
3 TN Cav	I	Farr	Rogers, James A.	Lived, Soldiers'
3 TN Cav	I	Sadlr	Somey, George	Died
3 TN Cav	I	Pvt	Abshur, Wilson	Died
3 TN Cav	I	Pvt	Baggart, M.	(?)
3 TN Cav	I	Pvt	Baley, William J.	Lived, Adams
3 TN Cav	I	Pvt	Bean, James R. P.	Lived
3 TN Cav	I	Pvt	Cooper, Robert	Lived
3 TN Cav	I	Pvt	Gibson, David G.	Lived, Soldiers'
3 TN Cav	I	Pvt	Gibson, Joseph	Died
3 TN Cav	I	Pvt	Hackney, Rice Levi	Lived
3 TN Cav	I	Pvt	Hines, Joseph	Lived, Gayoso, exhaustion
3 TN Cav	I	Pvt	Legan, Daniel	Died
3 TN Cav	I	Pvt	Lindsay, John R.	Died
3 TN Cav	I	Pvt	Maples, Henry	Died
3 TN Cav	I	Pvt	McCain, Albert	Died
3 TN Cav	I	Pvt	McTeag, D.	(?)
3 TN Cav	I	Pvt	Reed, John	Died
3 TN Cav	I	Pvt	Romines, David R.	Died
3 TN Cav	I	Pvt	Romines, John	Died
3 TN Cav	I	Pvt	Romines, Laten	Died
3 TN Cav	I	Pvt	Romines, Samuel L.	Died
3 TN Cav	I	Pvt	Simpson, Adam A.	Died
3 TN Cav	I	Pvt	Simpson, John H.	Lived, Adams, incised wound, scalp; slight scald
3 TN Cav	I	Pvt	Stevens, Andrew John	Died

Paroled Union Prisoners, continued

Unit	Company	Rank	Name	Fate
3 TN Cav	I	Pvt	Teague, Pleasant	Died
3 TN Cav	I	Pvt	Thompson, Madison Isaac	Lived, Overton, contusion
3 TN Cav	I	Pvt	Wright, William	Lived, Gayoso, exhaustion
3 TN Cav	K	1st Sgt	Thompson, Russell W.	Died, Washington, May 1, 1865, skull fracture
3 TN Cav	K	Cpl	Atchley, Pleasant S.	Lived, Washington, exhaustion
3 TN Cav	K	Cpl	Cash, Henry W.	Died
3 TN Cav	K	Cpl	Caves, James P.	Died
3 TN Cav	K	Cpl	Lawson, George M.	Lived, Adams, slight scald
3 TN Cav	K	Cpl	Rule, John	Died
3 TN Cav	K	Farr	Rule, Caleb	Lived, Gayoso, slight scalds
3 TN Cav	K	Pvt	Allen, Daniel	Lived, Overton, contusion
3 TN Cav	K	Pvt	Badgett, James D.	Lived, Soldiers'
3 TN Cav	K	Pvt	Battles, Isaac	Died
3 TN Cav	K	Pvt	Battles, William F.	Lived
3 TN Cav	K	Pvt	Blane, William	Lived, Adams, chilled
3 TN Cav	K	Pvt	Bogart, Levi M.	Died
3 TN Cav	K	Pvt	Carney, George W.	Lived, Adams, chilled
3 TN Cav	K	Pvt	Chandler, Benjamin	Died
3 TN Cav	K	Pvt	Davis, William	Died, Washington
3 TN Cav	K	Pvt	Deerman, Lewis A.	Lived, Soldiers'
3 TN Cav	K	Pvt	Deerman, Solomon	Died
3 TN Cav	K	Pvt	Dougherty, Jason M.	Lived
3 TN Cav	K	Pvt	Jack, Francis M.	Lived, Soldiers'
3 TN Cav	K	Pvt	Johns, Wiley	Died
3 TN Cav	K	Pvt	Kinnamon, Samuel	Died
3 TN Cav	K	Pvt	Langley, James M.	Lived
3 TN Cav	K	Pvt	Leek, William	Died
3 TN Cav	K	Pvt	Lesley, John W.	Lived, Gayoso, serious scalds
3 TN Cav	K	Pvt	Nicholas, Daniel H.	Died
3 TN Cav	K	Pvt	Owens, George F.	Died

Paroled Union Prisoners, continued

Unit	Company	Rank	Name	Fate
3 TN Cav	K	Pvt	Pangle, Thomas	Lived, Adams, bruised right hand
3 TN Cav	K	Pvt	Ramsey, John W.	Died
3 TN Cav	K	Pvt	Reed, Jacob M.	Lived, Overton, bruised hand
3 TN Cav	K	Pvt	Smith, James Polk	Died
3 TN Cav	K	Pvt	Stephens, Jeptha B.	Died
3 TN Cav	K	Pvt	Williams, Edmund H.	Died
3 TN Cav	K	Pvt	Williams, Nathaniel G.	Died
3 TN Cav	L	QSgt	Rogers, William R.	Lived
3 TN Cav	L	Sgt	Fowler, Andrew E.	Died
3 TN Cav	L	Cpl	Barnett, Anderson F.	Lived
3 TN Cav	L	Cpl	Jenkins, Samuel W.	Lived, Adams, fever
3 TN Cav	L	Cpl	Lemings, Samuel	Lived, Gayoso, exhaustion, slight wound
3 TN Cav	L	Cpl	Wiggins, Mitchel C.	Died
3 TN Cav	L	Pvt	Cawood, Benjamin F.	Died
3 TN Cav	L	Pvt	Collins, Charles	Died
3 TN Cav	L	Pvt	Crawford, William P.	Lived, Washington, scalded eye
3 TN Cav	L	Pvt	Dailey, William M.	Lived, Gayoso, slight scald, clavicle fracture
3 TN Cav	L	Pvt	Givens, William A.	Died
3 TN Cav	L	Pvt	Haynes, David A.	Died
3 TN Cav	L	Pvt	Hill, William S.	Lived, Gayoso, exhaustion
3 TN Cav	L	Pvt	Inlow, Richard F.	Lived
3 TN Cav	L	Pvt	Johnson, Jacob	Died
3 TN Cav	L	Pvt	Land, Thomas	Died
3 TN Cav	L	Pvt	Matthews, John	Died
3 TN Cav	L	Pvt	Montgomery, John M.	Died
3 TN Cav	L	Pvt	Morrison, Gilford C.	Died, Adams, severe scalds
3 TN Cav	L	Pvt	Morrison, Isaac A.	Died
3 TN Cav	L	Pvt	Nelson, Jasper L.	Died
3 TN Cav	L	Pvt	Nichols, James	Lived
3 TN Cav	L	Pvt	Riddle, Francis	Died

Paroled Union Prisoners, continued

Unit	Company	Rank	Name	Fate
3 TN Cav	L	Pvt	Sartin, Lewis J.	Died June 9, 1865
3 TN Cav	L	Pvt	Scott, James K. P.	Lived, Adams, chilled
3 TN Cav	L	Pvt	Scrimpsher, George	Died
3 TN Cav	L	Pvt	Stancy, Monterville H.	Lived, Soldiers'
3 TN Cav	L	Pvt	Strickland, Madison	Died
3 TN Cav	L	Pvt	Swaggarty, Vance	Lived, Soldiers'
3 TN Cav	L	Pvt	Tilson, William	Died
3 TN Cav	L	Pvt	Waddle, Samuel M.	Died, Soldiers'
3 TN Cav	L	Pvt	Webb, William J.	Lived, Gayoso, severe head cut
3 TN Cav	L	Pvt	Whitman, William Riley	Died, Gayoso, bruised hip
3 TN Cav	M	Pvt	Common, Richard	Died, Overton, severe scalds
4 TN Cav	A	Pvt	Dickens, Newton	Lived, Washington, slight contusion
4 TN Cav	B	Pvt	Dykes, William H.	Lived
4 TN Cav	I	Sgt	Houston, William T.	Lived, Soldiers'
4 TN Cav	K	Pvt	Norman, John A.	Lived, Washington, uninjured
4 TN Cav	M	Pvt	Thomas, Henry H.	(?)
6 TN Cav	E	Cpl	Gray, Morgan L.	Lived, Soldiers'
6 TN Cav	E	Pvt	Shelton, Olynthus G.	Lived, Soldiers'
6 TN Cav	G	Sgt	Wolverton, James T.	Lived, Adams, chilled
7 TN Cav	A	Pvt	Derryberry, John C.	Lived, Gayoso, exhaustion
7 TN Cav	A	Pvt	Smith, John W.	Died
7 TN Cav	C	Pvt	Davenport, Isaac Noah	Lived, Soldiers', slight wounds
7 TN Cav	C	Pvt	Fowler, Green L.	Died
7 TN Cav	C	Pvt	Smith, Isaac	Died
7 TN Cav	D	Pvt	Harover, John	Died
7 TN Cav	H	Pvt	Small, Andrew J.	Died
7 TN Cav	K	Pvt	Campbell, William T.	Died
7 TN Cav	L	Pvt	Winslow, W. H.	Died
8 TN Cav	A	Pvt	Montgomery, C.	(?)
8 TN Cav	A	Pvt	Nevins, L.	(?)
10 TN Cav	C	Pvt	Darlin, James	Lived, Adams, chilled

Paroled Union Prisoners, continued

Unit	Company	Rank	Name	Fate
11 TN Cav	D	Cpl	White, James E.	Lived, Overton, severe scalds, face, arms, hands
13 TN Cav	B	Pvt	Byron, John H.	(?)
13 TN Cav	G	Pvt	Campbell, Nathaniel T.	Died
2 TN MI	A	Pvt	Emenery, W.	(?)
2 TN MI	C	Pvt	Grimes, John M.	Died
2 TN MI	C	Pvt	Dugget, James	(?)
2 TN MI	D	Pvt	Brannon, Benjamin N.	Lived, Soldiers'
2 TN MI	D	Pvt	Dicus, James	Lived, Gayoso, exhaustion
2 TN MI	E	Pvt	Bombley, Jasper P.	Died
2 TN MI	E	Pvt	Greer, John A.	Lived, Overton, chilled
2 TN MI	F	Pvt	Pierce, Richard R.	(?)
2 TN MI	G	Sgt	Reese, William A.	Lived, Adams, diarrhea
2 TN MI	G	Pvt	Culp, Andrew J.	Lived
3 TN MI	B	Pvt	Haun, John T.	Died
3 TN MI	D	Pvt	Brooks, Joseph	Died
4 TN MI	A	Sgt	Stahum, Henry V.	Lived, Washington, slight scald
4 TN MI	A	Pvt	Dromgoole, Rolla A.	Died
4 TN MI	A	Pvt	Hawshaw, Adam R.	Died
4 TN MI	A	Pvt	McMurry, William	Died, Gayoso, slight wound
4 TN MI	A	Pvt	Odum, Pleasant	Died
4 TN MI	A	Pvt	Sumners, James B.	Died
4 TN MI	L	1st Lt	McDowall, William	Died
4 TN MI	L	Pvt	Phillips, John M.	Lived, Adams, chilled
3 TN Inf	F	Pvt	Kirkpatrick, William C.	Lived, Gayoso, left clavicle fracture
3 TN Inf	G	Sgt	Creswell, Samuel A.	Died
3 TN Inf	I	Pvt	Draper, Prior L.	Lived, Gayoso, slight scald
3 TN Inf	I	Pvt	Kirkpatrick, John R.	Lived, Washington, uninjured
3 TN Inf	I	Pvt	Ramsey, McPherson	Lived, Washington, scalded arm

Paroled Union Prisoners, continued

Unit	Company	Rank	Name	Fate
5 TN Inf	A	Pvt	Everett, Luke L.	Lived, Soldiers'
5 TN Inf	B	Pvt	Hines, Samuel J.	Lived, Gayoso, exhaustion
5 TN Inf	B	Pvt	Mincey, Robert	Lived, Adams, chilled
(?) TN			Jones, Doc	Lived
44 USCT	F	Capt	Elliott, J. Walter	Lived, slight scalds, face, throat, lungs
58 USCT		Lt	Keeler, Lewis C.	Died
111 USCT		Lt	Mader, John	Died
1 WV L Art	D	Pvt	Craig, Anthony	Died
1 WV L Art	D	Pvt	Loy, George C.	Lived, Washington, bruised right side
1 WV L Art	D	Pvt	Smith, George G.	Lived, Soldiers'
1 WV L Art	D	Pvt	Stephens, Allen R.	Died
1 WV Cav	G	Pvt	Rupel, Charles	(?), Soldiers'
1 WV Cav	L	Pvt	Cruddes, William	Died
2 WV Cav	F	Cpl	Sharp, Thomas	Lived, Overton, chilled
4 WV Cav	F	Pvt	Woodyard, Taylor	Lived, Soldiers'
6 WV Cav	B	Sgt	Lyons, James H.	Died
6 WV Cav	B	Pvt	Lawless, Patrick	Lived, Gayoso, slight scald
6 WV Cav	H	Pvt	Talmadge, J.	(?)
6 WV Cav	K	Pvt	Walsh, John	Died
1 WV Inf	A	Cpl	Richardson, Theopholis	Lived, Soldiers'
1 WV Inf	A	Pvt	Foster, Henry C.	Lived, Soldiers'
1 WV Inf	K	Pvt	Manners, Alexander	Died
1 WV Inf	K	Pvt	McHenry, James	Lived, Washington, eye wound
5 WV Inf	C	Pvt	Steel, John W.	Died
9 WV Inf	K	Cpl	Buckbee, James	Lived, Adams, bruised left leg
(?) (?)	B	Pvt	Lipton, James	(?), Soldiers'

Notes

In 1892, *Sultana* survivor Chester D. Berry, fearing that the story of the *Sultana* would die with the death of the last survivor, collected the accounts of 134 fellow survivors and published them in *Loss of the* Sultana *and Reminiscences of Survivors.* Aside from a short introduction by Berry, the accounts are presented singularly and alphabetically by last names. The accounts, written in the first person, are independent of each other. The name of the survivor giving an account is included, where applicable, in each note that refers to Berry's work.

A number of other works present survivor accounts in the same manner, most notably Jesse Hawes, *Cahaba: A Story of Captive Boys in Blue,* and George S. Schmutz, *History of the 102nd Regiment, OVI.* Again, the name of the survivor is included in each applicable note.

Also, many survivors submitted their accounts of the disaster to the *National Tribune,* a nationwide post–Civil War newspaper for soldiers, published in Washington, D.C. *The National Tribune* was equivalent to the *Stars & Stripes* of World War II. In the Bibliography, the cited articles are listed by authors under the heading, "Journals and Periodicals," for ease of reference.

Shortly after the *Sultana* disaster, the U.S. Army conducted a number of investigations. Statements, taken wherever and whenever possible, were usually one page or less in length, and the various investigative bodies did not number pages or accounts. Consequently, notes for testimony given during the Washburn Inquiry, Dana Commission, and Hoffman Investigation lack page numbers. The material acquired during these investigations is contained in Record Group 153, National Archives.

Chapter 1   The *Sultana*

1. "River News," *Cincinnati Daily Commercial,* January 3, 1863, 4.
2. Ibid., February 4, 1863, 4.
3. Hunter, *Steamboats on Western Rivers,* 87.
4. "River News," *Cincinnati Daily Commercial,* February 4, 1863, 4; Witzig, "Report of Casualties and Violations," 216.
5. Hunter, *Steamboats on Western Rivers,* 155, 157, 263–64.
6. Witzig, "Report of Casualties and Violations," 216; J. J. Witzig, testimony, in "Transcript of Court-Martial of Captain Frederic Speed," 129 (hereafter cited as "Transcript"); "River News," *Cincinnati Daily Commercial,* February 4, 1863, 4; Inspector's Certificate of *Sultana,* April 12, 1865 (hereafter cited as Inspector's Certificate).
7. Details of the *Sultana*'s design, construction, and furnishings are

from "River News," *Cincinnati Daily Commercial*, February 4, 1863, 4; testimony of George A. Williams, William Kerns, and Witzig, in "Transcript," 43, 59, 136; Inspector's Certificate; Kerns, testimony, in Dana Commission, "Records of Commission Conducted by General Dana" (hereafter cited as Dana Commission). Also, see Bates, *Western Rivers Steamboat Cyclopoedium*, 53; Hunter, *Steamboats on Western Rivers*, 109, 138.

8. Quoted in Hunter, *Steamboats on Western Rivers*, 397.

9. Ibid., 395; Bates, *Western Rivers Steamboat Cyclopoedium*, 59.

10. Bates, *Western Rivers Steamboat Cyclopoedium*, 70.

11. Form C Enrollment; Witzig, testimony, in "Transcript," 129, 136–37; Witzig, "Report of Casualties and Violations," 216; Inspector's Certificate; U.S. War Department, *War of Rebellion;* 1st ser., vol. 48, pt. 1, 217; Berry, *Loss of the* Sultana, 77; William Snow, testimony, in Washburn Inquiry, "Records of Inquiry Conducted by Major General Washburn" (hereafter cited as Washburn Inquiry).

12. *Webster's New World Dictionary*, 3d college ed., s.v. "sultana."

13. Way, *Way's Directory of Western River Packets*, 279–80; Way, *Way's Packet Directory*, 435–36.

14. Hunter, *Steamboats on Western Rivers*, 443–44; Custer, "Officers of the Steamboat," 27–28.

15. Details of steamboat officers and crew and their duties are from Custer, "Officers of the Steamboat," 27–29; Watson, *Paddlewheel Steamers*, 80, 87; Twain, *Life on the Mississippi*, 118–19; Custer, "The Engine Room," 17; Hunter, *Steamboats on Western Rivers*, 446; Custer, "The Cabin and Deck Crew," 27–29.

16. "River News," *Cincinnati Daily Commercial*, February 4, 1863, 4.

17. "River Correspondence," *Daily Missouri Republican*, February 13, 1863, 4.

18. Ibid., February 19, 4; February 21, 4; February 25, 4; March 2, 4; and March 5, 1863, 4.

19. Rutter, "Bewitching News," 12.

20. U.S. War Department, *War of Rebellion*, 1st ser., vol. 48, pt. 1, 219; J. O. Lewis, testimony, and L. W. Perce, testimony, both in Washburn Inquiry; Witzig, testimony, in "Transcript," 137.

21. "River Correspondence," *Daily Missouri Republican*, March 19, 4, and April 4, 1863, 4.

22. Quotations, ibid., May 9, 1863, 4. Also, see ibid., May 5, 4.

23. Ibid., May 12, 4, and May 16, 1863, 4.

24. Faust, *Historical Times*, 781–83.

25. "Fire of Hate Brands Boat of Early Days," *Memphis Evening Appeal*, May 13, 1927.

26. U.S. Navy Department, *War of Rebellion*, 1st ser., vol. 25, 4; "River Correspondence," *Daily Missouri Republican*, May 22, 3, and May 29, 1863, 3.

27. "River Correspondence," *Daily Missouri Republican*, July 18, 4, and July 21, 1863, 4.

28. Stillwell, *Story of Common Soldier*, 149–50.

29. Samuel, Huber, and Ogden, *Tales of the Mississippi,* 128; U.S. Navy Department, *War of Rebellion,* 1st ser., vol. 25, 339; "River Correspondence," *Daily Missouri Republican,* August 5, 4, and August 6, 1863, 4.

30. "River Correspondence," *Daily Missouri Republican,* September 27, 4, September 29, 4, and November 18, 1863, 4; "Burning of Sultana in 1865 Is Recalled," *Memphis Commercial Appeal,* May 29, 1936; Way, *Way's Directory of Western River Packets,* 280; "Fire of Hate Brands Boat."

31. "Fire of Hate Brands Boat"; Way, *Way's Directory of Western River Packets,* 280.

32. Greve, *Centennial History of Cincinnati,* 869–70.

33. "River News," *Memphis Daily Bulletin,* May 4, 1865, 3; Form C Enrollment; "The *Sultana* Disaster," *Daily Missouri Democrat,* April 29, 1865, 4.

34. "*Sultana* Disaster"; Potter, *The* Sultana *Tragedy,* 6.

35. U.S. Navy Department, *War of Rebellion,* 1st ser., vol. 25, 332–37, 420–21, 426–27, 546.

36. Bryant, *Cahaba Prison and* Sultana *Disaster,* 122–23; Potter, *The* Sultana *Tragedy,* 6.

37. Quotations from "*Sultana* Disaster." Also, see "Victims of the Disaster—The Lost," *Memphis Argus,* April 28, 1865, 3.

38. "Fire of Hate Brands Boat"; "Burning of *Sultana* in 1865 is Recalled," *Memphis Commercial Appeal,* May 29, 1936; departure advertisements, *Tri-Weekly Missouri Republican,* February 6, 1, and February 21, 1865, 1; Way, *Way's Directory of Western River Packets,* 280.

39. Quoted in "Cairo News," *Tri-Weekly Missouri Republican,* March 6, 1865, 4. Note: The Cairo newspapers are no longer available for reference, but they were frequently quoted by the Saint Louis newspapers.

40. "Memoranda of Olive Branch," *Tri-Weekly Missouri Republican,* March 17, 1865, 1.

41. "Burning of *Sultana* Recalled"; Way, *Way's Directory of Western River Packets,* 280; Lyda's account in Berry, *Loss of the* Sultana, 28.

42. Departure advertisement, *Tri-Weekly Missouri Republican,* March 20, 1, "Cairo News," *Tri-Weekly Missouri Republican,* April 7, 1865, 3; Lyda's account in Berry, *Loss of the* Sultana, 28.

43. Quotation and details are in "Cairo News," *Daily Missouri Republican,* April 10, 1865, 3.

44. Quotations are from "River Correspondence," *Tri-Weekly Missouri Republican,* April 14, 1865, 1. Also, see "River Correspondence, *Tri-Weekly Missouri Republican,* April 17, 1, and April 26, 1865, 1.

45. Form C Enrollment; J. S. Nauson, testimony, and L. G. Mitchell, testimony, both in Washburn Inquiry; "*Sultana* Disaster."

46. Soper to Potter, August 10, 1982; Nauson, testimony, in Washburn Inquiry."

47. "*Sultana* Disaster."

48. "River Correspondence," *Tri-Weekly Missouri Republican,* February 8, 1865, 1. Also, see advertisements, *Daily Missouri Democrat* and *Tri-Weekly Missouri Republican,* both February 22, 1865, 4.

49. Long and Long, *Civil War Day by Day*, 663, 670; Berry, *Loss of the* Sultana, 47.

50. Departure advertisement, *Daily Missouri Democrat*, April 11, 1865, 4.

51. "*Sultana* Disaster"; departure advertisement, *Daily Picayune*, April 20, 1865, 10; Nathan Wintringer, testimony, and George Kayton, testimony, both in "Transcript," 168, 317.

52. Departure advertisements, *Daily Missouri Democrat*, April 11, 1865, 4.

53. Berry, *Loss of the* Sultana, 104–5, 225.

54. Witzig, testimony, and Wintringer, testimony, both in "Transcript," 129, 162; Witzig, "Report of Casualties and Violations," 216; Inspector's Certificate; "River Correspondence," *Daily Missouri Republican,* June 4, 1863, 4.

55. Departure advertisement, *Tri-Weekly Missouri Republican,* April 14, 1865, 1.

56. Wintringer, testimony, in "Transcript," 162; departure advertisement, *Tri-Weekly Missouri Republican,* April 13, 1865, 1.

Chapter 2   Delivered from Bondage

1. Long and Long, *Civil War Day by Day*, 711; Faust, *Historical Times*, 603; Francis Trevelyan Miller, *Photographic History of Civil War,* vol. 7, 24, 102, 345–46; U.S. War Department, *War of Rebellion;* 2d ser., vol. 1, 166.

2. Faust, *Historical Times*, 604; Francis Trevelyan Miller, *Photographic History of Civil War,* vol. 7, 108–10.

3. Bryant, *Cahaba Prison and* Sultana *Disaster,* 20; Walker, *Cahaba and* Sultana *Disaster,* 4–5.

4. Bryant, *Cahaba Prison and* Sultana *Disaster,* 23.

5. Ibid., 23–24; Francis Trevelyan Miller, *Photographic History of Civil War,* vol. 7, 74.

6. Bryant, *Cahaba Prison and* Sultana *Disaster,* 23, 31–32.

7. Eldridge, "In the *Sultana* Disaster," 7. Also, see Berry, *Loss of the* Sultana, 299.

8. Huffaker, "My Father," 3. Also, see Berry, *Loss of the* Sultana, 304.

9. Quoted in Berry, *Loss of the* Sultana, 380.

10. Quoted in Schmutz, *History of 102nd Regiment,* 250.

11. Quoted in Berry, *Loss of the* Sultana, 323.

12. Quoted in Schmutz, *History of 102nd Regiment,* 250.

13. Bryant, *Cahaba Prison and* Sultana *Disaster,* 12.

14. Myers, "Night the *Sultana* Blew Up"; Berry, *Loss of the* Sultana, 257.

15. Quoted in Berry, *Loss of the* Sultana, 367.

16. Williams to home, March 19, 1865.

17. Berry, *Loss of the* Sultana, 300.

18. Walker, *Cahaba and* Sultana *Disaster,* 15.

19. Williams to home, March 19, 1865; Berry, *Loss of the* Sultana, 102, 134.

20. Francis Trevelyan Miller, *Photographic History of Civil War,* vol. 7, 74, 76; Long and Long, *Civil War Day by Day,* 490.

21. Quoted in Berry, *Loss of the* Sultana, 339.

22. Quoted in Francis Trevelyan Miller, *Photographic History of Civil War,* vol. 7, 82, 84.

23. Faust, *Historical Times,* 474; Long and Long, *Civil War Day by Day* 565; Roth, "Andersonville," 11; Berry, *Loss of the* Sultana, 45, 95, 197, 234.

24. Isaac N. Davenport, "Story of *Sultana,*" 3. Also, see Berry, *Loss of the* Sultana, 113; J. Walter Elliott, "By Fire and Flood."

25. J. Walter Elliott, "By Fire and Flood." Also, see Elliott's account in Berry, *Loss of the* Sultana, 113–14.

26. Quoted in Berry, *Loss of the* Sultana, 247–48.

27. Isaac N. Davenport, "Story of *Sultana,*" 4.

28. J. Walter Elliott, "By Fire and Flood."

29. Joseph Taylor Elliott, "*Sultana* Disaster," 164.

30. Horan to McCutchan.

31. Henderson, "Lincoln's Assassination and Camp Fisk," 170.

32. Details of the exchange in ibid.; Morgan L. Smith, testimony, in Washburn Inquiry; U.S. War Department, *War of Rebellion,* 2d ser., vol. 8, 284–85.

33. Goodrich's account in Berry, *Loss of the* Sultana, 154; also, see 325, 343.

34. Smith's account in Berry, *Loss of the* Sultana, 325; also, see 82, 211, 281, 319, 347.

35. U.S. War Department, *War of Rebellion,* 2d ser., vol. 8., 382, 378, 404–5.

36. Eldridge, "In the *Sultana* Disaster." Also, see Eldridge, "Some Events at Close of War."

37. Winters, *In the 50th Ohio,* 154.

38. Ibid. Also, see Berry, *Loss of the* Sultana, 145.

39. Joseph Taylor Elliot, "*Sultana* Disaster," 164–65. Also, see Horan to home; J. Walter Elliott, "By Fire and Flood."

40. Joseph Taylor Elliott, "*Sultana* Disaster," 165.

41. Ibid. Also, see J. Walter Elliott, "By Fire and Flood."

42. J. Walter Elliott, "By Fire and Flood."

43. Winters, *In the 50th Ohio,* 161.

44. Ibid; J. Walter Elliott, "By Fire and Flood."

45. Faust, *Historical Times,* 656; Winters, *In the 50th Ohio,* 158; "Relief for the *Sultana* Sufferers," *Memphis Daily Bulletin,* May 4, 1865, 3.

46. Walker, *Cahaba and* Sultana *Disaster,* 16.

47. Winters, *In the 50th Ohio,* 156.

48. George A. Williams, testimony, in Washburn Inquiry.

49. Ibid.; Potter, *The* Sultana *Tragedy,* 27–30.

50. Quoted in U.S. War Department, *War of Rebellion,* 2d ser., vol. 8, 425–26.

51. George A. Williams, testimony, in Washburn Inquiry.

52. Faust, *Historical Times,* 114, 474–75, 834; U.S. War Department, *War of Rebellion,* 2d ser., vol. 8, 483–84, 488–89.

53. George A. Williams, testimony, and H.A.M. Henderson, testimony, both in "Transcript," 23, 275; Frederic Speed, testimony, in Washburn Inquiry.

54. "Camp Fisk," *Tri-Weekly Missouri Republican,* April 12, 1865, 2.

55. U.S. War Department, *War of Rebellion,* 2d ser., vol. 8, 477–78; Henderson, testimony, in "Transcript," 277; Berry, *Loss of the* Sultana, 330.

56. Long and Long, *Civil War Day by Day,* 663, 670–71.

57. U.S. War Department, *War of Rebellion,* 2d ser., vol. 8, 483–84, 488–89.

Chapter 3   Messenger of Death

1. *Memphis Argus* quotation in "From Memphis," *Tri-Weekly Missouri Republican,* March 22, 1865, 1. Details of the flood are from "River News," *War Eagle,* April 14, 1865, 1; Winters, *In the 50th Ohio,* 167; Berry, *Loss of the* Sultana, 65–66, 373–74.

2. Kayton, testimony, in "Transcript," 321; departure advertisement, *Daily Missouri Democrat,* April 13, 1865, 4.

3. Speed's telegram quoted in U.S. War Department, *War of Rebellion,* 2d ser., vol. 8, 488–89.

4. James Wells, *Personal Memoirs,* 83; Miles Sells, testimony, in "Transcript," 127.

5. Sells, testimony, in "Transcript," 127; "Paroled Prisoners," *Daily Missouri Democrat,* April 4, 4, and April 10, 1865, 3.

6. Potter, *The* Sultana *Tragedy,* 31–32.

7. Winters, *In the 50th Ohio,* 156–57; Horan to McCutchan; Foley to Price.

8. Hinds to parents.

9. Foley to Price.

10. Winters, *In the 50th Ohio,* 158.

11. Joseph Taylor Elliott, *"Sultana* Disaster," 158.

12. Hinds to parents.

13. Winters, *In the 50th Ohio,* 158.

14. Spencer Harrison Williams to home, April 17, 1865.

15. McCrory's account in Berry, *Loss of the* Sultana, 244.

16. Brown's account in ibid., 76.

17. Foley to Price.

18. Spencer Harrison Williams to home, April 17, 1865.

19. Horan to home.

20. Ely, unpublished diary.

21. Hinds to friends at home.

22. Departure advertisement, *War Eagle,* April 14, 1865, 2.

23. Dana's telegrams quoted in U.S. War Department, *War of Rebellion,* 2d ser., vol. 8, 492–93.

24. Long and Long, *Civil War Day by Day,* 675–77.

25. Headline in *Cairo Democrat,* April 15, 1865, 1; "Explanatory," *War Eagle,* April 15, 1865, 2; "Cairo News," *Tri-Weekly Missouri Republican,* April 17,

1865, 1; Berry, *Loss of the* Sultana, 25; Sells, testimony, in "Transcript," 120, 122.

26. Berry, *Loss of the* Sultana, 25; "Colonel William S. Friesner of Logan Commanded Detail on Ill-Fated Sultana," *Logan Daily News,* June 27, 1966, 26.

27. "River News," *Memphis Daily Bulletin,* April 16, 3, and April 17, 1865, 4.

28. Special Order No. 132, in "Transcript," 352–53.

29. J. Warren Miller, testimony, in "Transcript," 215–16, 223; U.S. War Department, *War of Rebellion,* 1st ser., vol. 48, pt. 1, 210.

30. Special Order No. 133, in "Transcript," 354–57.

31. *Tri-Weekly Missouri Republican,* May 1, 1865, 4; Berry, *Loss of the* Sultana, 25.

32. Sells, testimony, in "Transcript," 121.

33. Potter, *The* Sultana *Tragedy,* 32.

34. Primary details of Hatch's military career and quotations from Lincoln's letter and report of examining board are in Potter, *The* Sultana *Tragedy,* 32–42.

35. Sells, testimony, in "Transcript," 121–22; Miles Sells, testimony, in Dana Commission.

36. Sells, testimony, in "Transcript," 121.

37. Ibid.; Morgan L. Smith, testimony, in Washburn Inquiry.

38. Sells, testimony, in "Transcript," 121–22.

39. Henderson, "Lincoln's Assassination and Camp Fisk," 171.

40. Ibid.; Winters, *In the 50th Ohio,* 161–62.

41. Roziene, "The Overloaded *Sultana,*" 7; James Wells, *Personal Memoirs,* 71–72.

42. "River News," *Tri-Weekly Missouri Republican,* April 26, 1865, 4; Henderson, "Lincoln's Assassination and Camp Fisk," 171.

43. Ely, unpublished diary.

44. Winters, *In the 50th Ohio,* 157; Dougherty, *Prison Diary,* 67; Horan to McCutchan; J. Walter Elliott, "By Fire and Flood," 2.

45. Special Order No. 134, in "Transcript," 357–58.

46. *Daily Picayune,* April 19, 1865, 1; East, *Sarah Morgan,* 606.

Chapter 4   Greed and Deception

1. Special Order No. 134, in "Transcript," 357–58; U.S. War Department, *War of Rebellion,* 1st ser., vol. 48, pt. 1, 211.

2. James Wells, *Personal Memoirs,* 73; Edwin L. Davenport, testimony, in "Transcript," 294, 295, 313.

3. Kerns, testimony, in "Transcript," 47–48, 80, 82.

4. U.S. War Department, *War of Rebellion,* 1st ser., vol. 48, pt. 1, 211.

5. George B. Denton, testimony, in Washburn Inquiry.

6. "A Sad Case" and "Caring for the Living and Dead," both in *Memphis Daily Bulletin,* April 28, 1865, 2.

7. "Statement of Mr. Long, A Passenger," and "Victims of the Disaster—

The Lost," both in *Memphis Argus,* April 28, 1865, 3; "Supposed Recognition," *Memphis Argus,* April 29, 1865, 3.

8. McLeod's account in Berry, *Loss of the* Sultana, 254–55; Charles E. Compton, testimony, in "Transcript," 147–48; McKesson to Clerk of Circuit Court; Bent family headstone, Wilmot Cemetery, Wilmot, Wisc.

9. Joseph Taylor Elliott, testimony, in "Transcript," 143; Nathan Wintringer, testimony, in Washburn Inquiry.

10. Nauson, testimony, in Washburn Inquiry.

11. Departure advertisement, *Daily Picayune,* April 21, 1865, 1, 8.

12. Kayton, testimony, in "Transcript," 321.

13. Compton, testimony, in ibid., 148; Wintringer, testimony, in Washburn Inquiry.

14. James Wells, *Personal Memoirs,* 73.

15. *Tri-Weekly Missouri Republican,* April 26, 1865, 3; U.S. War Department, *War of Rebellion,* 1st ser., vol. 48, pt. 1, 211.

16. Rex Miller, *Croxton's Raid,* 140.

17. Special Order No. 138, in "Transcript," 359–60.

18. Conversations of McGuire and Jones with Tillinghast are quoted in William Tillinghast, testimony, in Washburn Inquiry; and James P. McGuire, testimony, in Dana Commission.

19. "Arrivals—*Henry Ames,*" *Tri-Weekly Missouri Republican,* April 26, 1865, 3; Berry, *Loss of the* Sultana, 254.

20. Tillinghast, testimony, in Washburn Inquiry.

21. Kerns, testimony, in "Transcript," 62–63.

22. Jameson Cox, deposition, in ibid., Exhibit N.

23. U.S. War Department, *War of Rebellion,* 1st ser., vol. 48, pt. 1, 211.

24. Cox, deposition, in "Transcript," Exhibit N.

25. Tillinghast, testimony, in Washburn Inquiry.

26. William C. Jones, testimony, in "Transcript," 90–91.

27. Kerns, testimony, and William C. Jones, testimony, both in ibid., 63–64.

28. Frederic Speed, testimony, in Washburn Inquiry; Kerns, testimony, in "Transcript," 62–63.

29. Compton, testimony, in "Transcript," 148.

30. Wintringer, testimony, in Washburn Inquiry.

31. Speed, testimony, in ibid.

32. Speed, testimony, and Reuben B. Hatch, testimony, both in ibid.

33. U.S. Sanitary Commission, *The Sanitary Reporter,* vol. 1, 187.

34. Speed, testimony, in Washburn Inquiry; U.S. War Department, *War of Rebellion,* 1st ser., vol. 48, pt. 1, 211.

35. Details of Speed's conversations with Kerns and Hatch are in Kerns, testimony, in "Transcript," 63–64, 66, and Speed, testimony, in Washburn Inquiry.

36. George A. Williams, testimony, in "Transcript," 13; Speed, testimony, in Washburn Inquiry.

37. Compton, testimony, and Wintringer, testimony, both in "Tran-

script," 147¼, 169; Wintringer, testimony, and R. G. Taylor, testimony, both in Washburn Inquiry.

38. Account of Taylor's inspection of boiler is from Taylor, testimony, in Washburn Inquiry.

39. Denton, testimony, in ibid.

40. Sells, testimony, in "Transcript," 122.

Chapter 5   The Loading

1. Sells, testimony, in Dana Commission.

2. Ibid.

3. Sells, testimony, in "Transcript," 123, 126.

4. Account of conversation between Mason and Speed is in Sells, testimony, in ibid., 119, 123, 125–26.

5. Speed, testimony, in Washburn Inquiry.

6. Sells, testimony, in "Transcript," 123.

7. George A. Williams, testimony, and Sells, testimony, both in ibid., 14, 23–24, 40–41, 124. Note: Although Sells was not present at meeting between Mason and Williams, his testimony about it was allowed by the court on the assumption that the hearsay evidence had come directly from Mason.

8. George A. Williams, testimony, in ibid., 14, 24 and 40–41; Speed, testimony, in Washburn Inquiry.

9. Speed, testimony, in ibid. Note: Speed constantly changed his numbers when discussing the number of men to be transported.

10. U.S. War Department, *War of Rebellion,* 1st ser., vol. 48, pt. 1, 211.

11. George A. Williams, testimony, in "Transcript," 22–23, 25, 29.

12. Details of conversation between Speed and Hatch are in William H. H. Emmons, testimony, in ibid., 193–94; Also, see Speed, testimony, in Washburn Inquiry.

13. J. Warren Miller, testimony, Emmons, testimony, and Special Order No. 140, all in "Transcript," 194–95, 216–17, 361–62; Speed, testimony, in Washburn Inquiry.

14. George A. Williams, testimony, in "Transcript," 29, 37.

15. Details of conversation between Williams and Speed are in Speed, testimony, in Washburn Inquiry.

16. George A. Williams, testimony, and Cox, deposition, both in "Transcript," 29, 31, Exhibit N; Edward D. Butler, testimony, in Hoffman Investigation, "Records of the Investigation Conducted by General Hoffman (hereafter cited as Hoffman Investigation).

17. Edwin L. Davenport, testimony, in "Transcript," 283.

18. Quoted in "Reminiscence of the War," *Wayne County Democrat,* April 28, 1880.

19. James M. McCown, testimony, in "Transcript," 95, 100.

20. Cox, deposition, in "Transcript," Exhibit N.

21. Taylor, testimony, in Washburn Inquiry.

22. Account of conversation between Tillinghast and Jones is in Tillinghast, testimony, in ibid.

23. Kerns, testimony, in ibid.

24. Kerns, testimony, in "Transcript," 54–55, 59, 75, 80.

25. "Colonel William S. Friesner of Logan Commanded Detail on Ill-Fated *Sultana*," *Logan Daily News*, June 27, 1966, 25.

26. Edwin L. Davenport, testimony, and Cox, deposition, both in "Transcript," 284, 293–94, 305, Exhibit N.

27. Edward D. Butler, testimony, in ibid., 154;

28. The first trainload was known to include about 800 men; however, the men from Ohio on the first train numbered slightly more than 650.

The men from Kentucky, Tennessee, and West Virginia, totaling almost 700, were placed on the third and last train, but that last trainload was known to carry close to 800 men. A few of the survivors from the 2d and 5th Michigan Cavalry Regiments specifically stated that they went into Vicksburg on the last train. The author believes that all of the men from the Michigan cavalry units, approximately 100 in number, were held over for the last train.

The author also believes that the Michigan infantrymen, numbering about 170, and the Indiana cavalrymen, a total of approximately 250, were placed on the second train and that the Indiana infantry soldiers, numbering about 150, account for the missing number of men from the first trainload.

29. George A. Williams, testimony, and Cox, deposition, both in "Transcript," 13, Exhibit N.

30. George A. Williams, testimony, and Edwin L. Davenport, testimony, both in ibid., 30, 36, 285, 306, 314.

31. Kerns, testimony, in ibid., 46; Kerns, testimony, in Washburn Inquiry.

32. "Colonel William S. Friesner."

33. George A. Williams, testimony, in "Transcript," 20, 25, 32; Berry, *Loss of the* Sultana, 57; William D. Butler, testimony, in Hoffman Investigation.

34. Jones's account in Berry, *Loss of the* Sultana, 190.

35. Boor's account in ibid., 57. Also, see Jacob W. Rush, testimony, in Washburn Inquiry.

36. Brown's account in Berry, *Loss of the* Sultana, 76.

37. Newhouse to author; Anderson to author.

38. George S. Kemble, deposition, in "Transcript," Exhibit O.

39. George A. Williams, testimony, in ibid., 32, 35, 38, and in Washburn Inquiry.

40. U.S. War Department, *War of Rebellion*, 1st ser., vol. 48, pt. 1, 211; George A. Williams, testimony, in "Transcript," 35, 42, and in Washburn Inquiry.

41. Telegram quoted in Miller, testimony, in "Transcript," 219. Also, see George A. Williams, testimony, in "Transcript," 42.

42. Telegram quoted in Edwin L. Davenport, testimony, in "Transcript," 292–93. Also, see George A. Williams, testimony, in "Transcript," 42.

43. Speed, testimony, in Washburn Inquiry.

44. Edward D. Butler, testimony, and Cox, deposition, both in "Transcript," 153, Exhibit N; Edward D. Butler, testimony, in Washburn Inquiry.

45. George A. Williams, testimony, and Edward D. Butler, testimony, both in "Transcript," 15, 152.

46. Christian M. Nisley, testimony, in Washburn Inquiry; Nisley's account in Berry, *Loss of the* Sultana, 263.

47. Peacock's account in Berry, *Loss of the* Sultana, 285.

48. Taylor, testimony, in Washburn Inquiry; Wintringer, testimony, in "Transcript," 164–65.

49. Kerns, testimony, in Dana Commission; William C. Jones, testimony, in "Transcript," 86, 88.

50. Kerns, testimony, in "Transcript," 49; Hatch, testimony, in Washburn Inquiry.

51. Kerns, testimony, in "Transcript," 49–50.

52. Speed, testimony, in Washburn Inquiry.

53. Ibid.; Edwin L. Davenport, testimony, in "Transcript," 292–93, 314–15.

54. Edward D. Butler, testimony, in Washburn Inquiry.

55. McCown, testimony, in "Transcript," 104.

56. Speed, testimony, in Washburn Inquiry.

57. Speed, testimony, in ibid. McCown, testimony, and Edwin L. Davenport, testimony, both in "Transcript," 94, 287; Cox, deposition, in "Transcript," Exhibit N; James Wells, *Personal Memoirs,* 13.

Chapter 6   The Overcrowding

1. Kemble, deposition, in "Transcript," Exhibit O.

2. Kerns, testimony, in ibid., 50–51.

3. Edwin L. Davenport, testimony, in ibid., 289–90, 310.

4. Isaac N. Davenport, "Story of *Sultana,*" 5. Also, see Johnston, "*Sultana* Disaster;" McCown, testimony, in "Transcript," 96.

5. Kerns, testimony, in "Transcript," 51, 71–72.

6. James Wells, *Personal Memoirs,* 74.

7. Conversation quoted in Speed, testimony, in Washburn Inquiry.

8. Kerns, testimony, in "Transcript," 51, 62.

9. Speed, testimony, in Washburn Inquiry.

10. Quoted by Williams, testimony, in "Transcript," 38–39. During cross-examination, Speed's attorney asked Williams whether he remembered Speed inquiring if the men should be divided. Williams stated, "I cannot remember of any such remark."

11. Williams was quoted by Speed, testimony, in Washburn Inquiry.

12. Speed, testimony, in ibid.; Kerns, testimony, in "Transcript," 62–71.

13. Tillinghast, testimony, in Washburn Inquiry.

14. Account of conversation between Kerns and Williams is in Kerns, testimony, in "Transcript," 51–52.

15. Jones, testimony, in ibid., 86, 88, and in Washburn Inquiry.

16. Miller, testimony, in "Transcript," 222–23.

17. Smith, testimony, in Washburn Inquiry.

18. Hatch, testimony, in ibid.

19. McCown, testimony, in "Transcript," 98, 101.

20. Jeremiah Mahoney, testimony, in Hoffman Investigation.

21. Sharp, "The *Sultana* Disaster."

22. Simeon W. Dickenson, testimony, in Hoffman Investigation.

23. Sanders's account in Berry, *Loss of the* Sultana, 309.

24. William Butler, testimony, and Mahoney, testimony, both in Hoffman Investigation.

25. McCurdy, "The *Sultana* Explosion."

26. Fies's account in Berry, *Loss of the* Sultana, 125.

27. Edgar Talkington, "Survivor from the *Sultana*," 124.

28. McGuire, testimony, in Dana Commission.

29. Tillinghast, testimony, in Washburn Inquiry.

30. Kerns, testimony, in "Transcript," 52, 72.

31. Quoted in William Butler, testimony, in Hoffman Investigation.

32. Louis Bean, testimony, in ibid.

33. Clinger and Morgan quoted in Berry, *Loss of the* Sultana, 97, 258.

34. Hunter, *Steamboats on Western Rivers,* 314, 523–24.

35. Ibid., 532–35; Havinghurst, *Voices on the River,* 146.

36. Quoted in Hunter, *Steamboats on Western Rivers,* 526.

37. Ibid., 526–27, 529.

38. Ibid., 537, 542–44; Havinghurst, *Voices on the River,* 147.

39. Hunter, *Steamboats on Western Rivers,* 548–61; Witzig, testimony, in "Transcript," 197; Perce, testimony, in Washburn Inquiry.

40. Elbert J. Squire, testimony, in Hoffman Investigation.

41. Brown's account in Berry, *Loss of the* Sultana, 76–77.

42. "Minstrel Concert," *Memphis Daily Bulletin,* April 29, 1865, 3.

43. Anna Annis, testimony, in Hoffman Investigation.

44. Details about Safford are from J. Walter Elliott's account in Berry, *Loss of the* Sultana, 122.

45. Nauson, testimony, in Washburn Inquiry.

46. McCown's account is in McCown, testimony, in "Transcript," 101.

47. George A. Williams, testimony, in Washburn Inquiry.

48. Conversation between Williams and Speed is in Speed, testimony, and George A. Williams, testimony, both in ibid., and in Williams, testimony, in "Transcript," 17, 39.

49. Speed, testimony, in Washburn Inquiry; George A. Williams, testimony, in "Transcript," 17, 39.

50. Kerns's conversation with Mason and Gambrel is in Kerns, testimony, in ibid., 52–53, 74, and in Washburn Inquiry.

51. Speed's conversation with Mason and his observations are in Speed, testimony, in Washburn Inquiry.

52. Speed, testimony, in Hoffman Investigation; Edwin L. Davenport, testimony, in "Transcript," 292.

53. Kerns, testimony, in "Transcript," 53; William Gaud, testimony, in Washburn Inquiry.

54. Elias Shull, testimony, in "Transcript," 145–46.

55. Wintringer, testimony, in ibid., 163.

Chapter 7   Homeward Bound

1. Dixon, "Aboard the *Sultana*," 38. Also, see William C. Jones, testimony, in "Transcript," 90.

2. McCown, testimony, in "Transcript," 100; Michael, "Explosion of *Sultana*," 253.

3. Quoted in Berry, *Loss of the* Sultana, 76.

4. Ibid., 76–77.

5. Joseph Taylor Elliott, "*Sultana* Disaster," 168, 171. Also, see J. Walter Elliott, "By Fire and Flood."

6. Quoted in Berry, *Loss of the* Sultana, 191.

7. Waters to author.

8. William S. Friesner, testimony, in "Transcript," 111; also, see "Colonel William S. Friesner of Logan Commanded Detail on Ill-Fated *Sultana*," *Logan Daily News,* June 27, 1966, 25.

9. Winters, *In the 50th Ohio,* 163.

10. Louis Bean, testimony, in Hoffman Investigation; Wintringer, testimony, in Washburn Inquiry.

11. U.S. War Department, *War of Rebellion,* 1st ser., vol. 48, pt. 1, 212.

12. McCown, testimony, in "Transcript," 99, 107.

13. Franklin Barker, testimony, in Hoffman Investigation.

14. Barker, testimony, and Bean, testimony, both in ibid.

15. McCown, testimony, in "Transcript," 102; Barker, testimony, in Hoffman Investigation.

16. Quoted in "The *Sultana* Slaughter," *Indianapolis Daily Journal,* May 4, 1865, 4.

17. "Colonel William S. Friesner."

18. McCown, testimony, in "Transcript," 99.

19. Quoted in "The *Sultana* Slaughter."

20. Bean, testimony, in Hoffman Investigation.

21. Ibid.; McCown, testimony, and Friesner, testimony, both in "Transcript," 100, 110. Note: There is no record of the doctor's name; McCown did not give it in his testimony.

22. McCammon, *Loyal Mountain Troopers,* 144, 152; numbers derived from author's list of Union soldiers on board the *Sultana* (see Appendix B).

23. *Official Roster of Soldiers of Ohio,* vol. 8, 146; Berry, *Loss of the* Sultana, 45, 73, 80, 85, 94, 186, 196, 199, 247, 267, 270, 329, 336, 356; Rex Miller, *Croxton's Raid,* 140; Colvin, military records; author's list (see Appendix B).

24. Holmes to author; Hardesty, *Presidents, Soldiers and Statesmen.*

25. Bright, military records.

26. George Downing, military records; Jonathan Downing, military records.

27. Alexander Hall, military records; Anderson Hall, military records.

28. Humphress, "Sinking of the *Sultana*," 8–9.

29. Maxey, interview.

30. Blazier to author; Anderson, *John Pickens Family.*

31. Keeble, Sultana *Disaster.*

32. Wade to author; Ward to author.

33. George Millsaps, interview.

34. K. R. Hamilton, interview.

35. Best, "Members of 3d Tennessee Cavalry," 28g.

36. "From Memphis," *Tri-Weekly Missouri Republican,* April 26, 1865, 1, 3.

37. Winters, *In the 50th Ohio,* 163.

38. Dixon, "Aboard the *Sultana,*" 38.

39. Bean, testimony, in Hoffman Investigation.

40. Aldrich, *Cahawba Prison,* 14–15.

41. Bean, testimony, in Hoffman Investigation.

42. Quoted in "Colonel William S. Friesner."

43. Joseph Taylor Elliott, "*Sultana* Disaster," 168; also, see Squire, testimony, in Hoffman Investigation; McCown, testimony, and Compton, testimony, both in "Transcript," 101, 147½.

44. Quoted in "The *Sultana* Slaughter."

45. Squire, testimony, in Hoffman Investigation.

46. Lewis F. Hake, testimony, in Washburn Inquiry.

47. Joseph Taylor Elliott, "*Sultana* Disaster," 168.

48. Jones's and Stewart's accounts in Berry, *Loss of the* Sultana, 189, 344.

49. Ibid., 91, 104–5, 128, 180, 225.

50. Eldridge, "In the *Sultana* Disaster," 6; also, see "Minstrel Concert," *Memphis Daily Bulletin,* April 29, 1865, 3.

51. Winters, "In the 50th Ohio," 163.

52. Aldrich, *Cahawba Prison,* 29; Schmutz, *History of 102nd Regiment;* Joseph Taylor Elliott, "*Sultana* Disaster," 168.

53. Friesner, testimony, in Washburn Inquiry; McCown, testimony, in Hoffman Investigation.

54. "Colonel William S. Friesner"; Dixon, "Aboard the *Sultana,*" 38; Davis, *Touched by Fire,* 293.

55. J. Walter Elliott, "By Fire and Flood."

56. "Colonel William S. Friesner."

57. Berry, *Loss of the* Sultana, 200; Compton, testimony, in "Transcript," 147½.

58. Friesner quoted in "Colonel William S. Friesner."

Chapter 8   Prelude to Destiny

1. Account of Wooldridge farm from J. H. Curtis, "Only Living Eye-Witness Details Sultana Explosion," *Memphis Commercial Appeal,* January 25, 1920.

2. Twain, *Life on the Mississippi,* 181–82, 250; LaPointe, "Military Hospitals," 337–39.

3. Ratekin, Duke, and Young, "Awful *Sultana* Disaster," 7.

4. Friesner, testimony, in Washburn Inquiry; "Arrivals—*Sultana*," *Memphis Daily Bulletin,* April 26, 1865, 4.

5. Quoted in Berry, *Loss of the* Sultana, 287.

6. Ibid.; Aldrich, *Cahawba Prison,* 15.

7. Berry, *Loss of the* Sultana, 210; Hass, "The *Sultana,*" 3; Isaac N. Davenport, "Story of *Sultana,*" 5; U.S. Sanitary Commission, *The Sanitary Reporter,* vol. 1, 187.

8. Wintringer's account in Berry, *Loss of the* Sultana, 26; also, see Joseph Taylor Elliott, testimony, "Transcript," 143.

9. Raudebaugh's account in Berry, *Loss of the* Sultana, 293.

10. Aldrich, *Cahawba Prison,* 15.

11. Winters, *In the 50th Ohio,* 164.

12. Gaston's account in Berry, *Loss of the* Sultana, 150.

13. Ibid., 162.

14. Compton, testimony, in "Transcript," 147–48; "The Chicago Opera Troupe," *Memphis Daily Bulletin,* April 28, 1865, 3; "Minstrel Concert," *Memphis Daily Bulletin,* April 29, 1865, 3.

15. Lock, "Women on the *Sultana,*" 6.

16. McIntosh's account in Berry, *Loss of the* Sultana, 252.

17. Snow, testimony, in Washburn Inquiry; *Who Was Who in America,* 1154.

18. McFarland's account in Berry, *Loss of the* Sultana, 248–49.

19. Wintringer, testimony, in Washburn Inquiry; Kayton, testimony, in "Transcript," 317; Floyd, "Burning of the *Sultana,*" 70.

20. Quotation in Bean, testimony, in Hoffman Investigation. Also, see Kayton, testimony, in Washburn Inquiry; Hunter, *Steamboats on Western Rivers,* 269; "Testimony of the Pilot," *Memphis Daily Bulletin,* April 28, 1865, 2.

21. Joseph Taylor Elliott, "*Sultana* Disaster," 170.

22. Wintringer, testimony, in "Transcript," 167–68; Wintringer, testimony, in Washburn Inquiry.

23. Joseph Taylor Elliott, "*Sultana* Disaster," 177; story and quotation of Downing in Kline's account in Berry, *Loss of the* Sultana, 210.

24. Quoted in Berry, *Loss of the* Sultana, 210.

25. Fies's account in ibid., 126.

26. Kayton, testimony, in "Transcript," 321.

27. Samuel Clemens, testimony, in Washburn Inquiry; "The Chief Mate's Testimony" and "Testimony of the Pilot," both in *Memphis Daily Bulletin,* April 28, 1865, 2.

28. Berry, *Loss of the* Sultana, 48.

29. Bean, testimony, in Hoffman Investigation.

30. Berry, *Loss of the* Sultana, 95.

31. Ibid., 254–56.

32. Talkington, "Survivor from the *Sultana,*" 124.

33. J. R. Curtis, "Only Living Eye-Witness Details *Sultana* Explosion," *Memphis Commercial Appeal,* January 25, 1920; "Testimony of the Pilot"; Guer-

ney and Alden, *Harper's Pictorial History of Civil War,* 429; "To the Editor of the *Republican," Daily Missouri Republican,* May 1, 1865, 2.

34. Davis's account in Berry, *Loss of the* Sultana, 103.

Chapter 9   The Explosion

1. Rowberry quoted in "The Chief Mate's Testimony," *Memphis Daily Bulletin,* April 28, 1865, 2.

2. Clemens, testimony, in Washburn Inquiry.

3. Hunter, *Steamboats on Western Rivers,* 163–64; Cooper, interview.

4. Hunter, *Steamboats on Western Rivers,* 164–65.

5. Witzig, testimony, in "Transcript," 131–32.

6. Cooper, interview.

7. Witzig, testimony, in "Transcript," 131–32; Witzig, "Report of Casualties and Violations," 217.

8. Hunter, *Steamboats on Western Rivers,* 157–58, 158n, 263n.

9. Clemens quoted in Wintringer, testimony, in Washburn Inquiry; Isaac West, testimony, in Hoffman Investigation.

10. Kayton, testimony, in "Transcript," 318.

11. Witzig, testimony, in ibid., 133.

12. Cooper to author.

13. Hunter, *Steamboats on Western Rivers,* 292.

14. Winters, *In the 50th Ohio,* 165.

15. J. Walter Elliott, "By Fire and Flood."

16. Linginfelter, pension records.

17. Johnston, "*Sultana* Disaster."

18. Wolverton's account in Elliott and Moxley, *Tennessee Civil War Veterans Questionnaires,* vol. 1, 145–46.

19. Horner's account in Berry, *Loss of the* Sultana, 179.

20. Raudebaugh's account in ibid., 295.

21. Schmutz, *History of 102nd Regiment,* 239–40. Also, see "Reminiscence of the War," *Wayne County Democrat,* April 28, 1880.

22. Horn's account in Berry, *Loss of the* Sultana, 175.

23. Kochenderfer's account in ibid., 211–12.

24. "William Warner—Soldier—Pioneer," *Monitor-Press,* May 25, 1933; "Wellingtonian in *Sultana* Disaster Sixty Years Ago," *Wellington Daily News,* April 27, 1925.

25. Fox, pension records.

26. Eldridge, "Some Events at Close of War," 6. Also, see Eldridge, "In the *Sultana* Disaster," 7; "Union Veteran, Hamilton Native, Recalls *Sultana* River Disaster," *Chattanooga Daily Times,* August 2, 1931.

27. Brock, *Civil War Experiences.*

28. "*Sultana* Survivor is Taken by Death," *Knoxville News-Sentinel,* July 2, 1929; Deaderisle to Potter.

29. Anderson, *John Pickens Family,* 188.

30. Quoted in McCurdy, "The *Sultana* Explosion," 3.

31. McIntosh's account in Berry, *Loss of the* Sultana, 252–54.

32. Lahue's account in ibid., 215.

33. "Statement of Pilot George J. Cayton [Kayton]," *Memphis Argus*, April 29, 1865, 3. Also, see "Chief Mate's Testimony."

34. "Testimony of the Pilot," *Memphis Daily Bulletin*, April 28, 1865, 2; "To the Editor of the Republican," *Daily Missouri Republican*, May 1, 1865, 2.

35. Shummard's account in Berry, *Loss of the* Sultana, 315.

36. Horan, military records; Isenogle to Potter.

37. "Horrible Disaster on the River," *Memphis Daily Bulletin*, April 28, 1865, 1. Also, see Elliott and Moxley, *Tennessee Civil War Veterans Questionnaires*, vol. 1, 142.

38. "McMinn Countian Recalls Escape from the *Sultana* Fifty-Eight Years Ago When 1,238 Lost Lives," *Knoxville Sentinel*, December 9, 1923.

39. Crisp's letter in Elliott and Moxley, *Tennessee Civil War Veterans Questionnaires*, vol. 1, 151.

40. Madden's account in Berry, *Loss of the* Sultana, 229–30.

Chapter 10   Panic on the Bow

1. Johnston, "*Sultana* Disaster."

2. Chelf's account in Berry, *Loss of the* Sultana, 88–89.

3. Brunner's account in ibid., 81.

4. Gambill's account in ibid., 143.

5. Winters, *In the 50th Ohio,* 165.

6. Brady's account in Berry, *Loss of the* Sultana, 63–64.

7. Winters, *In the 50th Ohio,* 166.

8. Quoted in Berry, *Loss of the* Sultana, 64.

9. Ibid., 143.

10. McCrory's account in ibid., 244–45.

11. Karns's and Russell's accounts in ibid., 197, 308.

12. Ibid., 50–51.

13. Gregory's account in ibid., 156.

14. Young's account in Hawes, *Cahaba,* 183–84.

15. Boor's account in Berry, *Loss of the* Sultana, 58.

16. Norris's account in ibid., 266. Also, see "*Sultana* Survivor Called by Death Native of Country," *Daily Times and Recorder,* January 2, 1936.

17. Robinson's account in Berry, *Loss of the* Sultana, 301.

18. Lee's account in ibid., 220.

19. Patterson's account in ibid., 283–84.

20. Rosselot's account in ibid., 305–6.

21. Fies's account in ibid., 126–27.

22. Lugenbeal's account in ibid., 225–26.

23. Jones's account in ibid., 191–93; also, see "The *Sultana* Affair—Further Particulars," *Summit County Beacon,* May 18, 1865, 2.

24. Quoted in Berry, *Loss of the* Sultana, 100–01; also, see "James Cook of Kent Was on the *Sultana*," *The Cleveland Plain Dealer,* October 20, 1938.

25. Norton's account in Berry, *Loss of the* Sultana, 275–76.

26. Walker, *Cahaba and* Sultana *Disaster,* 18–19.

27. Berry, *Loss of the* Sultana, 169–70.
28. Walker, *Cahaba and* Sultana *Disaster,* 19–20.
29. Ibid.
30. Helminger's account in Berry, *Loss of the* Sultana, 170–71.
31. Norton's account in ibid., 271–72.
32. Wintringer, testimony, in Washburn Inquiry. Also, see Wintringer's account in Berry, *Loss of the* Sultana, 26–27; Wintringer, testimony, in "Transcript," 168–69.
33. Gaston's account in Berry, *Loss of the* Sultana, 149–50.
34. Peacock's account in ibid., 285–86.

Chapter 11   Devastation on the Stern

1. Quoted in Berry, *Loss of the* Sultana, 39.
2. Ibid., 319.
3. Ibid., 316.
4. Ibid., 237–38.
5. Hawes, *Cahaba,* 192–93; "River News," *Daily Missouri Democrat,* May 1, 1865, 4.
6. Foglesong's account in Berry, *Loss of the* Sultana, 136.
7. Hamblin's account in ibid., 162.
8. Allen's account in ibid., 32.
9. Bardon's account in ibid., 40.
10. "Andrew T. Peery's Story of the Sinking of the *Sultana* April 27, 1865," *Maryville Enterprise,* April 30, 1975, 1.
11. Quoted in Berry, *Loss of the* Sultana, 165.
12. Pangle's account in ibid., 281.
13. King's account in ibid., 201–02.
14. Smith to author.
15. Aldrich, *Cahawba Prison,* 16–17; Aldrich's account in Berry, *Loss of the* Sultana, 109–10.
16. Conversation between Aldrich and Dunsmore in Dunsmore's account in Berry, *Loss of the* Sultana, 109–10.
17. Aldrich, *Cahawba Prison,* 16–17; Aldrich's account in Berry, *Loss of the* Sultana, 109–10.
18. Dunsmore's account in Berry, *Loss of the* Sultana, 110.
19. McLeod's account in ibid., 256. Also see, J. Walter Elliott, "By Fire and Flood," and Winters, *In the 50th Ohio,* 175.
20. Joseph Taylor Elliott, "*Sultana* Disaster," 170–72.
21. Account of McCown and Fidler is from "The Wreck of the *Sultana,*" *The News-Leader,* October 8, 1896, 1. Also, see McCown, testimony, in Hoffman Investigation and in "Transcript," 103; McCown, pension records.
22. "Statement of Sergt. L. B. Hinckley," *Memphis Argus,* April 28, 1865, 3.
23. J. Walter Elliott, "By Fire and Flood."
24. McLeod's account in Berry, *Loss of the* Sultana, 256.

25. Dixon, "Aboard the *Sultana*," 38–39.

26. "Victims of the Disaster—The Lost," *Memphis Argus,* April 28, 1865, 3; "Colonel William S. Friesner of Logan Commanded Detail on Ill-Fated *Sultana,*" *Logan Daily News,* June 27, 1966, 26.

27. Account of Saffords in Joseph Taylor Elliott, "*Sultana* Disaster," 172–73. Also, see J. Walter Elliott, "By Fire and Flood."

28. Joseph Taylor Elliott, "*Sultana* Disaster," 172–73.

29. J. Walter Elliott, "By Fire and Flood."

30. "The *Sultana* Disaster," *Chicago Tribune,* May 13, 1865, 2.

31. Friesner's account in "Colonel William S. Friesner." Also, see Friesner, testimony, in "Transcript," 112–13.

32. "Statement of Mr. William M. Long, a Passenger," *Memphis Argus,* April 28, 1865, 3.

33. "Hon. W. D. Snow's Statement," *Memphis Daily Bulletin,* April 28, 1865, 1. Also, see Snow, testimony, in Washburn Inquiry.

34. "A Sad Case," *Memphis Daily Bulletin,* April 28, 1865, 2.

35. Account of Annis family is in Annis, testimony, in Hoffman Investigation.

Chapter 12   Death on the Hurricane Deck

1. Kline's account in Berry, *Loss of the* Sultana, 210–11.

2. Stewart's account in ibid., 344.

3. Rush's account in Hawes, *Cahaba,* 192–95.

4. Colvin's account in Elliott and Moxley, *Tennessee Civil War Veterans Questionnaires,* vol. 1, 147.

5. White's account in Berry, *Loss of the* Sultana, 377, and in Hawes, *Cahaba,* 177–78.

6. Haines's account in Berry, *Loss of the* Sultana, 159.

7. Van Vlack's account in ibid., 368.

8. Stevens's account in ibid., 341–42.

9. McFarland's account in ibid., 249–50.

10. Lockhart's account in Baughman, *History of Ashland County,* vol. 1, 217. Also, see Graham, *History of Richland County,* 173–75.

11. Sprinkle's account in Berry, *Loss of the* Sultana, 331.

12. King's account in ibid., 205.

13. Keeble, "*Sultana* Disaster," 3. Also, see "Andrew T. Peery's Story of the Sinking of the *Sultana* April 27, 1865," *Maryville Enterprise,* April 30, 1975, 2.

14. Lockhart's account in Baughman, *History of Ashland County,* vol. 1, 217. Also, see Graham, *History of Richland County,* 174–75.

15. Bardon's account in Berry, *Loss of the* Sultana, 40.

16. Squire's account in Day, *Story of 101st Ohio Infantry,* 344–45.

17. Carver's account in Berry, *Loss of the* Sultana, 82–83.

18. Van Nuys's account in ibid., 364–65.

19. Ibid., 51–52.

Chapter 13   The Horror of Fire

1. J. H. Curtis, "Only Living Eye-Witness Details *Sultana* Explosion," *Memphis Commercial Appeal,* January 25, 1920.

2. Michael, "Explosion of the *Sultana*," 254, and "*Sultana* Explosion."

3. Floyd, "Burning of the *Sultana*," 70–71.

4. McCown, testimony, in Hoffman Investigation. Also, see "Wreck of the *Sultana*," *The News-Leader,* October 8, 1896.

5. McCown, testimony, in Hoffman Investigation and in "Transcript," 102–3.

6. Wintringer, testimony, in Washburn Inquiry and in "Transcript," 168–69.

7. Account of McDonald brothers in Humphress, "Sinking of the *Sultana*," 8–9.

8. Quoted in Berry, *Loss of the* Sultana, 202.

9. Ibid., 163.

10. Smith's account in ibid., 319–21.

11. Morgan's account in ibid., 259.

12. Nisley's account in ibid., 263.

13. Alexander, "Civil War Experiences of Perry Alexander."

14. Foglesong's account in Berry, *Loss of the* Sultana, 137–38.

15. Annis, testimony, in Hoffman Investigation. Also, see Lahue's account in Berry, *Loss of the* Sultana, 215.

16. King's account in Berry, *Loss of the* Sultana, 202.

17. Horner's account in Schmutz, *History of the 102nd Regiment,* 244–45.

18. Fies's account in Berry, *Loss of the* Sultana, 127–28.

19. Gregory's account in ibid., 156.

20. Leake's account in ibid., 218.

21. Walker, *Cahaba and* Sultana *Disaster,* 20–22.

22. Berry, *Loss of the* Sultana, 219.

23. Account of the sister and her decision in ibid., 10.

24. Wooldridge's account in Curtis, "Only Living Eye-Witness." Also, see Joe Curtis, "In the Pilothouse—What Caused Tragedy on River Back in '65," *Memphis Commercial Appeal,* April 27, 1950.

25. Lee's account in Berry, *Loss of the* Sultana, 221.

Chapter 14   The Cold Mississippi

1. Hulit's account in "The *Sultana* Disaster," *Kansas City Star,* May 14, 1905.

2. Quoted in Berry, *Loss of the* Sultana, 208.

3. "The *Sultana* Disaster," *Chicago Tribune,* May 13, 1865, p. 2.

4. Porter's account in Berry, *Loss of the* Sultana, 288.

5. J. Walter Elliott, "By Fire and Flood."

6. Quoted in Hawes, *Cahaba,* 188.

7. Walker, *Cahaba and* Sultana *Disaster,* 21–23.

8. Schmutz quoted in "Reminiscence of the War," *Wayne County Democrat,* April 28, 1880. Also, see Schmutz's account in Berry, *Loss of the* Sultana, 311.

9. McCrory's account in Berry, *Loss of the* Sultana, 245.

10. Robinson's account in ibid., 301–2.

11. Summerville's account in Hawes, *Cahaba,* 181–82.

12. Horn's account in Berry, *Loss of the* Sultana, 177.

13. Deaderisle to Potter.

14. "Wellingtonian in *Sultana* Disaster Sixty Years Ago," *Wellington Daily News,* May 25, 1933.

15. Quoted in Berry, *Loss of the* Sultana, 104–5.

16. Ibid., 179–80.

17. Joseph Taylor Elliott, "*Sultana* Disaster," 178–79.

18. Norton's account in Berry, *Loss of the* Sultana, 272–73.

19. Hiram C. Wells, untitled manuscript.

20. "River News," *Memphis Argus,* April 28, 1865, 3; "River News," *Memphis Daily Bulletin,* April 28, 1865, 3.

21. William B. Alwood, Jr., testimony, in Washburn Inquiry.

22. "Appalling Marine Casualty," *Memphis Argus,* April 28, 1865, 3.

23. Alwood, testimony, in Washburn Inquiry; Kimberlin, "Destruction of the *Sultana,*" 3.

24. Cook's account in Berry, *Loss of the* Sultana, 101.

25. Alwood, testimony, in Washburn Inquiry.

26. Quoted in Berry, *Loss of the* Sultana, 152.

27. Norris's account in ibid., 266.

28. Rush's account in Hawes, *Cahaba,* 195–97. Also see, Rush testimony, in Washburn Inquiry.

29. Friesner's account in "Colonel William S. Friesner of Logan Commanded Detail on Ill-Fated *Sultana,*" *Logan Daily News,* June 27, 1966, 27.

30. Chelf's account in Berry, *Loss of the* Sultana, 89–90.

31. Alwood, testimony, in Washburn Inquiry.

32. "River News," *Memphis Daily Bulletin,* April 28, 1865, 3.

33. "Acts of Daring," *Memphis Argus,* April 28, 1865, 3.

34. "Statement of Mr. Henry Seman," *Memphis Argus,* April 29, 1865, 3.

35. Schmutz's account in "Reminiscence of the War." Also, see Berry, *Loss of the* Sultana, 311, and Schmutz, *History of 102nd Regiment,* 239–40.

36. Floyd, "Burning of the *Sultana,*" 71–72.

37. Love's account in Berry, *Loss of the* Sultana, 222.

38. Quoted in "Ensign Berry's Report," *Fort Wayne Sentinel,* April 29, 1902, 8.

39. Berry quoted in "Work of the Crew of the Gunboat Essex," *Memphis Argus,* April 28, 1865, 3.

40. Michael, "Explosion of the *Sultana,*" 254–56. Also, see Michael, "*Sultana* Explosion," 2.

Chapter 15   Help from Memphis

1. Johnston, "*Sultana* Disaster."
2. King's account in Berry, *Loss of the* Sultana, 203.
3. Chelf's account in ibid., 90.
4. Clarkson's account in ibid., 96.
5. Morgan's account in ibid., 259–60. Also, see "Findlay Survivor Tells Story of Sultana Wreck," *Toledo Daily Blade,* May 1, 1912, 10.
6. Madden's account in Berry, *Loss of the* Sultana, 231–33.
7. Bardon's account in ibid., 41.
8. Dougherty, *Prison Diary,* 70; Lawler to author, September 22, 1990; Sharp and Dunnigan, *Congressional Medal of Honor,* 765.
9. "The *Sultana* Disaster" and "The Gallant *Bostona,*" both in *Memphis Daily Bulletin,* April 28, 1865, 2; Alwood, testimony, in Washburn Inquiry.
10. Norton's account in Berry, *Loss of the* Sultana, 273. Note: Norton did not give the young soldier's name.
11. "The *Sultana* Disaster," *Memphis Daily Bulletin,* April 28, 1865, 2. Note: The soldier is not named in the newspaper article.
12. William Rowberry, testimony, in Washburn Inquiry. Also, see Madden's account in Berry, *Loss of the* Sultana, 233.
13. "Horrible Disaster on the River," *Memphis Daily Bulletin,* April 28, 1865, 1.
14. Account of the *Tyler*'s cutters in Michael, "Explosion of the *Sultana,*" 256. Also, see "A Woman and Child," *Memphis Daily Bulletin,* April 28, 1865, 2.

Frances Ackley was credited with pulling more than forty people from the river. In 1902, Congress granted her a pension of $20 a month for her help in rescuing the *Sultana* victims.

15. Love's account in Berry, *Loss of the* Sultana, 233; "Work of the Crew of the Gunboat *Essex,*" *Memphis Argus,* April 29, 1865, 3.
16. "The *Sultana* Disaster," *Chicago Tribune,* May 13, 1865, 2.
17. Love's account in Berry, *Loss of the* Sultana, 233–24.
18. Rescue of Safford in Elliott's account in Berry, *Loss of the* Sultana, 122.
19. U.S. Sanitary Commission, *Sanitary Reporter,* vol. 2, 3; "The Sanitary Commission," *Memphis Daily Bulletin,* May 4, 1865, 3.
20. Signor, "An Old Death Ship," 11. Also, see LaPointe, "Military Hospitals," 337.
21. Quoted in Elliott and Moxley, *Tennessee Civil War Questionnaires,* vol. 1, 152.
22. "Incidents of the Disaster," *Memphis Argus,* April 29, 1865, 3.
23. B.J.D. Irwin, testimony, in "Transcript," 116.
24. "Caring For the Living and the Dead" and "Two Brave Fellows," both in *Memphis Daily Bulletin,* April 28, 1865, 2.
25. "Drowning of a Little Girl," *Memphis Daily Bulletin,* April 28, 1865, 2.
26. Joseph Taylor Elliott, "*Sultana* Disaster," 173–76.

27. Quoted in Berry, *Loss of the* Sultana, 226–27.

28. Episode involving Swain and King is described by Kline in ibid., 210.

29. Horner's account in ibid., 178.

30. Smith's account in ibid., 327–28.

31. Jones's account in ibid., 193–95.

32. Quoted in "Statement of Mr. William Long, a Passenger," *Memphis Argus*, April 28, 1865, 3.

33. Sprinkle's account in Berry, *Loss of the* Sultana, 332.

34. Bringman's account in ibid., 71–72.

35. Maes's account in ibid., 235.

36. Quoted in "Ensign Berry's Report," *Fort Wayne Sentinel*, April 29, 1902, 8.

Chapter 16   The *Sultana*'s Last Minutes

1. U.S. War Department, *War of Rebellion*, 1st ser., vol. 48, pt. 1, 225.

2. Wood to Potter.

3. Berry's report in U.S. War Department, *War of Rebellion*, 1st ser. vol. 48, pt. 1, 220–21.

4. Horn's account in Berry, *Loss of the* Sultana, 175–76.

5. Berry's report in U.S. War Department, *War of Rebellion*, 1st ser., vol. 48, pt. 1, 220–21.

6. Yates's report in ibid., 225.

7. George Millsaps, interview.

8. Berry's report in U.S. War Department, *War of Rebellion*, 1st ser., vol. 48, pt. 1, 220–21.

9. Yates's report in ibid., 225.

10. Berry's report in ibid., 220–21.

11. Ibid.

12. Yates's report in ibid., 225.

13. Ibid., 222–24.

14. Berry's report in ibid., 220–21, 225.

15. Dixon, "Aboard the *Sultana*," 39.

16. Talkington, "Survivor from the *Sultana*," 125.

17. Hiram C. Wells, untitled manuscript.

18. Lugenbeal's account in Berry, *Loss of the* Sultana, 227; Lugenbeal, pension records.

19. Quoted in Berry, *Loss of the* Sultana, 279.

20. Garber's account in ibid., 147–48.

21. Ibid., 176; Twain, *Life on the Mississippi*, 182.

22. Berry's report in U.S. War Department, *War of Rebellion*, 1st ser., vol. 48, pt. 1, 220–21.

23. Long and Long, *Civil War Day by Day*, 312; Mound City, roadside marker.

24. Story of the Berry family in "Sunday Is Anniversary of Sultana Explosion," *West Memphis Evening Times*, April 25, 1969. Also, see "The Survivors," *Memphis Argus*, April 28, 1865, 3.

25. Atchley's account in Berry, *Loss of the* Sultana, 36.

26. Young's account in Hawes, *Cahaba*, 188–90.

27. Quoted in Berry, *Loss of the* Sultana, 163. Also, see Young's account in Hawes, *Cahaba*, 190.

28. King's account in Berry, *Loss of the* Sultana, 203–4.

29. "To the Editor of the Republican," *Daily Missouri Republican*, May 1, 1865, 2; "Acts of Daring," *Memphis Argus*, April 28, 1865, 3; U.S. Sanitary Commission, *The Sanitary Reporter*, vol. 1, 189.

30. "Horrible Disaster on the River," *Memphis Daily Bulletin*, April 28, 1865, 1; "Sunday is Anniversary."

31. Boor's account in Berry, *Loss of the* Sultana, 60.

32. "Statement of Sergt. L. B. Hinckley," *Memphis Argus*, April 28, 1865, 3.

33. Foglesong's account in Berry, *Loss of the* Sultana, 138.

34. Peery's account in "Andrew T. Peery's Story of the Sinking of the Sultana April 27, 1865," *Maryville Enterprise*, April 30, 1975, 2.

35. Hamilton's account in Berry, *Loss of the* Sultana, 166.

36. Quoted in ibid., 357.

37. Patterson's account in ibid., 284.

38. Fast's account in Hawes, *Cahaba*, 171–72.

39. Quoted in "Andrew T. Peery's Story."

40. Quoted in Berry, *Loss of the* Sultana, 166.

41. "Andrew T. Peery's Story." Also, see Fast's account in Hawes, *Cahaba*, 166.

42. Fast's account in Hawes, *Cahaba*, 166.

43. "Andrew T. Peery's Story."

44. Quoted in Hawes, *Cahaba*, 166.

45. "Andrew T. Peery's Story."

46. Fast's account in Hawes, *Cahaba*, 172.

47. Isaac N. Davenport, "Story of the *Sultana*," 7.

48. Thrasher's account in Berry, *Loss of the* Sultana, 357.

49. Isaac N. Davenport, "Story of the *Sultana*," 7–8.

50. Berry, *Loss of the* Sultana, 166; "A Horrid Scene," *Memphis Argus*, April 28, 1865, 3.

51. Fast's account in Hawes, *Cahaba*, 172–73.

52. Thrasher's account in Berry, *Loss of the* Sultana, 357.

53. Quoted in Hawes, *Cahaba*, 174.

54. Quoted in Berry, *Loss of the* Sultana, 209.

55. Quoted in Schmutz, *History of 102nd Regiment*, 245.

56. Quoted in Berry, *Loss of the* Sultana, 166.

57. Quoted in "Andrew T. Peery's Story."

58. Quoted in Hawes, *Cahaba*, 175.

Chapter 17   The Final Rescues

1. Wintringer's account in Berry, *Loss of the* Sultana, 27.

2. Quoted in ibid., 242–43.

3. Wintringer's account in ibid., 27.

4. Winters, *In the 50th Ohio,* 167.

5. Quoted in Berry, *Loss of the* Sultana, 67.

6. Quoted in ibid., 143.

7. Winters, *In the 50th Ohio,* 167; Fox's injuries also described in Fox, pension records.

8. Brady's account in Berry, *Loss of the* Sultana, 66.

9. Winters, *In the 50th Ohio,* 170–71.

10. Quoted in Berry, *Loss of the* Sultana, 66–67.

11. Winters, *In the 50th Ohio,* 171.

12. J. Walter Elliott, "By Fire and Flood."

13. Walker, *Cahaba and* Sultana *Disaster,* 24. Also, see McLeod's account in Berry, *Loss of the* Sultana, 256.

14. Walker, *Cahaba and* Sultana *Disaster,* 23–24.

15. McFarland's account in Berry, *Loss of the* Sultana, 250.

16. "Hon. W. D. Snow's Statement," *Memphis Daily Bulletin,* April 28, 1865, 1. Also, see Snow, testimony, in Washburn Inquiry.

17. Gregory's account in Berry, *Loss of the* Sultana, 156–57.

18. Walker, *Cahaba and* Sultana *Disaster,* 24.

19. Alwood, testimony, in Washburn Inquiry.

20. Potter, *The* Sultana *Tragedy,* 107.

21. Sharp, "The *Sultana* Disaster."

22. Berry, *Loss of the* Sultana, 54–55.

23. Fies's account in ibid., 130–31.

24. Quoted in ibid., 246.

25. Quoted in Elliott and Moxley, *Tennessee Civil War Veterans Questionnaires,* vol. 1, 147.

26. Clemens, testimony, in Washburn Inquiry.

27. McCrory's account in Berry, *Loss of the* Sultana, 246.

28. "To the Editor of the Republican," *Daily Missouri Republican,* May 1, 1865, 2.

29. "A Horrid Scene," *Memphis Argus,* April 28, 1865, 3.

30. Norris, "The *Sultana* Disaster." Also, see Norris's account in Berry, *Loss of the* Sultana, 269.

31. "The Survivors," *Memphis Argus,* April 29, 1865, 3; "The Picket-boat," *Memphis Daily Bulletin,* April 28, 1865, 2. Also, see Isaac N. Davenport, "Story of *Sultana.*"

32. "Caring for the Living and Dead" and "Two Brave Fellows," both in *Memphis Daily Bulletin,* April 28, 1865, 2.

33. "A Touching Incident," *Memphis Argus,* April 28, 3; "Supposed Recognition," *Memphis Argus,* April 29, 1865, 3; "Horrible River Disaster," *Memphis Daily Bulletin,* April 28, 1865, 1.

34. Joseph Taylor Elliott, "*Sultana* Disaster," 177–78.

35. Hiram C. Wells, untitled manuscript.

36. Floyd, "Burning of the *Sultana,*" 73.

37. McIntosh's account in Berry, *Loss of the* Sultana, 253.

38. Keeble, *The* Sultana *Disaster,* 4. Also, see Warner Ogden, "1700 Died When *Sultana* Sank," *Knoxville News-Sentinel,* April 28, 1929.

39. Eldridge, "Some Events at Close of War." Also, see "Union Veteran, Hamilton Native, Recalls *Sultana* River Disaster," *Chattanooga Daily Times,* August 2, 1931.

40. Lee's account in Berry, *Loss of the* Sultana, 221–22.

41. "Singular," *Memphis Argus,* April 29, 1865, 3.

42. "An Incident," *Memphis Daily Bulletin,* April 29, 3.

43. Walker, *Cahaba and* Sultana *Disaster,* 24–25.

44. "Sanitary Commission," *Memphis Daily Bulletin,* May 4, 1865, 3.

45. Elliott and Moxley, *Tennessee Civil War Veterans Questionnaires,* vol. 1, 152–53.

46. McFarland's account of the Tennessean and quotations from his account in Berry, *Loss of the* Sultana, 250–51.

A number of people have tried to ascertain the identity of the tall Tennessean, but no positive identification has ever been made.

47. Schmutz, *History of 102nd Regiment,* 240. Also, see Schmutz's account in Berry, *Loss of the* Sultana, 311.

48. J. Walter Elliott, "By Fire and Flood."

49. Horner's account in Schmutz, *History of 102nd Regiment,* 245.

50. "Appalling Marine Casualty," *Memphis Argus,* April 28, 1865, 3; Walker, *Cahaba and* Sultana *Disaster,* 194; Rush's account in Hawes, *Cahaba,* 194; Winters, *In the 50th Ohio,* 169; "From Cairo," *Daily Missouri Republican,* April 29, 1865, 3; U.S. Sanitary Commission, *Sanitary Reporter,* vol. 1, 189; Michael, "*Sultana* Explosion."

51. "Investigation of the *Sultana* Disaster," *Memphis Argus,* May 11, 1865, 3. Also, see "Charitable," *Memphis Daily Bulletin,* April 29, 1865, 2.

52. "Appalling Marine Casualty." Also, see "To the Ladies of Memphis," *Memphis Daily Bulletin,* April 30, 1865, 2.

53. "Appalling Marine Casualty." Also, see "From Cairo"; "Reminiscence of the War," *Wayne County Democrat,* April 28, 1880; Graham, *History of Richland County,* 175; "The *Sultana* Disaster," *Chicago Tribune,* May 13, 1865, 2.

54. "Victims of the Disaster—The Lost," *Memphis Argus,* April 28, 3; "Another Search after the Sultana Victims," *Memphis Argus,* May 13, 1865, 3; "A Sad Case," *Memphis Daily Bulletin,* April 28, 1865, 2.

55. "*Sultana* Victims on Both Sides of the River Exposed," *Memphis Argus,* May 12, 1865, 2. Also, see "A Touching Incident"; "Supposed Recognition"; "The *Sultana* Disaster," *Memphis Argus,* April 28, 1865, 2.

56. "A Sad Case."

57. "List of Certain Persons Supposed to Have Been Drowned," *Memphis Daily Bulletin,* April 29, 1865, 3.

58. "Appalling Marine Casualty"; "The Explosion of the *Sultana,*" *Daily Missouri Democrat,* April 29, 1865, 1.

Chapter 18   The Living and the Dead

1. List of persons in Memphis hospitals, reported in *Memphis Daily Bulletin,* April 28, 2; "More Survivors from the *Sultana,*" *Memphis Daily Bulletin,* April 29, 1865, 3; "The Survivors," *Memphis Argus,* April 28, 3 and "List of Survivors Continued," ibid., April 29, 1865, 3; "List of Persons in Memphis Hospitals," *Daily Missouri Democrat,* May 1, 1865, 2.

Lt. Col. B.J.D. Irwin, medical director and superintendent of military hospitals in Memphis, testimony, in "Transcript," 116, reports that he placed "five hundred and thirty into the general hospitals, most of whom were soldiers," and an additional "two hundred and sixty-odd, that went to the Soldiers' Home."

Sgt. Christian M. Nisley, testimony, in Washburn Inquiry, states that there were "2 commissioned officers, 234 non-commissioned officers and privates, 2 deckhands and 1 steamboat employee" at the Soldiers' Home—a total of 239 people.

2. "The *Sultana* Disaster," *Memphis Daily Bulletin,* April 28, 1865, 2.

3. LaPointe, "Military Hospitals," 341; Hawes, *Cahaba,* 167.

4. Fies's account in Berry, *Loss of the* Sultana, 131–32.

5. Winters, *In the 50th Ohio,* 171–75. Also, see McLeod's account in Berry, *Loss of the* Sultana, 156–57.

6. "Left Alone," *Memphis Daily Bulletin,* April 28, 1865, 2.

7. Quoted in Berry, *Loss of the* Sultana, 265.

8. Ibid., 140.

9. Ibid., 55.

10. Ward, "Survivors of the *Sultana,*" 126.

11. Quoted in "William Warner—Soldier-Pioneer," *Monitor-Press,* May 25, 1933.

12. Pickens to Cynthia and Mary Pickens.

13. J. Walter Elliott, "By Fire and Flood." 2.

14. McCown, testimony, in "Transcript," 103.

15. Varnell's account in Berry, *Loss of the* Sultana, 370.

16. Young's account in Hawes, *Cahaba,* 191.

17. P. Steve Millard to author.

18. Quoted in Berry, *Loss of the* Sultana, 166.

19. *Memphis Argus,* April 30, 1865, 3.

20. Walker, *Cahaba and* Sultana *Disaster,* 25–26.

21. Letter quoted in "The *Sultana* Affair—Further Particulars," *Summit County Beacon,* May 18, 1865, 1.

22. J. H. Curtis, "Only Living Eye-Witness Details *Sultana* Explosion," *Memphis Commercial Appeal,* January 25, 1920.

23. Aldrich, *Cahawba Prison,* 18.

24. Friesner, testimony, in "Transcript," 114; "From Cairo," *Toledo Daily Blade,* May 1, 1865, 3.

25. Quoted in Berry, *Loss of the* Sultana, 148. Also, see accounts of Lugen-

beal and Rule, both in Berry, *Loss of the* Sultana, 227, 307; Hiram C. Wells, untitled manuscript; "From Cairo," *Indianapolis Daily Journal,* May 1, 1865, 1.

26. Hiram C. Wells, untitled manuscript; "The *Sultana* Disaster," *Kansas City Star,* May 14, 1905.

27. Hamilton's account in Berry, *Loss of the* Sultana, 166–67. Also, see Johnston, "*Sultana* Disaster."

28. Berry, *Loss of the* Sultana, 148; Hiram C. Wells, untitled manuscript.

29. Accounts of Garber and Hamilton in Berry, *Loss of the* Sultana, 149, 167; Hiram C. Wells, untitled manuscript.

30. J. Walter Elliott, "By Fire and Flood"; James Wells, *Personal Memoirs,* 77; Berry, *Loss of the* Sultana, 56, 219, 253, 332.

31. J. Walter Elliott, "By Fire and Flood."

32. Walker, *Cahaba and* Sultana *Disaster,* 28.

33. "A Generous Deed," *Memphis Daily Bulletin,* May 10, 1865, 2.

34. J. Walter Elliott, "By Fire and Flood."

35. Brady's account in Berry, *Loss of the* Sultana, 67–68.

36. J. Walter Elliott, "By Fire and Flood."

37. Quoted in Berry, *Loss of the* Sultana, 67–68.

38. Quoted in "The *Sultana* Disaster," *Kansas City Star,* May 14, 1905.

39. Quoted in Berry, *Loss of the* Sultana, 67–68.

40. Quoted in "The *Sultana* Disaster," *Kansas City Star,* May 14, 1905.

41. Quoted in Berry, *Loss of the* Sultana, 67–68.

42. Details of stops in Terre Haute and Indianapolis in J. Walter Elliott, "By Fire and Flood." Also, see accounts of Chelf, McIntosh, and Thayer in Berry, *Loss of the* Sultana, 91, 254, 354.

43. Quoted in Berry, *Loss of the* Sultana, 68.

44. Hulit's account in "The *Sultana* Disaster," *The Kansas City Star,* May 14, 1905. Also, see accounts of Berry, Fies, Garber, and Hamilton in Berry, *Loss of the* Sultana, 56, 132, 149, 167.

45. McFarland's account in Berry, *Loss of the* Sultana, 251–52.

46. Haines's account in ibid., 160.

47. "By the U.S. Telegraph Line," *Illinois Daily State Journal,* April 29, 1865, 2.

48. "From Cairo," *Toledo Daily Blade,* May 1, 1865, 3; "River News," *Memphis Daily Bulletin,* May 6, 1865, 3.

William Dunham Snow, senator-elect from Arkansas, reached Washington, D.C., shortly after the disaster but according to *Who Was Who in America,* vol. 1, 1154, he was never admitted to a seat. Because he had been elected under a special proclamation of President Andrew Johnson, the Radical Republicans refused to recognize Snow because Arkansas had yet to petition to return to the Union.

49. "To the Ladies of Memphis," *Memphis Daily Bulletin,* April 30, 2; "A Laudable Enterprise," *Memphis Daily Bulletin,* May 3, 1865, 3; "Contributions," *Memphis Argus,* May 11, 1865, 3.

50. "*Sultana* Survivor Called by Death Native of County," *Daily Times and Recorder,* January 9, 1936.

51. David Hites, testimony, in Hoffman Investigation.

52. "McMinn Countian Recalls Escape from the *Sultana* Fifty-Eight Years Ago When 1,238 Lost Lives," *Knoxville Sentinel,* December 9, 1923.

53. Leppke to author.

54. Witzig, "Report of Casualties and Violations," 217.

55. Quoted in "The *Sultana* Disaster," *Daily Missouri Democrat,* June 19, 1865, 4. Also, see Way, *Way's Steamboat Directory Abridged,* 212.

56. "The *Sultana* Disaster," *Daily Missouri Democrat,* June 19, 1865, 4; Way, *Way's Steamboat Directory Abridged,* 212.

57. "From Cairo," *Daily Missouri Democrat,* April 29, 1865, 1. Also, see "River News," *Memphis Daily Bulletin,* May 4, 1865, 3.

58. Reward offers and inquiries in *Memphis Daily Bulletin,* April 28–May 3, May 13, May 23, 1865, and *Memphis Argus,* April 28–May 7, 1865.

59. *Memphis Daily Bulletin,* April 28 ("Reward—Mason"), 3, May 2 ("Reward—Mason, Gambrel, Stratton"), 2, and May 3, 1865 ("Reward—Ingraham"), 2; "Lost—Barkeep," *Memphis Argus,* April 29, 3; and "The Body of George Slater," May 10, 1865, 3.

60. "Incidents of the Disaster," *Memphis Argus,* April 29, 1865, 3.

61. "Bodies Found," *Memphis Daily Bulletin,* May 4, 1865, 3.

62. "River News," ibid., May 5, 1865, 3.

63. "River News," ibid., May 6, 1865, 3. Bodies on the barge also mentioned in Clough, "Burning of the Flagship."

64. "A Funeral of Eleven," *Memphis Argus,* May 6, 1865, 3.

65. "Body of George Slater." Also, see "More Victims," *Memphis Argus,* May 7, 1865, 3; "The Wreck of the *Sultana,*" *Memphis Daily Bulletin,* May 7, 1865, 3.

66. "Investigation of the *Sultana* Disaster," *Memphis Argus,* May 11, 1865, 3.

67. "More Dead Bodies," *Memphis Argus,* May 14, 1865, 3.

68. "Dead Bodies," *Memphis Argus,* May 19, 1865, 3.

69. "Health Report," *Memphis Argus,* May 9, 3, and May 16, 1865, 3; "The Dead of the *Sultana,*" *Memphis Daily Bulletin,* May 27, 1865, 3.

70. Hereford, *The Old Man River,* 83.

71. Quoted in Raudebaugh, "*Sultana* Disaster."

72. Ibid.

73. "Dead Bodies Below," *Memphis Argus,* May 11, 3; and "*Sultana* Victims on Both Sides of River Exposed," *Memphis Argus,* May 12, 1865, 2.

74. Floyd, "Burning of the *Sultana,*" 74. Also, see, "From Helena," *Daily Bulletin,* May 12, 1865, 1.

75. "River News," *Memphis Daily Bulletin,* May 3, 3, and May 6, 1865, 3; "A Funeral of Eleven"; "More Victims"; "James Cook of Kent Was on the *Sultana,*" *Cleveland Plain Dealer,* October 20, 1938.

According to records of the National Cemetery, Memphis, Tennessee, when the bodies of many of the identified *Sultana* victims were moved in 1867 from Elmwood Cemetery to the National Cemetery, the names of the dead, which had been written in chalk on the tops of the wooden coffins, were washed off during a driving rainstorm. This added to the list of "unknown" U.S. soldiers buried in the National Cemetery.

76. "Minstrel Concert," *Memphis Daily Bulletin,* April 29, 3; "The Sultana Benefit," *Memphis Daily Bulletin,* May 2, 3; "Friends for the Relief of the Sultana," *Memphis Daily Bulletin,* May 4, 3; "Relief of the Sultana Sufferers," *Memphis Daily Bulletin,* May 27, 1865, 3; "Relief Fund for the Sufferers," *Memphis Argus,* May 27, 1865, 3.

77. Quoted in "Relief Fund." Also, see "Calvary," *Memphis Argus,* May 2, 1865, 2.

78. Young's account in Hawes, *Cahaba,* 191.

79. Spafford, pension records.

80. Horner's account in Berry, *Loss of the* Sultana, 181.

81. Norwood to author.

82. Hill, *History of Ashland County,* 301–2.

83. Adams to author.

84. Braunwart to Survivors of Sultana Association.

85. Stella to author.

86. "James Cook."

87. Isenogle to Potter.

Chapter 19   The Investigations

1. U.S. War Department, *War of Rebellion,* 1st ser., vol. 48, pt. 1, 213; *Memphis Daily Bulletin,* April 28, 1865, 2.

2. Clemens, testimony, in *Washburn Inquiry.*

3. Quoted in U.S. War Department, *War of Rebellion,* 1st ser., vol. 48, pt. 1, 233.

4. William C. Postal, testimony, and John Curlic, testimony, both in *Washburn Inquiry.*

5. Thomas to Stanton.

6. U.S. War Department, *War of Rebellion,* 1st ser., vol. 48, pt. 1, 247.

7. Parsons, circular.

8. U.S. War Department, *War of Rebellion,* 1st ser., vol. 48, pt. 1, 213–14.

9. In addition to Kerns and Mitchell, the commission took statements from G. Gordan Adams, chief clerk for Kerns; Miles Sells, agent for the Merchants and People's Steamboat Line; and James P. McGuire, agent for the Atlantic and Mississippi Steamship Line.

10. Kerns, testimony, in *Dana Commission* and in *Washburn Inquiry.*

11. Mitchell, testimony, in *Dana Commission* and in *Washburn Inquiry;* Adams, Sells, and McGuire, testimony, all in *Dana Commission.*

12. Tillinghast, testimony, in *Washburn Inquiry.*

13. Williams, Speed, and Hatch, testimony, all in ibid.

14. Hatch, testimony, in ibid.

15. Smith, testimony, in ibid.

16. U.S. War Department, *War of Rebellion,* 1st ser., vol. 48, pt. 1, 210, 214.

17. Ibid., 210–12.

18. Quoted in ibid., 212.

19. Quoted in ibid.

20. "River News," *Memphis Daily Bulletin,* May 11, 1865, 3.

21. Wintringer, testimony, in *Hoffman Investigation.*

22. "River News," *Memphis Daily Bulletin,* May 7, 1865, 3; U.S. War Department, *War of Rebellion,* 1st ser., vol. 48, pt. 1, 217.

23. Cited in U.S. War Department, *War of Rebellion,* 1st ser., vol. 48, pt. 1, 440.

24. Details of Hoffman's report in ibid., 213–17.

25. "The *Sultana* Disaster," *Chicago Tribune,* May 24, 1865, 2.

26. Ibid.

27. Quoted in U.S. War Department, *War of Rebellion,* 1st ser., vol. 48, pt. 1, 212–13.

28. Boatner, *Civil War Dictionary,* 221, 892.

29. Meigs to Adjutant General of the Army.

30. Speed to Badeau.

31. Details of Hatch's military career following the *Sultana* disaster are from Potter, *The* Sultana *Tragedy,* 158–60.

32. Boatner, *Civil War Dictionary,* 773; Potter, *The* Sultana *Tragedy,* 160.

33. "Transcript," 156.

34. Ibid., 1–2.

35. Speed to Badeau.

36. Ibid.

37. Kerns, testimony, in "Transcript," 45.

38. "Transcript," 5–9.

39. Ibid., 10.

40. "Transcript," 369–71; U.S. War Department, *War of Rebellion,* 1st ser., vol. 48, pt. 1, 217–18.

41. "Transcript," 369–71.

42. Quoted in U.S. War Department, *War of Rebellion,* 1st ser., vol. 48, pt. 1, 218–19.

43. Ibid.

44. Ibid.

45. Kayton, testimony, in "Transcript," 319.

46. Quoted in U.S. War Department, *War of Rebellion,* 1st ser., vol. 48, pt. 1, 219.

47. Holt's summation in ibid., 219–20.

48. Ibid., 220.

Chapter 20   Too Soon Forgotten

1. "The *Sultana* Disaster," *New York Times,* May 3, 1865, 1.

2. "The Wreck of the *Sultana,*" *Harper's Weekly,* May 13, 1865, 291; "Explosion of the Steamer *Sultana,* April 28, 1865," *Harper's Weekly,* May 20, 1865, plate 316.

3. "City News," *Daily Missouri Democrat,* May 1, 1865, 4.

4. Graham, *History of Richland County,* 365.

5. *Brownlow's Knoxville Whig and Rebel Ventilator,* May 17 and May 31, 1865.

6. Long and Long, *Civil War Day by Day,* 661–87.

7. U.S. War Department, *War of Rebellion,* 1st ser., vol. 48, pt. 1, 214, 217. (See Appendix B.)

8. Ibid., 217; "The *Sultana* Disaster," *Memphis Daily Bulletin,* April 28, 1865, 2; LaPointe, "Military Hospitals," 341; U.S. Sanitary Commission, *Sanitary Reporter,* vol. 1, 187; Hawes, *Cahaba,* 167.

9. U.S. War Department, *War of Rebellion,* 1st ser., vol. 48, pt. 1, 217.

10. Ibid.; Way, *Way's Directory of Western River Packets,* 279–80.

11. "Survivors Disagree," *Fort Wayne Sentinel,* April 29, 1902, 7.

12. Sanders, military records; Lancaster to author. Also, see "Loss of the Third Tennessee Cavalry on the Steamer Sultana," *Brownlow's Knoxville Whig and Rebel Ventilator,* May 31, 1865; McCammon, *Loyal Mountain Troopers,* 157.

13. Berry, *Loss of the* Sultana, 55–56.

14. "James Cook of Kent Was on the *Sultana,*" *The Cleveland Plain Dealer,* October 20, 1938. Also, see Raudebaugh, "*Sultana* Disaster," April 18, 1889, 7.

15. "Hint of a 'Whitewash' ", *Fort Wayne Sentinel,* April 29, 1902, 7.

16. Hunter, *Steamboats on Western Rivers,* 158. Also, see Wintringer's account in Berry, *Loss of the* Sultana, 25–26.

17. Details about the company from Hartford Steam Boiler Inspection and Insurance Company desk calenders, 1979, 1990.

18. "Was It a Fiendish Atrocity?" and "River News," *Memphis Daily Bulletin,* May 2, 1865, 4.

19. Raudebaugh's account in Berry, *Loss of the* Sultana, 294.

20. "The Wreck of the *Sultana,*" *Memphis Daily Bulletin,* May 7, 1865, 7.

21. "A Terrible Disaster," *Daily Missouri Republican,* April 29, 1865, 2.

22. Potter, conversations.

23. Witzig, testimony, in "Transcript," 131, 139–40. Also, see "River News," *Memphis Daily Bulletin,* May 11, 1865, 3.

24. Nauson, testimony, in *Washburn Inquiry;* "Statement of Mr. William Long, A Passenger," *Memphis Argus,* April 27, 1865, 3.

25. Potter, conversations.

26. Figures on losses compiled by author (see Appendix B). Also, see "Third Tennessee Cavalry," May 17, 1865, and "Loss of the Third Tennessee Cavalry on the Steamer *Sultana,*" May 31, 1865, both in *Brownlow's Knoxville Whig and Rebel Ventilator.*

27. Quoted in McCammon, *Loyal Mountain Troopers,* 236.

28. Pontius to Marral.

29. "The *Sultana* Disaster," *Indianapolis Daily Gazette,* May 8, 1865, 4.

30. Berry, *Loss of the* Sultana, 11.

31. Raudebaugh, "*Sultana* Disaster."

32. Ibid.

33. "Survivors of *Sultana* Meet," *Knoxville Journal and Tribune,* April 27, 1892.

34. Berry, *Loss of the* Sultana, 7–11, 56, 383.

35. National *Sultana* Survivors' Association, Proceedings of annual reunions. "*Sultana* Survivors Tell of Escapes from Death," *Toledo Daily Blade*, April 28, 1910; "Want Monument to Sultana Dead," *Toledo Daily Blade*, May 1, 1912, 10; *Knoxville Journal and Tribune*, various dates, 1901–32; *Knoxville News-Sentinel*, various dates, 1901–32.

36. "Survivors of the Ill-Fated *Sultana*," *Knoxville News-Sentinel*, April 27, 1901, 9.

37. "Want Monument to *Sultana* Dead."

38. "Beautiful Monument Unveiled to Memory of the *Sultana's* Men," *Knoxville Journal and Tribune*, July 5, 1916, 8; "*Sultana* Victims' Shaft Unveiled," *Knoxville News-Sentinel*, July 4, 1916, 2.

39. Tommy Martin, "Keeble Holds All Offices in the *Sultana* Survivors' Association, for He's Last One," *Knoxville Journal and Tribune*, April 27, 1930.

40. "Last *Sultana* Disaster Survivor, Pleasant M. Keeble, Dies at 88 Here," *Knoxville Journal and Tribune*, March 5, 1931.

41. "Union Veteran, Hamilton Native, Recalls *Sultana* River Disaster," *Chattanooga Daily Times*, August 2, 1931; "Recalls Facing Death in *Sultana* Disaster," *Knoxville News-Sentinel*, September 4, 1931.

42. "Dr. Jenkins' Death Recalls *Sultana*," *Chattanooga Daily Times*, January 19, 1933.

43. Harris to author.

44. William Warner—Soldier-Pioneer," *Monitor Press*, May 25, 1933.

45. "Philip L. Horn, Last *Sultana* Survivor, Dies," *Wooster Daily Record*, April 2, 1934.

46. "*Sultana* Survivor Called by Death Native of County," *Daily Times and Recorder*, January 9, 1936.

47. Quoted in McCammon, *Loyal Mountain Troopers*, 156.

Afterword

1. Lynch and Marschall, Titanic—*Illustrated History*, 193; *Toledo Daily Blade*, April 27, 1912, 4.

2. "Wrecks of *Sultana* and *Titanic* Show Similarities," *Toledo Daily Blade*, April 27, 1912, 4.

3. Lord, *A Night to Remember*, 193; "River News," *Cincinnati Daily Commercial*, February 4, 1863, 4.

4. "Wrecks of *Sultana* and *Titanic* Show Similarities."

Appendix B

1. Berry, *Loss of the* Sultana, 383–426.

Glossary

boiler deck   second deck, the one above the boilers, that supports the main cabin, or saloon, and staterooms

bow   front of the boat

cabin   enclosed space on the second or boiler deck that contains the main saloon and staterooms

chimney   smokestack

cross chain   system of wrought-iron rods used for holding up the guards

cutter   ship's boat for carrying stores or passengers

gangplank   plank used as a bridge to span the space between a boat and shore or boat to boat; when suspended from above, called a stage or stageplank

gig   ship's boat that is long and light

guards   portion of the main deck that extends out beyond the hull

guy   line used to hold a mast, boom, or stack

hog chains   wrought-iron rods used to hold up the ends of the hull

hold   inside of the hull

hull   frame, or floating portion, of the boat that supports the upper decks

hurricane deck   flat, open deck, above the second deck, that forms the ceiling of the main saloon and staterooms

jackstaff   flagpole at the bow of the boat

ladies' cabin   usually the last fifty feet or so of the main cabin that is designated by a rich carpet and is off limits to male passengers

lines   term used for all ropes, cables, and wires on a boat

main cabin   long cabin on the second, or boiler, deck that is used as a dining hall at mealtime and a social hall the rest of the time

main deck   first deck, which supports the boat's machinery and boilers; stern of the first deck usually used for cargo storage

midship gangway   cross hallway between the main cabin saloon and second deck guards

paddlewheel   component of the machinery that propels the boat

pilothouse   uppermost structure of the boat that shelters the pilot and pilotwheel

pilotwheel   mechanism used to steer a steamboat

saloon   main cabin, which is flanked on either side by staterooms

scantling   any board used in framing

sidewheeler   boat with the paddlewheels located on the sides of the hull

skiff   small rowboat

skylight   row of small transom windows, encircling the main saloon, that provide light and ventilation

skylight roof   component that provides both covering for the skylights and support for the texas deck

smokestack   another name for chimney; also called stack

spar   heavy wooden timber used for lifting the boat over sandbars

spreader bar   solid rectangular piece of metal used for holding apart such components as masts or smokestacks

stageplank   hanging gangplank used as a bridge between the boat and the shore; also called stage

stanchion   vertical post used to support a deck

stateroom   Sleeping room for use of passengers or crew

stern   rear of the boat

texas   cabin situated on the skylight roof; usually occupied by the boat's officers

texas deck   topmost deck supporting the pilothouse and forming the ceiling of the texas cabin

wharfboat   floating warehouse/office, usually constructed on an old steamboat hull, that was moored to the riverbank of a city or large town; steamboats tied up to it for loading and unloading

wheel housing   wooden casing around a paddlewheel of a steamboat; sometimes referred to as a wheelhouse by survivors quoted in this book

yawl   rowboat

Bibliography

Primary Sources

Aldrich, Hosea C. *Cahawba Prison: A Glimpse of Life in a Rebel Prison.* Jerome, Mich.: Hosea C. Aldrich, Printer, n.d.

Alexander, Belle. "Civil War Experiences of Our Grandparent Perry Howard Alexander." Unpublished memoirs.

Berry, Chester D. *Loss of the* Sultana *and Reminiscences of Survivors.* Lansing, Mich.: Darius D. Thorp, 1892.

Brock, Samuel D. "The Civil War Experiences of James J. Brock." Manuscript, n.d.

Cogley, Thomas Sydenham. *History of the Seventh Indiana Cavalry Volunteers.* Laporte, Ind.: Herald Co., 1876.

Comstock, Daniel Webster. *Ninth Cavalry, One Hundred and Twenty-First Regiment Indiana Volunteers.* Richmond, Ind.: J. M. Coe, 1890.

Davenport, Isaac N. "Story of the *Sultana* Steamboat." Manuscript, n.d.

Day, Lewis W. *Story of the 101st Ohio Infantry.* Cleveland: W. M. Bayne Printing Co., 1894.

Dougherty, Michael. *Prison Diary of Michael Dougherty.* Bristol, Pa.: C. A. Dougherty, Printer, 1908.

Elliott, Colleen Morse, and Louis Armstrong Moxley, eds. 3 vols. *The Tennessee Civil War Veterans Questionnaires.* Easley, S.C.: Southern Historical Press, 1985.

Ely, John Clark. Unpublished diary, 1864–65.

Gaskill, Joseph W. *Footprints through Dixie.* Alliance, Ohio: Bradshaw Printing Co., 1919.

Hawes, Jesse. *Cahaba: A Story of Captive Boys in Blue.* New York: Burr Printing House, 1888.

Keeble, Edgar Rhea. "The *Sultana* Disaster, April 27, 1865 and Some Experiences of Pleasant M. Keeble." Manuscript, 1989.

Kimberlin, J. H., "The Destruction of the *Sultana*." Manuscript, 1919.

McIntosh, Epenetus W. *Off for the War.* Private printing, n.d.

Michael, William H. C. "Explosion of the *Sultana*." In *Civil War Sketches and Incidents.* Omaha: Commandery, 1902.

National *Sultana* Survivors' Association. Proceedings of annual reunions. Toledo, Ohio, 1910, 1914, and 1915. Personal files of Helen A. Kerr, Knoxville, Tenn.

Schmutz, George S. *History of the 102nd Regiment, OVI.* Wooster, Ohio: George S. Schmutz, 1907.

Walker, John L. *Cahaba Prison and the* Sultana *Disaster.* Hamilton, Ohio: Brown & Whitaker, 1910.

Wells, Hiram C. Untitled manuscript, 1886 or 1887.

Wells, James. *Personal Memoirs of James Wells.* San Diego, Calif.: James Wells, 1908.

Winters, Erastus. *In the 50th Ohio Serving Uncle Sam.* East Walnut Hill, Ohio: Erastus Winters, 1905.

Witzig, J. J. "Report of Casualties and Violations of Steamboat Laws, Fourth District." In *Report of the Secretary of the Treasury on the State of the Finances for the Year 1865.* Washington, D.C.: Government Printing Office, 1865.

Secondary Sources

Alphabetical General Index to Public Library Sets of 85,271 Names of Michigan Soldiers and Sailors Individual Records. Lansing, Mich.: Wynkoop Hallenbeck Crawford Co., 1915.

Anderson, Nellie Pickens. *The John Pickens Family.* Knoxville, Tenn.: S. B. Newman Co., 1951.

Annual Report of the Adjutant General of the State of Michigan for the Years 1865–6. 3 vols. Lansing, Mich.: John A. Kerr & Co., 1866.

Annual Report of the Adjutant General of the State of Tennessee for the Years 1861–6. Nashville: 1866.

Annual Report of the Adjutant General of West Virginia for the Year Ended December 31, 1865. Wheeling: John Frew, 1866.

Bates, Alan L. *The Western Rivers Steamboat Cyclopoedium.* Leonia, N.J.: Hustle Press, 1968.

Baughman, A. J. *History of Ashland County, Ohio.* 2 vols. Chicago: S. J. Clarke Publishing Co., 1908.

Boatner, Mark M., III. *The Civil War Dictionary.* New York: David McKay Company, Inc., 1959.

Bryant, William O. *Cahaba Prison and the* Sultana *Disaster.* Tuscaloosa: University of Alabama Press, 1990.

Civil War Centennial Commission. *Tennesseans in the Civil War.* Vol. 2, Nashville: Civil War Centennial Commission, 1965.

Davis, William C., ed. *Touched By Fire, Photographic Portrait of the Civil War.* Vol. 2. Boston: Little, Brown & Company, 1986.

East, Charles, ed. *Sarah Morgan, the Civil War Diary of a Southern Woman.* New York: Touchstone Books, 1992.

Faust, Patricia L., ed. *Historical Times Illustrated Encyclopedia of the Civil War.* New York: Harper & Row, 1986.

Graham, A. A. *History of Richland County, Ohio.* Ashland, Ohio: A. A. Graham & Co., 1880.

Greve, Charles T. *Centennial History of Cincinnati and Representative Citizens.* Vol. 2. Chicago: Biographical Publishing Co., 1904.

Guerney, Alfred H., and Henry M. Alden. *Harper's Pictorial History of the Civil War.* New York: Fairfax Press, 1977.

Hardesty, H. H. *Presidents, Soldiers and Statesmen.* Chicago: H. H. Hardesty, 1889.

Havighurst, Walter. *Voices on the River.* New York: Macmillan, 1964.

Hereford, Robert A. *The Old Man River—The Memories of Captain Louis Rosche, Pioneer Steamboatman.* Caldwell, Iowa: Caxton Printing Ltd., 1943.

Hill, George W. *History of Ashland County, Ohio.* Ashland, Ohio: A. A. Graham & Co., 1876.

Hunter, Louis C. *Steamboats on the Western Rivers.* New York: Octagon Books, 1969.

Long, E. B., and Barbara Long. *The Civil War Day by Day.* New York: Doubleday, 1971.

Lord, Walter. *A Night to Remember: Illustrated Edition.* New York: Bantam Books, 1979.

Lynch, Don, and Ken Marschall. Titanic: *An Illustrated History.* New York: Hyperion, 1992.

McCammon, Charles S., ed. *Loyal Mountain Troopers: The Second and Third Tennessee Volunteer Cavalry in the Civil War.* Maryville, Tenn.: Blount County Genealogical and Historical Society, 1992.

Miller, Francis Trevelyan, ed. *The Photographic History of the Civil War.* 10 vols. New York: Castle Books, 1957.

Miller, Rex. *Croxton's Raid.* Fort Collins, Colo.: Old Army Press, 1979.

Official Roster of the Soldiers of the State of Ohio in the War of the Rebellion. 12 vols. Akron, Ohio: Werner Co., 1886–90.

Potter, Jerry O. *The* Sultana *Tragedy.* Gretna, La.: Pelican Publishing Company, 1992.

Report of the Adjutant General of the State of Indiana, 1861–1865. 8 vols. Indianapolis: Alexander H. Conner, 1865–69.

Report of the Adjutant General of the State of Kentucky, 1861–1866. 2 vols. Frankfort, Ky.: John H. Harney, 1866–67.

Record of Service of Michigan Volunteers in the Civil War, 1861–1865. 46 vols. Kalamazoo: Ihling Bros. & Everard, 1905.

Samuel, Ray, Leonard V. Huber, and Warren C. Ogden. *Tales of the Mississippi.* New York: Hastings House, 1955.

Sharp & Dunnigan. *The Congressional Medal of Honor: The Names, The Deeds.* Chico, Calif.: Sharp & Dunnigan, 1984.

Stillwell, Leander. *The Story of a Common Soldier of Army Life in the Civil War 1861–1865.* 2d ed. Erie, Kans.: Franklin Hudson Pub. Co., 1920.

Stuber, Johann. *Mein Tagebuch uber die Erlebnisse im Revolutions-Kreige von 1861 bis 1865.* Cincinnati, Ohio: Druck von S. Rosenthal & Co., 1896.

Twain, Mark. *Life on the Mississippi.* New York: Harper & Brothers Publishers, 1930.

U.S. Navy Department. *War of the Rebellion: The Official Records of the Union and Confederate Navies in the War of the Rebellion.* 30 vols. Washington, D.C.: Government Printing Office, 1894–1922.

U.S. Quartermaster General's Department. *Roll of Honor (No. XXI) Names of Soldiers Who Died in Defense of the American Union Interred in the National*

Cemeteries at Memphis, Tennessee and Chalmatte, Louisiana. Washington, D.C.: Government Printing Office, 1869.

U.S. Sanitary Commission, Western Department. *The Sanitary Reporter.* Vol. 2. Louisville, Ky.: U.S. Sanitary Commission, 1865.

U.S. War Department. *War of the Rebellion: A Compilation of the Official Records of the Union and Confederate Armies.* 70 vols. Washington, D.C.: Government Printing Office, 1880–1901.

Watson, Ken. *Paddlewheel Steamers.* New York: W. W. Norton & Co., 1985.

Way, Frederick, Jr. *Way's Directory of Western River Packets.* Sewickley, Pa.: Frederick Way, Jr., 1950.

————. *Way's Packet Directory, 1848–1983.* Athens: Ohio University, 1983.

————. *Way's Steamboat Directory Abridged.* Sewickley, Pa.: Frederick Way, Jr., 1944.

Who Was Who in America. Vol. 1. Chicago: A. H. Marquis Co., 1943.

Journals and Periodicals

Best, Edwin J. "Members of the 3rd Tennessee Cavalry Regiment, USA." *Blount Journal* 5, no. 1 (May 1989): 13–34.

Clough, B. F. "The Burning of the Flagship *Black Hawk.*" *National Tribune,* September 3, 1885, 3.

Custer, Jack E. "The Cabin and Deck Crew." *The Egregious Steamboat Journal* 3 (September/October 1991): 27–29.

————. "The Engine Room." *The Egregious Steamboat Journal* 2 (July/August 1991): 17, 26.

————. "Officers of the Steamboat." *The Egregious Steamboat Journal* 2 (July/August 1991): 27–29.

Dixon, William F. "Aboard the *Sultana.*" *Civil War Times Illustrated* 12 (February 1974): 38–39.

Eldridge, Charles M. "In the *Sultana* Disaster." *National Tribune,* June 26, 1924, 7.

————. "Some Events at Close of the Civil War." *National Tribune,* August 1, 1929, 6.

Elliott, J. Walter. "By Fire and Flood." *National Tribune,* June 30, 1887, 2.

Elliott, Joseph Taylor. "The *Sultana* Disaster." *Indiana Historical Society Publication* 5, no. 3 (1913): 161–99.

"Explosion of the Steamer *Sultana,* April 28, 1865." *Harper's Weekly* 9, no. 438 (May 20, 1865): 316.

Floyd, William B. "The Burning of the *Sultana.*" *The Wisconsin Magazine of History* 11 (September 1927): 70–76.

Hass, George. "The *Sultana.*" *National Tribune,* November 15, 1888, 3.

Henderson, Howard A. M. "Lincoln's Assassination and Camp Fisk." *Confederate Veteran* 15 (April 1907): 170–71.

Huffaker, Elsie. "My Father." *The* Sultana *Remembered: Newsletter of the Association of* Sultana *Descendants and Friends* 4, no. 10 (Summer 1992): 2–3.

Humphress, Stephen B. "The Sinking of the *Sultana.*" *Kentucky Heritage Magazine* (Fall-Winter 1981): 8–9.

Johnston, Benjamin F. "*Sultana* Disaster." *National Tribune,* May 10, 1900, 7.

LaPointe, Patricia M. "Military Hospitals in Memphis, 1861–1865." *Tennessee Historical Quarterly* 43, no. 4 (1983): 325–42.

Lock, G. Monroe. "Women on the *Sultana,*" *National Tribune,* May 31, 1923, 6.

McCurdy, J. H. "The *Sultana* Explosion." *National Tribune,* August 30, 1888, 3.

Michael, William H. "*Sultana* Explosion." *National Tribune,* July 26, 1888, 3.

Myers, John L. "The Night That the *Sultana* Blew Up." *National Tribune,* February 19, 1925, 5.

Norris, Joseph B. "The *Sultana* Disaster." *National Tribune,* December 17, 1885, 3.

Ratekin, J. R., William Duke, and J. P. Young. "Awful *Sultana* Disaster: A Symposium." *National Tribune,* May 10, 1923, 7.

Raudebaugh, Samuel H. "*Sultana* Disaster." *National Tribune,* April 18, 1889, 4.

Roth, David E. "Andersonville: The Story of an American Tragedy." *Blue and Gray Magazine* 3, no. 3 (January 1986): 5–20, 48–52.

Roziene, F. A. "The Overloaded *Sultana.*" *National Tribune,* May 16, 1912, 7.

Rutter, J. W. "Bewitching News." *S & D Reflector* 2, no. 3 (September 1965): 12.

Sharp, Thomas. "The *Sultana* Disaster." *National Tribune,* November 12, 1912, 7.

Signor, George W. "An Old Death Ship." *National Tribune,* November 19, 1914, 11.

Talkington, Edgar. "A Survivor from the *Sultana.*" *Indiana Historical Bulletin* 32 (July 1955): 123–25.

Ward, Dewyda L. "Survivors of the *Sultana.*" *The Ohio Genealogical Society,* Report 26, no. 3 (Fall 1986): 126.

"The Wreck of the *Sultana.*" *Harper's Weekly* 9, no. 437 (May 13, 1865): 291.

Newspapers

Adrian (Michigan) *Weekly Press,* May 2, 1890.

Ashland (Ohio) *Union,* May 3, 1865.

Ashtabula (Ohio) *Sentinel,* May 24, 1865.

Brownlow's Knoxville (Tennessee) *Whig and Rebel Ventilator,* May 17 and May 31, 1865.

Cairo (Illinois) *Democrat,* April 14, 1865.

Chattanooga (Tennessee) *Daily Times,* August 2, 1931; January 19, 1933.

Chicago Tribune, May 11, 13, and 24, 1865.

Cincinnati Daily Commercial, January 5 and February 4, 1863; April 29, May 1, and May 2, 1865.

Cincinnati Daily Gazette, April 29, 1865; various dates, May 1865.

Cincinnati Daily Enquirer, May 1, 3, and 9, 1865.

The Cleveland Plain Dealer, October 20, 1938.

Daily Missouri Democrat (Saint Louis), February 22, 1865; various dates, April and May 1865; June 19, 1865.

Daily Missouri Republican (Saint Louis), various dates, February–May 1863; April 10, 1865.

Daily Ohio State Journal (Columbus), May 3, 1865.

Daily Picayune (New Orleans), April 19–21, 1865.

Daily Times and Recorder (Zanesville, Ohio), January 2 and 9, 1936.

Delaware County Free Press (Muncie, Ind.), May 4, 1865.

Detroit Advertiser and Tribune, June 15, 1865.

Detroit Free Press, June 15, 1865.

Fort Wayne (Indiana) *Sentinel,* April 29, 1902.

Holmes County Farmer (Millersburg, Ohio), May 4, 1865.

Illinois Daily State Journal, April 29, 1865.

Indianapolis Daily Gazette, May 3 and 8, 1865.

Indianapolis Daily Journal, May 1 and 4, 1865.

Kansas City (Missouri) *Star,* May 14, 1905.

Knoxville (Tennessee) *Journal and Tribune,* April 27, 1892; April 27, 1901; April 28, 1915; July 5, 1916; April 27, 1917; April 27, 1919; April 27, 1930; March 5, 1931.

Knoxville (Tennessee) *News-Sentinel,* April 28, 1927; July 2, 1929; September 4, 1931.

Knoxville (Tennessee) *Sentinel,* July 4, 1916; April 26, 1919; April 15, 1920; December 9, 1923.

Logan (Ohio) *Daily News,* June 27, 1966, Sesquicentennial edition.

Louisville (Kentucky) *Daily Journal,* April 29 and 30, May 3 and 7, 1865.

Mansfield (Ohio) *Herald,* May 3 and 10, 1865.

Maryville (Tennessee) *Enterprise,* April 30, 1975.

Memphis Argus, various dates, April and May 1865.

Memphis Commercial Appeal, January 25, 1920; May 13, 1927; May 29, 1936; April 27, 1950.

Memphis Daily Appeal, May 8, 1888.

Memphis Daily Bulletin, various dates, April and May 1865.

Memphis Evening Appeal, May 13, 1927.

Monitor-Press (Wellington, Kans.), May 25, 1933.

The News-Leader (Springfield, Ky.), October 8, 1896.

New York Times, April 29, May 1–4 and 28, 1865.

Summit County Beacon (Akron, Ohio), May 18, 1865.

Toledo (Ohio) *Daily Blade,* April 29, May 1, 3, 6, and 12, 1865; April 28, 1910; April 27 and May 1, 1912.

Tri-Weekly Missouri Republican (Saint Louis), various dates, February–May 1865.

War Eagle (Cairo, Ill.), April 14 and 15, 1865.

Wayne County Democrat (Wooster, Ohio), April 28, 1880.

Wellington (Kansas) *Daily News,* April 27, 1925.

West Memphis (Arkansas) *Evening Times,* April 25, 1969.

Wooster (Ohio) *Daily Record,* April 2, 1934.

Unpublished Government Documents

Bright, Isaac. Military records. National Archives.

Colvin, Winfield Scott. Military records. Courtesy of Joseph C. Colvin, Medway, Ohio.

Dana Commission. "Records of the Commission Conducted by General Napoleon Jackson Tecumseh Dana." Records of the Adjutant General's Office, Record Group 153, National Archives.

Downing, George. Military records. National Archives.

Downing, Jonathan. Military records. National Archives.

Form C Enrollment, March 24, 1865, Official Steamboat Enrollment in Conformity to an Act of Congress of the United States Entitled "Act of Enrolling and Licensing Ships or Vessels" Approved Feb. 18, 1793, and of "An Act to Regulate the Admeasurement of Tonnage of Ships and Vessels of the United States" Approved May 6, 1864. National Archives.

Fox, John, Jr. Pension records. Courtesy of Richard L. Waters, Jefferson, Ohio.

Hall, Alexander. Military records. National Archives.

Hall, Anderson. Military records. National Archives.

Hoffman Investigation. "Records of the Investigation Conducted by General William Hoffman." Records of the Adjutant General's Office, Record Group 153, National Archives.

Horan, Thomas. Military records. W. H. Smith Memorial Library, Indiana Historical Society.

Inspector's Certificate of *Sultana,* April 12, 1865. Records of the Adjutant General's Office, Record Group 153, National Archives.

Linginfelter, Henry Tolbert. Pension records. Courtesy of Judith Tucker, Kingsport, Tenn.

Lugenbeal, William. Pension records. Courtesy of Bonnie Knox, Wooster, Ohio.

McCown, James M. Pension records. Courtesy of Stephen L. Wright, Louisville, Ky.

Meigs, Gen. M. C. Letter to Adjutant of the Army. June 16, 1865. Records of the Judge Advocate General's Office, Record Group 153, National Archives.

National Cemetery Burial Records, National Cemetery, Memphis, Tenn.

Parsons, Col. Lewis. Circular. May 2, 1865. Records of the Judge Advocate General's Office, Record Group 153, National Archives.

Sanders, David Nahum. Military records. Courtesy of Dr. Richard M. Lancaster, Melbourne, Fla.

Spafford, Harrison. Pension records. Courtesy of H. Lloyd Cornelius, Wooster, Ohio.

"Transcript of the Court-Martial of Captain Frederic Speed." Records of the Judge Advocate General's Office, Record Group 153, National Archives.

Tennessee Soldiers' Records. Microfilm Publications, Microcopy 395, Rolls 1–220. National Archives.

Thomas, Gen. Charles. Telegram to Edwin Stanton, April 29, 1865. Records of the Judge Advocate General's Office, Record Group 153, National Archives.

Washburn Inquiry. "Records of the Inquiry Conducted by Major General Cadwallader C. Washburn." Records of the Adjutant General's Office, Record Group 153, National Archives.

Correspondence and Interviews

Adams, Gail L. Letter to author. May 9, 1993.

Anderson, Randall M. Letter to author. October 4, 1990.

Blazier, Dorothy. Letter to author. May 9, 1989.

Braunwart, Hannah. Letter to Survivors of the *Sultana* Association. April 24, 1901. Courtesy of Helen Kerr, Knoxville, Tenn.

Cooper, Donald, Hayes Boiler & Mechanical, Inc. Interview by author. Chicago, Ill., June 1993.

———. Letter to author. June 17, 1993.

Deaderisle, Judith. Letter to Jerry O. Potter. April 24, 1984. Courtesy of Potter, Cordova, Tenn.

Foley, Richard Jordan. Letter to Sara Catherine Price. April 8, 1865. Courtesy of Nancy Foley Johnson, Lexington, Ky.

Hamilton, K. R. Interview by author. Knoxville, Tenn., April 1990.

Harris, Dave. Letter to author. March 8, 1989.

Hinds, Thomas J. Letter to parents. March 25, 1865. Courtesy of T. Fazzini, Hamilton, Ohio.

———. Letter to friends at home. April 14, 1865. Courtesy of T. Fazzini, Hamilton, Ohio.

Holmes, Gary. Letter to author. February 26, 1993.

Horan, Thomas. Letter to home. March 27, 1865. W. H. Smith Memorial Library, Indiana Historical Society, Indianapolis, Ind.

———. Letter to Samuel McCutchan. April 18, 1865. W. H. Smith Memorial Library, Indiana Historical Society, Indianapolis, Ind.

Isenogle, Ruth Provine. Letter to Jerry O. Potter. May 31, 1989. Courtesy of Potter, Cordova, Tenn.

Lancaster, Dr. Richard M. Letter to author. November 26, 1990.

Lawler, James M. Letters to author. September 22, October 12, and November 30, 1990.

Leppke, Don. Letter to author. September 4, 1990.

Maxey, Robert. Interview by author. Knoxville, Tenn., April 1993.

McKesson, William A. Letter to Clerk of the Circuit Court. April 12, 1866. Kenosha County Historical Society and Museum, Kenosha, Wisc.

Millard, P. Steve. Letter to author. January 8, 1994.

Millsaps, George. Interview by author. Knoxville, Tenn., April 1988.

Newhouse, Pam. Letter to author. July 7, 1990.

Norwood, Helen. Letter to author. August 9, 1990.

Pickens, Samuel. Letter to Cynthia and Mary Pickens. April 28, 1865. Courtesy of Helen A. Kerr, Knoxville, Tenn.

Pontius, William A. Letter to Annie Marral. May 1, 1865. Courtesy of William D. Pontius, Evansville, Ill.

Potter, Jerry O. Conversations with author. Various dates.

Smith, Maxine H. Letter to author, November 26, 1993.

Soper, Mrs. A. B., Sr. Letter to Jerry O. Potter. August 10, 1982. Courtesy of Potter, Cordova, Tenn.

Speed, Frederic. Letter to Col. Adam Badeau, December 13, 1865. Courtesy of Bill Mason, Morehead City, N.C.

Stella, Rachel. Letter to author. January 6, 1992.

Wade, Paul. Letter to author. May 1, 1993.

Ward, Charles M., Jr. Letters to author. May 6 and June 15, 1993.

Waters, Dr. Richard L. Letter to author. November 11, 1988.

Williams, Spencer Harrison. Letter to home. March 19, 1865. Courtesy of Jim Joplin, Springfield, Missouri.

Williams, Spencer Harrison. Letter to home. April 17, 1865. Courtesy of Jim Joplin, Springfield, Mo.

Wood, Ralph C. Letter to Jerry O. Potter. June 7, 1984. Courtesy of Potter, Cordova, Tenn.

Index

ABOUT THE AUTHOR

Gene Eric Salecker is a police officer at Northeastern Illinois University, Chicago, who has been compiling data on the *Sultana* disaster since 1978. He has written numerous articles for periodicals including *Blue and Gray Magazine* and *The Egregious Steamboat Journal,* and he has perhaps the most comprehensive computerized database of Union prisoners connected with the disaster yet assembled. Mr. Salecker has displayed his collection of artifacts and photographs at Civil War collectors' shows around the Midwest, and he was for many years a member of a Civil War reenactment group. He holds a B.A. in history from Northeastern Illinois University.